The Power of the Sacred Name:

V. Raghavan's Studies in Nāmasiddhānta and Indian Culture

Studies in Indian Tradition No.—4

The Power of the Sacred Name:

V. Raghavan's Studies in Nāmasiddhānta and Indian Culture

Edited by
William J. Jackson

Sri Satguru Publications
A Division of
INDIAN BOOKS CENTRE
Delhi-India

Published by:
Sri Satguru Publications
Indological and Oriental Publishers
A Division of
Indian Books Centre
40/5, Shakti Nagar,
Delhi-110007
(INDIA)

First Edition: Delhi, 1994

ISBN 81-7030-395-8

Printed in India.

To the three rose windows
in my life:
Roselle, my mother,
whose faith includes the rosary;
Rose, my daughter,
singer of love in many names;
Marcia Plant, my wife,
beautiful bright woman

Contents

Preface *vii*

I. Introductory Essay on the Name and Nāmasiddhānta Saints
Reading the Signs of the Times and Beyond: Kāverī Delta Nāmasiddhānta Saints' Lives (by William J. Jackson) 1

II. Cultural Overviews: V. Raghavan's Essays on the Name in Indian History and Culture
1. Indian Culture and Its Creative Revivers: Singer-Saint Integrators 47
2. Praise of the Name: Highlights from Ṛg Vedic Times to Tyāgarāja 64
3. Perennialism and the Name, V. Raghavan's Foreword to Frithjof Schuon's *Language of the Self* (and Passages from that Book) 90

III. Leaders of Kāverī Delta Nāmasiddhānta
1. Bodhendra and Sadgurusvāmī (by N. Raghunathan) 109
2. Śrīdhara Veṅkaṭeṣa Āyyāvāl 119

	3. Sadāśiva Brahmendra	131
	4. Nārāyaṇa Tìrtha Part One	142
	Part Two	148
IV.	Creative Exponents of the Name and Related Studies	
	1. Vāk Devatā	155
	2. Bhagavata Purāṇa	159
	3. Encountering Tulasidās	166
	4. Guru Nānak	169
	5. Bhadrācalam Rāmadās	186
	6. Upaniṣad Brahmayogin	200
	7. Tyāgarāja	217
	8. Mahatma Gāndhi	231
V.	V. Raghavan's Translation of *Viṣṇu Sahasranāma*	234
VI.	1. Beads on Strings: Concluding Reflections on the Power of the Name (by William J. Jackson)	247
	2. Passages in Praise of the Name	294
VII.	Appendices on V. Raghavan	
	1. Autobiographical Reflections by V. Raghavan	317
	2. Dr. V. Raghavan, A Personal Reminiscence by Milton Singer	328
VIII.	Bibliography	345
	Index	355
	Map, Illustrations and Chart	

Preface

Devotion via the Name

This study is about devotion to holy names – names such as Rāma, Krishna, or Devī – in India, especially in the Kāverī delta from 1650 to 1850 A.D. During that time leaders such as Veṅkaṭeṣa Āyyāvāl, Bodhendra, Sadāśiva Brahmendra, Nārāyaṇa Tīrtha and Sadgurusvāmī sang, repeated and taught about the holy names as a Hindu way of religious life leading ultimately to *mokṣa*. These *Nāmasiddhānta* (path of attainment through the name) leaders practised revolving the name in their minds and singing holy names aloud as ways to keep a hold on the ultimate amid an everchanging world of disturbance and confusion. They saw the name as a simple direct way to taste *bhakti*, to plunge the individual into contact with the holy through evocative utterance.

Sitting in a temple holding a *japamāla* (rosary of 108 beads) or engaged in one's daily labor, devotees kept the name as their constant companion; it offered stability in this world and hope of transcendence beyond. For years they would repeat such mantras centered on names as "Om namo Nārāyaṇāya" or "Om namaḥ Śivāya" or "Rām Rāmāya namaḥ." Singing songs composed of divine names along with others in public places or meditating on the beloved form of the deity alone at home in the quiet predawn hours, devotees of the name dwelt on this focal point which was intimately individual yet in long continuity with ancient Hindu traditions. Its simplicity gave humble people access to holy presence, and its depth gave philosophers and yogis a wealth of lore and metaphysics to consider. To musicians and enjoyers of the beauty of art it gave an entry to the ancient metaphors of supreme harmony as the base of the universe, and the sweetness of *ānanda* which can be tasted through discernment.

The *bhakti* saints of the era under scrutiny and those of the few centuries preceding it (Jñānadev, Caitanya, Ānnamācārya, Rāmadās, Kabīr, Tukārām, Nānak, for example) were like bees returning to the hive: after discovering a great store of sweetness they had to communicate to the rest of their communities how all could reach that source of *ānanda.* Bees perform a dance which encodes directions to the honey; the saints composed songs, guided listeners by suggesting practices, of which repeating and singing the name were central ones. In the Kāverī delta, saints such as Bodhendra, Sadāśiva Brahmendra, Tyāgarāja and Upaniṣad Brahmayogin are typically pictured as *sādhakas* devoted to the name, seekers who after years of striving tasted realization or had a vision (*darśan*) of the divine, before they began singing songs and guiding others through their spoken words and poetry.

It has been said that poetry measures being.[1] Divine names, called on over a lifetime can be said to be markers in consciousness which also "measure being." The *sādhana* of name repetition measures obstacles and resistances to one's effort, offering a standard in the face of moods and the unknowns of change in the life-experiences of name devotees. Holding onto the name over long years the devotee can be said to measure the power of fate and transcendence, and to measure human weaknesses and limits as well as potential for perseverance. Repeating the name helps measure more of human life in spiritual terms than most other events and repeated practices which are of briefer duration. The name is said to be a companion which helps the devotee measure the meaning and rewards of self-sacrifice. In other words by reciting the name for so many millions of times, it is not just the number of names that is measured. Though it is a measure of one's *tapas*, one's *sādhana* and commitment, recitation of the name millions of times, such as was done by Tyāgarāja, it is also a measure of being – a fathoming of human being in time; it indicates vast being beyond the human and beyond time; it is an instrument for winning a vision of the holy in one form or another.

As "bad luck" is one form entropy takes, name devotion is one form of striving for upward evolvement, right-mindfulness overcoming chaos. Beauty is one way to experience truth, and the path of *bhakti* skilfully employs it. The "sweet path" (*mādhurya*) of *bhakti* is a heart-centered mode of spiritual practice. The name is said to be one way to engender in the psyche the beauty and glory of the holy – *nāmasiddhānta* promotes this, offering a way of concentration and refinement for the simple. Nāmasiddhānta's goal is to saturate the whole brain, the whole psyche, the whole memory, the whole life with what the name connotes. *Nāmasiddhānta* is a method directed toward an experience. The primacy of experience in Indian religions, from the earliest yoga schools onward is of significance here. Like Zen masters and Sufis, like the iconoclastic Kabīr and other mystics, *Nāmasiddhāntins* were often skeptical toward panditry which is no substitute for spiritual practices and religious experience.

Name and Sound

For millennia there has been continual widespread use of holy names and invocations not only in South Asia but in Egypt, Rome, Africa, Arabia and many other parts of the world. Historically, whether for "conjuring the gods by magic formula" (the probable original meaning of the ancient term for Tibetan indigenous shamanic religion – Bön[2]), or used in pious monotheistic prayer to cultivate remembrance and longing, the Name has long been a preferred mode to reach inspiration, dream, trance, and mystical vision, among seekers worldwide. In India repeating the name is one form of mantra, a "mind tool" for breaking down conditioned perceptual structures of time, and the built up patterns of language and mental concepts in human consciousness, measuring the limits of the realms of the unconscious. Rhythmic repetition affects the human organism when performed mentally; and acoustic vibrations make an impact on the nervous system. Rhythm potentially can re-empattern a person's thoughts, feelings, perceptions.

A theory and practice of the sacredness of sound and its effects on the human nervous system was developed further in mystical directions by Indian musician-yogis. For example, in a traditional Hindu music treatise it is said that "In the center of the body is the *prāṇa* (life-force, breath); in the center of the *prāṇa* is the *dhvāni* (sound); in the center of the *dhvāni* is *nāda* (musical sound, harmonious primordial vibration); and in the center of the *nāda* is Sadāśiva– the Supreme Lord."[3] Thus, in *nāda-yoga* the vibration of chanting the name ultimately participates in the nature of that which is named. The mantra sound which tunes one in to the mystery of the ultimate *nāda* – the cosmic "music of the spheres," the sound of the name ringing in one's heart and voice–harmonizes one with the infinite eternal hum of Being. (In keeping with this concept, chants and songs are called the deity's clothing in a Tyāgarāja lyric.) The idea of the magical power inherent in the recited name and in the mantric vibrational force of sound was developed and culminated in masterpieces of devotional music created by Nāmasiddhānta and *bhajana sampradāya* saints of the Kāverī delta. In India we find that ritual, yogic, musical and *bhakti* beliefs all have tended to impel Indians of various persuasions to repeat sacred names and powerful sounds as means to spiritual realization.[4]

Nāmasiddhānta

The word "siddhānta," which forms part of the term *Nāmasiddhānta* (used by V. Raghavan to denote the movement of devotees of the Name in the Kāverī delta, gives the followers a unity which might otherwise be elusive), is intriguingly ambiguous. *Siddha*, meaning "accomplished," is the past passive participle of the root *sidh*, which means to succeed or to attain, and *anta* means "end." Thus, Siddhānta means "final result," or "established supreme attainment," or "settled opinion or doctrine; accepted truth." Śaivasiddhānta means Śaiva orthopraxy, expounding final liberation through devotion to Śiva, but I have found no indications that affiliation with the Nāmasiddānta path involves the kind of sectarian exclusiveness associated with Śaivasiddhānta. Advaitasiddhānta is a term used to designate Śaṅkara's path, "the way of non-dualism," and *Nāmasiddhānta* is used in this way by Raghavan, to mean "the way of salvation by means of the name." Or, because "salvation" is so associated with Christianity, "the way to perfection or complete spiritual attainment through the power of the name."[5]

V. Raghavan has interpreted it both as the practice of "recital of God's name as the most potent means of salvation" (the ultimate attainment of *mokṣa*), and also as the means to *siddhi*, full spiritual attainment or empowerment.[6] Possibly because it has such a range of meanings and associations, and hence is a word with powerful overtones, it appealed to Raghavan, who popularized it by identifying mystic exponents of the name in the Kāverī delta as Nāmasiddhānta saints. In the tales of their lives the leaders of Nāmasiddhānta are depicted as having attained wonderous powers.[7] Sadāśiva Brahmendra, the mysterious naked *sadhu*, especially seems to be associated with *siddha* characteristics, as we shall see.

Nāmasiddhānta is not exactly a sect, though one aspect of the multilingual *bhajana sampradāya* was oriented to particular congregations of villagers along the banks of the Kāverī river. Sadgurusvāmī (1776-1817), for example, after years of "itinerant ministry" established the Ramakrishna Bhajana Math at Marudanallur, near Kumbakonam, and initiated followers into the practice of Rāma-*nāma*. He was a householder, and he named as his successor someone in the family which first welcomed him to settle in that village. That *matha* and others established in Tāñjāvūr by Sadgurusvāmī, and by Bodhendra generations before him, have been institutional centers for the promulgation of Nāmasiddhānta. But these halls largely serve as meeting places for local non-sectarian bhajan singing. In general, Nāmasiddhānta practices tend to de-emphasize sectarian differences. The obliteration of differences and even motives is stressed in a passage by Bodhendra, in his Sanskrit work *Nāmāmṛitarasāyana*:

> In whatever way, under any circumstances, by the performance of the chanting and singing of the Name, all sins get destroyed and release does happen, whether the Name is recited by woman or man. It may be by any man [of any caste or position], or by one insane, by one having faith or without faith . . ."[8]

While this is the professed doctrine, Bodhendra himself repeated his mantra 108,000 times per day – a strict and strenuous discipline following a specific rule. Bodhendra also fostered the musical expression of loving devotion to the name. But the cited passage hyperbolically stresses the merciful offer of maximum openness and laxness, saying any repetition of the name has saving power. The intention is to encourage hope of free access. Any person is free to recite the name, just as many kinds of people can be bhajan singers; in actual practice some groups singing bhajans may be composed of members of certain castes more than others. In India the professed ideal of free access has often not made for a homogenized or random composition of communities of worship. *Nāmasiddhānta* in its most extended sense would seem to mean the faith of any and all who are involved in the repetition of the name, whether they sing or say it, and more specifically the forms it took in the Kāverī delta under the promotion of the five leaders. Nāmasiddhānta is probably best thought of as a *bhakti* discipline which many different kinds of people have enthusiastically followed. It was one of the ways in which *bhakti* has tended to offer experiences which cut across or include *varnāśrama dharma* ("caste and life-stage obligation") differences. In the Tāñjāvūr District villages, and in Madras and other cities today, Nāmasiddhānta does not denote a well-organized community with hard and fast rules, the members of which assert an identity in contradistinction to or alongside of other sects. To what extent Nāmasiddhānta enthusiasts aspired to re-order the existing Hindu communities by harmonizing antagonistic forces, or by offering new group activities, is difficult to say. Spokesmen I met say Nāmasiddhānta has sought to spread fervency of interior practice and personal sincerity in *bhakti*, not to build a new sect or push for external change.[9]

The leaders of Kāverī delta Nāmasiddhānta, in part because they lived in Tamil Nadu, often wrote not in their mother tongue, Telugu, but in Sanskrit, like the *smārta* writers of the Purāṇas, and unlike many sectarian *bhakti* leaders who used their mother tongues for religious writing. In their spoken teachings they employed the regional languages. Being conservative innovators they also sought, as earlier *smārtas* had, to carry forward essential traditions, yet to adapt to meet the chaos of changing times, the turbulence in society.

These leaders seemed to take seriously the idea expressed as early as the *Maitri Upaniṣad*: "Some contemplate one Name, and some another. Which of these is the best? All are eminent clues to the transcendent, immortal, unembodied Brahman: these Names are to be contemplated, lauded, and at last denied. For by them one rises higher and higher in these worlds; but where all comes to its end, there he attains to the Unity of the Person."[10] But they believed not only in the transparency of all names and forms; they also had a faith in the miraculous power of the name to bring protection and salvation.

The Delta Region in Tamil Nadu

The Kāverī delta is a "nodal region" which for centuries has attracted cultivators and radiated culture. V. Raghavan wrote affectionately of the Kāverī as "the silver anklet at the feet of Mother India," a golden stream enriching the soil "with juicy crops, and the natives of that soil with superior qualities of intellect and speech." The Kāverī delta is an important generative core of South Indian regional culture and economy. The singing and saying of the name which became important there was declared by the *purāṇas* to be the primary mode of access to the holy for Hindus in this "fallen age," the *Kali Yuga*. The *bhakti* path, which features devotion to the name as a central practice, is thought of as a gift of grace, a pleasant, easy way and "special offer" extended in difficult times to troubled people in need of a path to God. As such it is still immensely popular in South India, while other paths – of meditation, Vedic ritual and *haṭha yoga* – have fewer followers. The roots of name-devotion may offer a key to understanding Vedic kathenotheism ("one-God-at-a-time-ism") and to reconciling bewildering strands of Hinduism – polytheism and monotheism, *advaita bhakti* and *tantra*. V. Raghavan's work helps us focus on the role of name-devotion in Hinduism's diverse past. While translators and scholars such as Ram Mohan Roy, Vivekananda, and S. Radhakrishnan have presented the philosophical *advaita vedānta* side of Hinduism to the West, which served as a corrective to prevailing onesided opinions (e.g., that Hinduism is only polytheistic with no unifying concepts), V. Raghavan brought out the full range of rich religious life expressed organically in cultural creativity. His studies have helped bring out the rich treasury of Kāverī delta culture: aesthetics, *bhakti* poetry and music, narratives and philosophies, dance dramas, hagiography and musical discourse (*Harikathā*). Nāmasiddhānta's social impact has been significant in Tamil Nadu. As a rather broad-minded path it seems well-suited to the new democratic era, fostering a sense of equality and harmony, it has sanctioned greater interaction among previously separated communities.

Tāñjāvūr, as a thriving playground for the enactment of these concepts, has been a region known for producing literature in several languages. It is thought of as a hospitable cradle for development in *bhakti* music because of unique historical conditions. The Chola dynasty used Tāñjāvūr as capital until 1320 when Muslims from the North invaded. They ruled South India for nearly fifty years, until defeated by forces of the Vijayanagara empire. During that half century many Urdu words were added to the Tamil vocabulary. During the succeeding Vijayanagara reign, the Nāyak chieftains or viceroys representing the Vijayanagara emperor ruled from Tāñjāvūr and Madurai, and they brought into those provinces Telugu and Kannada scholars, musicans, dancers and artists. After the Vijayanagara empire fell, the Nāyaks or viceroys who continued ruling in Tāñjāvūr and Madurai became independent rulers, and they continued to support culturally creative Telugu and Kannada speakers and scholars. When the Nāyak kingdoms were overrun by Marātha forces the Marāthi language was added to the forms of expression used there. The Marātha regime began in Tāñjāvūr in 1676 and ended in 1855. During the Marātha rule scholars, dancers, musicians and *Harikathā* performers from Mahārāṣtra added to the layers of Tāñjāvūr culture. The Marātha descendants of Śivajī inherited his mission of arousing a sense of Hindu identity by encouraging popular *bhakti* and the arts. The Marātha kings introduced some Hindustani music to Tāñjāvūr, and patronized musicians speaking Marāthi, Telugu, Tamil and sponsored other regional artists and scholars.[11] Thus, in Tāñjāvūr a rich mixture of regional cultures and languages thrived under Hindu rulers who themselves were connoisseurs, *bhaktas* and sometimes poets and composers.

V. Raghavan's Contribution

V. Raghavan conducted in-depth research into the lives, documents, Sanskrit texts, history and cultural vitality of this fertile region, focusing on the Nāmasiddhānta saints and their background as one of his favorite areas of exploration. His studies on Nāmasiddhānta, scattered over the decades in various journals, music society publications and scholarly booklets, have not been very accessible to Western scholars. Though these articles have a thematic unity Raghavan did not unite them or place them systematically in the context of world religions. It was as if he prepared the materials and information to make a lens with which to focus on the topic of Nāmasiddhānta, but he did not live to grind and polish the lens as a completed instrument. He also wrote comprehensive overviews on Indian religious culture, but did not bring those together with his Nāmasiddhānta studies, perhaps because he died rather suddenly. (He died of a massive heart attack in the middle of the night on April 5, 1979 – auspicious Rāmanavami day. In fact he had just a few hours earlier delivered a lecture on the greatness of Rāma at the Kuppuswami Sastri Research

Institute.) Raghavan was a world-renowned Sanskritist who conducted many important Indological research projects, especially concerned with to religious aesthetics and Sanskrit literature. He published over 120 books and 1100 papers. His work, like that of other devoted scholars, is anti-entropic. That is, it retrieves neglected aspects of culture, organizes, preserves, keeps alive reflections of useful and beautiful accomplishments which have evolved in the course of Indian civilization. By bringing together some of his studies on this particular topic and arranging them and discussing them in larger historical and comparative contexts, my goal has been to complete what he began, but also to update it, to take an important subject a step further and bring it to the attention of today's students of world religions. In the following introduction to religious veneration to sacred names and to the history of Nāmasiddhānta, as well as in footnotes and a speculative conclusion, I have tried to bring out the relevance of name traditions and related religious phenomena, rather than leave them as disconnected and isolated topics of academic curiosity. As the American Sanskritist Daniel H.H. Ingalls said, Raghavan "earned by his discoveries the admiration of all Sanskritists and has won their deep gratitude for his making possible by his researches still further discoveries that may be their own." He successfully combined precision and breadth of knowledge, and thus as Ingalls said, became "a living example of those different abilities, the exact and the broad, or call them the traditional and the modern, which when combined form the only adequate basis for interpreting the complexity of Sanskrit literature,"[12] and the diverse and complex life of India.

What V. Raghavan left in disparate locations I have brought together and organized in one volume. Some of the pieces assembled here were written for a popular audience (for example the essay on Sadāśiva Brahmendra); others are more technical and detailed (for example the essay on Upaniṣad Brahmayogin). All of them are careful assessments of significant topics which should prove valuable to students of Indian religions and comparative studies. The "lens" which V. Raghavan prepared to make but left unfinished has determined in large part the "optics" under consideration in this volume. I have supplied translations of words to clarify the text, omitted passages when constraints of space demanded it, and placed some matter in footnotes, and augmented some footnotes. I have changed phraseology to current American forms of English to make for an easier reading. I have tried in all of these editorial tasks to preserve what I took to be V. Raghavan's original intentions and presentation of information, and to make his work more accessible to the interested reader of today.

I am grateful to V. Raghavan's daughter Nandini Ramani for helping me locate rare publications and translating Tamil pieces; to Professor Charudattan, V. Raghavan's son, and to V. Raghavan's wife for information and encouragement. Thanks to Professors Klaus Witz, Raymond Williams, and Charles Hallisey for their suggestions; to Evelyn Oliver, Kathryn Engstrom and Kimberly Long, for typing and other manuscript preparation assistance, to Ruth Barker for inter-library loan help, and to Indiana University for a summer faculty fellowship, and manuscript preparation funding. Thanks to R. Krishnamurthy for permission to use his photographs as illustrations.

Before turning to V. Raghavan's studies, let us consider the historical and religious context of the Nāmasiddhānta saints' lives and works.

Notes

[1]Spanos, *Heidegger and the Question of Literature*, Bloomington: Indiana University, 1979. p. xiv. Martin Heidegger, " . . . Poetically Man Dwells . . . " in *Poetry, Language, Thought*, tr. A. Hofstadter, New York: Harper and Row, 1971.

[2]Helmet Hoffman, *Religions of Tibet*, New York: Macmillan, 1961, p. 14.

[3]*Sloka 6, Svarārṇava* manuscript found among Tyāgarāja's books. Journal of the Music Academy of Madras. *Rāmarahasyopaniṣad*, cited by V. Raghavan, *Spiritual Heritage of Tyāgarāja*, ed. C. Ramanujachari and V. Raghavan (Madras: Ramakrishna Mission, 1966, 2nd ed.). See Śārṅgadeva's *Saṅgīta Ratnākara* I.iii.

[4]Charlotte Vaudeville asserts belief in the Name and in its infinite potency as a means of salvation is common to the Sant and medieval Vaiṣṇava tradition: "it is evidently a Tantric conception inherited by both." *Kabīr* (London: Oxford Univ., 1974), p. 141. A.K. Coomaraswamy in *Yakshas*, describes bhakti practices, including the repetition of the name, as originating with Yakṣa worship.

[5] Some scholars have taken "siddhānta" in the term Nāmasiddhānta in the more conventional meaning of philosophical "doctrine;" for example T.K. Venkateswaran translates *Nāmasiddhānta* as "the philosophy of the Divine Name and its singing." *Krishna: Myths, Rites and Attitudes*, ed. Milton Singer, p. 164.

[6]V. Raghavan in *Cultural Heritage of India*, vol. IV, p. 512., and in *Spiritual Heritage of Tyāgarāja*, p. 122.

[7]It would seem that Raghavan popularized the term "Nāmasiddhānta." The name "Nāmasiddhānta" is used by Dr. Seetha in *Tanjore as a Seat of Music* (Madras: Madras Univ, 1981). R. Krishnamurthy in *Saints of the Cauvery Delta* (Delhi, Concept Pub., 1979), and T.K. Venkateswaran's essay in *Krishna: Myths, Rites, and Attitudes*, ed. M. Singer (Chicago: Univ. of Chicago, 1966), pp. 139 ff. N. Raghunathan, "Bodhendra and Sadguru Swami," pp. 133 ff, *Seminar on Saints*, ed. Mahadevan, Madras: USGR, 1960.

[8]Raghavan's Translation quoted by T.K. Venkateswaran in Singer's *Krishna: Myths, Rites, and Attitudes*. In that book Singer discusses social background of Madras bhajan groups. See R. Rangaramanuja Ayyangar's *History of South Indian (Carnatic) Music* (Madras: Author, s.d.), pp. 213-214.

[9]Madras Hindus whom I interviewed said most people who take part in

bhajanas and name-recitation do not identify themselves as *nāmasiddhantins* but identify themselves as Vaiṣṇava or more generally, *bhaktas* devoted to the name and form of their *iṣṭadevatā*.

[10]Tr. by A.K. Coomaraswamy, *The Bugbear of Literacy*, p. 57. One could also see in their lives the application of the teaching found in the *Bhagavad Gītā*: "Let not the one who knows all confuse the one who knows little."

[11]This background on Tāñjāvūr is based largely on an explanation received from T.S. Parthasarathy, Madras, July 21, 1981.

[12]Daniel H.H. Ingalls, introduction to *Bibliography of the Books, Papers and other Contributions of Dr. V. Raghavan*, ed. A.L. Mudaliar (Ahmedabad: New Order Book Co., 1968), p. x.

I

Reading the Signs of the Times and Beyond:

Kāverī Delta Nāmasiddhānta Saints' Lives

by William J. Jackson

Traditions of Transcendence

Naitāvad enā paro anyad asti
"Beyond this world there is a transcendent."
Ṛg Veda X.31.8

In the earliest surviving literature of India, the Vedas, there are many symbolic indications of vision and mystical experiences "transcending the human condition."[1] *Rg Veda* hymn X.136 pictures long-haired sages (*munis*): "When gods get in them, they ride with the rush of the wind. 'Crazy with wisdom we have lifted ourselves to the wind. Our bodies are all you who are merely mortal can see.' He [the sage] sails through the air, seeing appearances spread out below."[2] In the *Ṛg Veda* there are also many references to an orientation in which transcendent reality gives proportion to life on earth. Three-fourths of the cosmic Puruṣa is beyond this world (RV X.90), and Viṣṇu's third step is beyond the mortal realm and the flight of birds (ṚV I.154-5; VII.99-100). The *Brihadarnayaka Upaniṣad* (II.3.6; III.9.26; IV.2.4; IV.4.22) employs remotion ("*Neti neti*" – "Not this") to suggest that the ultimately real is not to be confused with this perishable world. This shows an ancient focus of religious experience in India: the consciousness of eternal being beyond time and change. The problem of access to the transcendent has been an ongoing soteriological concern for Hindus.

In classical Hinduism, humans are thought of as born in the noise of *samsāra*, but with an inborn restlessness for the peace of the eternal. Amid fluctuating cycles of rebirth, Hindus seek "the other shore." They follow a trajectory beyond this life's desires and joys, aiming at release from the wheel of re-death. To attain *mokṣa* or *nirvāṇa* is the goal of yoga. Paths of ritual, dedicated action and philosophy aim at finding the timeless. The *tāraka mantra* invoking Rāma's name with devotion *(bhakti)* is an "enabler of crossing." These are a few indications of an extensive strand of Hindu faith concerned with the hope of transcending this world. "Asceticism, not only as a way of salvation, but as a general orientation, the tendency towards a negation of the world – ultramundaneity – has deeply imbued Hinduism," as Louis Dumont wrote.[3]

In Hindu culture there are also many life-affirming symbols, images of *rasa*, for example, the divine vegetal sap bespeaking the holy's immanence in the organic life of this world. To be sure, there are religious actions performed in the hopes of enjoying this world's offerings. Yet, there is also much mention of "burning the seeds" of karma, and cutting the roots of thralldom to this world. The *Bhagavad Gītā* mentions the unmanifest (*avyakta*) as man's true self and goal. In India, in each system which has two or three manifest parts, there is also a third or fourth part which is transcendent: The Ganges and Jumnā are visible rivers; the Sarasvatī is the unseen third. The legitimate ends of human life: *kāma* (pleasure), *artha* (success), and *dharma* (duty), are followed by *mokṣa* (release), the transcendent fourth. The *varṇāśrama* system is crowned with *sannyāsa*, in which the first three stages are left behind. The tripartite mantra *prānava*, A-U-M, has *turīya*, a fourth dimension which is infinite, dissolving in silence. *Sattva*, *rajas*, and *tamas* are the finite strands of nature; Brahman is the changeless eternal consciousness on which they are superimposed.

Śaṅkara, the *smārta* Brahman *advaita* philosopher and reformer of Hindu traditions, who lived in the ninth century, distinguished between two levels: *Vyāvahārika*, the relatively real "this-shore" world, and *paramārtha*, the Absolute beyond, "the other shore." "I am not mind, ego, senses, elements, I am Śiva, Sat-cit-ānanda, changeless, all-pervading," he wrote in his verses on *Nirvāṇa*.[5] Śaṅkara took one of India's ideals to its logical and mystical conclusion, and popular Hinduism did not disown him, but held him all the closer, attributing to him hymns of praise as well as philosophical treatises, humanizing him but not ignoring the extreme of transcendence-realization associated with his life. Śaṅkara is a classic example of a Brahman of cultural initiative, a renunciate who was also an active worker in this world, drawing on popular *bhāgavata* traditions in culturally creative ways. Sanskritist Daniel H.H. Ingalls warns: "Do not jump to conclusions about Indian philosophy and religion" from the work of such individuals as Śaṅkara.[6] Yet without the world-renouncer and the transcendent Brahman for which he lived, one would have a much reduced and faulty picture of the Hindu religious worldview. Faith in such subjective religious experiences as *samādhi*'s super-consciousness has given India some essential aspects of her character.

Furthermore, there are many other examples of yogis like Śaṅkara who did not merely sit on the periphery absorbed in *samādhi*, but who were "great integrators" who sought to convey access to the transcendent through a thousand names of the divine, setting them to music and leading the dance. In India there is a mutual interaction of inward and outward realms of religion, a blurring of distinctions between *advaita* and *bhakti*. That such blurring makes the Western mind uncomfortable may say as much about the limits of the modern Western mind, as it does about the Hindu synthesis.

In any case, illiterate sense-bound villagers have been much taken by saints in whose lives the Absolute, *paramātma*, was experienced, and the saints themselves often willingly served as "rafts" to help others, including simple villagers, cross *saṃsāra*'s inevitable flux of pains and change. In India the saint whose authority and inspiration came from *samādhi* or vision was often at the center generating the ideals, values, religious and cultural life of society. The authors of scriptures, leaders of sects, keepers of traditional *mores*, tenders of the sacred fires of Hindu faith are often pictured as inspired by vision and *samādhi* in the minds of the masses: their charisma comes from signs of their experience of the transcendent. The logic being: who but one who has seen the farthest and known the deepest is fit to guide?

Religion as Reaching Beyond

Though historical conditions vary, the saintly life can be considered in terms of a striving beyond, a yearning toward the reality which saves from the unsatisfactory conditions of mortal life. The urge toward one or another kind of solution which saves or offers access to the transcendent seems to be at the heart of many of the intense lives of those who are remembered as saints. The saint is *homo religiosus* par excellence, and J.L. Mehta has suggested that

> Going beyond, the movement of self-surpassing, is as much constitutive of the human state as defining and setting up boundaries. It is this self-transcending movement, this reaching out and reaching down within, inherent in man, which defines him as *homo religiosus*, a bridge thrown across, from the realm of the visible to another shore. It is part of this movement to give itself a symbol or concept of that toward which it strains, its mode of being, its nature, its nearness or remoteness...[7]

For Nāmasiddhānta *bhaktas* the "symbol or concept" of the holy was the *Name* – of Rāma, Śiva, Krishna or the Goddess – the Name was a *means* to the transcendent, and also a way that shared the very nature of the goal – divine being. Through the Name its sayers and singers are linked to the Supreme which is named. By purifying practices, by cultivating devotional longing, and dwelling on divine reality through repetition of the Name, the Nāmasiddhānta leaders of the 17th and 18th centuries demonstrated that the devotee could experience the divine – in dream, trance or vision. Thus rather than being merely a representational sign, the Name is thought of as a symbol through which the holy is made present; the sayer and singer participate in holiness, through the calling of the beloved's Name.

Bodhendra, Nāmasiddhānta leader of the 17th century, describes the unconditional power of the Name: "In whatever way, under any circumstances, by the performance of the chanting and singing of the Name, all sins are destroyed and release is effected, whether the Name is recited by woman or man . . . ."[8] An entrance to a new mode of being is pictured here: a purifying transformation and release – *mokṣa*.

Release is one example, but there are also other experiences of self-forgetfulness in Nāmasiddhānta *bhakti*, which would qualify as forms of transcendence. Participating in, attaining awareness of realities greater than one's solitary self, can take many forms. There are various ways in which individuals are subsumed in something greater or have their egos eclipsed. "He who loses himself shall find himself," is a principle found in non-Hindu piety as well.[9]

There are various kinds of experiences noted in the history of religions which may be considered as relating to transcendence, from spiritual love and transpersonal socializing which widens horizons and multiplies capacities, to the solitary

Taoist sage described by Chuang Tzu as "returning to the origin" in stillness. There is the *satori* of a Zen monk. And, a recent study by Frank Clooney points out, there is the Hindu transcendence involved in Jaimini's *mīmāṁsā* interpretation of sacrifice in which the individual view is surpassed in relation to the sum total of values and viewpoints in a religious ritual which precludes the supernatural.[10] There is the "crossing over" of Jain *tīrthaṅkaras*, and the prophetic encounter with God as radically Other, and many other modes of reaching beyond as well.

Though experiences of transcendence would seem to be a universal human capacity it would seem that the forms the experiences take depend in part on cultural conditioning by tradition, and on the historical times of the world in which one lives. I believe that an examination of the signs of transcendence in the Nāmasiddhānta leaders' lives will firstly illuminate continuities with earlier Indian religious traditions, and secondly reveal aspects of the new situation to which their lives are an answer. But before considering specific *signs of a reach beyond*, and images of a reality not reducible to mind, senses, words, which is pictured as *reaching into* the lives of Nāmasiddhānta leaders, let us look at the general social and political conditions in which they lived. A better grasp of the background, the historical conditions in which the leaders lived, helps us understand better the responses they developed and the experiences for which they are remembered.

Historical Conditions During Nāmasiddhānta's Flourishing

Nāmasiddhānta leaders Āyyāvāl, Bodhendra, Sadāśiva Brahmendra, Nārāyaṇa Tīrtha and Sadguru Svāmī lived during the 17th, 18th and early 19th centuries in the Kāverī delta kindgom of Tāñjavūr. The Dutch were active in establishing settlements on the Coromandel Coast from 1612 onward, the Danes from 1618, the English from 1639, and the Portuguese settled and then lost their footholds during the first half of the 17th century. The French occupied Puducheri before the end of the century. European rivalry for coastal trade advantages led to deeper foreign involvement in the region.

During this period the Mughal empire expanded Southward into Karṇāṭaka and the Coromandel coast, becoming a destabilizing element, upsetting the economic relationships and trade patterns already in place, undermining political and administrative systems and preparing the way for deeper and wider European entrenchment. In the North the Mughals brought unity to the monetary system. They standardized customs duties, and communications, and integrated regional economic growth. In the South, the Mughal presence was a different story. The Mughals could not draw the region together under one rule, but their aggressive presence helped rip it apart.[11]

The Tāñjavūr rulers during this time – first Nāyaks of the period toward the end of the Vijayanagara empire, and then after 1675, Marāṭha kings – faced political threats to their authority from all sides, as well as natural destabilizing forces. For example, famine – there was a major famine in 1659. The Nāyaks of Madurai and Tāñjavūr were unsteady allies – to each other and to the other powers around them, both Hindu and European. The Tāñjavūr Nāyaks soon developed a "healthy respect" for the Dutch, granting them concessions and accepting their naval dominance, leasing ports and villages after staging an ineffective siege against the Dutch in the 1660s.

In the 1670s Tāñjavūr suffered from the war between the Nāyak of Madurai and the Nāyak of Tāñjavūr, and the Dutch profited from the situation by extending their own rights and privileges during that time. When the Marāṭha raja Ekojī drove out the Madurai Nāyak and established his rulership in Tāñjavūr in 1675 he cancelled previous concessions granted to the Dutch. After strife with the Dutch he learned to respect their strength. He returned their previous concessions in exchange for annual revenue of gold and elephants, but he at least recovered two important ports. Ekojī also made a costly peace with Sivājī, his half-brother. It was during this time that two Nāmasiddhānta leaders, Bodhendra and Āyyāvāl, were born.

In 1677 and 1680 Kāverī floods played havoc with the region. Despite Ekojī's war efforts he seems to have found the resources to promote Hindu culture also. The royal family of which he was a part was Śaivite, especially devoted to Śiva as Tyāgeśa in the Tiruvārūr temple, not too far from the Tāñjavūr city capital.

In 1689 when the Mughal emperor Aurangzeb's forces overran the area, the Dutch renegotiated their rights with the Muslims. Tāñjavūr Marāṭha rulers after Ekojī had serious financial problems and relied heavily on Dutch funds, for which they willingly exchanged concessions. Marāṭha King Śāhajī (1684-1710 or 1712) attacked Nagapatnam villages in 1691 when Dutch gifts were deemed inadequate. Śāhajī laid siege to the city and harassed Dutch trade. The Dutch attacked and broke the siege in August 1691. Śāhajī sued for peace and signed a treaty returning old privileges. In 1698 Mughal authority was established up to the frontiers of Tāñjavūr state, and the rāja had to pay an annual tribute of 30 *lakh* rupees. (A *lakh* is 100,000.) In the 18th century Tāñjavūr rulers were weakened militarily and financially, paying large tributes to the Mughals to keep them at bay. They were also kept busy fighting Madurai and Ramnad forces, while the Dutch presence gradually grew stronger during these years.[12]

Āyyāvāl, one of the Nāmasiddhānta leaders, wrote a long work in Sanskrit about the Marāṭha royal family, especially Śāhajī II, who was his patron when he was a young man. During the rule of Śāhajī II in the latter 17th century, there was recurrent, almost constant, fear of Muslim invasion. Śāhajī II sent troops to aid Rājarām, son of Śivājī and the ruler of Ginjee in the fight against Kulfikar Khan, Aurangzeb's commander. V. Raghavan has interpreted Śāhajī II's attacks on Christians and Muslims as a heroic defense of Dharma. Not surprisingly, Śāhajī appears far more successful in this venture in Sanksrit literature than in Muslim, Dutch or English records. Raghavan writes in his introduction to Āyyāvāl's *Sāhendra Vilāsa* that the way Śāhajī fought against "the new menace of the Christian missionaries masquerading as Roman Brahmans, weaning away the masses and reviling Hindu faith and worship. . . [shows] that our hero's zeal for the safeguarding of the Country's religion was really comprehensive in its sweep. No wonder that Nallā, alias Bhūminātha takes Śāhajī's biography as a holy chronicle and record of Dharma in his *Dharmavijaya Campū*."[13]

To help buttress Hindu culture, Śāhajī II in 1693 gifted Tiruviśanallūr village on the banks of the Kāverī to Brahman scholars, authors and *bhaktas*. Nāmasiddhānta leaders Āyyāvāl and Bodhendra were associated with this village.

According to historians David Ludden and Kathleen Gough, slave labor played a part in South Indian economy during this period. A major famine in 1729 made the slave trade brisker, with European Companies buying slaves for work in their ports and settlements. Both Mughal and Marāṭha rulers alike frowned on the growth of a large scale slave trade in the Coromandel, but they were unable to halt it altogether. It was during this time of famine and distress that Sadāśiva Brahmendra and NārāyaṇaTīrtha, two of the major Nāmasiddhānta leaders, were active. But historical references do not show up in their works – they were poets, not historians.[14]

After 1740 Tāñjavūr seemed to teeter on the brink of financial collapse year after year. The rulers had to make repeated indemnity payments to the Mughal rulers in 1741 and 1750. During this time the rājas mortgaged large areas of coastal territory to the Dutch for cash. The Dutch were not strong enough to fully exploit the situation by deepening their involvement with Hindu allies. The Dutch had commitments in Java and Ceylon which prevented them from giving hinterland rulers the military aid they desired.

During the period of the earlier Nāmasiddhānta leaders – Āyyāvāl and Bodhendra – the British rivalled the Dutch for trade privileges, sometimes siding with the Muslims against the Nāyaks. Gradually the English response to challenges became bolder. The British had gained a foothold in Chennapatnam (1639), and they strengthened their stand by building Fort Saint George (1641) which became a planning center and staging area for landward ventures. Then the British expanded their holdings, acquiring Devanampatnam in 1690, and in the early 1700s they began negotiating agreements with Mughal rulers.[15]

Thus, political change, social instability and economic distress, as well as increasingly disruptive foreign encroachment, mark the time of the Nāmasiddhānta leaders. From Ekojī's reign to the end of Śāhajī's reign, 1675-1711, over 824,000 tons of rice were produced annually in Tāñjavūr, some of which was exported. From Śarabhojī's reign to the end of Tukojī's reign, 1711-1735, over 617,000 tons of rice were produced annually. In Tulajī's reign, beginning in 1735, the usual rice production was 514,285 tons. In 1744 only 96,000 tons were produced and famine ensued. There were other catastrophic lowpoints, such as the period around 1781, when the Muslim leader Haidar Ali, father of Tippu Sultan, invaded and there was famine. In 1781 the gross yield dropped to 1/7 of the previous year's yield causing extreme distress. A Christian missionary, F. Schwartz, active in Tāñjavūr at this time described healthy persons as rarities and said most people looked like "wandering skeletons." It was during and following this time that Tyāgarāja, the culminative Nāmasiddhānta composer grew to manhood, and Sadgurusvāmī, the last "ācārya" of the movement, appeared on the scene. They must have felt the impact of the catastrophic famine in their formative years. From 1771 to 1860 the British conquest of South India re-shaped the production mode and Tāñjavūr became an agricultural hinterland of the British empire, and Tāñjavūr's traditional crafts died as exports dwindled under British policies. Villagers were in distress in the region off and on from 1812 to 1850, with severe famines in 1811-12 and 1823-26.[16]

Responses to these historical conditions varied, and it is no simple task to summarize what the time meant for all the Hindu communities trying to survive or keep their way of life afloat as the tides of fortune changed. Invasions, famines, demands for exorbitant tribute were but some of the destabilizing sources of insecurity. During the initial phase of the European Companies setting up business on the Coromandel coast there were new co-operative ventures organized and launched. New groups of Indian merchants entered into trade partnerships among diverse social and religious groups. Strategic reorganizing went on at various levels of Hindu society; at the level of poor peasants, subsistence and survival were still the perennial concerns. In mid-17th century European Companies found Coromandel trade "a major growth area." Dutch intrusion and agressiveness made a strong impact along the Coromandel Coast in the 18th century, as in Tāñjavūr and other "hinterland" capitols Hindu administrations weakened and faltered.[17] The Nāmasiddhānta movement, in part, may be seen as a response to these conditions – a way offered to Hindus amidst the waves of change.

Two Telugu Brahman Patterns of Response: Niyogi and Vaidiki

A pattern of response to the increasing presence of powerful alien forces is evident among Telugu Brahmans in South India: two models of adaptation and response seem to have existed in association with two types of Brahmans: *Niyogi* and *Vaidiki.*[18]

The *Niyogis*, (literally, "functionaries or commissioned officials") who often worked as village accountants, adapted to fit new administrative positions which were opened up by the Muslim and European powers. During the 17th and 18th centuries they worked as clerks, administrators and translators for Muslim rulers and zamindars and for European companies, and often found the professional bureaucratic lifestyle agreeable. They incorporated some new ideas from the Westerners, and this gradually had a modernizing impact on Hindu society. The Niyogi survival strategy appears to have been "You can't beat them, so join them." Ashis Nandy has pointed out that by co-operating and serving the Muslims and the Companies, these Brahmans at least survived (unlike the Aztec priests uncompromisingly facing Spanish invaders[19]). This strategy could include humoring and acting agreeable to the new masters, even when the situations were not humorous, and inwardly the servant disagreed with the colonizers.

The second group of Telugu Brahmans, the *Vaidikis*, were traditionalists who learned and preserved the scriptures. They chanted the Sanskrit texts and studied the *śāstras* – the books of knowledge and rules of conduct. The *Vaidikis* had a different response. We might say that they imitated Satyavrata (the "Hindu Noah" who nurtured a fish which grew to save him and others during dissolution, *pralaya*; the fish saved Satyavrata by advising him to build an ark stocked with seeds for new life).[20] The *Vaidikis* were concerned with preserving essentials of tradition, sometimes with the help of creative adaptiveness. Some of these knowers of the orthodox code chose elements from resources of the past, fashioning a creative answer in response to the changing times brought about by the presence of Muslim and European powers. While traders, Kings and the wealthy, as well as the Niyogi Brahmans progressively learned to co-operate with Europeans and Muslims in order to survive, the Vaidiki Smārta Brahmans were more conservative. They tended to be less assimilationist more communal. They avoided much contact with the "others" and remained protective of the cultural religious heritage being endangered by historical change and interaction with colonialist civilizations.

In this category are the five Nāmasiddhānta leaders, most of whom were Telugu *Vaidiki smārta* Brahmans. Also in this category was the "culmination" of the tradition, Tyāgarāja. These men's lives tell us something about their ideals and hopes, their thrust toward the transcendent, their holding on to what seemed to them most valuable and essential. For them, the Name was the "*tāraka mantra*," enabling the crossing. Like Satyavrata's boat, it carried the condensed minimum cargo necessary for the survival of Hindu faith. The Name was simple enough for all to use, holy enough to uplift and save, able to link this world and the person in it to the ultimate security of a transcendent reality beyond change. The designation "Smārta" deserves more attention than many historians have given it. Farquhar, in *Outlines of Religious Literature in India*, traces the term *smārta* to Gupta times, when it was used to distinguish followers of the *Gṛihya śāstras* who kept up household rites from those Brahmans who kept up all the elaborate vedic (*śrauta*) rites. As I mentioned earlier, *Smārtas* were creative re-shapers of the *Purāṇas*, incorporating folk devotion into Sanskrit texts, and were known for *pañcāyatana* worship, in which five deities are represented, with the worshipper's favorite form in the center. *Smārtas* possessed of a more universalist vision synthesized regional rites and practices into a larger pan-Indian system. *Smārta* in South India is also a term associated with Ayyars or Aiyars, distinguishing them from Ayyangārs (Vaiṣṇavas), and hence has sometimes been oversimplified to mean Śaiva, though in actuality there seems to be a strong non-sectarian side to the community.[21]

The Five Nāmasiddhānta/Bhajana Sampradāya Leaders: Stories Reflecting Signs of Transcendence in Their Lives

The term "signs of transcendence" is meant to indicate incidents or symbolic occurrences which point to faith in, or experience of, a reality beyond mere individual physical existence. These signs in hagiography often stand for some extraordinary moments of inspiration in the saints' lives, or reflect some unusual power which later generations find inspiring to recall. The sources for these stories are oral traditions and written literature about Kāverī delta *bhakti*.

In terms of modern scholarship, the Kāverī Nāmasiddhānta movement has been researched most influentially by V. Raghavan, who based his publications on Sanskrit texts as well as written and oral Tamil hagiography available during the first seven decades of this century. Raghavan gathered these traditions and wrote articles for journals, book introductions, newspapers, music society and *maṭh* publications, and he prepared talks for seminars, conferences and festivals, placing the Nāmasiddhānta leaders on the map of modern scholarship, and keeping them in public awareness as a viable part of the 20th century Hindu cultural self-image. Raghavan's studies of Nāmasiddhānta saints' lives and works represent the "standard" traditions about the saints current during the first half of this century. His accounts add musicological information to the popular accounts, as do P. Sambamoorthy's and R. Rangaramanuja Iyengar's.[22] None of these scholars' accounts seem very concerned with contextualizing the lives historically, as I have found it necessary to do in the foregoing section. It is the exception rather than the rule to find specific "historical" references in the saints' stories; in part this may be due to an attempt to calm and not disturb memories of communal conflict between Muslims and Hindus, as well as a reflection of Hindu ahistoricism. I have sought out and highlighted episodes reflecting *both* historical conditions and "signs of the transcendent" which make religion religion and not history, sociology, anthropology, linguistics and economics.

1. Bodhendra, who was named Puruṣottaman at birth, was born in Kāñcīpuram, west of Madras in the early 17th century to a *smārta* Brahman couple who had hoped for a child for a long time. The boy's birth was interpreted as a reward for the parents' faithful service to the 58th Jagadguru ("pontiff" or "head") of the Kāñcīpuram monastery. An early sign associated with transcendence concerns a vow he took as a boy.

After studying *śruti* and *smṛiti* scriptures, and practicing *nāmasankīrtana* and repetition of Rāma's name 100,000 times a day, Bodhendra was told by his guru to follow him to the holy city of Banāras, far away in the North, where the guru desired to bathe in the Ganges. Bodhendra was to travel with a young companion, Jñānasekharan. As they were leaving Kāñcīpuram the two made a suicide pact: if one died en route, the other would proceed to Banāras and inform the guru of the agreement, and then take his own life in the Ganges. As fate would have it, Bodhendra's friend Jñānasekharan died en route. Bodhendra wanted to live up to the agreement, but when he arrived in Banāras the guru dissuaded him, saying he could accomplish something better by doing good on earth. The guru cited a story from the Rāmāyaṇa to justify breaking the vow, and argued that the best alternative would be for the boy to become a dedicated *sannyāsin*, asserting that this change was a kind of "death" at ones own hand, because it would be a signal of the end of one's current worldly *janma* or birth.[23]

Though most Hindus today would not share the value, Bodhendra's, willingness to commit suicide is a sign related to the transcendent in Hinduism in those times. Taking an action which results in losing one's life in this world in pursuit of a higher purpose is a most dramatic indication of faith in a realm and life *beyond*. In the case of a religious vow, suicide means not just to "end it all" but to take leave of this for *that* – affirming the transcendent. Jains fasting to death are another example of this practice in India. Ritual suicide in rivers is described approvingly in the *Matsya Purāṇa* and in other scriptures, and Chinese and Muslim travellers to India noted witnessing such acts. For example, Chinese pilgrim Hiuen Tsiang in the 7th century wrote of the Prayāg Kumbha Mela, "the sacred rivers confluence festival." He saw ascetics clinging to tall posts embedded in the river while staring at the sun until blind, then jumping into the water. The idea was to force one's own ultimate "confluence" with the divine at this auspicious site. Others deliberately plunged headlong from a sacred banyan tree, or entered fires of burning cowdung cakes, seeking an auspicious end and transition. Philosophers and kings followed by their wives drowned themselves, and *sādhus* slaughtered each other in a frenzy of self-violent renunciation at certain times. A Muslim traveller of the middle ages described voluntary drownings in Cambay (Gujarat) and Śrī Laṅka. Self-inflicted death at a holy place or time – under the wheels of the Jagannath festival chariot, or in the flames of a widow's *satī* – was for a long time a religiously approved way to transcend earthly conditions.[24]

It is significant that Bodhendra's contemplated suicide – the death he had accepted in principle – was transcended by an unexpected new life at the guru's direction. Bodhendra received a new lease on life, a different life from the one he sought, a life revealed through circumstances which were beyond his control.

The second extraordinary event recounted in Bodhendra's life story concerns a miracle demonstrating the power of the holy Name. This event is said to have occurred after Bodhendra became a *sannyāsin.* His guru told him to return to Kāñcī after stopping in Jagannātha *kṣetra* (in Puri, Orissa) to get a text on the Name from Lakṣmīdhara (who in fact is thought by historians to have lived during the 16th century).[25] Lakṣmīdhara was "away from home" when Bodhendra arrived at midnight, so the traveller waited on the porch. A Brahman couple arrived, also seeking Lakṣmīdhara. It seems that during their travels the wife had been kidnapped from her husband by Muslims; she later found her husband again, but by then had been "polluted," converted by the Muslims to their faith, though not voluntarily. Lakṣmīdhara's son, the Jagannātha Pandit Lakṣmīkānta Kavi, told the couple that saying Rāma Nāma would be sufficient *prāyaścittam* or expiation for the loss of ritual purity and status. Surprised, Bodhendra asked the authority for this teaching and was told it could be found, supported by orthodox references, in Lakṣmīdhara's text *Bhagavannāma Kaumudi.* Bodhendra said "If the Name is really that powerful, it should cause the woman's Muslim clothes and ornaments to be replaced by Hindu ones if she prayerfully says the Name while bathing in the Jagannāthasvāmì temple pool." Lakṣmīkānta did not disagree. He showed his guests the way to the pool. Saying Rāma's name the woman bathed and emerged a Hindu *sumaṅgali* or "auspicious married woman" with her *maṅgala sūtra, tilak* and her necklace of black beads and other emblems of Hindu tradition restored. The story goes that this miraculous occurrence convinced Bodhendra of the power of the Name and set him on his path of enthusiasm for spreading devotion to it.

The pilgrimage was thus for Bodhendra an initiation of sorts into full faith in the power of the Name. In this depiction of the origins of Bodhendra's belief in the power of the Name, it is noteworthy that the larger than life episode of Hindus seeking to recover from overpowering Muslim forces sets the stage for his later career. The story communicates an experience of wonder at the Name's power in the face of an anxiety-producing historical challenge: Islamic threats to the survival of Hindu traditions. It points to Kāverī delta Nāmasiddhānta's origins and concerns for legitimate authority – scriptural citations on the Name – and it also has to do with hope for survival of a religious lifeway in a disturbing transition time.

A third sign of transcendence comes later, after Bodhendra had grown older, having composed one *lakh* (100,000) *ślokas* (verses) based on Lakṣmīdhara's work about the Name at his guru's behest, and finally having succeeded his guru as head of the Kāñcīpuram monastery and serving for years in that capacity. An old man now, Bodhendra went to Govindapuram village, in the Kāverī delta, where he remained, living a life of renunciation and yoga. It is said he would go into *samādhi* after burying himself in the Kāverī river bed sands. In the evening, as per agreement, children would come and uncover him, rousing him from his higher state of consciousness. (*Samādhi* is the meditative experience of transcendent consciousness – reaching beyond the usual mind characteristic of human conditioning.) One evening the children came to uncover the holy man and a divine voice told them Bodhendra had attained *mahāsamādhi*, the final liberation. To commemorate this event, the voice advised, devoted people should build a memorial structure and perform an *arādhana* (worship celebration) yearly. At night the ethereal sound of the name "Rāma" is said to be audible to believers there.[26] Bodhendra died in 1692, leaving a legacy of scholarship, devotion, and a long life dedicated to service of the Name.

2. Āyyāvāl, as Srīdhara Veṅkaṭesa Ārya came to be called, was born around 1650. He was a married Telugu *smārta* Brahman. He refused the offer of a Mysore rāja to serve as minister, a position his father had held. Instead he went South, settling in Tiruviśanallūr because of his fondness for the nearby Mahāliṅgasvāmī temple. Āyyāvāl met Bodhendra in Tiruviśanullūr. They were like-minded in their enthusiasm for the Name, and offered each other encouragement. Together they are considered the launchers of Nāmasiddhānta in the Kāverī delta.

Āyyāvāl enjoyed the patronage of Śahajī II for reciting and expounding on the Sanskrit epics – *Rāmāyaṇa* and *Mahābhārata*.

There is a miracle story told of Āyyāvāl which demonstrates that genuine devotion partakes of a mode beyond forms and conventional sectarian categories. It seems that a Krishna devotee at first wanted Āyyāvāl to attend a Rādhākalyānam festival, in which Krishna's marriage to Rādhā is celebrated with song. Then, some time later the Krishna devotee sent a message saying "No, don't come, you're a Śiva bhakta, so we're starting without you and your disciples." The Krishna devotee and his guests realized their folly when they heard from observers that Krishna publicly appeared to Āyyāvāl soon thereafter, as proof of the holy man's worthiness. Genuine devotion (*sadbhakti*) transcends the petty-minded categorizations humans habitually make, Krishna's appearance would seem to say. The story implies that one should not underestimate the non-sectarian or inter-sectarian *bhakti* of a devout *smārta*, and that Krishna's grace overflows the neat boundaries people habitually use.

Another story relates that when the Kāverī was flood-swollen, Āyyāvāl instead of crossing as usual to worship in the temple decided to pray at home, offering praise inwardly, and in so doing transcended ordinary space. That he overcame the distance between himself and the temple deity is shown in the story by a priest from the temple appearing and offering *prasād* to him; Āyyāvāl is said to have given the priest a shawl to protect him from the cool monsoon dampness. Later, the temple image was seen wearing the same shawl when the inner sanctum was opened, and the priest there seemed to know nothing about the shawl. It soon dawned on everyone concerned that it had been the deity who had visited Āyyāvāl in the form of a priest.

The third and most memorable miracle story – one for which Āyyāvāl is best known – concerns his feeding a starving outcast food intended for *śrāddha* rites. When local Brahmans criticized him for breaking caste rules by feeding an outcast, and pronounced as penalty a bath in the Ganges river to expiate his sin, Āyyāvāl stood his ground. He prayed at home and the Goddess Gaṅgā appeared in his backyard well, to satisfy any ultraconservatives' ritual requirements, and to prove Āyyāvāl's superior compassion toward a man starving to death.

All of the Kāverī Nāmasiddhānta saints must have

experienced the distress of periodic famine which plagued Tāñjavūr during their lifetimes and they must have seen the effects of starvation, in the lower castes especially. In India, in modern times and before, the needy are a fact of life and this is reflected in religious expression. There are many stories of Śiva disguised as a beggar outcast, rewarding those who serve him in that form. The ideal response of Āyyāvāl to the need of a starving man was preserved in stories still current in the Kāverī delta. Devotees still celebrate the appearance of "Ganges water" Āyyāvāl's well, bathing in the *maṭh* built at that site during the annual Āyyāvāl *arādhana* day festival.

Āyyāvāl, as previously mentioned, wrote a long Sanskrit poem praising the Maratha king Śivaji for protecting Hindu tradition by destroying the invading Muslims, and praising king Śāhajī as divine. Thus, Āyyāvāl's life shows that his *bhakti* enabled him to envision Śiva in both *cāṇḍāla* and rāja, with a sensibility which transcended usual social categories. Like Bodhendra, Āyyāvāl promoted Nāmasiddhānta in individual practice and group *bhajana* singing. Unlike the *sannyāsin* Bodhendra, Āyyāvāl felt no qualms about accepting court patronage.[27] In fact, Āyyāvāl's life shows more dependence on the support of a king than is seen in the other leaders' lives. Rejecting one king's offer he bacame poet-laureate of another. He profited from praise and his girth in portraits bears testimony to his being well-fed. Yet the overall evidence is not one-sided. The householder Āyyāvāl was also remembered for siding with the poorer and middle class, and almost colluding with Robin Hood-like outlaws. One harvest-time, it is said, when *thivatti kolaikutam* – "robbers with torches" – threatened Tiruviśanallūr at night, Āyyāvāl told the poor and middle classes to gather and sing Nāma *bhajanas* on the Kāverī shore. They did so, while the rich busied themselves at home trying to hide their wealth. The bandits who approached were converted by the saint and the poor people singing by the river. The thieves, to show their submission, gave part of the loot they had stolen from the rich to be used at Āyyāvāl's discretion. He accepted it and gave it to Mahaliṅgasvāmī temple for a golden serpent ornament to be made for the deity. This ornament is still on display there.

3. Sadāśiva Brahmendra, or "Sadāśivendra, disciple of gracious Parama Śivendra," as he referred to himself, was born around 1675. His Telugu *smārta* Brahman father, Mokṣam Somasundara was a native of Tiruviśanallūr but he was born farther South in Madurai. He was also called Bhikṣu Guptan, a name meaning "gift of the Lord." He married young, but did not remain in the wedded state. At the feast held in celebration of his wife's attainment of puberty he grew hungry, and then became angry at being kept waiting so long for something to eat. Self-consciousness of this agitation disturbed him so much he came to the conclusion that only a renunciate's life would be one of peace. He left home and studied first with Āyyāvāl, then with the Saṅkarācārya of the Kāmakoṭi Pīṭha in Kumbakoṇam, who initiated him into the *sannyāsin*'s life. During his years of wandering he composed songs to Śiva, Rāma and Krishna and *advaita* verses. An *avadhūta* ("discarder of worldly attachments") he was a renunciate without possessions – even without clothes to cover his frame. Brahmendra has more "signs of the transcendent" clustered in his lifestory than any of the other Nāmasiddhānta leaders. That is, more episodes and symbolic images pointing to belief in experiences of a reality beyond the conventions and limited surfaces of this world are found associated with his life and works. He is thought of as enjoying transcendent consciousness – *sat-cit-ānanda* – as an experience more real than his physical life in the material world.[28]

Sadāśiva Brahmendra's vow of silence is a sign of

awareness which is beyond language and discursive thought. What conventional people deem "overreactions" to worldly incidents were occasions which pushed Brahmendra into the realm of the transcendent. Criticized by his guru for displaying clever debating skills to villagers, he took a vow never to speak again. His customary *nakedness*, which may have resulted from someone casually mentioning that possessions were a bar to release, represents a return to primal simplicity before and beyond ordinary social convention. Pictured in clothesless silhouette, Brahmendra is popularly called "the ghost" or "the shadow," and is remembered for his *avadhūta* childlike purity. He is described as sitting in *samādhi* for weeks, so that a shifting riverbed covered him with sand. The image of obliviousness to time and the elements of nature also indicates otherworldly experiences: so absorbed was he in *that*, he lost all sense of *this*.

Sadāśiva Brahmendra blessed king Śarabhojī I (also spelled Serfoji), who reigned from 1712 to 1729, with the gift of a book on Vedānta which he had written, and this auspicious act of benediction is thought to have enabled the king to have the children he had long desired. Of course, from the king's view Sadāśiva Brahmendra was an aid in getting ordinary worldly desires satisfied – but his power was respected because it was extraordinary – it seemed to come from contact with a realm *beyond ordinary material control*. Vijaya Raghunātha Tondaiman learned the meaning of the *Dakṣiṇamūrti mantra* when Sadāśiva Brahmendra wrote it on the sand. The ruler kept the sand in a gold casket and venerated it as a sacred keepsake of the lesson; it is still kept in the Pudukoṭṭai palace today.

Brahmendra generally is remembered for showing an unconcern for social status or other matters pertaining to this world. For example, he fearlessly or absentmindedly entered the court of Chanda Sahib, Muslim Nawāb of Arcot, it is said. The Nawāb interpreted the stranger's bold intrusion into these private precincts as a threat to his harem's safety, and attacked the intruding saint with a sword. Brahmendra is recalled in tales as exhibiting detachment from pain and physical comfort. When the Nawāb slashed his arm off, the naked saint calmly, almost absent-mindedly, re-attached it. (Somewhat like the New Testament story in which Jesus restores the High Priest's servant's ear which Peter cut off –John 18.10, Luke 22.50-1.) His life is depicted with characterizations of mysterious power obtained from beyond the ordinary man's realm (the power of trance) as when he temporarily paralyzed harvest workers who were about to attack him on a threshing floor. They had feared he was a bandit and struck out against him, only to find themselves immobilized. Later, after others begged him to break the spell, he released the human statues from their rigid stances.

Mistaken identity figures in the plot of yet another story about Brahmendra, which is set in a village near Tiruchirāpalli. There, village officials were gathered to collect taxes, and fuel was being heaped up to cook food for them. The naked silent holy man was passing through just then and the arrogant officials mistook him for an outcast because of his nakedness, and made him carry a bundle of wood on his head. When he arrived at the kitchen and dropped the wood, it burst into flames, damaging goods, scaring everyone present and causing the tax men to regret their presumption. In other stories the saint is pictured as the favorite visitor of little children, whom he often fed and entertained with wonders – such as an instant trip to Madurai and back. There are many signs of people's awe at this imagination-capturing figure, including a story of his reviving a dead bride.

Brahmendra's lyrical works are also marked with

suggestions of a transcendent reality reached through deep inner realization. In one song for example,[29] to clear up misconceptions about literalism and geographical interpretations of the Rāma story, he sang that Rāma is playing in his heart; Rāma's lady is Serenity, and she rejoices in Ayodhyā, the unassailable capital which is *dahara*, the ethereal center of the subtle heart-realm, the "beyond within." Here transcendence is not found in the geography of this world, to which Brahmendra was often oblivious, or beyond the world, out there somewhere, but in the timeless inner realm. His poem *Ātmavidyavilāsa*[30] is full of descriptions of the realized soul absorbed in transcendental consciousness. For example, he describes the ideal life as follows:

"The sage wanders, desires crushed, knowing the universe is unsubstantial" and that it has come into existence from *māyā*, the clouding illusion of the mind (v. 12). The sage "sports like a child;" he has plunged into "the Ocean of pure Bliss" and is "delighted with the diverse actions of men, without any feeling of 'you' or 'I' "(v. 14). Wandering in jungle outskirts he is like a deaf, blind idiot, karmaless and delighting in the Self (v. 15). Immersed in bliss, "he remains in another world, as it were," and depending on his mood he thinks, sings or dances (v. 21). Abandoning the dry "desert region" of the worthless world, the sage is a "good swan" who plays freely in the lake which is absolute bliss (v. 30). The ascetic meditates on Truth on riverbanks, withdrawn from names (v. 34).

More than any of the other Nāmasiddhānta saints Sadāśiva Brahmendra is pictured as revelling in a realm of awareness where names and forms are not taken seriously, and are left behind. He further depicts the life he lived in this manner: With the humor of poverty, bare existence is sufficient wealth to the desireless sage. The cupped palm of his hand is his begging bowl; under a tree he finds his resting place; he wears the "jewel" of non-attachment; the riverbank bush is his home, his bed is the sand (v. 36). "Having dissolved the entire world" under the power of the eternal, he puts in his mouth through *prārabdha karma* (reaping karmic results from actions before his realization experience) the food that comes his way (v. 40). The yogi does not unduly regard nor does he disregard anything (v. 41). He remains in a state of spiritual plenitude like an unflickering lamp, rid of conventional *śāstraic* injunctions and free from obligatory acts (v. 42). To him the universe is a grassblade. His body is smeared with mud and decked with straw. He "enjoys secret Bliss in regions beyond death and old age." (v. 43). Not seeing, speaking, hearing, he is steady in bliss like a still log (v. 44). He wanders like a fool, unnoticed, seeing only perfection everywhere (v. 45). He rejects nothing as bad, accepts nothing as good (v. 50). He is unconcerned with past, future, and with what is in front of him; he is bliss (v. 51). The ascetic roams beyond the senses (v. 52). Independent of all, "mind lost in That which is beyond the entire universe of Līlā," divine play (v. 55), he becomes absolute Brahman (v. 58), the One Truth, the Ultimate Shore, *Tat*, shining unperceived by the senses (v. 62). If these and similar pointers toward transcendence do not indicate the values of ultramundaneity, nothing does. Yet the sage plays a part in this world.

It is no wonder that the more Sadāśiva Brahmendra approximated his ideal, the more the folk memory immortalized him with such mysterious titles as "the shadow" and "the ghost," and pictured him simply as the empty silhouette of a naked man's form. Such charisma also made people prize his catchy songs, which are still very popular in South India today, thanks to such seminal Karṇāṭaka musicians as Semmangudi Srinivasa Iyer, who is himself a *smārta* brahman.

4. Nārāyaṇa Tīrtha, another Telugu *smārta* Brahman, is remembered in the *bhajana sampradāya* of South India – the

inter-sect multilingual tradition which worships via codified bhakti songs from a variety of Indian languages representing different bhakti composers. The *bhajana sampradāya* which grew out of the Nāmasiddhānta movement was organized in group singing form by Sadgurusvāmī, the last of the five leaders to appear chronologically, as we shall see. Nārāyaṇa Tīrtha was born in the 17th century in Guntur, Andhra Pradesh, and died in 1735 or 1745. Nārāyaṇa Tīrtha is known especially for his Sanskrit lyrical drama *Krishnalīlā Taraṅgiṇī* ("Waves of the Sports of Krishna"). He was an *advaitin sannyāsin*, like Brahmendra, who was his senior, and like Upaniṣad Brahmayogi, the guru and founder of a Kāñcīpuram *maṭh* who came later.

According to traditional stories,[31] Nārāyaṇa Tīrtha entered the *gṛihastha* or householder stage of life, and the first sign in his biography concerning the extraordinary is related to the manner in which he left the householder stage of life. Once, swimming across the Krishna river in Andhra Pradesh to be with his wife, Nārāyaṇa found that the current became so violent it threatened to drown him. He heard a *voice from beyond*, it is said, telling him to take the vow of *sannyāsa* immediately.

So, in panic, he discarded his sacred thread, pulled out a token hair (since he could not shave), and hurried through the necessary *mantras*. But much to his dismay, he survived. He was now in the uncomfortable state of being a married *sannyāsin*, a renunciate with a wife. Being both, he could be neither. The *sannyāsin*'s role is one of asceticism, detachment from conventional roles and activities. The *sannyāsin*'s life is associated with the extraordinary – it is a life devoted to seeking *mokṣa*, beyond worldly conventions. He must be possessionless, dependent on the charity of others whose lives he passes through momentarily as he wanders. Nārāyaṇa

Tīrtha longed for that life, but had tied the marriage bonds. What to do? Finally Nārāyaṇa Tīrtha's wife and her family generously released him from family obligations, so he could follow the new life he seemed destined to live. (Like Sadāśiva Brahmendra's wife, Tīrtha's wife was a person displaced by her husband's transformation, and her life does not seem to have been considered especially important, next to his.)

A second sign of the transforming influx of grace from beyond or spiritual destiny becoming manifest is found in the story of Tīrtha's stomach-ache. He was suffering from chronic intestinal pain in the village of Naḍukkāverī, and he prayed for a cure. In a dream *a voice told him* to follow an animal which would appear to him when he awoke. If followed, it would lead the seeker to a place where he would be free of his gut-ratcheting pain. A boar (*varaha*) appeared next day and ran along the banks of the Kodamurutti river, a branch of the Kāverī, for three miles, into Varahūr village (also known as Bhūpatirājapuram) with Tīrtha following. The boar disappeared into the temple of Veṅkaṭeśvara there. Nārāyaṇa Tīrtha believed he had been led by Viṣṇu's boar incarnation, through whose intervention he had been saved from a torturous affliction. The sign from beyond the human condition had come in the inspiring dream, in the form of a wild animal, and in discovering a village with that animal's namesake, which would become his home. Through surrender (*prapatti*) his future was made known to him and peace was secured.

In Varahūr village, Nārāyaṇa Tīrtha established a *bhajana sampradāya*, composing many songs and teaching them to others. His disciples sang and danced the Krishna play he was inspired to write. Raghavan writes that Nārāyaṇa Tīrtha "augmented the *bhāgavata* (devotional) tradition in Tāñjāvūr with *bhajana* songs promoting bhakti through arts and discourse." In the *Krishnalīlā Taraṅgiṇī*, elegant Sanskrit lyrics express Vedāntic ideas as well as the ever-appealing Krishna-and-*gopī* stories of love. In the first *taranga* Nārāyaṇa Tīrtha encourages listeners to bathe in the supreme *Prayāg* or confluence of the three great rivers of divine Names: the Name Rāma being the Ganges, the Name Krishna being the Yamunā, and the name Govinda being the Sarasvatī river. The inner processes of *bhakti* are said to give the same merit as the outer actions of ritual, and Nārāyaṇa Tīrtha, with verve and imagination cultivated these among the people of the Kāverī delta.[32]

Promoting *bhakti* in popular forms (which are still being celebrated), Nārāyaṇa Tīrtha was later thought of as a reincarnation of Jayadeva, the 12th century author of Sanskrit love songs about Krishna. Yet Hindus never forgot Nārāyaṇa Tīrtha as the afflicted one transformed by unusual experiences. It would be speculation to suggest that the original pain of stomach ache was caused by famine or food problems of the time, but the episode could stand for the problems and traumatic memories of many, – a time of uncertainty and unease resolved by providential guidance. Again, the story tells of a turning point, a hopeful new start – survival, as well as inspired creative efflorescence.

5. Sadgurusvāmī was born in Tiruviśanallūr in 1776.

At the start of the *bhajana sampradāya* or devotional song program performed by groups in many parts of Tamil Nadu, the *bhaktas* recite verses on Bodhendra, Āyyāvāl, Nārāyaṇa Tīrtha and Sadgurusvāmī. V. Raghavan calls these "the four ācāryas" or masters of this tradition which has preserved in recent centuries both the religious discipline of *bhakti* and the fine art of music in Tamil Nadu. Sadgurusvāmī believed that the Name alone would not suffice– *bhakti* song was also part of the full devotional regimen needed to provide salvation for Hindus in the present age, and so he organized and codified a program of singing to be followed.

An early sign of the transcendent in stories of Sadgurusvāmī's life is seen in the effect which the miraculous power of the Name of Rāma had upon him. As an infant and toddler it is said that he was unable to speak. Then, while still a child, he heard his guru whisper the name Rāma in his ear, and from then on he was able to speak. The extraordinary power of the Name allowed him to take part in the otherwise closed world of human language. It is a way of saying that he only spoke *because* of the Name.

In another episode from Sadgurusvāmī's lifestory, when Bodhendra's *samādhi* memorial was once washed away by river floods, Sadgurusvāmī went to the riverbank and sought a sign. He attentively walked and listened until he could hear the still-vibrating echo of the transcendent name of Rāma. Thus he located the original site of his hero's resting place so it could be built anew. The story has symbolic meaning: Sadgurusvāmī is pictured as re-discoverer, renewer, rebuilder of an old faith.

There are fewer miracles associated with Sadgurusvāmī, who appears as a more practical-minded organizer than some other leaders– he is much more of an institution builder than Sadāśiva Brahmendra, for example. If Brahmendra stands for spontaneity, Sadgurusvāmī stands for routine. He gave initiation in the Name to the weak Marāṭha King Sarabhojī II, (also known as Serfoji) puppet of the British East India Company, and received a Kerala king's help in building Bodhendra's memorial, as the architecture of the structure testifies. He also founded a "lay maṭh" and codified the *bhajanas* into a set program that included songs in various languages dedicated to various divine forms. He regularized practices and instituted the six rules to be followed in the tradition.[33] Perhaps Weber's "routinization of charisma" is a concept useful in understanding his function. That is, with his influence the public, institutional form of Nāmasiddhānta takes on a shape closer to that of sects with their own set forms of community worship – yet it is important to remember that it also remains non-sectarian, very inclusive, in terms of intersectarian membership and multilingual expression in song.

Sadgurusvāmī is said to have repeated his Rāma mantra 108,000 a day. He was married, yet lived by *uñchavṛitti* or mendicancy, as Tyāgarāja, his contemporary, also did. This means of livelihood is intended to ensure humility, poverty and dependence on the community of devotees rather than on the king. Though a householder, Sadgurusvāmī appears to be associated with a transcendence of worldly emotional attachments– he was not overcome by grief at his wife's death, according to his biographies. Sadgurusvāmī died in 1817, at the age of forty-one, thirty years before Tyāgarāja's death.

Reflections on the Nāmsiddhānta Lives

Taken together as a cluster or "family resemblance" group the Nāmasiddhānta leaders' lifestories reflect faith in and religious experiences of several kinds of transcendence. Significant motifs recur: varied indications of faith in the transcendent power of the Name, as would be expected. The *river* as a transformative presence in these saints lives is also noteworthy. Like Śaṅkara, two of these Brahmans became *sannyāsins* when they came into contact with the perilous waters. Appearances of divine beings – Krishna, The Goddess Gaṅgā, the boar incarnation of Viṣṇu, Śiva disguised as a priest, etc. – are common episodes. For Kāverī delta hearers, stories told by *bhāgavatars* (performers of musical discourse on *bhakti* themes), such as the story of Bodhendra learning of the Name, and of Āyyāvāl witnessing the Goddess Gaṅgā in his own backyard, arouse faith and wonder in listeners. These symbols make a higher reality present to the imagination of the hearers, inviting participation through faith. Such stories encourage practices offering hope that the *sādhaka* (aspirant) who likewise takes the Name as a path will reach similar ends.

In the gestalt of the saints' lives taken altogether, there is a symmetry or balancing effect. Sadāśiva Brahmendra has an experience with his guru which shuts his mouth for good; Sadgurusvāmī has a guru experience which opens his mouth to speak for the first time. Sadāśiva Brahmendra seems beyond all dependence: silent, bare, innocent, wise and blissfully oblivious; Nārāyaṇa Tīrtha, at the mercy of a painful existence, relies on self-effacing trust in non-human intervention – complete surrender.

As a group these men were not exclusively *sannyāsins* or householders, but had involvement in both realms. They were *siddha*-like yogis, sometimes lost in *samādhi* and found by others, inspirers through contagious song, and yet they were able to function as builders of spiritual communities in a time of recovery. Thus, these saints combine dynamic contrasts. There are interrelations within the group – "members" were friends (Āyyāvāl and Bodhendra), helpers in a mutual enterprise (Bodhendra and Sadgurusvāmī), re-constructors supporting each others' works. Their interdependence, and the historical time in which they lived, both contribute to their identities, and dictate certain standards. Perhaps all saints fulfil an historical function, responding to some gripping need of the time, appealing to contemporaries with archetype-developing lifeways. In the *bhajana sampradāya* movement into which which Nāmasiddhānta seems to have evolved, the saints' names and works are celebrated in the program of devotional songs. Their works live on, activating further religious activity, and in a sense, their lives still "work," promoting faith in the Name.

It was V. Raghavan, a *smārta* Brahman himself, who made a strong case for this cluster of unique individuals with similar backgrounds and concerns and divergent personalities, as a group of saints. Yet Raghavan was an intellectual spokesman who could articulate the leaders' importance only because the common people of the delta region already had accepted their teachings and kept popular the oral tradition of their lives, and the *bhajana sampradāya* program maintained this self-composed sense of the past. Unless they are embraced by the people who carry on the traditions, "saints" (whether Brahman or not) are the custodians of nothing vital. The ritual telling of their leaders lives enacts a faith in the transcendent. Interactions between the folk and the intellectual guardians of tradition are dramatically illustrated by the process of the development of the lifestory of Tyāgarāja, who is said to be the culmination of the Nāmasiddhānta tradition.[34] The musician-saint's life as told by the people of the Kāverī delta and Tamil Harikathā performers, became associated with motifs found in the lives of earlier Nāmasiddhānta and pan-Indian singer-saints.

The *smārta*hood of the leaders is significant. Some Tamilians, including scholars and members of the tradition say it was "just a coincidence" that all five were *smārta* Brahmans, and insisted that saying and singing the Name is a religious practice which transcends caste and other bounds. Outsiders cannot help but notice, however, that *smārtas* had an unusual freedom to encourage worship of a variety of names and forms, a freedom which some Hindus now take for granted. Being *smārtas*, the leaders knew and wrote their works in Sanskrit, embodying high culture. But like some other *smārtas*, they showed with their lives a love of popular and vernacular culture, including messages and melodies singable by all. Modern Hindus often downplay the old designations – of being a member of a *smārta* family, for example.[35]

Smārta Brahmans such as Lakṣmīdhara, the five leaders, Tyāgarāja, and Upaniṣad Brahman, (who founded a *maṭh* in Kāñcīpuram, wrote commentaries on 108 Upaniṣads, and composed *bhakti* songs) are all somewhat inconvenient in terms of sect categorization. The *smārta* option of choosing a favorite name and form for worship, the concept of images used in worship being non-absolute vehicles to a divine reality which is ultimately formless, can be traced to the Upaniṣads. The relatively real is used to attain the divine absolute. As a thorn is used to remove a thorn, the guru uses *māyā* as an instrument – relatively real names, forms and methods are used to dissolve worldly *māyā*. Practices propagated by *smārtas*, such as worship of the five focal points of *pañcāyatana pūjā* and the tradition of having a reservoir of various *iṣṭadevatās*, any one of whom may be chosen as a focus for devotion to the divine Name, gave a broad-based encouragement to the updating of pan-Indian Hindu faith, generating for the survival of their lifeway something like "a buffer of diversity that will protect the human being against obsolescence," to use Gregory Bateson's words.[36]

South Indian Hinduism in the time immediately preceding the period of the Nāmasiddhānta leaders – during the Vijayanagara era (1350-1600) – was a "faith that had undergone an ordeal." The ordeal was a series of violent Muslim invasions and a period of military occupation during the first part of the 14th century. Earlier heterodox challenges from Buddhists and Jains, as well as Hindu sect differences now seemed to Hindus to be relatively insignificant doctrinal divergences, compared with the conflicts with Muslim foes who invaded with force and put infidels to death. Hence, after personally experiencing this extreme enmity, Hindus developed a more tolerant mood toward the variety of sects within their own homegrown traditions. Vijayanagara rulers encouraged this spirit and new sects found fertile soil for development. "The birth and evolution of Smārtas, the Bhāgavata community, Mādhavas, Viṣṇusvāmīs, Nimbārkas, Vallabhāchāryas, Rādhā-Vallabhis, Svamī Nārāyaṇis, Śrī Vaiṇṇavas, Sātānis [non-Brahman Vaiṣṇavites who cannot wear the holy thread and who are sometimes non-vegetarians], Menbhaus and Rāmānandis can be traced to this period," Job Thomas states.[37] In my view, members of already long-existing *smārta* and *bhāgavata* traditions were in a position to know the needs of the time and responded creatively, appealed anew and gained momentum during that stimulating era. North Indian saint Narasī Mehtā's life also shows a progressive and creative *smārta* response in relation to *bhāgavata* enthusiasm.[38]

Nāmasiddhānta was one strand in the pan-Indian scheme of reformulation in early modernity. In the 15th century in North India, the saint Rāmānanda and a variety of others, at the dawn of a new age of popular piety, called for fuller participation by the illiterate, the downtrodden, and untouchables in the community life of religious devotion. Caitanya (1486-1534) taught his disciples that Krishna could become present via his Nāma, and that chanting the Name was a great purifier, helping win grace and release. Likewise, in other regions, Name enthusiasts with "non-sectarian" teachings transcended caste and community barriers. Kabīr, Purandaradās, Tulsidās, Annamācārya, Mīrābāī became voices to sing along with and exemplars to follow. The neat schemes of sects, *jatis* and *varṇas* were not the final word or reality to these more free-floating agents, these border-crossers and tricksters confronting the rigidities of convention. They sometimes delighted in bursting barriers, or at least in challenging the ultimacy of caste boundaries with the anomalies of their devotion-centered existence. Whether with a mysterious smile or a brittle break, they eluded some of the old lines of demarcation, opening up the field of religion to all who could feel with enthusiasm. Nāmasiddhānta leaders, like many of these other *bhaktas* did not seek to destroy sect affiliations, but wanted to emphasize and promote a harmonious *bhakti* way open to the many through saying and singing holy Names. With an eye to the future and a rejection of short-sighted petty limits, *nāmasiddhānta* answered exasperating social strictures through expansiveness. The leaders performed a corrective function in the system of Hindu society as a whole, operating within the limits of their own world view. Though they did not achieve perfect impartiality there are signs of a vision of a more inclusive neutrality than is found in some earlier forms of Hinduism, such as availability of the name to all and songs in various languages calling on different holy names.

The impulse of openness, of declaring free access via the Name, seems to be in tune with developments in India which were coming to fruition in the seventeenth century; it seems more in tune with modern times and hence more viable than a narrow sectarian response. The old traditional tripartite division of society – Brahmans, clean non-Brahmans, unclean non-Brahmans –changed with modernization, developments in politics and economy, and such influences as *niyogis* borrowing from Western lifestyles. The way of the Name offered a stable and simple staple in the midst of complex change and spiritual hunger.

The earlier Kāverī Nāmasiddhānta leaders fulfilled the Marātha king's wishes to reaffirm and strengthen Hinduism against the Mughals and Europeans, and Āyyāvāl especially depended on the king for his livelihood. But some of the leaders saw the danger of too close a dependence on the king, who himself was soon to become a dependent of the British, and eventually a thing of the past. One sign of this is the fact that the leaders sometimes chose the path of renunciation and *uñchavṛitti*, which bound them to poverty. These saints, like other *bhaktas*, had their own tradition of skepticism, and sang scornful criticism, heckling devotional hypocrites, men of "belly *vairāgya*," and all who made a prosperous career of showing off their *bhakti*. To interpret their lives in purely political terms would leave out much that is significant.

The Telugu *smārtas* of Nāmasiddhānta combined practical adaptability with ideals of preservation and creativity. They straddled the householder-*sannyāsin* ideals which still compel many conscientious modern Hindus at least in theory. The founding of a "lay maṭh" is an institutional example of this. Those leaders who were associated with the village of Tiruviśanallūr, near the temple town of Kumbakoṇam, were supported by the king, and felt free to co-operate with the court. They could bless the king with spiritual advice and, in the case of Sadgurusvāmī, seek a king's help in a building project. Those who were renunciates were free to abandon all dependence on the court. The composite portrait is of a group of men for all seasons, thermostats of Hinduism, popularizers of age-old spirituality. Women figure in their lifestories (for example Bodhendra accepted a prostitute as a follower despite gossipers, and when she died her head burst and the name of Rāma was heard – proof of Bodhendra's rectitude); but no prominent woman saint came to rank among the great leaders. In the times after Tyāgarāja's death, Bangalore Nagaratnāmmāl became an important figure, a saintly promoter of Nāmasiddhānta, but no counterpart to Mīrābāī in the North shares the stage with the male leaders.

There is an ancient strand in Indian religious traditions, a sentiment which promotes tolerance for and encouragement of various faiths. In Aśoka's 12th Rock Edict, for example, it is said that Aśoka wanted to encourage "growth in the qualities essential to religion in men of all faiths."[39] This characteristic strand or inclusive tendency affirms service to and support of religious practices not because they are Buddhist or Hindu, Vaisṇava or Śaiva, but because they tend to ennoble human life. In terms of the motivation behind the Nāmasiddhānta leaders' work, I see no reason to underestimate this motive, or the motive of sheer enjoyment which the creative participants found in composing poems and songs; neither should we underestimate the genius and will of the Hindu spirit to hold to the sacred at all costs.

The Nāmasiddhānta teachers and their lifestories demonstrate a spectrum of religious modes – for the harassed and overburdened any calling on the name is beneficial; for the devoted and musically inclined regular singing of enjoyable songs spreads joy and well-being; for the dedicated yogi or specialist, recitation of the Name many millions of times leads to *siddhi*. Thus, with undemanding minimalism, enthusiastic celebration, and the promise of high attainments, faith in the Name offered defenses against invading forces, promising a sense of continuity, a feeling of *communitas* and ultimately, access to *mokṣa*. Beyond the merely "within" of the lone ascetic, or the unsatisfying mundane – the public historical crisis – the Name partakes of transcendent glory, offering a way well-suited to unpredictable times, a flexible way to resolve dichotomies, a way bridging people and the ultimate through simple utterance in song or sigh. The leaders of Nāmasiddhānta were saints, charismatic renewers of faith whose lives seemed linked to a reality beyond chaos. Like the mythical Satyavrata, they fostered a way to keep a bond to the primordial sacred despite all else. Like earlier holy men – *ṛiṣis* and yogis – their lifestories preserve signs of transcendence.[38]

Let us turn now to V. Raghavan's studies of the Name and Indian culture.

Notes

[1]Jan Gonda, *The Vision of the Vedic Poets* (The Hague: Mouton and Co., 1963). Mircea Eliade, in *The Sacred and the Profane* (New York: Harvest, 1959), p. 175, writes that in India "the fundamental mystical experience – transcending the human condition – is expressed in a two-fold image, breaking the roof, and flight."

[2]This translated passage is based on one found in J. Frits Staal, *Exploring Mysticism* (London: Univ. of California, 1975), p. 197. See also Mircea Eliade, *Yoga: Immortality and Freedom* (Princeton: Princeton University Press, 1958), p. 102, and Ralph T.H. Griffith, tr. *The Hymns of the Ṛg Veda* (Delhi: Motilal Banarsidass, 1973 reprint), pp. 636-637.

[3]Louis Dumont, tr. M. Sainsbury, *Homo Hierarchicus* (Chicago: Univ. of Chicago, 1970), pp. 184-7., in 1980 edition see Appendix B, "World Renunciation and Indian Religions," p. 273.

[4]*Bhagavad Gīt* , II.25; VIII.18.

[5]Śankara, *Thus Spoke Śrī Śankara* (Madras: Rāmakrishna Mission, 1969), pp. 47-50.

[6]D.H.H. Ingalls, "Dharma and Mokṣa," *Philosophy East and West*, Vol. VII, nos. 1 and 2, April-July 1957, p. 48.

[7]J.L. Mehta, *India and the West: The Problem of Understanding* (Chicgo: Scholars Press, 1985), p. 203.

[8]V. Raghavan, ed. tr. *Nāmāmṛtarasāyana* quoted in the introduction to *Ākhyāṣaṣṭi* (Kumbakoṇam and Madras: Kāmakoṭi Kośasthānam, 1944).

[9]The human capacity to experience life as a threshold, or to travel a path from the seen and known here to an unknown sphere or "shore" beyond, may explain why in China the human has been called the "middle creature," and in Western thought is the pivotal hinge-like being between the animal world and the realm of angels – the link between matter and spirit. What does it say about the human being's condition that he or she always has the capacity for trance and ecstasy? Such experiences as love, nostalgia for roots, obsession with power, the need to escape pressures, the attraction of fantasies promising temporary freedom, the impulses of humor and heroism, the addiction to drink and drugs – all of these can be interpreted as unconscious forms of the impulse to reach beyond, to seek further. Transcendence may be an active motive point in people's

lives, without being consciously recognized as such. The ultimate meaning of human actions seems more intelligible in light of this.

In *The Meaning of Transcendence: A Heideggerian Reflection* (Chicgo: Scholars Press, 1981). Robert P. Orr points out "Transcendence, from the Indo-European root *skand*, names passing-beyond with respect to what is fixed, determinate, delimited" (p. 6). The isolated individual can experience interconnectedness, growth, depth. "The demise of the experienced meaningfulness of any transcendental reality is due precisely to the current cultural sovereignty of the task of world-appropriation" (p. 12). The mastery of surfaces, purposiveness, the calculative mode of thought, utilitarian materialism, technology, I/it attitudes diminish the sense of transcendence. Purposive rationality forgets the systemic nature of reality – cosmos with realms of nature, the network of human culture, and the life of individual man – mental, physical, emotional, and their interrelationships. The interrelated levels of the whole, the "interconnectivities" demand a depth detector to do justice to the realities. Crude determinisms ignore the depths and explain motives in caricature.

Humans still have the capacity to surpass, to reach out, to become more than yesterday's definition. This non-static view can include the awareness of some power or mystery beyond the individual's calculative brain and limiting skin. What Ken Wilber calls the "Atman Project" is the yearning which man naturally feels for wholeness, the need to realize the nature of being infinite and eternal. In the face of death, and with no means to reach the infinite, people use symbolic substitutes: sex, food, money, fame, power, drugs and knowledge as substitute gratifications for the true release possible in wholeness.

Robert Bellah's essay "Transcendence in Contemporary Piety" is an example of his thought on this topic. *Beyond Belief: Essays on Religion in a Post-Traditional World* (New York: Harper & Row, 1970). Dietrich Bonhoeffer (*Letters and Papers from Prison*, New York: MacMillan, 1971) and Paul Tillich ("Religion and Secular Culture" in *The Protestant Ethic*, Chicago: Chicago Univ., 1957) are cited by Orr as opening new discussions on transcendence. See also W.C. Smith's "Transcendence" Ingersoll Lecture in *Harvard Divinity Bulletin*, Fall 1988, Vol. XVIII, no. 3., pp. 10-15.

[10]See N.J. Girardot, *Myth and Meaning in Early Taoism* (Berkeley: University of California, 1983). Frank Clooney, "Jaimini's

Contribution to the Theory of Sacrifice." *History of Religions*, vol. 25, no. 3, Feb, 1986. See also Carman on Rāmānuja's concept of Viṣṇu's *paratva* (transcendence) and *saulabhya* (accessibility). *Ānvikṣiki* (Research Bulletin of the Centre of Advanced Study in Philosophy), Banaras Hindu University, Vol. I, nos. 1-2, Aug.-Dec. 1968, pp. 77-78. And Coomaraswamy, *Selected Papers*, Vol. I (Princeton: Princeton Univ., 1977), p. 75.

[11]Sinnappah Arasaratnam, *Merchants, Companies and Commerce on the Coromandel Coast, 1650-1740* (Delhi: Oxford Univ. Press, 1986), p. 91.

[12]Ibid., pp. 77-79, 45.

[13]V. Raghavan, ed. *Śāhendra Vilāsa* (Tiruchi: Kalyan Press, 1952), p. 74. Manucci, *Storia do Mogor or Mogul India 1653-1708*, Vol. III (London: J. Murray, 1907-8), pp. 327-332.

[14]In *The Religions of Man*, Huston Smith states ". . . India never sank to slavery . . . " (New York: Harper and Row, 1958), p. 67. Srinivasa Aiyangar, in *Tamil Studies, Second Series* (Delhi?: Abhinav (South Asia Books), 1986), p. 66 writes "Slavery as an institution of the type that existed in ancient Greece and Rome has never prevailed in Tamil Nadu. But kings, chieftains and landed magnates here had such complete power over the people, that for the bulk of them feudal subjection was a common lot." For a discussion of slaves (adimai alukal) in Tamil Nadu see Kathleen Gough, *Rural Society in Southeast India* (Cambridge: Cambridge Univ., 1981), pp. 105-106. Though slavery was legally abolished in 1843, the conditions of many Harijan laborers' lives changed little during the British rule. p. 131. See also Sinnappah Arasaratnam, *Merchants and Companies on the Coromandel Coast* (Delhi: Oxford University Press, 1986), p. 211. And David Ludden, *A Peasant History of South India* (Princeton: Princeton Univ. Press, 1985.)

[15]Sinnappah Arasaratnam, *Merchants and Companies* . . . , pp. 90-91.

[16]Kathleen Gough, *Rural Society in Southeast India* (Cambridge: Cambridge Univ. Press, 1981), pp. 120 and 410-411. Pearson, ed. *Memoirs of Schwartz*, Vol. I, pp. 348 ff. C.K. Srinivasan, *Marāṭha Rule in the Carnatic* (Annamalainagar: Annamalai Univ., 1945), pp. 308-310.

[17] Sinnappah Arasaratnam, pp. 354-5.

[18]V. Nārāyaṇa Rao, "Telugu Intellectuals," South Asian *Intellectuals and Social Change*, ed. Y.K. Malik (New Delhi: Heritage Pub., 1982), p. 315.

[19]Ashis Nandy, *The Intimate Enemy: Loss and Recovery of Self Under Colonialism* (Delhi: Oxford University Press, 1983), p. 113.

[20]*Bhāgavata Purāṇa* VIII 24, 32-37. According to legend, Satyavrata was a royal sage who lived on nothing but water. He ruled over the Dravida territory. One day an strange fish appeared in his hands while he offered handfuls of water to his ancestors at the river; the helpless fish was fearful and Satyavrata resolved to protect it. The fish expanded rapidly, outgrowing each container – coconut shell, jar, lake, ocean. When the fish was 800 miles long Satyavrata could no longer contain himself. "Who are you?" he asked, guessing Lord Hari had come himself in this form to help. What was the huge whale's mission? "At the *kalpa*'s end the dissolution of the universe comes," the fish told the sage. "Seven days from now the three worlds will be submerged in the ocean. I will send a mysterious boat to you. Take herbs, plants, seeds, animals and the seven seers, and sail, guided by the seers' light. Tie the boat to my horn with Vasuki the cosmic serpent. I will roam in the water throughout the night of Brahmā, and you will realize my glory as Para Brahmā." The king did so, and in the ark preserved a way of life. In *Śatapatha Brāhmaṇa* I, 8.1.1-6, Manu is the "Noah" who saves the fish and builds an ark.

A more modern analogy of the endeavor of preservers and revivers is that of the hologram. The creative conservator seizes means which produce a kind of hologram image, which memory researchers use to explain how information is distributed in the brain. The interrelations are such that if "part" is lost the whole is still available in other "parts". e.g. a song of Tyāgarāja holds essentials of *sanātana dharma*, the ancient tradition.

[21]J.N. Farquhar, *An Outline of Religious Literature in India* (London: Oxford, 1920) which places the term *smārta* in Gupta times. p. 141. Yoshitsugu Sawai, "Faith of Ascetics and Lay Smārtas," 1984 Harvard Ph.D. thesis on Smārta traditions and the Śringiri Maṭh. See also V.S. Pathak, *Smārta Religious Tradition* (Meerut: Kusumanjali Prakashan, 1987). Milton Singer makes very helpful observations about *smārtas* in *Krishna: Myths, Rites and Attitudes* (Chicago: Univ. of Chicago Press, 1966, 1971). See also my forthcoming "Questions About the Rememberers: Smārta Brahmans as Renewers of Tradition."

[22]V. Raghavan, "Sadāśiva Brahmendra," *The Hindu*, Feb. 18, 1970. "Tīrtha Nārāyaṇa," *The Hindu*, Jan. 4, 1970. "Introductory Thesis"

to *The Spiritual Heritage of Tyāgarāja*, C. Ramanujacari (Madras: Ramakrishna Math, 1981). P. Sambamoorthy, *Great Composers,* Book I, Madras: The Indian Music Publishing House, 1978. R. Rangaramanuja Ayyangar, *History of South Indian (Carnatic) Music* (Madras: Author, 1978).

[23]R. Krishnamurthy's acknowledges his debt to V. Raghavan for his accounts of the Nāmasiddhānta leaders in *The Saints of the Cauvery Delta* (New Delhi: Concept Pub. Co., 1979). See V. Raghavan's introduction to *Śāhendra Vilāsa*, and T.M.P. Mahadevan's *Seminar on Saints* (Madras: Ganesh, 1960), and S. Seetha, *Tanjore as a Seat of Music* (Madras: University of Madras, 1981).

[24]*The Book of the Wonders of India: Mainland, Sea and Islands* by Captain Buzurg ibn Shahriyar of Ramhormuz, tr. G.S.P. Freeman-Grenville (London and the Hague: East-West Publishers, 1981), pp. 4, 71-72, 81. Eleanor Munro, *On Glory Roads* (London: Thames and Hudson, 1987), pp. 52-53. V.S. Pathak, *Smārta Religious Traditions*. pp. 78-79. "The German poet, Ferdinand Freilgrath (1810-1876), recounted for his readers how hundreds of Hindu pilgrims in Puri, India, crushed themselves to death in religious ecstasy under the wheels of the Juggernaut (Jaganath) chariot . . . " Joseph W. Elder, ed. *Chapters in Indian Civilization,* Vol. II (Dubuque: Kendall/Hunt, 1970), p. 28. See also S. Settar, *Inviting Death: Indian Attitudes Towards the Ritual Death* (Leiden: E.J. Brill, 1989).

[25]Not much is known about Lakṣmīdhara, author of the commentary on the *Saundarya Laharī*. In a colophon to his Śiva *nibandha* he says he is a devotee of Śiva at Ekāmra – Bhuvaneśvar, Orissa, and that he lived in the court of Pratāparudra Gajapat of Orissa (C.E. 1497-1539). He was an advocate of "fiercely puritanical and Brahmin dominated Śrīvidya tantrism" whose work solidified views on the *Saundarya Laharī*–later commentators follow his cues. He is responsible for certain vocabulary usages (such as right/left) and some ideas in Śrīvidya that have persisted. But he advocated a ritual and theological *sādhana* especially involving Śrīcakra which has no following, though like the Kaulācāra Bhāskarāya's followers, some *sādhakas* identify themselves with his work and views without strictly following his literal teachings. An "ardent proponent of the Śrīvidya Śākta tantric tradition, centering on the beneficient *Lalitāmahātripurasundarī*, the Śrīcakra, and the 15 or 16 syllable *śrīvidya mantra* known usually as the *pañcadaśī*. It is not uncommon in South India for Śrīvidya *upāsakas* to be Śaivas for 'public'

purposes, Śāktas privately and socially and religiously rooted in Brahmin communities (such as the Ayyar communities of Tamil Nadu, strongly identifying themselves with the Śaṅkara maṭhs and the traditional ascription of Śākta works, including Saundarya Laharī, to Śaṅkara)." So *Śrī vidya upāsakas* such as Lakṣmīdhara could have written a Śiva *nibandha*. "There is precedent, in fact, among other historical Śrīvidya adepts to 'cross' sectarian lines (artificial lines, for most part, when you speak of *smārtas*)." I am indebted to Prof. Douglas Brooks, University of Rochester, New York, for much of this information (personal correspondence, Jan. 20, 1988). Teun Goudriaan and Sanjukta Gupta, in *Hindu Tantric and Śakta Literature* (Wiesbaden: Harrassowitz, 1979), and Ch. Chakravarti, *The Tantras: Studies on Their Religion and Literature* (Calcutta: Punthi Pustak, 1963), p. 72, ff. also provide some information on Lakṣmīdhara's background.

[26]The image of the yogi in *samādhi* underground is familiar in the North as well. For example, there is a Banāras legend of a yogi in trance in an underground cavern unearthed by engineers. Awakened from his meditation, he was shocked to hear Rāma and Sītā were gone and that is was now the Kali age. He plunged into the Ganges and vanished. Diana Eck, *Banāras: City of Light*, p. 247. Oral tradition says Āyyāvāl was a Karṇāṭaka Brahman of Mysore. V. Raghavan calls him an Andhra; his father's name was Lingaryar. Śrīdhara is an *intiperu* or housename. Bodhendra in *Nāmāmṛitarasāyana* calls Āyyāvāl "Veṅkaṭeśa Śāstri."

[27]Biographical traditions about Āyyāvāl are found in R. Krishnamurthy's *The Saints of the Cauvery Delta*, which follows Raghavan quite closely. (New Delhi: Concept Pub. Co., 1979). Also V. Raghavan's introduction to *Śahendra Vilasa* (Tiruchi: Kalyan Press for Saraswati Mahal Library, 1952). Biographical traditions about Bodhendra are found in R. Krishnamurthy's *The Saints of the Cauvery Delta* (New Delhi: Concept Pub. Co., 1979) and in Mahadevan's *Seminar on Saints*, p.133.

[28]V. Raghavan, "Sadāśiva Brahmam," in *Seminar on Saints*, ed. T.M.P. Mahadevan (Madras: Ganesh, 1960). V. Raghavan, "Sadāśiva Brahmendra," The Hindu, Feb. 18, 1970. "Śrī Sadāśiva Brahmendra's Ātmavidyavilāsa," *Vendānta Keśari*, Dec. 1950. p. 301-304. Shuddhananda Bharati, *Sadāśiva Brahman (The Silent Sage)* (Madras: Shuddhananda Library, [s.d.]).

[29]Sadāśiva Brahmendra, song on Ayodhyā. *Compositions of Śrī Śadāśiva Brahmendra* (Madras: Semmangudi Srinivasa Iyer Golden Jubilee Trust, 1979). Also found in *Śivamānāsikapūjā Kīrtanāni Ātmavidyāvilāsa* (Madras: Śrī Kāmakoṭi Kośaṣṭhānena Prakāsitam, 1951), p. 47.

[30]Sadāśiva Brahmendra, *Ātmavidyāvilāsa*, in *Śivamānāsikapūja Kīrtanāni Ātmavidyāvilāsa*, p. 79 and ff. *Avadhūtas* are described in the *Bhāgavata Purāṇa* XI.7-8-9 and the *Avadhūta upaniṣad.* An English translation of this is found in *Samnyāsa Upaniṣads*, Vol. 104 Adyar Library Series (Madras: Theosophical Society, 1978), pp. 1-7.

Manu Dharmaśāstra VI.1 describes the life of a renunciate, and the *Crest Jewel of Discrimination* (*Viveka Cūḍāmani*), tr. Prabhavananda and Isherwood (N.Y: New Am. Lib., 1947), attributed to Śaṅkara, this text describes one who lives continually illumined by consciousness of Brahman: " . . . unattached . . . he may wear costly clothing or none . . . He may seem like a madman, or like a child, or sometimes like an unclean spirit. Thus, he wanders the earth." pp. 96, 111.

[31]Nārāyaṇa Tīrtha, *Krishnalīlātaraṅgiṇī*, Telugu script version (Madras: Vavila, 1967).

[32]V. Raghavan, "Tīrtha Nārāyaṇa," The Hindu, Jan. 4, 1970. R. Krishnamurthy, *The Saints of the Cauvery Delta*, pp. 63-67. Saints Narasimha Mehta and Jñāneśvara used similar imagery in earlier centuries.

[33]The rules or practices are as follows: The devotee (*bhāgavata*) should remember to repeat the name, ritually awaken and worship the Lord each day, live by alms, perform *pūjā*, sing the praise of God with others, and ritually put the Lord to sleep each night.

[34]See my article "A Life Becomes a Legend: Tyāgarāja as Exemplar," *Journal of the American Academy of Religion*, L X, 4, 1992, winter.

[35]In present-day India it is bad manners to ask someone in public if he is a Brahman, and *smārta* is a term fast becoming unrecognizable to many in the younger generation. Even the older generation of *smārtas* usually have had no particular connection with *smṛiti* texts. J.L. Mehta, personal correspondence, Jabalpur, July 23, 1987. S. Ramaswāmī, personal correspondence, Madras, Feb. 19, 1986, and Savitri Rajan, personal correspondence, Madras, March 9, 1986.

[36]Gregory Bateson and Mary Catherine Bateson, *Angels Fear: Towards an Epistemology of the Sacred* (N.Y.: Macmillan, 1987), p. 52. In the 10th

century a *smārta* named Bhaskara in his introduction to a *Bhagavad Gītā* commentary seems to carry over social elitism into soteriology – or vice versa. Thus, not all *smārtas* were invariably expansive and progressive in their philosophy toward the lower castes; some were rigidly conservative.

[37]Job Thomas, "Cultural Developments in Tamil Nadu During the Vijayanagara Period," in *Vijayanagara–City and Empire: New Currents of Research*, ed. A.L. Dallapiccola and S.Z. Lallemant (Stuttgart: Steiner Verlag, 1985). Farquhar, Van Buitenen, Pathak and others do not consider the *smārtas* to have originated at this time, but earlier. I agree with them. Perhaps Thomas means a noticeable phase of *smārta* development is traceable to this time.

[38]John S. Hawley, "Morality Beyond Morality in the Lives of Three Hindu Saints," in *Saints and Virtues* (Berkeley: Univ. of California, 1987), pp. 59-63.

[37]Eugen Hultzsch, ed. and tr., *The Incriptions of Asoka*, Vol. I of *Corpus Inscriptionum Indicarum* (Delhi, 1925, reprint 1969), Twelfth Rock Edict.

[38]Today in 1990, such expounders of the Name as Krishna Premi of Paranur and Venkataramana Bhagavatar of Tiruvidaimarudur continue to keep up the tradition in the Kāverī delta and in Tamil Nadu generally.

II
CULTURAL OVERVIEWS

Part One
Indian Culture and Its Creative Revivers: Singer-Saint Integrators[1]

The thoughts and teachings of a culture have a two-fold basis, first, the spoken words and written texts, and the living exemplars who speak and write. In the most ancient stage, the two were represented by the Vedas and the seers or *ṛiṣis*. Then came as personal exemplars the *avatārs*, incarnations such as Rāma and Krishna, and then the ācāryas, the master teachers. At all times, the person of the guru was emphasized, and even when one was literate and capable, the imparting of a *mantra*, the mystic formula of syllables to be repeated, or the teaching, *upadeśa*, had to be personally done. For when a thing is taken from a book, it is like firewood without a flame, but when the guru imparts it he transmits also a part of his power and grace. After the age of the great *ācāryas*, in the post-classical period, when Sanskrit and the Prākrits derived from Sanskrit were yielding place to Apabhraṃśa (the early medieval vernaculars with incorrect grammar and corruptions in language), and the early phases of the modern Indian languages were yet to come into existence, there appeared all over the country a succession of men of divine grace and realization who mediated between the hoary heritage and the future generations, and who translated and interpreted the ancient heritage from the learned levels to the people at large, using for this mission the local languages and the art of music. But for them the heritage would have been fossilized; they were as great as the original *ṛiṣis* or *ācāryas* for what they did. In the words of Sister Nivedita: "Greatness is but another name for interpretation. . . . Every profound truth waits for the life that shall be all its voice, and when that is found, it comes within the reach of multitudes to whom it would have remained inaccessible."[2] These saint-singers in the Indian languages had to appear to make the heritage live again, gaining in the process fresh dimensions and widening participation.

Overview of the Emergence of Bhakti Scholars and Saints

The learned and popular traditions have had a parallel development from remote times, alternately blossoming forth and influencing each other. If the Vedas represented the former, the *Itihāsa* and *Purāṇas*, stories of the past and legends, stood for the latter. Within the classical tradition itself *Kāvya* (poetry) and *Śāstra* (scriptures and lawbooks) represented the former while drama and the arts addressed themselves to the people at large. The rise of temples and depiction of myths and legends in sculpture were a further attempt to take the masses into the sweep of this culture. Classifying the periods of Indian culture Śrī Aurobindo describes this post-classical period as "a lifting up of the whole lower life and the impressing upon it of the values of the spirit. This was the sense of the *purāṇic* and *tāntric* systems and the religions of *bhakti*."[3] Popular religious movements and forms of worship prevalent or growing in various parts of the country were taken up, and they were given a proper setting and incorporated into the *Purāṇas*. As successors of the ancient *āśramas* of the *ṛiṣis*, *maṭhs* and cave-retreats associated with religious teachers, particularly the Śaiva saints, appeared in historical times. Śaṅkara's activities also led to the formation of orders of monks who moved about and ministered to the spiritual needs of the people. At this time the classical language had given rise to the Prākrits and their literatures and these in turn had ushered in the Apabhramśa dialects (derived from classical Sanskrit) in which literatures had begun to bloom. From earliest times, there was a floating popular didactic poetry, a mass of wise sayings, *subhāṣitas*, in simple Sanskrit, employing similes and other devices enabling easy memorization by the people. Part of this store of *subhāṣitas* went into Buddhism, part into Jainism and the rest continued to be in the main stream of Sanskrit literature.

All these popular aspects of Sanskrit literature have to be borne in mind while tracing the origin and growth of the saints and their songs in the spoken languages of India. In Jainism, there was the mystic tradition represented by Yogīdu, author of the *Paramārtha Prakāśa*, and certain others, who, unlike the scholastic Jain dialecticians, spoke a universal language and freely referred to the Supreme Power in cosmopolitan terms such as Jina, Buddha, Brahmā, Haṃsa, Śiva and Viṣṇu, and to the state of salvation as *mukti* and unity, without any sectarian differences. The Yoga which cut across the different contending schools and which was, as a *sādhana* or spiritual discipline, cherished by all of them was a great solvent of the differences. Along with yoga, *tāntra* was also resorted to by Jainism and Buddhism, as much as by Hinduism. While in the west of India the Jain mystics were producing this kind of eclectic literature, in the east the Buddhist *siddhas* of the *Sahāja* movement were composing in symbolic language (*Sandhā-bhaṣha*) philosophical songs called *Caryā-gītas*. As *padas* these *Caryā-gītas* were all set to music, and in a way, may be considered to have paved the way for the emergence of the Hindu saints and their songs in the Indian languages. From the allusions in the songs of the saints, and from records about some of them, we are led to relate the rise of these saints in the north to the *nāth* movement. One notable figure who popularized yoga is Gorakhnātha who stands at the threshold of the age of the popular saints. The whole of North India up to Nepal and the lower Himalayan areas were pervaded by Gorakhnātha and his teaching on Hathayoga and the esoteric practice of *nāda* or *śabda*—the spirituality of mystical vibrations in mantra and music. To all of these teachings we find references in the songs of the later North Indian saints, Kabīr, Nānak and others. Jñāneśvara, the pioneer in Mahārāṣṭra, is said to have belonged to the *nāth sampradāya*.

The Rich Traditions of Tamil Saints

In the South, the movement started with Pallava times when South India was a stronghold of Buddhism and Jainism. It was the effort to reclaim the country for the Vedic, Purāṇic and devotional path that threw up the Śaiva and Vaiṣṇava saints in Tamil. This movement began in the 6th century and gathered momentum in the next few centuries by which time the whole of the South had been completely swept back into the older faith. This was a two-fold renaissance: one adopting the medium of Sanskrit, the other that of Tamil. The two streams of the new activity should be mentioned as the Sanskrit works composed at the time became masterpieces of the greatest import and played an unprecedented part in influencing the North and effecting its spiritual and devotional reclamation. The *Bhāgavata Purāṇa*, which was the equivalent of the Bible to the later schools of *bhakti* in the North, was a product of this momentous creative period in South India.

Śaṅkara towered above all the geniuses of these times in the South. The force of his personality and the spectacular success of his mission can be gauged by the reference made by another South Indian Śaiva saint, Māṇikkavāchakar, to Śaṅkara's philosophy as "raging in the country like a tempest."[4] After Śaṅkara, South India produced Rāmānuja, and it was a follower of the devotional school of *vedanta*, Rāmānanda, who was responsible for the *bhakti* movements of the North, Kabīr,

Tulasi and others owing allegiance to him.

Rāmānuja's work coalesced with the earlier work of the Tamil hymns of the Vaiṣṇava saints called *āḻvārs* who had built up the movement of devotion to Viṣṇu. The *āḻvār*s are ten in number counted also as twelve with the addition of two more, including the woman known as "the Lord's bride," Āṇḍāl. These came from different parts of the Tamil region including the Chera kingdom. They flourished between A.D. 700 and 900. Five of them may be said to be more important than the rest– Poihai, Pey, Bhūtam, Nammāḻvār and Periyāḻvār. The songs of the twelve *āḻvārs* are together called "The Divine Composition" (*Divyaprabandham*), as also "Four Thousand" (*Nālāyiram*) from the number of verses. Twenty-four separate compositions are included in the four parts in which the collection is arranged and a whole fourth of it is the composition of Nammāḻvār, called *Tiruvāimozhi*, meaning "sacred utterance" or the Veda (in Tamil). All these were collected and arranged by Nāthamuni from whom the Sanskrit tradition of Śrīvaiṣṇavism starts. The poems in the collection are all set to different *rāgas* or melodies.

The Śaiva saints, *nāyanārs*, are sixty-three in number and their period too ranges from 700 to 900 A.D. They were first listed by one of them Sundaramūrti, and their detailed biography was written by the Chola minister Śekkizhār. The greatest of these are Appar, Sambandhar and Sundarar, referred to as "the trinity" (*Mūvar*). With Māṇikkavāchakar, author of the collection *Tiruvāchakam*, they form the four Śaiva *samaya gurus*. Seven are the greatest composers of the Śaiva hymns called *Devāra*, meaning "adoration of the Lord," and of them the most prolific were the trinity. Appar sang 49,000 verses of which 3,110 are extant, Sambandhar 16,000 of which 3,840 are available, and Sundarar 38,000 of which only 1,000 have survived. As in the case of the Vaiṣṇava hymns, the Śaivite ones, too, had to be salvaged and organised; this was done by Nambi Andar Nambi, at the instance of Rājarāja Chola I in the 10th century A.D. Including the hymns of the first three *nāyanārs* and the poems of Māṇikkavāchakar, the entire Śaiva religious poetry as then available was arranged in twelve books, the last one being Śekkizhār's biography of the saints. These books included the hymns of seven later saints too. (Recently a set of eleven hitherto unknown *Devāram* hymns has been discovered in a 12th century temple inscription.[5])

The hymns of the *Devāram* are not only rich in their devotional fervour and religious and philosophical ideas, but they were all composed as music, set in different ragas, and as such form the earliest corpus of South Indian music compositions. Endowments came to be made very early for their regular recital in temples with flute, string and drums accompaniments – from the time of Pallava Nandvarman III (844-66 A.D.). Even to this day the moving strains of the *Devāram* songs are to be heard in the temples and in concert halls; conferences are held and research is being done on their *rāgas* known as *pan*. In Sambandhar's songs alone a hundred rhythmic varieties are to be found. The three peaks of south Indian spiritual revival, Śaṅkara (32 years), Sambandhar (16 years) and Sundarar (18 years), all passed away very young, after galvanizing the people.

The poetry and music of *Devāram* and *Divyaprabandham* are closely linked to South Indian temples, the building of which was taken up on a large scale by the Pallava rulers and on a larger scale by the Cholas later. The temples proved to be the physical citadels of devotion and the arts as also sources of inspiration to other saints and their devotional outpourings.

The service that the *nāyanārs* and *āḻvārs* rendered cannot be estimated merely by their life-work or their hymns; for the spirit they generated gathered force through the centuries. New galaxies of saints came into being and new geniuses arose to add further impetus.

The Tamil *siddhas*, of whom little is known outside Tamil Nadu, must be mentioned. The Tamil *siddha* tradition is seen in medicine alchemy and religion. Among the religious *siddhas*, eighteen in number, there were Tirumūlar, the *vedāntin* author of the *Tirumantra*, and counted also among *nāyanārs*, Paṭṭinattār, known too for his saintly life and compositions, Śivavākyar, the largest composer in this group and considered to be identical, in his earlier life, with the Vaiṣṇava saint, *āḻvār* Tirumazhiśai, and a group of mystics who have fanciful names and sobriquets based on the characteristic features of their songs, e.g., "the Snake-Charmer *siddha*" whose songs are couched as addresses to the dancing snake. The *siddhas* adopt symbolic language. It is interesting to note that in the South Indian *siddha* tradition there was one Bhoga who lived in Kāñcīpuram talking a strange language according to saint Appar; Bhoga is considered to have been a Chinese.

The 15th century produced the most remarkable personality – Aruṇagirināthar, whose heart, bursting with devotion to Kumāra, broke out into 16,000 songs on Him as enshrined in 225 temples in Tamil Nadu and Śrī Laṅka, which shrines the saint-singer visited. His songs are set to a marvellous variety of rhythmic patterns in which South Indian musicians, adept in *laya*, are continuously exercising their imagination and rhythmic skill. Aruṇagiri handled also a unique language which freely passed from Tamil to Sanskrit and without the mechanical appearance of the well-known mixed bi-lingual diction in Tamil and Malayalam called *maṇi-pravāla*.

The passage of time did not mean that the ages of the great saints were over in South India. The 17th century produced Tāyumānavar, belonging to a family of officials of the Nāyak Court in Madurai; this saint was a prolific composer and he has left a legacy of songs of *vedāntin*-cum-Śaivite flavour which are full of his Sanskrit and Tamil erudition. The latest was Rāmāliṅgasvāmī, a contemporary of Rāmakrishna Paramahaṁsa. Born in 1823 near Chidambaram, he disappeared in 1874; but there are not wanting devotees and admirers who believe that he will appear again. His annual festival is celebrated. He was a Pillai by birth but drew followers and admirers from all classes. At Vadalūr near Chidambaram, he built a temple with only a lamp as symbolic of the Great Light of Divine Grace (*arut-perum-jyoti*) and poured forth a large volume of songs on Divine Grace (*arut-pā*). He desired to establish a Brotherhood of Man and his school is called *Śuddha samarasa mārga*, the pure path of harmony.

This sustained spiritual and religious fervor in South India which led to the long and continuous flowering of saintliness, devotion, hymns and songs in the Tamil region may be studied against an all-India background. Its North Indian contacts were many. The appellations *nāyanār* and *ālvār* mean the same thing as *nātha*, and the *siddha* is an all-India phenomenon. There were affiliations between South Indian Śaivism and Vaiṣṇavism and the forms of these two sects as practiced in Kashmir and other parts of the North. Saints and scholars like Tirumular and Nathamuni were from the North. Aruṇagirinātha, author of the *Tiruppughazh* on Kumāra, belonged to a Bengali family from Varendra and settled in the days of the Vijayanagara empire at Mulluṇḍrum near Aruṇāchala.

The Creative Saints of Karṇātaka

The new impulse spread from Tamil Nadu to adjacent Karṇāṭaka, where comparable to the Nāyanārs and Āḻvārs, two groups of saints arose, the Vīraśaivas or Liṅgāyats, and the Haridāsas. The former movement began in the 12th century with Basava the Brahman Minister of the Kalachuri King Bijjala of Kalyāna, or as it is held by some, with Ekāntada Rāmāyya. Besides Basava, other noteworthy figures in this tradition are Allama Prabhu and the "God's bride" in this school, Akkā Mahādevī; but from sayings left by the saints of this school we come to know of over two hundred of them, men and women. That this was a popular movement which transcended all caste-distinctions among its votaries is borne out by the variety of avocations from which the saints were drawn: from the Brahman Minister and the intellectual Allama to cobbler, washerman, cultivator, oil-monger, watchman, weaver of mats, etc. The literature of this school is of special significance as it took the form of sententious prose, called *vacana*. These *vacanas* show that Vīraśaivism was a call to get over all formalism, ritual and castes and to vow for oneself the higher life of virtues. The name Vīraśaiva underlines their being worshippers of Śiva; their other name, *Liṅgāyata* refers to their wearing always on their body a replica of the Śivaliṅga. The organization includes monasteries, gurus, and reference of the five founders, Ekorāma, Paṇḍitārādhya, Revaṇa, Marula, and Viśvāradhya. Wandering Vīraśaiva mendicants, the *jaṅgamas*, chanted the *vacanas* in simple tunes. (The musical affiliation of the *vacanas* may be seen in these lyrics from a *vacana* of Basava: "My Lord Kūḍala Saṅgama! make my body the *daṇḍi* of the *viṇā*, my head the sound-box, and my nerves the strings, and play the thirty-two *rāgas* on me.")

The Karṇāṭaka movement based on Viṣṇu-devotion, that of the Haridāsas, became widely known in non-Kanarese areas also, chiefly through its association with music. The greatest of the devotional lyric or *pada*-singers of this school, Purandaradāsa (1480-1564), is revered as the founder of modern Karṇāṭaka music. The Haridāsas became affiliated to the *dvaita* or dualist school of Madhvācārya, and thus, too, the songs of the Haridāsas spread in other areas. Purandara is believed to have composed an incredible number of *padas*, 475,000. What has survived is itself large in number and distinguished by a variety of forms of musical composition. His *padas*, the model and the source of inspiration for Tyāgarāja, are remarkable for their devotion, moral teachings, popular sayings, wit and satire and philosophical truths. There were other *Dāsas* ("servants of the Lord") in this group, the *Dāsa-kuṭa*, who composed *padas*: Kanaka, Vijaya, Jagannātha and Gopāla. That Kanakadāsa was a shepherd and that this teacher was the pontiff Vyāsarāya shows that the Haridāsa movement, too, was a popular one. The *dāsas* also popularized in South India the practice of holy mendicancy, going about with the *tambura* on the shoulders, bells on feet, the *chipals* for rhythm in hand, singing the *padas* and receiving handfuls of rice (*uñcha-vṛitti*) from willing house-holders. Similarly, in the Western world William James quotes an Italian mystic who says: "The true monk takes nothing with him but his lyre."[6]

Mahārāṣṭran and Gujarāti Singer Saints

The sweep of the *bhakti* movement over Mahārāṣṭra and the areas of old Rajasthāni, Hindi, Bengāli, etc., has been made known by scholars by systematic historical accounts, monographs and translations into English. The activities of the Mahārāṣṭra saints, who number about fifty, cover a period of five hundred years. The saints of this region, too, are drawn from the highest intellectual classes as well as the "lower" classes including outcastes, and some women and Muslims too. Jñāneśvara, the pioneer and the foremost among these, who wrote his gloss on the *Bhagavad Gītā* in 1290 A.D., is advaitic. The work of Bopadeva on the elucidation and popularization of the *Bhāgavata Purāṇa* under the Yādavas of

Devagiri, under whom Jñāneśvara too flourished, gave to this part of the country devotion to Krishna oriented to *advaita*; Jñāneśvara adopted this approach. The most important of the Mahārāṣṭra saints are, besides Jñānadeva, Nāmdeva (1269-1344), a tailor, Tukārām (1608-49), a shopkeeper, and Samārtha Rāmdās (1608-81) author of *Dāsabodha*, and Śivājī's guru, who popularized devotion to Rāma in Mahārāṣṭra. There are many edifying and miraculous stories related in the *Bhaktamālā* of Mahīpati about these saints, each of which has its own significance, exemplifying as it does a truth or a tenet of the doctrine of devotion or of knowledge. There are some parallelisms in the lives of the saints of the different regions, e.g., Ekanāth feeding a hungry *mahar* at his house and Veṅkaṭeśa Āyyāvāl of Tāñjāvūr District (C. 1700 A.D.) feeding a *caṇḍāla* with the *śrāddha* food for his ancestor-rite and the story of the Tamil pariah saint Nandanar and that of Cokamela with reference to entering the temple. The message of these stories is that true devotion alone matters and that caste, station, pomp and mere learning are of little moment. The Mahārāṣṭran devotional institution of musical *sankīrtan* had far-reaching effects, and the new stimulus to the practice of *bhājana* or congregational singing of the Lord's name or of songs of devotion which Tāñjāvūr District in Tamil Nadu got especially, was largely the cultural outcome of Marātha rule in Tāñjāvūr in the 17th and 18th centuries.

In Gujarat too, the same typical devotional activity and poetry manifested themselves; there were the twin strains of *advaita* and Krishna-*bhakti*. The two most important figures who sanctified this part of the country are Narasimha Mehtā of Junagadh, author of the song dear to Mahātma Gandhi, *Vaiṣṇava jana to*, and Mīrābāi of Rājasthan, the princess who became Lord Giridhar's bride. This spirit pervaded Sindh also, as the lives of Shah Karim and Shah Inayat and the poems of Shah Abdul Karim show.

Kashmīri, Punjābi and Other Northern Bhaktas

Kashmir was the home and meeting-place, in classical times, of different systems of philosophy and religion, Buddhism, Śaivism and *advaita*, and held the premier position as the touchstone of Sanskrit scholarship for centuries. At the end of the classical period, Kashmir gained a new position as the meeting-place of traditional Hindu thought and culture and the new Islamic thought and culture. Sufism and Vedānta provided the bridge and mystics arose who spoke in a language which drew followers from both sections of the people. Lallādevī, the lady mystic of the 14th century, whose monistic utterances form a large collection, is the best representative of Kashmir's contribution to this corpus of the poetry of *vedānta* and *bhakti* in the Indian languages.

Punjab's outstanding contribution is Nānak and the Sikh faith. As Toynbee says: "The Sikh religion might be described, not inaccurately, as a vision of this Hindu-Muslim common ground. To have discovered and embraced the deep harmony underlying the historic Hindu-Muslim discord has been a noble spiritual triumph; the Sikhs may well be proud of their religious ethos and origin."[7] After Nānak (1469-1539), there was a succession of nine gurus, Angad, Amar Dās, Rām Dās, Arjan, Har Govind, Har Rai, Har Kishan, Tegh Bahadur and Gobind Singh, down to 1708. The songs of these gurus are collected in the *Granth Saheb* which, after the tenth guru, became the permanent "guru" for later generations. The *Granth Saheb* is a storehouse of songs of the sings, some of them from the earlier saints of Mahārāṣṭra, Varanāsi, etc., all of them glorifying divinity, in an impersonal form, without any particular name, advocating the higher forms of abstract and non-sectarian worship and the sincere practice of spiritual *sādhanas*.

The ultimate inspiration of all the saints of the Hindi-speaking areas is Rāmānanda, who had twelve disciples. The greatest figures of this tradition were Kabīr and Tulasi; both of them were *vedāntins* and adored Rāma, but Kabīr was more strictly advaitic. In the words of Sir G. Grierson: "The words of two men of the past can be still heard in every village of Hindustan. These are Tulasi Dās, the abandoned child of a beggar Brahman tribe, and Kabīr, the despised weaver of Benāres."[8] Kabīr's influence extended up to Punjab, his songs being included in the Sikh sacred writings; other sects, besides individual writers, inspired by Kabīr are the Dādūpanthis, Lāldāsis, Bābālalis, Sadhu Charandāsis, Garibdāsis, Rāmāsanchis, Paltupantis, Prānnāthis, Rādhāsvāmis. Different from the schools of Rāma-devotion which had an *advaita* background and denounced forms and rituals, there were schools of Krishna-devotion of which Vallabhacharya was the inspiration. Sūrdās, the blind-singer of Agra, was the greatest personality in the tradition of Krishna-devotion. The most prominent feature of the popular movement in the area was the background of Hindu-Muslim relations; as a result, many of these popular saint-singers became the apostles of a synthesis and rapprochement, aided by the common points in *advaita* and Sufism. This commingling produced also Krishna-devotees among Muslims who sang fine lyrics in their Krishna-*prema* (love), for example, Raskhan and Abdul Rahim Khankhana.

If we turn East, it is the land of Krishna and Śakti. The early stirrings of Rādhā-Krishna devotional literature go back to Jayadeva and his masterpiece of Sanskrit lyric, the *Gītagovinda*, which became the main inspiration of a flowering of musical dance-drama composition all over the east, the Deccan and South India. Krishna-*bhakti* bloomed in Western India too. In the East, Vidyāpati of Mithilā (14th cent. A.D.), a distinguished Sanskrit writer, was the pioneer of the *pada* compositions in the spoken languages on the theme of Rādhā-Krishna *bhakti*; his songs were sung by Caitanya and they form the common heritage of Bihar and Bengal. He was followed by Śaṅkaradeva of Assām whose literary output as well as the organization of devotional institutions in his part of the country was most impressive. Śaṅkaradeva (1449-1558), son of a Kāyastha local chief, became learned in Sanskrit; under the influence of the *Bhāgavata Purāṇa*, he turned from his family tradition of Sakti-worship to Krishna. He propagated Krishna-*bhakti* by writing a Sanskrit text on devotion, by poetic versions in his language of portions of the *Bhāgavata Purāṇa*, by composing songs and creating a type of drama of *Bhāgavata Purāṇa* themes called *Aṅkia-Nat*, by writing prayer-formulae for congregational recitation (*nāma-ghoṣha* and *kīrtana-ghoṣha*), and by setting up centres for devotional exercises called *sattras* and *nāmghars*. His pilgrimage included South India and the influence of his work extended beyond Assām and embraced areas of Tibeto-Burman peoples. Here again the movement was cosmopolitan and Śaṅkaradeva had Brahmans as also Muslims as pupils.

Bengali Singers and the Return to the South

In neighboring Bengal where already the Buddhist *caryāgītas* and later different kinds of *mangal* songs had paved the way, the new *pada*-compositions on Kālī or Krishna arose with Caṇḍīdās (14th century), who was a Śakta and then became a Vaiṣṇava. The *Caṇḍi* or *Devī-mahātmya* in Sanskrit was the ultimate source of inspiration for the Śakta lyrics of Bengal. Rāmāprasad (1718-75), of whom Sister Nivedita, after comparing his songs with aspects of the writings of Blake, Burns and Whitman, observes that "the radiant white heat of childlikeness" in his songs, has really no parallel,[9] is perhaps the best of the Śakta *pada*-composers of Bengal. However, Rāmāprasād was not an exclusive worshipper of Devī as his

Krishna and Śiva *kīrtanas* show. A fresh upsurge of Krishna-*bhakti* in Bengal flowed from Caitanya (1486-1534). Caitanya wrote only two short Sanskrit *stotras* (poems) but his disciples and followers put out a large body of literature in Sanskrit and Bengali in song, poem, play, aesthetics and biography of Caitanya which attest to the hold of his gospel of Krishna devotion on the Bengali people. Caitanya's sway extended to Orissa also.

The cycle came full circle and reached South India again. Through music, dance and dance-drama, the influence on Jayadeva spread southwards and in Telugu, Kannada, Tamil and Malayālam, musical stories and plays on devotional themes were composed in Sanskrit and these languages. *Kīrtana* and *bhajana* flowed from Mahārāṣṭra chiefly, and from Bengal to some extend, so that on a soil already the seed-bed of *bhakti* the flow of these fresh waters from other areas led to a rich new crop of devotional music and dance-drama. With Nāyak and Marātha rule at Tāñjāvūr, many devout teachers and gifted music-composers from Āndhra and Mahārāṣṭra went there; it was as if for a time all literary and cultural roads led to Tāñjāvūr. This was the golden age of Karṇāṭaka music. In Āndhra, Bhadrāchala Rāmādas was a local officer under the Sultans of Golcanda. For spending the revenue collection on Lord Rāma in the temple at Bhadrācala he was thrown into prison, from where he sang his songs on Rāma. In his footsteps and those of Purandaradās of Karṇāṭaka, Tyāgarāja, a Telugu domiciled in Tāñjāvūr District in Tamil Nadu, followed. Tyāgarāja, the greatest of the Karṇāṭaka music-composers, was also a great devotee of Rāma. His compositions take an important place in the Rāma-literature of India. Among music-composers or saint-singers who adopted a single theme, Tyāgarāja stands foremost for literary appeal, richness of ideas and fancies, endless emotional variations and intensity of feeling.

Name, Guru, True Bhakti, Oneness

In an over-all comparative study of this song-literature of the saints, we find some common features in the religious and philosophical doctrines as well as expression. All the saints, from the 7th century *nāyanārs* and *āḻvārs* of the South to the most recent ones, inclusive of the Muslim mystics who sang on Krishna or Rāma, hold the name of the Lord, *nāma*, as the savior and as fundamental to their approach. Many ideas and illuminating analogies are offered by the saints to bring out the importance of the Name (*nāma*) and its relation to the form (*rūpa*) of the Lord.

The next is the uniform emphasis on guru which we find even in the songs of Muslim devotees. Here again many striking and suggestive similes are used to bring out the nature and role of the guru in relation to God and realization. The third is the stress on the uniqueness of *bhakti* as a democratic doctrine which consolidates all people without distinction of caste, community, nationality, or sex. The fourth is the repeated clarification of the true form of devotion or worship. The fifth is their reformist zeal and denunciation of sham and deception as also of empty formalism. The sixth is the comprehension, catholicity and the sense of unity of all paths. Nānak adopts not only a Hindu-Muslim eclecticism but also assimilates Buddhistic terms from Tibet like *śūnya* and *mahaśūnya*. The seventh is, barring some stray cases of exclusive allegiance to Śiva or Viṣṇu, the generally prevailing *advaita* tone and the preference for monism and, ultimately, unity. Not only are many descriptions of the abstract Brahman in the *Upaniṣads* echoed or adopted, but actual assertions are made with this conviction. Some of the saints like Tulasidās try to harmonize the concepts of *jñāna* and *bhakti*, and of *sākāra* and *nirākara*, the Personal and the Impersonal, with the aid of meaningful analogies. This is one of the many integrations of the faiths, paths, modes, and *sādhanas* which the saints achieved by repeated emphasis on this old and principal Indian belief. In doing this, they did only what mystics of all climes have done. Says William James in his *Varieties of Religious Experience*: "Mystical states of mind in every degree are shown in history, usually though not always. to make for a monistic view."

Notes

[1]From *The Great Integrators: The Singer Saints of India* (New Delhi: Pub. Div., Ministry of Information, Govt. of India, 1966, 1969, 1976, 1979), pp. 4-19.

[2]Margaret E. Noble (Sister Nivedita), *Kālī, the Mother* (Mayavati [Almore]: Advaita Ashrama, 1950), p. 43.

[3]Sri Aurobindo Ghose, *Renaissance in India* (Chandernagore: Prabartak Publishing House, 1920), p. 21.

[4]IV. *Porri-t-tiru-ahaval*, II. 54-55.

[5]*Annual Report of Epigraphy*, Madras, 1918, p. 149.

[6]W. James, *The Varieties of Religious Experience* (New York: Random House, 1902), pp. 266-7.

[7]*The Sacred Writings of the Sikhs* (New York: UNESCO and Sahitya Akademi, 1960), Foreword, p. 10.

[8]F.E. Keay, *Kabīr and His Followers*, The Religious Life of India Series (Calcutta, 1931), p. 67.

[9]Margaret E. Noble (Sister Nivedita), *Kālī, the Mother*, p. 48.

CULTURAL OVERVIEWS

Part Two:

Praise of the Name: Highlights from Ṛg Vedic Times to Tyāgarāja[1]

What is there in a name, one may ask. It is name that is everything. Name is fame. It is by using somebody's name that one has to get on. When one is highly enraged or highly pleased, one calls names, of abuse or of praise. In the excess of one's hate or love, what comes out of one is mere name. In those short exclamations that break forth, the entire surcharged feeling stands compressed.

A name is therefore a condensed "tablet" form of a *guṇa*, an attribute of a person. The *Viṣṇu sahasranāma* ("Thousand Names of Viṣṇu" in the Mahābhārata epic) says that *nāmas* are based on *guṇas*, the qualities or strands of nature. The *Bhāgavata Purāṇa*, a *bhakti* text, says that the names of the Lord are each marked with fame, exploit and quality of the Lord.[2] And of the Lord who is possessed of infinite excellences, the names are also infinite.

The earliest outpourings of man praying to the divine powers are seen in the *Ṛg Vedic* hymns, in the form of praises of the names and qualities of different deities, Agni, Indra etc. In the *Śatarudrīya*, the same deity Rudra, who is conceived as everything, is praised with different and numerous names. Even in the *Upaniṣads*, Brahman, which is really without qualities, *nirguṇa*, is yet characterised by expressions like *satya*, *jñāna*, *ananta.*[3]

It is a matter of common experience, as the *Bhāgavata Purāṇa* says, that when one keeps on muttering the name of a thing, one's mind develops a love for it and a gradual absorption in it.[4]

It is with the help of a word, the name of an object, that one can recollect and fix an object in one's mind. Names, therefore, serve as fasteners attaching the Lord's personality in our mind and heart.[5]

In seeking a person through praise, there are three forms: firstly to describe in varied and poetic manner the greatness of the person sought; secondly, to refer to his varied glory by several significant attributes in the form of manifold names; and lastly, to call him forth for our help by the repitition of only one name of his. Under the first category come all poetic hymns. Under the second come the *sahasra nāma*, *astottara nāma* hymns and the *nāmāvalis* sung in *bhajans*, and under the last comes *nāma pārāyaṇa* or the repetition of a single name: Rāma, Śiva, Krishna, or the Goddess.

It has been held that with the gradual deterioration in the faculties and abilities of men, as ages passed on towards *Kali* (the fourth age, an age of strife in the Hindu time cycle), the sages devised further and further easier paths, for the salvation of suffering humanity. It is with this purpose in view that the path of *bhakti* or devotion was developed. *Kali* is predominantly an age of emotion and it is through this emotion that man has to be saved. This is achieved by turning the flow of his emotion in the direction of a Supreme saving Personality. To draw man's heart in love towards the Supreme Being, the emphasis was shifted from knowledge to devotion and from an abstraction to a Personality endowed with infinite excellences, in fact the human form itself in which Divinity frequently incarnated. When *bhakti* was thus evolved and developed, further processes of simplification were introduced, so that anybody and everybody, in whatever standard of equipment of mind and character, might have some means to take to.[6]

Along with temples, worship of images, adoration with acts of worship, singing the Lord's glory, reading and listening to writings on divine glory, and even mere recitation of divine names developed. Thus were the Himālayan waters of the *Upaniṣads* brought to the plains, to irrigate the hearts of the masses of the entire country. All glory to these spiritual engineers who undertook these works, the *paurāṇikas*, the *bhāgavatas*, the *āḻvārs*, and *nāyanārs*, the saints and bhaktas and musicians of this country, to which galaxy Jñāneśwara and Rāmānanda, Caitanya and Tyāgarāja belonged.[7]

The literature of *bhakti* bearing in particular on the doctrine of the Lord's Name as the supreme means of salvation is quite considerable. Besides some of the later *Saguṇa Upaniṣads*, portions of the *Mahābhārata*, the *Bhagavad Gītā*, the *Viṣṇu Sahasranāma*, the *Purāṇas* and especially the *Viṣṇu-* and the *Bhagavata Purāṇas* form the main authorities of this school of thought. A number of religious writers contributed treatises on the theory of the subject of *Nāmamahātmya*, in which they seek support not only in the above-mentioned texts, going up to the later minor *Upaniṣads*, but also to the *Ṛg Vedic* hymns themselves. The basic *Vedic* text on which they take their stand is *Ṛg veda*, 2.2.26: "O Praisers, knowing them, express every one of his names. O Viṣṇu, we desire the goodwill of you who are great."[8] (*āsya jānanto nāma cidviviktana mahatte viṣṇo sumatim bhajāmahe*)

Of the *Upaniṣads* referred to, I shall mention briefly here only one, the *Kalisantaranopaniṣad*, which specially concerns itself with the means of salvation appropriate or most efficacious in the *Kali* age or to get over *Kali*. According to this text, at the end of the *Dvāpara* age and the opening of *Kali*, Nārada asked his father Brahmā how he could cross over the *Kali* age. Brahmā gave him the remedy: "You can shake off *Kali* by reciting the Name of the Lord Nārāyaṇa, the Prime Being."

The *Bhagavad Gītā* added its weight to this school of thought when it said that of all forms of *yajña*, the Lord was of the form of *japa-yajña*: "Among sacrifices, I am the sacrifice of repeating the mantra." (*yajñānām japayajno 'smi*)

The full significance of this exaltation of *japa-yajña* in the *Bhagavad Gītā* is brought out later in the Mahābhārata epic, in the introduction to the *Viṣṇu Sahasranāma*. Having listened to all sorts of *dharma*, Yudhiṣṭhira, still not satisfied, asked Bhīṣma again: "What do you consider to be the greatest, the *dharma* of all *dharmas*, the most righteous action of all? By reciting what will beings as such be liberated from the cycle of birth and transmigration?" Bhīṣma replied that in his view, the devoted adoration of the Lord with hymns of praise and through the thousand divine Names is the *dharma* which is superior to all other *dharmas*. It was in reply to this question of Yudhiṣṭhira that Bhīṣma gave the world the thousand Names of the Lord. (See the translation of the *Viṣṇu Sahasranāma* in a later part of this book.)

The superiority of this *japayajña*, sacrifice of repetition, or *nāma-stotra*, hymn in praise of holy names, over other *dharmas* and *yajñas* which is meant here is well explained by the master teacher *ācārya* Śaṅkara in his commentary on the *Viṣṇu Sahasranāma*. Śaṅkara says: "What is the ground of superiority of this adoration in the form of the hymn? Its superiority over other kinds of *yajñas* consists in the following points in its favor: It does not involve injury to a being in the form of sacrifice; it is an *ahimsā-yāga*, a sacrifice of non-violence. For doing it, you need no collection of men, money or material, nor need you observe any particular time, place or procedure."[9]

And Śaṅkara then quotes a large number of verses from several *Purāṇas* to bear out his explanation. The *Viṣṇu Purāṇa* says: "Meditation in *Kṛita Yuga*, sacrifices in *Tretā Yuga*, worship in *Dvāpara Yuga*, – what these give, that one attains in *Kali Yuga* by merely uttering the Name of the Lord."[10]

> One can cast off this sheath of sin by uttering the Lord's Name even as one walks, stands, lies down, drinks, eats or bends down. In every *karma*, gaps or lapses occur and expiations for them have to be done; if those expiations are further *Karmas* of penance etc., further lapses are in store and there is infinite regress, *Avavasthā*. So, the expiation of all expiations is the thought of the Lord with the uttering of His Name. The singing of His Name reduces all sins, even as fire, all dross. In *Kali*, Name alone is the means; there is no other path.[11]

Furthermore, there is the insistence that "You need not recite Vedic chants – the *ṛiks*, *yajus* or *sāmans*. Sing the Lord's Name. There is the Lord's name available to men, there is the human tongue which men themselves can control – still, men fall into hell – what a wonder!"[12]

The *Bhāgavata* is the *Purāṇa* of *Purāṇas* for this school of *bhaktas* and worshippers of the Lord's Name. Owing to the great facility of attaining salvation through Name, the *Kali* age becomes meritorious, in spite of its many defects and indeed those that know hold *Kali* in great regard for this.

> Indeed there is one great virtue which the *Kali* age possesses, O Pariksit, though it is the storehouse of all the evils that exist. By merely chanting the names and glories of Lord Krishna, one is released from all one's attachments and reaches the ultimate . . . . Mature and discriminating persons who appreciate the merits of the Kali age and recognize the essence of things, extol this age, in which by merely chanting the names of the Lord one can attain all the desired

objects (which could otherwise be attained through efforts in a variety of other ways).[13]

According to the *Bhāgavata Purāṇa*, even the great *jñānins* (wise men) and *paramahaṃsas* (great sages, who like the mythical swans of their namesake separate milk from water, the eternal from the temporary) though they have nothing to do or gain, revel in the Personality, Names and songs of the Lord. In fact, the *Purāṇa* holds that the liberated state of pure *jñāna*, without any act, if it is to be devoid of the love of the Lord, is not good. To sing of the Lord's glory is the only beautiful thing; it is eternally fresh and charming; it is an incessant festivity for the mind; it alone removes men's sorrows completely. The speech and writing, in which the glorious Names of the Lord are imbedded, is the flood that washes away the sins of humanity, though every verse of it may be full of grammatical lapses. That literature, however wonderful, which is barren of the glorification of the Lord, is like the pool where crows splash dirty water, not the *mānasa* lake in which the swans of liberated souls sport and delight.

> That speech alone is pleasant, which constantly gives newer and newer delight, that alone is a perennial source of great rejoicing to the mind and finally that is the only means of drying up the ocean of man's grief, through which Viṣṇu's glory is continuously being sung." . . . Speech, which though full of figurative expressions, never utters the praises that possess the virtue of sanctifying the whole world, is considered to be the delight of voluptuous men who wallow in the pleasures of sense like crows that feed upon the dirty leavings of food. Like swans, which are believed to have their abode in the lotus beds of *Mānasarovar* lake, devotees who have taken shelter at the lotus feet of the Lord

> and therefore ever abide in His heart never take delight in such speech (v. 10). On the other hand, that composition which, though faulty of diction consists of verses each of which contains the names of the immortal Lord, bearing the impress of His glory, wipes out the sins of the people; it is such composition that pious men love to hear, sing and repeat to an audience (v. 11).
>
> That wisdom too which is free from blemish and is a direct means to the attainment of liberation does not adorn one's soul so much, if it is devoid of devotion to Lord Acyuta. How then, can sorrow at every stage (both while it is being performed and at the time of its fruition), and even disinterested action that has not been dedicated to God serve to heighten one's glory (v. 12).[14]

It is in accordance with this that great *advaitic* teachers from Śaṅkara onwards have all been *bhaktas* and have sung many a hymn of devotion. It is in accordance with this that many distinguished scholars, *bhakta*s and *sannyāsin*s gave a fresh stimulus to the school of *Nāmasiddhānta* in Cola Deśa, the Southern areas including Tāñjāvūr District, in the seventeenth and eighteenth centuries. The most noteworthy amongst these propagators of this *Nāma bhajana* is Sridhara Veṅkaṭeśa, popularly known by the revered name "Āyyāvāl" who wrote the *Ākhyāṣaṣṭi*, or Sixty verses on the Lord's Name, and another treatise on this subject entitled *Bhagavan nāma Bhūṣana*. He was accompanied in his enthusiasm by Śrī Bodhendra, a *sannyāsin* who wrote four works expounding the details of this doctrine, using titles associating the name with nectar: the *Nāmāmṛita Rasāyana*, the *Nāmāmṛita Rasodaya*, the *Nāmāmṛita Sūryodaya* and the *Bhagavan Nāmāmṛitārṇava*. The guru saluted by Tyāgarāja in his *Naukā Carita*, Śrī

Rāmakrishnānanda, was also probably an expounder of this *Nāma māhātmya*. "Nāma-paras," adherents of the path of Name, are mentioned separately from those who take to the six philosophical systems, by Tyāgarāja in his piece *Nijamarmamulanu*. And it is significant to note here that one of the manuscripts in Tyāgarāja's library, which has come down to us, is of a work called *Devatā Nāma Māhātmya*.

It is necessary to look more closely at this kind of background to understand the literary and historical influences on Tyāgarāja, which helped form his devotion to *Rāma nāma*, and the ideas he expressed on this subject in the course of some of his songs.

* * *

It is well known that in the wake of the *bhakti* movement, the worship of Rāma attained great importance, and the movement spread widely and gave rise to a considerable literature taking the form of *Upaniṣads*, sections of *Purāṇa* and independent *purāṇic* compilations called *Samhitas*, philosophical and devotional versions of the *Rāmāyana* epic such as the *Adhyātma Rāmāyaṇa*, the *Adbhūta Rāmāyaṇa* and the *Ānanda Rāmāyaṇa*, and independent digests on the methods and details of worship, recitation of Rāma's name, and so on. In the process of this magnification, stories came up to explain such incidents in Vālmīki which obviously called for an explanation; thus a series of "earlier stories" (*pūrva-vṛitta*) arose, some of these being necessitated by the supposedly vulnerable points in the acts of Rāma. The mass of such stories of praise of Rāma's glories, *Rāmamāhātmya* grew so much and got spread over so wide a literature that today anyone who wants to have a collection of all these is faced with the formidable task of collation of material scattered in numerous works, many of which are in manuscripts. But fortunately for the student of Rāma literature, a recluse named Rāmabrahmānanda Sarasvatī set himself to the task and produced a compendium of such Rāma stories in a work called the *Tattva-saṁgraha-rāmāyaṇa*. This work is very useful to votaries of Rāma and students of history and the development of Rāma stories and their impact on the literatures of the different parts of the country, particularly works like the *Rāma-carit-manasa* of Tulsidās, produced under the spell of the Rāma movement that gained a momentum at the hands of Rāmānanda of Banāras. In South India one of the greatest and most popular figures to follow this movement of Rāma-*bhakti* and to have attained *siddhi* or spiritual realization by the prescribed mode of repeating Rāma's name was Tyāgarāja. His elder, Upaniṣad Brahman was another devotee of this tradition, a pupil of Vasudevendra. Another disciple of Vasudevendra, who taught Advaita and Rāma-*bhakti*, was Svayamprakāśānanda. Svayamprakāśānanda was the guru of the author of the *Tattva-saṁgraha-rāmāyaṇa*.[15]

* * *

Of the later *Saguna Upaniṣads*, three deal exclusively with Rāma: the *Rāma Rahasya* and the *Pūrva-* and *Uttara Rāma Tāpanī-Upaniṣads*. In those as well as in the *Kali Santaranopaniṣad*, the doctrine of *Nāma* is given to us in the form of Rāma-*nāma*. After Brahmā told Nārada that *Kali* could be crossed over by the recital of the Lord's Name, Nārada asks again: "What is that Name?" and Brahmā replies: "*Hare Rāma Hare Rāma Rāma Rāma Hare Hare/ Hare Krishna Hare Krishna Krishna Krishna Hare Hare.*"

In the *Rāma Rahasyopaniṣad*, which is one of the later ones, Rāma says that one escapes from all sins by repeating his Name, nine hundred and sixty million times.[16] (The detailed procedure to be followed for the performance of the *koṭijapa* of Rāma-*nāma* is set forth in the *Tattvasaṁgraha Rāmāyaṇa, Kiṣkindhā Khāṇḍa*, 9, *Śiva-Pārvatī-samvada.*) Towards its close, the *Rāma Rahasyopaniṣad* expounds the significance of the syllabic constituents of the name, Rāma. It is said Śiva knows this significance well. The name Rāma is a synthesis of the essence of the Nārāyana eight syllable mantra and the Śiva five syllable mantra, its two syllables being extracted from the two separate mantras.[17]

It is because *Rāma nāma* is dealt with so fully in the *Upaniṣads* that Tyāgarāja describes that Name as *Veda-varṇanīyamau nāmamuto* in *Evarikai* and as *Vedasāramau nāmadheyamunu* in his song *Talacinantanē.*

The *Rāma uttara tāpanī* says that Rāma mantra is called *tāraka*, "enabler of the crossing," because it traditionally has been the utterance empowering aspirants to cross over *samsāra*, the sea of worldly existences, to the other shore of ultimate reality. (Rāma has been adored as the *nāma-tāraka* par excellence, by Muthusvāmī Dīkṣitar also in his song on Rāma, *Rāmacandram bhāvayāmi – Nāma-kīrtana-tārakam.* In the song *Raghupate Rāma*, Tyāgarāja characterizes Rāma as "tāraka-nāmadheya" meaning "He whose name saves one.") In fact *tāraka nāma* is a very common epithet of Rāma, found for example in the song *Sujana jīvana. Tāraka* is Brahman and Rāma is Brahman. And this *Rāma tāraka mantra* is given to every person who dies at the *Avimukta kṣetra* ("Sacred field of Liberation") in Banāras, at the *Maṇikarṇika tīrtha* shrine or any part of the Ganges bank, imparted by Lord Śiva Himself. Banāras or Varanāsi, where the two rivers Varanā and Asī meet, is an external correlative of the juncture of the brows and the nose, and here is the spot to be concentrated upon by yogis.[18] The imparting of the *tāraka mantra* of *Rāma nāma* by Śiva at Banāras is further dealt with in the *Kāśikhaṇḍa.*

The poet Kalidāsa wrote that when the guru Vasiṣṭha

gave the name "Rāma" to King Daśaratha's first son, he was prompted to suggest that name because of the charming personality of Rāma; and the poet immediately adds that the name became the foremest auspicious thing of the world. Tyāgarāja sang that the name chosen was as charming as the person: *Rāmabhirāma rāmaṇīyanāma. Rāma nāma* is also the Victorious Name which bestows success in the mundane as well as spiritual spheres: *Jayakāra-nāma*, Tyāgarāja sings in *Dīnajanāvana.*[19]

As already observed, one of the tenets of the worshippers of the Lord's Name is that the *Nāma* itself is the *Rūpa*, the Form. Accordingly, to the worshippers of Name with such a belief, the Name is not merely an *upāya*, a "means" to reach the Lord, but is *upeya*, the "end" – the holy goal itself. This tenet of Name itself being first the means and then the end, both *upāya* and *upeya*, is expounded in the treatise just referred to, the *Upeya nāma-viveka* by Upaniṣad Brahman, which Tyāgarāja must have read.

The Name has two phases even as the Brahman has the two phases, *saguṇa* and *nirguṇa*, with form and formless. The former is the *upāya*, the means, and the latter, the *upeya*, is the Absolute to be attained.

The *upāya-nāma* of the Name as normally understood has itself four phases, from the gross to the subtle: *sthūla* ("gross"), *sūkṣma* ("subtle"), *bīja* ("seed") and *turiya* ("fourth"), each of which forms, in an ascending order, the object of worship as the aspirant evolves higher and higher. In the fourth, the *turiya*, the devotee sees no difference between himself and that state which *Rāma nāma* would endow him with; that is, he has reached the non-differentiating advaitic stage here. On the attainment of this fourth stage, the aspirant becomes qualified to realise complete one-ness in which the body and the world cease to exist for him and he is just the "disembodied consciousness" itself, *vikalebaracaitanya*; this is the stage of *nāma* itself as the Brahman and the goal, the *upeya*.

The first three stages of adoration of *upāya-nāma* are stages of duality of the worshipper and the worshipped; the fourth is a stage of unity but the next stage of *upeya nāma* is the final realization where there is no question of duality or non-duality; it is the absolute impartite state of realization.

This detailed introduction is needed to understand Tyāgarāja's practice of *Rāma nāma japa* and the full meaning of his songs on *Rāma nāma*. Just as the wanderings and doings of Śrī Sadāśiva Brahmendra along the Kāverī banks, which are still a fragrant memory with us, are a proof to us in recent times of the glory of the high *avadhūta*[20] state, so is the life and *siddhi* (extraordinary yogic power) of Tyāgarāja, the master of music and *bhakti* saint, is a proof of the efficacy of *Rāma nāma* as a potent means of salvation.

Tyāgarāja was an exponent of the school that the *Nāma-japa* of the Lord is the most effective path and that the devotee of the name need not be concerned with other paths: *Rāma-nāmamu sāramē gāni anya-mārgavicāra mēṭike, O manasā* he sings in the song *Sāramē*. "O mind, only the name Rāma is most precious and all worthy – why be concerned with other roads and various ways?" According to a tradition of the Umayālpuram village "school" of Tyāgarāja's pupils, Tyāgarāja embarked in the prime of his youth, his twentieth year, on the great *tapas* of reciting *Rāma nāma* nine hundred and sixty million times; and it took him twenty-one years and fifteen days to finish this *japa*. In the end Tyāgarāja had the *darśan* or vision of Śrī Rāmacandra and he sang his first inspired piece, *Ēla nī dayarādu*, according to this school.

In this connection, we may bear in mind that the *Rāma Rahasya Upaniṣad* lays down that *Rāma nāma* has to be chanted ninety-six crores [one crore is ten million] times for the attainment of *siddhi* or extraordinary powers. Whether the form of the tradition in the Umayālpuram School is true exactly or not, there is no doubt that Tyāgarāja did attain *siddhi* through practicing the *japa* of *Rāma nāma*. In more than one song does Tyāgarāja refer to his having had the visit of Rāma or his sight; for example in the songs *Kanugoṇṭini* and *Bhavanuta*. To utter the Lord's Name became a second nature to him. If the Tamil Śaiva Saint prayed to his Lord that even if he forgot the Lord, his tongue should go on repeating the Lord's Name,[21] Tyāgarāja prays for nothing more than that his tongue should become used to continuous repetition of the Lord's Name, in his song *Śrī Raghuvara*.[22]

In *Ūrake*, another song, he affirms that this king of *mantras*, *Rāma-nāma*, was ever "shining" (*rājillu*) on the tongue of Tyāgarāja. He must have developed this practice of *nāma japa* very early. Attention may be drawn in this connection to those songs of his in which he himself tells us that he was devoted to Rāma from his early years, and even from birth.[23] He was thus a *garbha-bhāgavata*, "a devotee while still in the womb," like Prahlāda. In fact, his familiarity with devotion to the name from the time of his birth, is not unlikely, when we recollect the fact that his father Rāma Brahman was a classmate of Śrī Upaniṣad Brahman and both of them were Rāma *bhaktas*, and Upaniṣad Brahman Yogi, the author of the treatise on *nāma* called *Upeya-nāma-viveka*, was one of the teachers of the *bhakti* movement devoted to Rāma-*nāma* in South India.

In *Pāhi mām har* , quoted above, Tyāgarāja says that he secured early in his life the precious pearl of *Rāma nāma*. (*Pāhi rāma nāma muktāphalamul riti.*)

One of the doctrines of this *Rāma nāma siddhānta* which we saw mentioned in the *Rāma Upaniṣads* is that Śiva knows the value and taste of the sweet name of Rāma and that He imparts it to people dying in Banāras. This tenet is basic to the entire body of Tyāgarāja's songs. When the composer introduces his *mudrā* or signature at the end of all his pieces in expressions like *Tyāgarājanutuni*, the expression means "Rāma praised by both poet Tyāgarāja and by Lord Śiva," Tyāgarāja being the name and form of Śiva worshipped in the main temple at the composer's birth place. Tyāgarāja makes an explicit and full reference to this in a song (*Inta saukyamani*):

> Is it possible for me to describe the *ānanda*, the divine bliss one derives from chanting *Rāma nāma*? Who knows its measure and quality? Only true and great devotees know it. Lord Śaṅkara, who delights in drinking the nectar of music with the sugar-candy of *Rāma nāma*, knows it well.[24]

At the end of Tyāgarāja's song *Rāma raghukula jalanidhē*, there is another reference: "You made Śaṅkara utter your *tāraka mantra* in the ears of the people who live in this *Kali* age." In the song *Nityarūpa* Tyāgarāja says "The Lord Śiva of Kaśi knows your name." In *Kana kana rucirā* he cites Śiva as a witness to the efficacy of *Rāma nāma*: "Śiva, the one who lives in Kailāsa, is a witness . . ." In the well known piece *Vād rā* Tyāgarāja says that Śiva initiates the ignorant folk of the world in this *tārakamantra* so that they might cross over the sea of *samsāra*. *Sāramē gāni* is another piece in which he cites the example of Śiva. By making reference to the initiation of Vālmīki in Rāma-*nāma* by Nārada and to Śuka teaching Hari-*nāma* to King Parīkṣit, the song emphasizes to us the primary position which we should give to the *Rāmāyaṇa* and the *Bhāgavata Purāṇa*.

> Did not Śiva, the delighter in *Sāma gāna*, music of the *Sāma Veda*, drink with all earnestness the nectar

of Rāma-*nāma*, besides unceasingly uttering it to his holy consort Pārvatī and explaining to Her its great efficacy and significance?[25]

We noted above that the interpretation of the significance of Rāma-*nāma* given by the *Rāma Rahasyopaniṣad*, considers it an essence extracted out of both the *Nārāyaṇa astakṣari* (eight syllable mantra) and Śiva *pañcakṣari* (five syllable mantra). The doctrine is set forth fully by Tyāgarāja in his song *Evarani*:

> What do people determine you to be and how do they worship you? As Śiva, Mādhava, Brahmā or the Supreme Absolute? I prostrate before those wise ones who found the solution by extracting and combining the soul of each of the two mantras, "Rā" from "Om Namo Nārāyanāya" and "Ma" from "Om Na*ma* Śivāya."

In the song the actual order of the syllables as set forth by Tyāgarāja is not Rā-ma but Ma-rā which according to some imaginative interpreters is a reference to the sage Vālmīki of whom Tyāgarāja is adored as an incarnation and the story of Vālmīki, who unable to utter Rāma, was going on uttering "Marā-marā" so that in the concatenation, the correct name Rāma was automatically formed; even such an utterance is considered efficacious according to *Nāma-siddhānta*, as explained here below. This "Ma-rā" episode is seen in a Purandaradāsa song too.

A further point in this process of extraction of the essences of the two mantras is also suggested by Tyāgarāja when he sings *I vavaramu delisina* (literally "knowing this specification or detail") and calls the two extracted syllables the "*jīva*" or life of the two mantras. This *vivara* or further "detail" of how these two syllables constitute the *jīva* or life of the two mantras is that if "Rā" is taken out of "Nārāyanāya," the word becomes "Nāyanāya" which means "It helps not as the path for the aspirant" and if "Ma" is taken out of "Na*ma*s Śivāya" the expression becomes "Na Śivāya" meaning "not for good." This is all set forth by Upaniṣad Brahman at some length in his *Upeyanāmaviveka.*

One of the further developments in the direction of the glorification of *Nāma* as the easiest of means is the view that just as fire burns even if it is touched without knowledge, the Lord's Name saves one, if it comes from any quarter and in any form, even if it is uttered unconsciously or in play, in ridicule or whatever. Even if the letters constituting the name Rāma, Śiva, Krishna or the Goddess, occur as part of other sound-combinations in sentences of other meanings they are salvific. The *Viṣṇu Purāṇa* asserts this power of the name: "by the repetition of [Viṣṇu's] name man is undoubtedly liberated from all sins, which fly like wolves that are frightened by a lion" (VI.8.19). This and other similar verses are quoted by Śaṅkara in his *Viṣṇu sahasra nāma bhāṣya.*[26]

The *Bhāgavata Purāṇa* also upheld this view and illustrated it with the classic story of Ajāmila, who, having spent his life in dissipation, called out at the time of his death, the name of his last beloved son, which was Nārāyaṇa. The moment the sound "Nārāyaṇa" came out of that sinner's mouth, all his sins vanished, and the emissaries of Viṣṇu rushed to prevent those of Yama from claiming Ajāmila. It is declared on that occasion that whatever the spirit or manner in which one uttered the Lord's name, he is saved. The medicine does not require the sick man to have much knowledge about it to give him the cure.[27]

> The wise know that saying a name of Viṣṇu is able to cleanse all one's sins, even if it is intended to denote another, or when it is spoken in jest, or as an

exclamation during a song, or even disrespectfully (*Bhāgavata Purāṇa* VI.2. v.14). A man who says the word "Hari" involuntarily, spontaneously as he stumbles or falls, when suddenly bitten (by a snake or other creature, in fever, when an arm or leg is broken, no longer deserves to undergo sufferings (v. 15). Just as a medicine with the most potency is certain to produce the best effect, even if taken by chance, so too does the name of the Lord reveal its power to purify, even when someone is ignorant of it, and is uttered casually (v. 19).

Ajāmila, a character in the *Bhāgavata Purāṇa*, uttered the whole name, though he was only referring to his son. To illustrate the case, *bhāgavatas* (expounders and lead singers of devotion) tell stories and offer illustrations. One is the conversion of Vālmīki by Nārada, which incident is referred to by Tyāgarāja in *I menu galigi nanduku*. But the *bhāgavatas* say that Vālmīki the hunter could not, as already mentioned, utter "Rāma," but, as a man of the forest, could utter "Marā," the name of a tree. Therefore, Nārada ingeniously asked him to repeat quickly "Marā-Marā-Marā," so that in the sound chain the name "Rāma" automatically sounded.

Ayyāvāl, the predecessor of Tyāgarāja and one whose teaching on the subject of *Nāma-mahātmya* held the field in Coladeśa, the South land, subscribed to this view and in some verses in his hymn on the Lord's name, *Ākhyā ṣaṣṭi*, he referred to the name Śiva as saving one even if its sounds were somehow introduced in the everyday speech of a man, for instance, "Where does he l*iv*e?" asks one; "On the bea*ch*," says another; in the answer, something similar to the sound combination "Śi-va" occurs, even though the syllables are reversed.

This, Tyāgarāja felt, was carrying it too far. The uttering

of the Lord's Name, he insisted, should be informed by love for the Lord. Those who do not love the Lord know not the relish of His Name. "O Rāma, will people without love for you know the flavor of your name? O Sītā!" (*Rāma nīyeḍa prema rahitulaku/nāma ruci delusunā*)

Besides, "Rāma" means the essence of Śiva and Viṣṇu; Rāma is Brahman itself; what is the use of repeating the sound Rāma, without any knowledge of its meaning or as referring to another person or object? Tyāgarāja elaborates his view by means of a series of telling similes in his song *Telisi rāma cintanatō*.

> The Name must be uttered with a knowledge of its significance and with contemplation of Rāma. Closing the senses up for a minute and realising the real truth of the *tāraka-rūpa* of Rāma, one should utter the Name.
>
> Rāma means a woman; that leads to lust, etc. Rāma is the name of the Supreme Brahman too; that removes all the distress of mortal birth. *Arka* is the name of a poisonous plant; *Arka* means the Sun that dispels all darkness. *Aja* means a goat; *Aja* means also Brahman, who would bless you with success.

That *nāma kīrtana*, singing the divine names, is not a mechanical process, that a real practice of this means a full equipment of knowledge, self-control, purity of mind, devotion, concentration, etc., has also been emphasized in the books. In his comments on the name *Viśva*, (literally meaning "all") which leads the one thousand Names of Viṣṇu, Śaṅkara says that it is only one who has realized the truth that God is *Viśva*, Everything, who can utter the *nāma*. Śaṅkara's teaching in his comments on the Name *Viśva* is summarized by Tyāgarāja in the last part of his song *Intakanna yānanda – Ni japamulu vela nī jagamulu nīvai rājillunaya* – "Whenever I murmur again and again your name, the worlds seem to shine with your presence." Such a realization would make one completely refrain from *himsā* (violence), etc., and such a person deserves to sing the Lord's Name. Some texts go so far as to say that only the realized souls who have become one with the Lord can take the Name; others should not vainly take it.

We have already drawn attention to the fourth and fifth stages of *Nāma pārāyaṇa* which are stages of *advaita*. Upaniṣad Brahman says in his *Upeya nāma viveka* that the repetition of *Rāma nāma* should be attended with the non-dual contemplation, *advaita-bhāvanā*.

In the *Padma Purāṇa*, ten pitfalls for enthusiasts of *nāma kīrtana* are set forth and their avoidance is insisted upon. They are characterised as ten offences against the Lord's Name, *nāma-aparādhas*. The first is the deriding of good men, *nindā* of *sādhus*. The second is to see difference between one form of Deity and another, e.g., Śiva and Viṣṇu. Then, disregard for Gurus, denouncing the *Vedas* and *Śāstras* as needless, considering that the glorification of *Nāma* is in fact an exaggeration, committing sins on the strength of the *Nāma*, absence of purity of mind achieved through refraining from injury to others, from lying, stealing, incontinence and receiving gifts. The next is to desist from all *karmas* and *dharmas* on the excuse of the *nāma-japa*. Then, teaching the Name to the faithless and the un-interested. And lastly, failing to cultivate benevolence and continuing to be dominated by *ahaṁkāra* and *mamakāra*, the sense of "I" and "Mine."

Tyāgarāja was one of those who considered the recitation of *Nāma* a high form which only qualified people should resort to, if they are to reap the benefit. To the second and partly to the seventh *aparādha* referred to above, Tyāgarāja's *Sukhi evarō* gives expression:

> Who is the blessed one that enjoys the bliss of *Rāma-nāma*, the highest of *mantras* calculated to save men from bondage? Who is that blessed one who, unflinching from truth, serving all humanity and free from hatred towards other deities, sings sweetly the *Rāma-nāma*?

There is again reference to the second *aparādha* in the essentials of a true devotee described by Tyāgarāja in his *Bhaktuni cāritra* ("Conduct of the devotee"), *Śiva mādhava bh damu j yagarādu* ("You shouldn't make any difference between the names of Śiva and Viṣṇu"). In his song *Vinatāsuta*, Tyāgarāja condemns disputes about different faiths as useless. In the song on the Goddess, Dharmasamvardhanī, *Karuṇa jūdavamma*, Tyāgarāja addresses the Goddess as being Herself both Śiva and Rāma.

In a song on Śiva, *Śambho śiva Śaṅkara*, he describes the Lord as one who always puts down the pride of those inferior people who revel in sectarian differences: "God is the destroyer of the pride of a person who has fallen into the pit of differences of religions." (*Mata-bh da-patita-mānava-mada-santata-bhaṅga*)

In *Itaradaivamula*, Tyāgarāja says that without any prejudice against other faiths he is devoted to Rāma – *matabhēda-mulēka sadā madini marulu gonna tanaku*. "[I am] one whose mind without harboring any prejudice against other faiths is constantly and passionately in love with you. Only such a Rāma *bhajana* as is done with a mind free from the six inner enemies, lust, anger, and the others, will bring salvation, and free one from the ills of this world."

In the true spirit of one who, while adoring one form as his dearest, held in respect the rest as but other forms of Divinity, Tyāgarāja praised Subrahmaṇya as "unequalled among the Gods" (*Nīvanti daivamu sadanana*), and Devī as the "refuge of Tyāgarāja's family" –"*Tyāgarāja kulasaranye,*" in his song *Ammadharmasamvardhanī.*

The very fruit of *Nāma-japa* is that the Name purifies one's mind: "My mind has been cleansed by chanting your holy name." (*Nī nāmamuce nāmadi nirmalamainadi*, in the song *Jñāna-mosagarādā.*)

And hence is *Rāma nāma* "the most sanctifying name" (*Paramapāvana-nāma*) as he sings in *Rāmaramaṇa.* "If there is one who thus worships the Lord truly with His Name, – surely, who can equal him?" he asks in *Dāśarathānī ṛiṇamu.*

> Who can equal that worshipper of the Lord's Name, who has cleared his mind of all its manifold lumber, who has steadfast devotion, who discards sectarian disputes, who longs for the Lord, who has established the Lord's feet in his heart, who shuns like poison the company of those who do not enjoy this happiness, and who values the company of true devotees? Who can equal those who are transported to ecstasy meditating on the Lord?

And he asks what can equal our own human birth if we do this adoration of the Lord with the flowers of divine glorious names. "O mind, that human life is blessed in which the Lord is installed on the golden throne of thought and is worshipped with flowers of his holy names" (*Nāma kusumamulacē pujiñcē*). It is necessary to understand fully the significance when Tyāgarāja speaks more than once of *nāma-kusuma*, of the name of the Lord as the flower of His worship. According to the prescribed directions for the adoration of Rāma-*nāma* (*Rāma mantra puraścarana* and *Kriyāyoga*) Rāma mantra itself is to be used as the flowers for the *pūjā* (worship); *nāma-japa* is the flower worship (*puspa-arcana*).[28]

And if one cannot have true love for Rāma-*nāma*, of what

use is his life – "Of what use is a life without true love for your holy name, O Rāmacandra?" he asks in *Pāhi paramātma.* The Lord's Name brings prosperity here, and leading one on the right path, it brings one to the abode of Divinity or is itself all prosperity, all austerity and the abode eternal. "The name of Rāma brings one welfare, leads one always on the right path and is the abode of divinity," he asserts in *Vandanamu.*

The most elaborate expression or exclamation relating to the joys of uttering *Rāma nāma* is of course the long *Divya-nāma* in the auspicious *Sauraṣṭra raga* in which Tyāgarāja simply loses himself as it were: *Melu melu Rāma-nāma-sukham ī dharalō manasā.*

> Ah Mind! Exceedingly superior in this world is the bliss of Rāma's Name to the joy of a thirsty man getting water to drink, of a pauper coming by a treasure, of getting water in draught, of frightened person getting courage, of a hungry man getting a sumptuous feast, of an angry man calming down, of an ignoramus becoming suddenly learned.

Indeed, Tyāgarāja in this song exalts the bliss of the utterance of the Lord's Name above sweet devotional music, above even the bliss of contemplating God, or spiritual experience or the realization of Brahman itself:

> The pleasure one derives in meditation on Śrī Rāma the Bestower of prosperity, O mind! The happiness that Rāma-*nāma* gives to one is *higher than that*!
>
> The pleasure one derives after successful Vedāntic inquiry, O mind! The happiness that Rāma-*nāma* gives to one is *higher than that*!
>
> The bliss which one derives from the realization of *nirguṇa* Para Brahman, O mind! The happiness that Rāma-*nāma* gives to one is *higher than that*!

Notes

[1]Editor's note: This was first published as part of *The Spiritual Heritage of Tyāgarāja*, by C. Ramanujacari with an introductory thesis by V. Raghavan (Madras: Śrī Ramakrishna Math, 1966), pp. 109-137. Revised edition 1981, pp. 99-124. I have moved a number of Sanskrit passages to the footnotes and replaced them with English translations for the sake of easier reading.

[2]*Nāmānyanantasya yaso'dkitāni* in *Bhāgavata Purāṇa*, I.4.11.

[3]Paramaśivendra Sarasvatī, the guru of Sadāśiva Brahmendra, collected together as *Upaniṣan-nāma-sahasra*, to be of help in the contemplation and realization of the *svarūpa* of Brahman.

[4]Rāma nāma śravanamu valla nāma rūpamē
hṛidayamuninḍi prema buṭṭa jēyaga lēdā.

Tyāgarāja similarly says, in his song *Smaraṇe sukhamu*, that the constant listening to *Rāma nāma*, establishes the form of that name in the heart and fills the heart with love. "Listening to Rāma's name and filling the heart with the form being named, this causes love to be born, doesn't it?" In one of his visions of realization, the song *Nājīvādhāra* Tyāgarāja exclaims of his Lord, "Are you not the letters of the Name I repeat in my *japa*, taken shape like this?"

[5]Nī nāmāmṛita-pānamu yanu sōpānamu dorikenu.

Varying the metaphor, Tyāgarāja in his song *Veṅkaṭeśa ninu* compares the drinking of the nectar of the Lord's Name to something that lifts one to the presence of the Lord, verily the flight of steps leading one to God: "By drinking the nectar of Your name I have found that very staircase." The imagery is based on the local fact of the numberless steps of the Seven Hills of Tirupati which devotees mount and traverse uttering the Lord's Name.

[6]That the doctrine of Name redeems the humble and the learned alike is given expression to by Dīkṣitar in a song of his on Rāma, *Māmava raghuvara*: pāmarapaṇḍitapāvanakara-nāmadeya.

[7]Like the Maharatha saints in the South West, and Rāmānanda and his followers in the North, Śrī Caitanya in the East was responsible for making the whole country resound with "Hari-bōl." In their doctrines, the Caitanyaites hold "Name" itself as a form of the Lord; and though capable of other significances also, two passages in Tyāgarāja may lend themselves to an interpretation that the composer knew the tenet that *nāma* was itself a *rūpa* of the Lord: "My prayer is Your

form (*Nā japa varṇa rūpama*) in his song *Nājīvādhāra* and "The very form of your name is in my heart," (*Nāma rūpam hṛidayamuniṇḍi*) in his *Smaraṇē sukhamu*.

[8]I am indebted to Professor Robert Hueckstedt, University of Manitoba, Winnipeg, for this translation.

[9]asya stutilaksanasya arcanasya ādhikye kim kāraṇam?
ucyate–himsādipuruṣāntara-dravyāntara
deśakālādiniyamānapekṣatvamādhikye kāraṇam/

[10]dhyāyan krite yajan yajñaistretāyām dvāpare 'rcayan
yadāpnoti tadāpnoti kalau samkīrtya keśavam. *Viṣṇu Purāṇa* 6.2.17.

[11]gacchamstiṣṭansvapan vāpi piban buñjannamstathā/
kṛṣṇa kriṣṇoti saṅkirtya mucyate pāpakañcukāt//
prāyaścittānyaśesāni tapaḥkarmātmakāni vai/
yāni teṣāmaśeṣānām kriṣṇānusmaraṇam param//
yannām kirtanam bhaktyā vilāpanamanuttamam/
maitryāśeṣapāpānām dhātūnāmiva pāvakaḥ/
yāsya smṛtyā ca nāmoktyā tapo yajñakriyādiṣu/
nyūnam sampūrṇatāmeti sadhyo vande tamacyutam//
hare nāmaiva nāmaiva nāmaiva mama jīvanam/
kalau nāstyeva nāstyeva nāstyeva gatiranyathā//

[12]mā ṛico mā yajustāta mā sāma paṭha kimcana/
govindeti hare nāma geyam gāyasva nityaśaḥ//
nārāyaṇeti śabdo 'sti vāgasti vaśavartinī/
tathāpi narake ghore patantītyetadad bhutam//
kalerdoṣanidhe rājan asti hyeko mahan guṇaḥ/
kīrtanadeva kriṣṇasya muktasaṅgaḥ param vraget// XII.3.51.
kalim sabhājayantyāryāh gunajñāh sārabhāginaḥ/
yatra saṇkirtanenaiva sarvaḥ svārtho 'bhilabhyate// XI.5.36.

[13]tadeva ramyam ruciram navam navam
tadeva śaśvanmanaso mahotsavam/
tadeva śokārnavaśoṣaṇam nriṇam
yaduttamaślokayaso 'nugīyate XII.12.49.

[14] na yadvacaścitrapadam hareryaśah
jagatpavitram pragriṇīta karhicit/
tadvāyasam tīrthamuśanti manasāḥ
na yatra hamsa niramantyuśikṣayāḥ//
tadvāgvisargo janatāghaviplavo
yasmin pratiślokamabaddhavatyapi

nāmānyanantasya yaśo 'ṅkitāni yat
śṛiṇvanti gāyanti gṛiṇanti sādhavaḥ//
naiṣkarmyapyacyutabhāvavarjitam
na śobhate jñānamalam nirañjanam/ BP I.5 10-12.

[15]Editor's note: I have inserted this relevant paragraph from V. Raghavan's article on "The *Tattvasaṁgraha-Rāmāyaṇa* of Rāmabrahmānanda," *Annals of Oriental Research, University of Madras*, Vol. X, pt. 1.

[16]yo mama ṣaṇṇavatikotināmāni japati sa
tebhyaḥ pāpebhyaḥ pramucyate

[17]śrī rāmamantra rājasya samyagartho 'yamucyate/
nārāyaṇaṣṭaksare ca śivapañcakṣare tathā/
sārthakārṇadvayam rāmo ramante yatra yoginaḥ//

[18]Rāma tells Śiva:
mumūrṣordakṣiṇe karṇe yasya kasyāpi vā svayam/
upadeṣyasi manmantram sa mukto bhavitā śiva//

[19]Cf. the custom of *pārāyaṇa* ("summary") of the *Rāmāyaṇa* or the *Sundarakāṇḍa* that we do according to formulae like *rāghavo vijayam dadyāda mama sītāpatiḥ prabhuḥ.*

[20]*Avadhūta* – a possessionless, realized soul, from whom all has "fallen off."

[21][Editor's note: I have been unable to identify the "Tamil Śaiva Saint" referred to here. It may have been Maṇikkavācakar.]
Narravā unnai nān marakkinum sollu nā nāmasśivāyave.

[22]Cf. John Damascenus: "We must learn to invoke God's Name more often than we breathe, at all times and everywhere and during all our labours."

[23]*cinna nāḍe yanusariñcu* in the song *Pāhimām śrīrāmacandra*; *cinna nāḍe nīcelimi galuga gōri – cintimpa lēdā śrīrāma* in the song *Nannubrōva*; *ānāṭimodalu ninnu vēḍiti* in the *Bhairavi rāga* song *Ānandamānanda*; *nē cinnatanamu nāḍe* in his song *Ninnē nera namminānurā*; in *cinnanāṭa nuṇḍi ninnē gāni nēnanulu nammitinā*; in *Innāḷḷu dayarākunna*; in *Nivēgāni*, he describes the Lord as a treasure earned and handed down from the elders of his family (*Munu māvamśamuna galugu peddalu tapamulanu jēsi yārjiñcina dhanamu*); and in his *Pāhi mām harē*, a *Divyanāma* piece, he even says that he was born into this world with the name Rāma on his lips and had steadfastly kept it up. *Pāhi rāma yanucu bhuvini bāgabuṭṭidi! Pāhi Rāma yanucu gaṭṭi paṭṭu baṭṭiti.* ("Protect me; I was born uttering the name Rāma and have always kept saying it – save me.")

[24]Compare the words of the Christian St. Bernard: "The Name of Jesus is not only light; it is also nourishment. All food is too dry to be assimilated by the soul if it is not flavored by this condiment; it is too insipid unless this salt relieves its tastelessness. I have no taste for thy writings if I cannot read this Name there . . . it is *honey* for my mouth, melody for my ears, joy for my heart, but it is also a *medicine*."

[25]Sāma gāna lōluḍau
rajata-giri-dhāmuḍaina
Tyāgarāja Śivuḍu atinēmamuto
nāmāmṛita pānamu yēmarakanu
jēsi, Rāma Rāma Rāma yanucu
satatamu Śrīmadādi Gauriki
śṛṇgāriki yā mahimalan ā rahasyamulan
ati prēmanu upadēśiñca lēdā.

The reference to Śiva explaining to Pārvatī the greatness of Rāma *nāma* is to passages like the oft-quoted verse [Editor's note: This is possibly from the *Adhyātma Rāmāyaṇa*]:
śrīrāma rāma rāmeti rāme rāme manorame/
sahasranāmatastulyam rāmanāma varānane//

[26]avaśonapi yannāmni kīrtite sarvapātakaiḥ/
pumān vimucyate sadyaḥ simhatrastairmṛigairiva// VP 6.8.19.
jñānato 'jñānato vāpi vāsudevasya kīrtanāt/
tatsarvam vilayam yāti toyastham lavaṇam yathā//

[27]*Bhāgavata Purāṇa*:
saṁketyam pārihāsyam va stomam helanameva vā/
vaikuṇṭhanāmagrahaṇamaśeṣaghaharam viduḥ//
patitasskhalito bhagnaḥ sandastaṣtapta āhataḥ/
harirityavaśenāha pumānnārhati yātanām//
yathāgadam vīryatamaṁypayuktam yadṛicchayā/
ajānato 'pyātmaguṇam kuryānmantro 'pyudāhṛitaḥ//VI.2.14,15,19.

[28]See *Tattvasaṁgraha Rāmāyaṇa*, Sundara, Cantos 13, 14.

CULTURAL OVERVIEWS

Part Three:

Perennialism and the Name V.Raghavan's Foreword to Frithjof Schuon's *The Language of the Self*[1]

> "'Internally' every religion is the doctrine of the one Self and its earthly manifestation, as also the way leading to the abolition of the false self or the way of the mysterious reintegration of our 'personality' in the celestial Prototype." – Frithjof Schuon

The Perennialist Scholars

There is a class of writings which has contributed in a unique way to the true understanding of Hinduism in the West. This is a class of writings different from the more widely known one of the Orientalists, but may be considered the consummation of the work which these "Orientalists" had done since their discovery of Sanskrit and their subsequent study of the East by editing and translating Eastern classics and tracing the development of the different branches of Oriental thought. To adopt the language of the *Muṇḍaka Upaniṣad*, all that they have done may be called the *aparā vidyā*, non-transcendent knowledge, while the class of writings dealt with here may be deemed the *parā vidyā*, transcendent knowledge. An eminent figure who easily passed from the former to the latter[2] and who is not only well known in this country but widely admired is Ananda K. Coomaraswamy. Another name that comes in this line is that of the French savant René Guénon, the quintessence of whose teachings Coomaraswamy himself brings together in his essay, "Eastern Wisdom and Western Knowledge." Yet another member of the elite of authentic exponents in the West of Eastern wisdom is Frithjof Schuon.

In the works of these authors the words Tradition and Orthodoxy—quite unfashionable these days – have been used. At the outset a certain distinctiveness and distinction were also claimed for the class of writings these perennialists produced. What are the chief features of their approach?

Seven Features of Perennialism

Firstly, these writings bring out the fact that underlying the different religions of the world there is a common tradition and a basic unity. To quote Schuon, "explicitly to practice one religion is implicitly to practice them all."[3] This common tradition is the gnosis or the *philosophia perennis* which is the connecting link between the different religious languages.[4]

Secondly, while Truth is one, Revelation or Tradition or Form is naturally diverse, thanks to the infinity of divine possibility.[5] While orthodoxy, which represents divine necessity, is the conforming to this basic gnosis, originality, which represents divine freedom,[6] comprehends the different forms this gnosis puts forth at different times or in different parts of the world. "... the diverse revelations do not really contradict one another, since they do not apply to the same receptacle and since God never addresses the same message to two or more receptacles . . ."[7] In the words of Guenon, "differences in doctrines, in order to be legitimate, can only be a mere matter of adaptation, modifying the more or less external forms of expression but in no wise touching the principles themselves;"[8] according to men's varying capacity, God "taught them at one time one thing and at another time another, as circumstances required."[9] ". . . Every traditional form is superior".[10] To be more precise one should rather say that every traditional form specializes in a particular aspect. "That one enunciation may be less direct in its form than another is no proof whatever of a lesser wisdom but solely of a lesser receptivity on the part of the particular environment. To the others in a particular respect and it is this characteristic which in fact indicates the sufficient reason for the existence of that form."[11]

Thirdly, while a search in the writings of the different religions of the world has shown that this gnosis or knowledge of the Self forms the core of all religions, it is in Hinduism that it is found in a most pronounced form and has never been forgotten. Also, the Hindu heritage is precious for another reason: it is not only "the most ancient of the living traditional forms" but "it possesses a certain superiority or centrality with respect to later forms."[12] "Hinduism has the faculty of combining all the perspectives which elsewhere are mutually exclusive." While combining through the doctrine of *adhikāra-bheda* and *ruci* (spiritual temperament) the different perspectives (*darśanas*), "Hinduism does not lose sight of unity; it has a tendency to see unity in diversity and in each element of this diversity."[13]

Fourthly, the highest of these perspectives is Gnosis, the metaphysic of the Self, the Vedānta. "That the way of Knowledge, *jñāna-mārga*, is among spiritual ways the highest, and in a still more ultimate sense, that it is the spiritual way as such, the one in which all other ways finally must merge, is a fundamental truth to which all traditional teachings bear witness either openly or else by implication." Of "those doctrines and methods that keep closest to true knowledge as the 'highest' ways open to man," "the Hindu Vedānta provides an example that conforms in its presentation, as near as conceivably possible, to the goal it sets itself, which is Deliverance total and unqualified."[14] As to Śaṅkara and the Sufis, to these writers too, knowledge alone delivers. The doctrine of *bhakti*, Hindu or Christian, does not contradict that of *jñāna*, for "the conceptions of Rāmānuja are contained in those of Śaṅkara and are transcended by them." "Rāmānuja affirms against Śaṅkarācārya truths which the latter never denied on their own level."[15] Like faith, (*Śraddhāvān labhate jñānam*, *Bhagavad Gītā*, IV. 39. Cf. "It is for certain men who have been allowed to pass from faith to gnosis. . ." – (Clement of Alexandria) devotion is a pre-condition of knowledge; there have been no greater hymnists in India than Śaṅkara; for, to one who has realized the Self, it is more natural than not, as the *Bhāgavata Purāṇa* says, to be singing of the Lord.[16] Not only Rāmakrishna, but many a forebear of his has been this *bhakta-jñānin*, devotee-sage. Also, when the *Upaniṣad* says of the Supreme Self *yam evaiṣa vṛṇute tena labhyaḥ tasyaiṣa ātmā vṛṇute tanūm svām*, there is, as it were, a synthesis of *jñāna* and *bhakti*. It is in this light that statements such as that of St. Marcarius of Egypt, "Love is inseparable from knowledge," are to be understood. Between different approaches, e.g., *bhakti* and *jñāna*, it is, therefore, not a question of error and truth, but one of lesser truth and greater truth or of different gradations of the universal reality.[17] Reality affirms itself by degrees, but without ceasing to be "one," the inferior degrees of this affirmation being absorbed by metaphysical integration or synthesis, into the superior degrees. Furthermore, Being Itself, which is none other than the "Personal God," is in its turn surpassed by the "Impersonal."[18]

Fifthly, between the subject to be realised which is *sat*, *cit*, and *ānanda* and the objective world superimposed on it, "there is interposed a direct objectivation of the subject" which mediates in the re-integration, the trinity of the *avatāra*, the guru and the revelation or mantra.[19] "The Absolute reveals itself also, to the same sage, in an objective manner, by springing up suddenly in the mind in the form of sacred words; and the Absolute reveals itself also in the giving of inspired Texts which are to be the support of life and of spiritual realization to an entire civilization; in such a case the Absolute never reveals itself in subjective mode, except in the case of certain *avatāras* whose body and mind manifest the self in a manner eminently more direct than with the ordinary sage."[20]

Sixthly, the East and Hinduism in particular are noteworthy for preserving not only this tradition of gnosis, but what is very important today, the "techniques of realization." For "knowledge is not merely a matter of right theory. . .but is something to be 'actualized' with the help of a method running parallel to the doctrine . . . ."[21] Foremost among these techniques is yoga, which as described by Patanjali includes the virtues and that unique mode called *japa*, repetition of a holy name in a *mantra*, which runs like a golden thread through *karma*, *bhakti*, and *jñāna*, and assimilates the former two to the last.

Lastly, "as the *spiritual technique* is essentially the art of concentration,"[22] the traditional ideology favours art, which in origin was the imitation of divine act or the analogy used by revelation for exegesis, 'as a direct aid to spirituality,[23]; "the spiritual efficacy of aesthetic supports is in the very nature of things," for "apart from the intrinsic value of beauty" "the efficacy of art is to be found in the unifying power of aesthetic experience." As Schuon says in his *Spiritual Perspectives*: "There is something in our intelligence which wants to live at rest, something in which the conscious and unconscious meet in a kind of passive activity, and it is this element to which the lofty and easy language of art speaks. The language is lofty because of the spiritual symbolism of its form and the nobility of its style; it is easy because of the aesthetic mode of assimilation."[24]

A Vision of Underlying Unity

Perhaps the greatest gain from this study of world religions is the discovery of their underlying unity and of the fact that they are but diverse "paths that lead to the same summit." It is also clear that this unity could lie only in the doctrine of gnosis, for it is knowledge that has no history. The realization of this truth would obviate the evangelistic obsession of certain faiths, which by admixture of violence, exploitation or corruption of one kind or another or by dilution of the teaching, carry out their expansionism. As Aldous Huxley says: "Like any other form of imperialism, theological imperialism is a menace to permanent world peace. The reign of violence will never come to an end until, first, most human beings accept the same true philosophy of life; until, second, this perennial philosophy is recognised as the highest factor common to all the world religions; until, third, the adherents of every religion renounce the idolatrous time-philosophies, with which, in their own particular faith, the perennial philosophy of eternity has been overlaid. . . ."[25] This does not mean a watering down of faith or the growth of a religious indifference; it is only a curative of sectarianism. Every religion is unique and the aspirant devoted to it should strive within it with that faith; but when he has reached the goal, he no longer sees any diversity. This has been affirmed so far as the manifold perspectives within the Indian tradition are concerned continuously by the Veda, the *Upaniṣad*, the *Bhagavad Gītā*, and the hymns of saints and devotees, but it was left to Rāmakrishna Paramahaṃsa in modern times to demonstrate this in respect of the non-Indian religious traditions too, Christianity and Islam. For a correct estimate of Rāmakrishna, the following from Schuon cannot possibly be excelled. "In Rāmakrishna there is something which seems to defy every category; he was like the living symbol of the inner unity of religions; he was, in fact, the first saint deliberately wishing to penetrate 'foreign' spiritual forms. . . . In the present time of confusion, disarray and doubt, he was the saint called to 'verify' forms and 'reveal,' if one can so express it, their single truth."[26] In 1926, a European student of *vedānta* met his Holiness Śrī Śaṅkarācārya of Śringeri and at the end of the conversation wanted to know if Hinduism took converts. "No, rather it is needless for Hinduism to take converts," so saying, His Holiness explained why Hinduism was called *sanātana dharma*, the Eternal Law. The European said that he had no idea when he came that he would be going away from his Holiness with a desire to be a better Christian. His Holiness observed in conclusion that an artist howsoever capable required a stable background of canvas for his painting. "Apply your God-given gifts on the stable background of your own God-chosen faith, Christianity. When the painting is over and you are contemplating the beauty of the picture, the background may face away from your view of its own accord. . . ."

The Service of Perennialists to East and West

The service that this group of perennialist writers in the West has done is both to the East and the West. The integration they have achieved on the basis of a traditional and spiritual outlook is not exactly Oriental, for as they have shown, this outlook is common to medieval and scholastic West. "What we have in mind for the Christian," says Schuon,[27] "is a return to his own sources and not an orientalization of the West." "If Guenon wants the West to turn to Eastern metaphysics, it is not because they are Eastern, but because this is metaphysics. . . . It is only because this metaphysics still survives as a living power in Eastern societies, in so far as they have not been corrupted by the withering touch of Western, or rather modern, civilization. . .and not to orientalize the West, but to bring back the West to a consciousness of the roots of her own life and values. . .that Guenon asks us to turn to the East."[28]

The message of these writers is not less needed, nor ever

more opportune than today, for the East, which under the impact of different forces from the modern West is either "sleeping over its truths," or indulging in a "spiritual demogogy" busy preparing versions of its teachings acceptable to the modern West, or committing suicide by working itself up into a frenzy that it had been terribly mistaken down the centuries and that, cutting itself completely from its hoary moorings, it should now set itself, in the wake of the modern West, to work for the Utopia of increased production, improved standard of living and an equality instead of quality. That India and the greater part of the East are now free from Western colonialism is no guarantee that their traditions would be conserved. As Gai Eaton observes: "It is far too early to tell how profoundly Western ideas may have penetrated the basic structures of life in India, but it is clear that the process of penetration has by no means ceased with the abdication of the British Rāj; the country, now regarded as politically mature, because its traditional forms have been more or less undermined, has been left to the tender mercies of Westernized Indians who are unlikely to show such moderation as we did in tampering with the old way of life."[29] Both Guenon and Schuon have taken special pains to criticize modern Indian scholars or teachers who have had to "present," so to say, the orthodox tradition of India for Western acceptance. But one may not consider this the chief sin of modern India when one reflects on the long history of Hindu thought, during almost the whole course of which it had been submitted to the impact of forces both internal and external, and finds that, without sacrificing its fundamentals, Hindu tradition had always put forth adaptations of forms, and that indeed it is these diversified forms which justify the claim of this culture to "formal amplitude."

On the other hand, the real danger is from that total Westernization in which the East is fast, thoughtlessly, throwing away its precious heritage. In their denunciation of modern

Western civilization and in the way to regeneration that they have pointed out through the recovery of the traditional spirit, it is the East that these savants have shown as supplying the key to that treasure of spiritual wisdom. To many modern Indians and their leaders who are intensely allergic to the words Tradition and Orthodoxy, this growing school of Western thinkers should act as a shock-absorber. Their re-affirmation of the value of this ancient, in fact timeless, wisdom should lead to a reawakening in the East, and to an arrest of the spreading decay of its tradition. Let not that contingency arise in which, for this ancient wisdom, as for our antique artware, we would one day have to go to the West where it has been taken and treasured by a band of *vivekins*! (cognoscenti or discerning knowers). And for awakening us with their true and revealing exposition of this knowledge, these *vivekins* of the West are entitled to our gratitude and respect. "They resemble *ṛṣis* and are venerable," (*ṛṣivat te'pi pūjyās syuh*), as Garga of yore said of the *śāstra-jñas* of the West.

[The following passages from Schuon's book shed light on the place of the Name as an integral part of Hindu traditions.]

The Guru, the Name and the Self[30]
(From *The Language of the Self*) by Frithjof Schuon

> According to certain people's expressed views, the crucial question is not that of tradition, of initiation or of method, but the question of the Guru's own realization. Such a view leaves us with only two alternatives: either a man is not a perfect Sage, and in that case he has no means of knowing whether the Guru is a perfect Sage or not; or else a man is himself a perfect Sage, and in that case he has no means of knowing whether the Guru is a perfect

Sage or not; or else a man is himself a perfect Sage, in which case he has no need of a Guru. All that the disciple can know is that the Guru is spiritually superior to himself; and he is only able to know this thanks to the tradition to which he belongs and from which the Guru has issued. When the disciple has attained the degree of his Guru, he is at liberty to seek another Guru, and so on, as is shown by the example, among others of Śrī Rāmakrishna whose spiritual realization surpassed, not only that of the Brāhmini Bhairavi, but even that of his second Guru, the *jñānin* Totāpuri. In every case the one thing which is indispensable is an immediate relation with the embodied Absolute, which "embodiment" can and must in fact assume different forms and cannot depend on anything as conjectural as the personal realization of such and such a man. The Veda, the *praṇava* Om, the divine Name (Śiva, Hari and others) and the Guru, both as such and in virtue of his function, are so many embodiments of the Absolute.

We have heard it said that the Hindus are not in agreement as to the degree of realization of Śrī Rāmakrishna; one can thus have different opinions on this matter, which shows precisely the falsity of the principle according to which it is for the disciple to judge the spirituality of the Master and to determine the degree of his realization. On the other hand, it is evident that the disciple will seek a guru whose teaching, reputation and personal radiance betoken the highest wisdom. In any case, the fact that the guru Totāpuri was surpassed by his disciple Rāmakrishṇa in no way indicates that Śrī Totāpuri was a false guru or that Śrī Rāmakrishna was mistaken in allowing himself to be guided by him.

In the same line of thought is the question of the universality of tradition, which amounts in the last analysis to knowing whether the founders of great religions, such as the Buddha, Christ, Muhammad, possessed perfect wisdom, and whether as a consequence one finds within these religions the methods and Masters necessary to guide one towards the realization of the Self. Now the doctrine of the Self (in other words that which in Hinduism is called the *vedānta*) is plainly enunciated in certain teachings of these *avatāras*, and their identity with the Self has been affirmed by them with the greatest clarity; if this be so, there is not the slightest reason to doubt, first of all their own "realization," and secondly the existence, within the respective traditions, of doctrines and methods the purpose of which is to lead those qualified to the same perfect realization: such a doubt cannot possibly arise in any balanced mind. In actual fact among the Buddhists as among the Sufis, and also in the ancient Christian churches, there have always been sages who have proclaimed their identity with the Self, even though they have necessarily been rarer here than in the Hindu world where the most profound truths are enunciated much more openly and more directly than anywhere else. Be that as it may, the thing which matters is not the form but the meaning of the enunciations; that one enunciation may be less direct in its form than another is no proof whatever of a lesser wisdom but solely of a lesser receptivity on the part of the particular environment. The sage stands above forms and moreover no form as such is perfect; one cannot, therefore, measure wisdom according to the mental forms which it assumes. Whether one says "Who am I?" or "What am I?" is a matter of indifference, only the meaning is important.

We venture to hope, in any case, that there does not exist in India a guru who believes himself superior to the Buddha, the Christ or the prophet. The extrinsic proof of their identity with the Self resides not only in their own affirmations and in the existence of spiritual ways which derive from them, but also in the possibility of invoking the redemptive Name of the Avatāra. Thus, the fact that one can attain Deliverance by invoking Śrī Rāma, proves the perfection of his Wisdom; the avataric Name, whether isolated, or included in a formula, is the immediate vehicle of the eternal *sadguru*.

It is clear that, compared with the Truth, theory amounts to nothing; but in order to be able to say this one must take one's stand above theory, and not below it. For one who is not even capable of understanding it, theory will be his immediate need; it is theory which for him will represent the Self. If such a one presumes to scorn theory and to concern himself only with the realization he will be wasting his time. Only he who understands the doctrine can know that in the face of Reality it also counts for nothing.

If, as some maintain, the Self is so easily understood, how is it that It is not understood by all men? If on the other hand It is hard to understand, then it follows that one must possess in the first place rare intellectual and human qualifications in order to conceive of It, not to mention realizing It, if not to explain It, which may take on forms both subtle and complex, as well as apparently simple ones.

In conclusion, we are minded to add a few further remarks about the spiritual uses of Invocation, *japa*, as found in the great traditions practically without exception. Persons affected with intellectual pretensions have been prone to look down upon those who follow this method, whether in India or elsewhere, describing it as only suitable for the spiritually immature. This opinion, based as it is upon a complete failure to understand either the operative principle behind *japa* or the "technical" conditions governing its use at various degrees, is in its way rather characteristic of certain mentalities and will therefore provide a fitting conclusion to the present discussion; besides which the subject is of great importance in itself, since it relates to a spiritual means particularly related, as all the traditions agree, to the conditions of humanity in the latter days of the cycle.

How can one deny that the practice of *japa*, when it is accompanied by appropriate meditation, is able to bring about Self-realization, in view of the fact that the *Mānava-dharma-śāstra*, the books of yoga and other sacred texts bear witness to it? In order to understand that *japa* is not by definition a bhaktic method only (contrary to what certain people affirm) and that it can constitute an aid to the realization of Reality, one must understand that the divine Name does not refer by definition to an "objective God," but that it objectivates and actualizes the Self, exactly like the Sadguru, and that it is thus an embodiment of the Absolute; in Sufism, the divine Name (Allah) corresponds exactly to the *praṇava* "Om" with its mantras. *Japa* is not properly speaking a rite, otherwise the sacred texts would not say that for him who practices *japa* rites are no longer required. A rite is an act having a purificatory or sacrificial purpose; a Brahman could be, so to speak, crushed beneath an accumulation of rites; when it is said that rites cannot deliver from ignorance, it is evidently these sacrificial and purificatory rites which are in question, and not methodical invocation which even renders an elaborate ritualism impossible. *Japa* cannot be opposed to Knowledge – which alone delivers – because it is a relative support of it; apart from the fact that the divine Name "incarnates" the divine "Ego," absolute and infinite, of which it provides us *a priori* with the virtuality, it removes *a fortiori* all such obstacles as are opposed to knowledge, that is to say such obstacles as separate us in illusory fashion from That which we have in reality never ceased to be – That which we are. If Śrī Śaṅkara says that knowledge is the only direct means of obtaining Liberation, this indicates implicitly that there are other means, indirect no doubt, but none the less efficacious. For us human beings Knowledge always presents itself, at least *a priori*, in association with a support which is its vehicle; such a support can never be contrary to its own end. If the *japa* of a *jñānin* who has already obtained *tatvôpadeśa* constitutes an aid to preserving which has been assimilated spiritually, this also proves that *japa* is in no way opposed to Knowledge, no more than the respiration with which *japa* moreover must eventually become merged. It is clearly evident that, after a certain stage, the "materiality" of the divine Name becomes secondary; but this likewise implies no condemnation of *japa*, quite the contrary. The *jñānic japa*, as practiced in certain Islamic religious orders, is accompanied by meditations on unreality and reality and after that by pure and unitive contemplation, which means that in Sufism, as in *vedānta*, it is Knowledge which always and alone delivers.

Śrī Śaṅkarācārya says in his hymns: "I do not ask of Thee, O Mother! riches, good fortune, or salvation; I seek no happiness, no knowledge. This is my only prayer to Thee: that, as the breath of life forsakes me, still I may chant Thy holy Name." And also: "If one who feeds on the flesh of dogs can learn to speak with honeyed words, a beggar gain uncounted wealth and so live long and fearlessly, simply from hearing Thy magic Name, who can describe what must befall one who repeats it day and night?" And again: "Chanting Brahman, the Word of Redemption, meditating *Aham Brahmāsmi* ("I am Brahman"), living on alms and wandering freely, blest indeed is the wearer of the loin-cloth." And finally: "Control the soul, restrain the breath, sift out the transient from the True; repeat the holy Name of God, and quieten the restless mind within; to this, the universal rule, apply yourself with heart and soul."

* * *

There is a dispassion which transcends all conditions of existence: this dispassion, or this deliverance, lies to some extent at the center of existence like a kernel of peace and light; it is like a drop of redemptive spray in an ocean of flames. "The whole universe is on fire," said the Buddha; our misfortune lies in our not knowing that the substance of existence is fire, this substance into which we are woven while yet remaining alien bodies. For the "naive and unrepentent," the world is a neutral space from which he chooses the agreeable content while believing he has the power to avoid the disagreeable, provided he be clever enough and meets with good luck; but the man who does not know that existence is an immense brazier has no imperative reason for wanting to get out of it, and that is why an Arabic proverb says, "The crown of wisdom is the fear of God"– that is to say, the fear of divine afflictions, which are the fatal price of our state of remoteness.

The kernel of light at the centre of the current of forms is essentially the "remembrance of God"– which in the end demands all that we are–as the words of Muhammad declare: "All that is to be found on earth is accursed, save only the remembrance of God," and "There is no fault greater than that of existing." "None is good but one: God," said Christ. This implies that what comes from God–His Name–and what leads to Him–remembering His Name–share in his goodness. The virtual fire through which we live withdraws from things to the extent that we are centered on the mystery of this remembering; things then become transparent and transmit to us the rays of their immutable and blessed archetypes.

It could also be said that existence is fiery in so far as it is regarded as being outside God and, by this fact, it also leads to fire; it is a consuming blaze for the perverted will and illumination for the contemplative intelligence, and it is, thus, at once threat and "consolation," enslaving seduction and liberating vision. It is the changeless and blessed archetypes that man is seeking (did he but know it) when he attaches himself to shadows here below; and he suffers cruelly, first when these shadows disappear and later when, at death, he perceives the archetypes, from which his love for shadows had turned him away. (Music, like dancing, is the art of bringing terrestrial shadows back to celestial vibrations and divine archetypes. In the plastic arts an analogous function is performed by stylization.)

* * *

The divine name is thus a manifestation of the supreme principle, or to speak more plainly, it is not therefore in the first place a manifestation, but is the principle itself.[31]

Notes

[1]This introduction by V. Raghavan is dated Aug. 18, 1959. Frithjof Schuon, *Language of the Self* tr. by Marco Pallis and Macleod Matheson (Madras: Ganesh and Co. 1959). Elements of the introduction not bearing on *Nāmasiddhānta* have been omitted, and the selections from Schuon's *Language. . . .* have been made on the basis of their relevance to Name traditions.

[2]Like Truth, the same *sādhaka* or spiritual aspirant, may have modes and levels; and one can pass from one kind of study to the other without looking down upon the other, or fearing the loss of caste by mixing with those of another school, or being accused of having as if two distinct brains.

[3]Frithjof Schuon, *Gnosis* (London: John Murray, 19), p. 33.

[4]Ibid., p. 27.

[5]Ibid., p. 29.

[6]Frithjof Schuon, *Language of the Self*, p. 100.

[7]Frithjof Schuon, *Gnosis*, pp. 29-30.

[8]*Introduction to the Study of Hindu Doctrines*, p. 201. Compare Schuon, *The Transcendent Unity of Religions* (New York: Harper Torchbook, 1975), p. 124: "Every tradition is necessarily an adaptation. . . ."

[9]*Language of the Self*, p. 101.

[10]*Transcendent Unity*, p. 50.

[11]Ibid, p. 68.

[12]*The Transcendent Unity. . .* , p. 51. (Op. cit., p. 107, fn., " "Hinduism represents the Primordial Tradition. . . . ")

[13]*Spiritual Perspectives*, pp. 66, 68.

[14]*Language of the Self*, p. 46.

[15]Ibid., p. 24.

[16]See Ch. XLII, "From Bhakti to Jñāna and Back" in the *Call of the Jagadguru*, lectures by the Śaṅkarācārya of Kāñcī. (Madras: Ganesh & Co., 1961).

[17]*The Transcendent Unity*, p. 38. ("Reality affirms itself by degrees, but without ceasing to be 'one,' the inferior degrees of this affirmation being absorbed, by metaphysical integration or synthesis, into the superior degrees. Furthermore Being Itself, which is none other than the Personal God, is in its turn surpassed by the Impersonal. . . ."

[18]*The Transcendent Unity*, p. 53.

[19]*Language of the Self*, p. 18.

[20]Ibid., p. 57.

[21]Ibid., p. 229.

[22]Ibid., p. 89.

[23]Ibid., p. 108.

[24]Ibid., p. 29.

[25]Aldous Huxley, *The Perennial Philosophy*, New York: Harper & Row, 1970, p. 229.

[26]*Language of the Self*, p. 37.

[27]Ibid., p. 229.

[28]A.K. Coomaraswamy, "Eastern Wisdom and Western Knowledge," *Isis*, XXXIV:3, pp. 359-363.

[29]*The Richest Vein: Eastern Tradition and Modern Thought* (London: Faber and Faber), p. 17. See also *Language of the Self*, p. 198.)

[30]Selected from Frithjof Schuon, (tr. by Marco Pallis and Macleod Matheson) *The Language of the Self*, Madras: Ganesh & Co., 1959.

[31]Cited in C. Ramanujachari and V. Raghavan, *Spiritual Heritage of Tyāgarāja* (Madras: Śrī Rāmakrishna Math, 1966).

III

LEADERS OF KĀVERĪ DELTA NĀMASIDDHĀNTA:

One:

Bodhendra and Sadgurusvāmi (by N. Raghunathan)[1]

Bhajana and *nāma-sankīrtana* are among the most prominent items of congregational devotion practiced by Hindus. Chanting the many auspicious names of the Lord with form, *saguṇa* Brahman, who is the object of worship even of those who believe in the advaitic Absolute, the formless One without a second who is beyond word and thought, has been regarded as the most acceptable form of praise of the Most High. It is calculated to invoke His Grace and, by reminding the devotee of God's infinite Wisdom, Goodness, Beauty and Power, to instil in his mind a longing for intimate and loving communion with Him. For the past two hundred years neither the group singing of devotional songs (*bhajana*) nor the musical recital of litanies (*nāma-sankīrtana*) composed in honor of different aspects of the Godhead – Śiva, Viṣṇu, or Śakti – nor the repetitive chanting of the names of the great *avatārs*, Rāma and Krishna, has been begun in the Tamil country without the following panegyric verses being first sung in honor of the saints who are the subject of this paper:

> We beseech the Grace of Śri Bodhendra, the prince of yogis and most glorious of spiritual preceptors, who was the embodiment of the inexhaustable riches of the soul which is the empire the Lord's Name brings.

> We bow at the feet of Śri Veṅkaṭarama, [Sadgurusvāmī], the prince of spiritual guides, who was the incarnation in one person of the two great souls: Śri Bhagavan-nāma Bodhendra and Śrīdhara Ārya.

Bhagavan-nāma Bodhendra, to give him his full *āśrama*-name and Śrīdhara Veṅkaṭeśa Arya, universally venerated as "Āyyāvāl" in the Tamil country, were contemporaries who spent many years in the opening decades of the 18th century in adjacent villages near Kumbakoṇam in the Tāñjāvūr District on the banks of the Kāverī. They were chiefly responsible for the renaissance of *bhakti* in the South and of art as its handmaid, a movement which in due course produced many a flower of spiritual perfection, including the great saint-composers, Tyāgarāja, Śyāma Śāstri and Muttusvāmī Dīkṣitar who are among the peaks of Karnāṭaka music.

From the chronicles of Śri Kāñcīpuram Kāmakoṭi Pītham, the monastery which was founded by Śaṅkarācārya, it appears that Śri Bodhendra, a *sannyāsin* and Rāma *bhakta*, was a Telugu Brahman born in Kāñcīpuram who succeeded his guru in the headship of the Kāñcīpuram Kāmakoṭi Pīṭham. While on a pilgrimage to Rāmeśvaram, from Kāñcī, which was then the home seat of the *maṭh*, he met the great scholar, saint and Śiva *bhakta*, Āyyāvāl. The two godly men found such satisfaction in each other's holy company and in the propitious conditions for spreading the teaching of the divine Name which they found in the Tāñjāvūr countryside that Śri Bodhendra spent the rest of his life in and near Tiruvidaimarudur the great Śiva *kṣetra* or holy site. He attained beatitude at Govindapuram, a nearby village where his monument still attracts crowds of devotees every year at his anniversary.

Āyyāvāl, who came of a family in Telugu Brahmans

originally domiciled in Mysore, lived in Tiruviśanallūr, a village across the river, which was famous for its scholarship and piety. It had been founded by Śāhajī, the son of Ekojī of the Mahārāṣṭra dynasty. Āyyāvāl too was an *advaitin*, but he lived the householder's life. He had won the king's regard in his early years by his attainments as a poet and scholar and by his character. Settling down in the village of which his father was one of the original grantees he composed many hymns in praise of Śiva, his *iṣṭadevatā* or favorite form of the divine, and other deities. He composed a treatise of the efficacy of the divine Name as a *tārakamantra*, a saving utterance.[2] From references to it in Śri Bodhendra's tracts on the same subject we know it was called *Bhagavan-nāma bhuṣana* and was distinguished by its devotional fervour, learning and insight. Unfortunately no manuscript of the work has come to light.

Āyyāvāl is a household name in the Tāñjāvūr countryside because of a remarkable legend connected with his life. On a *śrāddha* day a starving untouchable came to his back-garden and piteously wailed for food. Without a moment's hesitation, the saint ordered the food cooked for ceremonial offering to the Brahmans to be given to him, though that involved a great violation of rule and practice. When the villagers remonstrated he prayed to the holy Gaṅgā, and forthwith the well in his back-yard began to rise and overflow. The onlookers were convinced that the holy Ganges stream had indeed issued from its Northern home, appearing here to testify to the loving compassion that had welled up from a good man's heart, and thus proclaimed to the world his superior sanctity.

A few decades after the passing away of both these saints there was born in another Telugu Brahman family of Tiruviśanallūr a child who was named Veṅkaṭarama but who was known to fame as Śri Sadgurusvāmī. An intense yearning for God developed in his from his earliest youth. Well-versed in the *Śāstras* and endowed with an extraordinarily fascinating personality he was cut out for success, but his mind turned away from worldly pursuits. He dutifully lived a householder's life for a short while, following the *uñchavṛitti dharma*;[3] and when he lost his dependents he went about the countryside, a real *mukta* (liberated soul), incessantly singing the glory of God and the power of the divine Name, in all of the divine aspects and *avatārs*, thus consciously carrying on the combined mission of Bodhendra and Āyyāvāl. It is to his self-dedication to the task of resuscitating the *bhāgavata dharma* that metaphorical reference is made in the verse I have quoted above, which speaks of him as the incarnation of these two sainted men. After some years of itinerant ministry he came to rest at Marudānallūr, another village near Kumbakoṇam, where he established the Rādhākrishna Bhajana Maṭh and initiated large numbers into the divine mystery of Rāma-*nāma*. The heads of that lay *maṭha*, whose succession he established in the family of the disciple who first welcomed him to that village, are looked upon as having authority, through the grace of Śri Sadgurusvāmī, to initiate the aspirant in Rāma *nāma japa*. That *maṭh* and other *bhajana-maṭhs* founded by his disciples in the Tāñjāvūr District and elsewhere carry on the *bhajana sampradāya* established by Bodhendra and Sadgurusvāmī and propagate the *Nāma-siddhānta* which teaches that salvation may be obtained by putting one's trust in the mercy of the Lord and the infinite potency of the divine Name. Though they were all mystics of a high order, Bodhendra was a philosopher as well, while Āyyāvāl was primarily a poet-his *Ākhya śaṣṭi*, on the potency of Śiva-*nāma* and his *Daya śaṭakam* (an invocation of the Compassion of Lord Śiva) show imagination as well as learning and piety, and Sadgurusvāmī was ecstatic with the power to impart touch that transforms.

Before he became a *sannyāsin* Bodhendra had been to Banāras and travelled widely in the North. Age-long tradition credits him with having received the text of *Bhagavan-nāma kaumudi* from the family of its remarkable fifteenth-century author Lakṣmīdhara, who may be said to have been the first theoretician who systematized the philosophy which is familiarly known as the *Nāma-siddhānta* and who, as the picturesque legend has it, prophesied that it would be given to a great *sannyāsin* to spread the faith in the divine Name in the Southland (*dākṣiṇa deśa*). Bodhendra was familiar with Ananta Deva's commentary on Lakṣmīdhara's work as well as works by later writers on the subject.

Lakṣmīdhara, who is described as a great authority on *pūrva mīmāṃsā*, the philosophical theory of ritual, seeks to establish in his terse treatise, by reference to scriptures – *Śruti* (Vedas), *Smṛiti* (Law books), *Itihāsa* (history and legends) and *Purāṇa* (devotional narrative scriptures), that there is no such large difference of opinion as had been supposed to exist between *Smṛiti* and *Purāṇa* in regard to the efficacy of the divine Name as the instrument for the destruction of sins and the opening of the way to salvation. He resolutely maintains that if the *Smṛitis* should differ from the Purāṇas in regard to any vital matter we would be justified in preferring the *Purāṇas*, as their recognised purpose, the "*upabrahmana*," making clear and explicit the teaching of the Veda, shows that they are superior to the *Smṛitis* which are merely ancillary and derivative. He traces thus the orderly evolution of spiritual progress by means of the practice of repetitions of the divine Name:

> The recital of the divine Name leads to the extinction of sin: the continued repetition of the Name strengthens the good tendencies (*vāsanas*) connected with the connotations of the name and the elimination

of the bad *vāsanas* which had strengthened the tendency to sin; this generates the impulse to serve the devotees of the Lord; their infectious zeal in describing His manifold glory induces *naiṣṭikī bhakti*, unshakable devotion; then follow in succession the abolition of sorrow, the exaltation of the soul, the realization of the Highest, which is Truth and therefrom *mukti*.

Lakṣmīdhara bases his view mainly on the *Bhāgavata Purāṇa*, which is the *bhakti* scripture par excellence. He describes *bhakti* as *rati*, love for the Divine. There is not, however, in his work any reference to the Rādha-Krishna devotional movement or the refinements of the teachings of *prema-bhakti* or devoted love which the Caitanya school developed. Lakṣmīdhara traces the exaltation of the divine Name to its source in the Veda itself, quoting the Ṛik of Dirghatamas: "O praisers, knowing them, praise every one of his names. O Viṣṇu, we desire the good will of you who are great."

āsyajānanto nāmacidvivaktana
mahatte viṣṇo sumatim bhajāmahe

This is relied upon by Śri Śaṅkara also in his commentary on the *Viṣṇu sahasranāma* to establish the potency of *Nāma-japa* and *Nāma-kīrtana*.

Bodhendra, in his turn, reinforces the authority of the Ṛig Vedic verse with a Yajur Vedic verse.[4] And he also relies largely on the great *ācārya* Śaṅkara's *Gītā Bhāshya* and *Sahasra-nāma Bhāsya* as on the *Bhāgavata Purāṇa*, the *Viṣṇu Purāṇa*, the *Bṛihan-naradīya*, the *Brahma-vaivarta* and other *Purāṇas*, to support a thesis which is broadly the same as that of Lakṣmīdhara. He does this with massive erudition, a logical subtley and nimbleness of mind which extort admiration. His mastery of *pūrva mīmāṁsā* and *nyāya*, and his undoubted authority as a great *advaitin* who has written his own commentary on Śri Śaṅkara's *Bhagavad Gītā Bhāṣya*, as well as the saintliness of his life, must have made him a formidable foe to the "frogs in the well" as he contemptuously terms those who thought that the exaltation of the Name as divine incarnation, *Bhagavan-nāma*, had no philosophical basis. One of them, in particular, roused his ire by writing a book which apparently gained some vogue even in areas outside the Tamil country, though even its name has not come down to us. His *Nāma-amṛita Rasodaya*, in six chapters, the longest of his treatises on the subject– he seems to have written many, as seen from the tribute of panegyrists who speak of him as *Nāma-nibandha-śatakarta*,–is a superb example of his polemical gift as well as of his practiced skill as a teacher; he uses iteration with great virtuosity. Of his other extant works, the *Nāma-amṛita rasāyana* is the most compendious as it seems to have been one of the earliest. It marshalls the six reasons given by this school of thought for regarding the utterance of the divine Name as superior to other means prescribed in the scriptures. (1) the practice of *nāma-japa*, which is open to everybody irrespective of caste, stage of life (*āśrama*) or sex, involves no injury; (2) it needs no ancillary aid; (3) it is not dependant on the intercession of another person; (4 to 6) its practice is not regulated by restrictions and prohibitions regarding time, or place or ritual. This tract also describes the ten kinds of "*Nāma-aparādhas*" or sins which retard the efficacy of *nāma-kīrtana*. These sins include that of cavilling against perfected men. Expiation for these sins is to be found only in the continued chanting of the divine Name till the propensity to sin is extinguished.[5]

Among these ten "Nāma-aparādhas" figures another which is of peculiar significance for a true understanding of the teachings of Bodhendra and his followers. The sectarian who exalts his *iṣṭa-devatā* at the expense of other comes in for vigorous trouncing as being guilty of *Nāma-aparadha*. Śri Bodhendra is credited with two other works, *Hari-hara bheda-dhikkāra* and *Hari-hara-advaita-bhūṣaṇam*, which aim to show that the scriptures which seem to exalt Viṣṇu and cry down Śiva, and vice versa, do this merely with a view to strengthening people's faith in the deity of their own allegiance and that the depreciation of others is not intended to be taken too seriously. By an elaborate review of all the relevant authorities he shows that the fundamental intention of all the scriptures is to emphasize the unity of the Godhead, the essential identity of Viṣṇu and Śiva. No less remarkable is the insistence, in an *advaitin* and a *sannyāsin* too, that *Mūrta-brahma upāsana*, the meditation or worship of the Brahman with attributes, is essential as a preparation for *advaita-anubhava*, the realization of oneness. He indeed stoutly declares that the foolish who deride *saguṇa upāsana* (devotion to the divine with qualities) can never hope to realize the *nirguṇa*, supreme formless reality. In this Śri Bodhendra does not depart from the spirit of the great Śaṅkara's teaching.

The influence of the *bhakti* movement started by Bodhendra and Āyyāvāl, strengthened by Sadgurusvāmī and fortified by the living example of many a realised soul still keeps alive the flame of spirituality in the hearts of the people. And it has been a most potent force for true toleration. This catholicity of outlook indeed characterizes all the mystics who have exalted the divine Name from the early beginnings of the movement. It can be traced to Lakṣmīdhara himself. One of the closing verses of *Bhagavan-nāma kaumudi* effects a magnificent imaginative identification of Śiva and Viṣṇu with each other, with the guru and with the *iṣṭa-devatā*. With that characteristic expression of the Indian synthesis this short account may appropriately end:

He who (as Viṣṇu) was the creator of the holy Gaṅgā, which flowed from his lotus-feet, fell so much in love with its redemptive virtues that (as Śiva) he bore it on his own head: he is our Guru, he is the divine ruler of our race.[6]

Notes

[1]First published in T.M.P. Mahadevan, ed. *A Seminar on Saints*. (Madras: Ganesh and Co., 1960). N. Raghunathan was a colleague and friend of V. Raghavan. This essay completes and complements the other sketches of *Namasiddhanta* leaders by V. Raghavan. It was influenced by V. Raghavan's studies, though it was not written by him. Without this piece a gap would be left in the study, and because it was written by Raghunathan after consultation with, and guidance from, V. Raghavan, I have included it here.

The *bhajana* program sequence codified by Sadgurusvāmī is as follows, according to Veṅkaṭaramana Bhāgavatar, the elder *bhajana* leader of Tiruvidaimarudur village, with whom I spoke in July 1989. First, Gaṇeśa invocation and verses invoking Bodhendra and Āyyāvāl. Then, 1. *Todayamaṅgalam kirtanas* by Chinnayya Tāllappakka. 2. Songs celebrating the gurus Bodhendra and 3. Āyyāvāl and 4. Sadgurusvāmī. 5. *Gita Govinda* lyrics. 6. Nārāyaṇa Tīrtha songs from Krishnalīlātaraṅgini. 7. Bhadrācalam Rāmadas *kirtana*. 8. Purandaradāsa song. 9. Sadāśiva Brahmendra songs. 10. Gopala Krishna Bharati song in Tamil. 11. Tyāgarāja songs in Telugu. Then songs in other languages: Kabīr, Tulsidās, Mahārāṣṭra *abhaṅgas*. Chidambaram Natarāja *kīrtanas*, Śaiva and Vaiṣṇava songs, *divyanāma saṅkīrtanas*, and finally a ritual in which the singers sing while circumambulating a lamp with five flames.

[2]A *mantra* or incantatory word or group of words which is believed to help the earnest seeker who repeats it to transcend the ocean of *karma* or transmigratory existence.

[3]This had originally referred to the vow that a man would live by picking up the stray unregarded ears of grain that had fallen in the field or by the wayside while harvesters were at work. Later it came to mean the practice of accepting the small offerings of rice the devout made as the *bhāgavata* (one who dedicated himself wholly to the life of

devotion) went along the village street of a morning singing or chanting the praises of the Lord.

[4]patatte adyasipivista nāmāryassamsamiva yunnani vidvān.

(This passage from the *Yajur Veda* is not identified by number in the original article.)

[5]Bodhendra is no formalist. He suggests that the man who has developed passionate devotion and would like to spend his time doing *nāma-saṅkirtana* could legitimately restrict himself to the minimum of ritual observances and duties enjoined by the *Smṛitis* provided he at the same time gives only the minimum of attention to worldly affairs and the earning of a livelihood.

[6]Lakṣmidhara, *Bhagavannāma Kaumudi*, Kasi: Prakāśasthānam Acyutagranthamālā Kāryālayaḥ, 1907. A copy of this book is available at Widener Library, Harvard University.

LEADERS OF KĀVERĪ DELTA NĀMASIDDHĀNTA

Two:

Śrīdhara Veṅkateśa Āyyāvāl: Poet and Legendary Enthusiast of the Name[1]

"He who has pure knowledge and strong devotion
toward the Almighty and
the Almighty's Name,
He who has love for the devotee, who is a worshipper
of the Name,
He who has detachment from all else, his heart
turned toward the Lord,
steadfast in his loving kindness –
I give my veneration to that human form of the
divine Parameśvara,
whose name is Śrīdhara Veṅkateśa Āyyāvāl, the
Guru."

It is with this prayer that *Bhajana sampradāya* sessions in South India begin. The divine form of Śrīdhara Veṅkateśa Āyyāvāl is worthy of this veneration; it is well known that this saintly man was referred to both by the common people and by the learned as "Āyyāvāl," meaning "the honored one, the respected sire." That he was known by this name shows their deep regard for him. Śrīdhara Veṅkateśa and Śrīmad Bodhendra were two important souls who gave life to the *bhajana* tradition and Name repetition movement throughout Chola Deśa.

The Mahārāṣtran rulers of Tāñjāvūr patronized the arts

and education on a large scale. Tāñjāvūr flourished very well during the reigns of Śāhajī, Śarabhojī and Tukojī, sons of Ekojī, who founded the Mahārāṣṭra dynasty there. The arts developed greatly during their reigns. Of the three rulers, Śāhajī (1684-1710) was foremost. Not only did he encourage talented poets, but he himself was also well-versed in arts and literature. He composed poems and musical dramas in Telugu, Marāthi and Sanskrit, and his devotion and generosity toward learned saints show that he was filled with spiritual discernment and yogic determination.

In 1693 King Śāhajī donated the sacred place of Tiruviśanallūr village to 46 learned families who were well-versed in various specialties of knowledge, and the place was renamed Śāhajirājapuram. Śrī Rāmabhadra Dikṣitar, Bhaskara Dikṣitar, Veda Kavi, Mahādeva Kavi, Periappa Kavi, Nallakavi, Śivarāmakrishnar alias Sadāśiva Brahmendra are all great people who belonged to these families. Among them were certain families from what is now Andhra Pradesh, too. Among the Telugu families one was that of Mokṣam Somasundara, and another was that of Śrīdhara Liṅgayariar. The great saint Śrī Sadāśiva Brahmendra was born of Somasundara, and it is thought by some that Śrīdhara Veṅkateśa was born of the latter, namely Liṅgayariar.

It is not known for certain if Śrīdhara Veṅkateśa, who was patronized by King Śāhajī, was one of the forty-five primary donees of the village of Tiruviśanallūr or not. That he was a resident of that village is amply borne out by the existence in that village of his house and the annual festival that takes place there in his honor. It would therefore appear that he was a subsequent donee. Śrīdhara Veṅkateśa, as his prefixed house-name shows, was evidently a member of a family originating in what is now Andhra Pradesh. It is definitely known that there were pandits from the Telugu country among the donees of this village; but none of these is noted in the list of donee names in the grant with his house-name. Our author was known to his contemporaries as Veṅkateśa or Veṅkateśvara Śāstrin, as can be seen in Bodhendra's references to him.[2] If Śrīdhara Veṅkateśa was one of the donees, he can only be the Veṅkateśvara Śāstrin mentioned as the 24th in the list, but the likelihood is that the *Nāmasiddhānta* author named Śrīdhara Veṅkateśa is different from this Veṅkateśvara.

Śrīdhara, as has been pointed out, is his house name; and in his colophonic verses in *Śāhendravilāsa* ("The Illustrious Acts of King Śāhajī") he mentions his father as Liṅgārya. That this Telugu Śrīdhara was patronized by the Tāñjāvūr court is evident from the *Cakorasandeśa* of Navīna Patañjali Śrīdhara Peru Suri.[3]

His Life

As mentioned before, Śrīdhara Veṅkateśa is more popularly known as "Āyyāvāl," meaning "the respected sire." In fact, few indeed will be the South Indians with any pretentions to culture or religious faith who have not heard of "Āyyāvāl" and the annual festival that is held in his name – the *Āyyāvāl utsava* at Tiruviśanallūr. There is hardly any *bhajana maṭh*, or prayer hall, where his portrait is not venerated; there are not only prayer-verses on him, but songs composed on him and sung regularly as part of the *bhajana* program. He, along with his contemporary Bodhendra, was responsible in the Kāverī delta region for the great spread of that phase of the *bhakti* devotional movement which believes in the singing of the Lord's glory and the repetition of the divine name, *Nāmasiddhānta*, as the most efficacious means of salvation, particularly in the present age. It is not only by his writings on this subject, both in the form of devotional hymns and critical treatise, but also by the high devotional and spiritual attainments of his life that he came to occupy this leading place in the pantheon of devotees of the Lord.

Several anecdotes are traditionally handed down in respect of Āyyāvāl and his spiritual attainments. It is said that with one of his hymns, the *Kulīrāṣṭaka*, he brought rains at a time when they had failed, and the last verse of the hymn itself has a bearing on this incident. With this hymn *Tārāvalīstuti*, he is said to have brought back to life or saved from imminent death a child, and the second half of each verse in this hymn has a direct reference to it.

More celebrated than these two miracles is the incident of Āyyāvāl and the hunger-stricken *caṇḍāla* or untouchable, which "canonized" Āyyāvāl and gave birth to the annual Āyyāvāl festival on the new-moon day in the month of Kārttika (November-December). Once, on the day on which he had to perform the annual *śrāddha* ceremony for his departed parent, Āyyāvāl, while going to the Kāverī river for bath, saw a *caṇḍāla* in the throes of death as a result of starvation; Āyyāvāl who saw the oneness of life everywhere and realized the universal presence of the Lord, was moved by the sight, and asked the consecrated *śrāddha* food made ready at his house for the Brahman invitees to be made over to the *candāla*. Custom demanded from him an expiation in the form of a bath in the Ganges; for this he uttered forth a prayer to Mother Gaṅgā.

Of contemporary references to Śrīdhara Veṅkateśa, two have come to my notice: As shown below, Bodhendra cites him in his work on *Nāmasiddhānta*. In the play, *Śṛṅgāramañjari śāharājīya* by Periappā Kavi alias Vainateya, the author refers to himself in the Prologue as having received approbation from Śrīdhara Veṅkateśa, among others. Our author is mentioned by Appākavi as a respected friend of the same age.[4]

Of the distinguished writers of the age who sat at our author's feet, we know now only one, Vīṇai Ayyaṇṇa Dīkṣita, a Telugu scholar and expert player on the *vīṇā*. Ayyaṇṇa's *Vyāsatatparya Nirṇaya* is a well known tract on *advaita*, conveying the correct import of the *Brahma sūtras*.[5] The author was the son of Veṅkateśa Kavi, author of Rādhāmādhavasamvāda and other Telugu *prabandas* and younger brother of Nṛihari, author of Telugu *prabandhas* like *Sudantā Kalyāna*. In the second introductory verse, the author salutes his guru, Śrīdhara Veṅkateśa Āyyāvāl.

His Works

As is only to be expected from the above given account of the life of Āyyāvāl, his devotional hymns became most popular. As early as 1895 the Śrī Vidyā Press of Kumbakonam, brought out a *grantha* script edition of all the *stotra*s composed by Śrīdhara Veṅkateśa. This collection which was edited by the well known Nṛisimha Bhāgavatar and Bhattaśrī Nārāyaṇa Śāstrigal consists of

1. Ākhyāṣaṣti
2. Dāyaśataka
3. Matṛibhutasataka
4. Stutipaddhati
5. Śivabhaktikalpalatikā
6. Śivabhaktalakṣaṇa
7. Tārāvalīstotra
8. Ārtiharastuti
9. Kulirāṣṭaka
10. Jambūnāthāṣṭaka
11. Dosapariharaṣṭaka
12. Krishnadvādaśamañjarī
13. Acyutāṣṭaka
14. Dolānavaratnamālā

and was based on manuscripts of these works collected from several places. Not only did the same Press subsequently reprint this collection, but other agencies too brought out similar collections.[6]

It is said that there is a hymn of his on Gaṅgā (the Ganges) associated with the miracle narrated above but, as already stated, it has not yet been recovered and identified.

On the subject of the sanctity and efficacy of uttering the Lord's Name and attaining salvation thereby, i.e., on the *Nāma-siddhānta* school of devotion to which he gave a great stimulus in the Kāverī delta, he had made contributions in the form of hymns mentioned already, the *Ākhyāṣaṣṭi* being particularly a work of importance in this respect. Besides these, Śrīdhara Veṅkateśa wrote a regular treatise called the *Bhagavan nāma bhūṣana* on this subject. This work has unfortunately not yet been found in manuscript. (The fifth *Śaṅkarabharaṇa-rāga* song in Gopālakrishna Bhārati's *Rāgamālikā* is on Śrīdhara Veṅkateśa and refers to this work of our author.)

Another work with which Śrīdhara Veṅkateśa was connected is the list of words called *Padamaṇimañjari* which he and two contemporaries and co-villagers of his, his namesake Veṅkateśvara Śāstrin and Nallādhavarin, compiled at the behest of their beloved patron, King Śāhajī.[7]

At the end of each canto of his *Śāhendravilāsa* he refers to himself as proficient in all *śāstras*, particularly in *nyāya*, but no work of his in this line has yet come to light.

The only *kāvya* or lengthy narrative poem of his is the *Śāhendravilāsa* on his patron Śāhajī.

The question has been asked, how was it that the great saint and devotee of the Lord Āyyāvāl composed the poem on King Śāhajī? That is, why did he indulge in *nara-stuti*, "praise of man" as it is usual to put it? It is hardly necessary to offer in explanation of this that the *Śāhendravilāsa* was, as is clear, a production of the earlier years of Śrīdhara Veṅkateśa. Even if the poem was written by him in his later years, there is nothing inappropriate in it. The close association of learned men and even *sannyāsins* with rulers has been a constant feature of Indian literary history; and as it happens quite often these rulers have been active litterateurs themselves. Rāmabhadra

Dīkṣita who was an exclusive devotee of God in the form of Rāma and would praise none else was the most intimate author friend of Śāhajī and has praised him many times. Bhāskararāya, also known as Bhāsurānandanātha, one of the senior and much respected personalities of this time, and an acknowledged *ācārya* of highest attainments in Śakta-worship, composed, as has already been pointed out, a eulogy of eight verses on Śāhajī, in which he anticipated the same criticism that we are considering here.[8]

Apart from his zeal for fostering culture, Śāhajī, as all his court-poets have pointed out and as the works ascribed to him show, was deeply imbued with devotion. He was such an ardent *bhakta* of God Tyāgarāja of Tiruvārūr that when a reference is made to his demise, it is said that he attained oneness with Tyāgeśa.

The *Śāhendravilāsa* is primarily a poem, though it incorporates a few historical facts and narrates the two important military events of Śāhajī's time, the aid given to the Setupati and Rājarām at Gingee. As is usual in such compositions, poetic descriptions progress in the well known order: childhood, youth and marriage, hero's prowess and the march of the army, hunting and sporting in garden and water, city and palace, sunset and sunrise, love and separation, and seasons and scenes of nature.

* * *

Śāhajī came to the throne very young and died young at 40; except for the few events already referred to, there was not much of political unsettlement to distrub the peace and prosperity of the decades during which Tāñjāvūr was under his rule. Our author by speaking of him not only as an incarnation of Śiva, but also by expressing it in so many words that the God-appointed role of his life was to free the country from the harassment caused by the Muslims (VII. 10) reflects but correctly the security and stimulus that the resilient Hindu Chiefs of the South from the Vijayanagar times onwards gave to Hindu religion and culture. At this time there was the new menace of the Christian missionaries masquerading as Roman Brahmans, weaning away the masses and reviling Hindu faith and worship. The European historian Manucci vouchsafes to us, in his reference to Śāhajī's persecution of the Christians, that our hero's zeal for the safeguarding of the Country's religion was really comprehensive in its sweep. No wonder that Nallā alias Bhūminātha takes Śāhajī's biography as a holy chronicle and record of *dharma* in his *Dharmavijaya Campū*. The concluding eulogy in that work presents a true picture of the plenty and all round richness of life that was vouchsafed to the people of the Kāverī delta in this period. The tradition of the cultural richness of this area goes indeed to the Chola times and even earlier, but credit is due to the successive rulers who realised the value of this culture, and not only preserved it but enriched it considerably. If the Nāyaks reinforced it with elements of value from Telugu, the Marāthas breathed some fresh life into it with the elements from the Mahārāṣṭra. In arts and letters, devotion and spiritual endeavour, the culture of the Kāverī delta attained a marvellous complexion, varied, brilliant and uplifting. In the making of this Kāverī river delta culture, the fragrance of which has not yet died out, Śāhajī played no small part, Śāhajī whom Āyyāvāl rightly hailed in this poem as "himself the heart and soul of the Muse."

Āyyāvāl in Praise of the Name

Śrī Āyyāvāl praised the holy name, which like a mother pours out so much welfare, love, generosity and nurturing care toward Name devotees, especially in verse like the following from the *Ākhyāṣaṣṭi*:[10]

Some who contemplate that divine form of Śiva

enjoy some good things in this world; others, O Mother, Compassion of Śiva, thanks to your support, delight in enjoying the ambrosial billows of Śiva's Name and casting away all anguish (v. 4).

O Compassion! When will the floods of your excellences, in which are immersed Śiva Himself, engulf me with the ambrosial billows of the auspicious Names incessantly recited, Names like Smararati (Enemy of the Love-god), Śambhu (Auspicious), Purahara (Destroyer of Tripura), Śiva, Umādhava (Lord of Pārvatī), Hara, Murari (Enemy of the demon Mura), Govinda, Chief of Gods, Mukunda (v. 22).

O Compassion of Śiva! You are capable of granting immediately the state of Brahmā or the fortune of Viṣṇu; why don't you give me the state of sitting somewhere, rid of all distress and concentrated in the continuous recital of the Name of Śiva? (v. 29)

"Let this man utter once the Name of Śiva even if it be through the guise of words like *(a)hara* ('Bring') and I shall take away all his distress." Which man, not stupid like me will not, without thought of another thing, resort to you who are thus constantly wakeful, O Compassion of Śiva? (v. 32)

O Compassion! If I am not taken up for support on the ground that I am a sinner, tell Śiva there will be ruin to his reputation as the protector of the distressed and as one the occasional utterance of whose Name destroys all sins (v. 56).

O Compassion! The occasional contemplation of Śiva, doing obeisance to Him or the mention of His Name, becomes the supreme means of removing

> the transmigratory toil, because of you. O Mother, your way is great indeed! (v. 91)
>
> O Compassion! Give me that steadfast mind that Śiva and Viṣṇu, who are both like Śiva to me, may never leave my mind; even so, make this tongue of mine utter "Śiva, Śiva," for, barring these two, there is nothing else that is the object of my desire (v. 99).
>
> O Compassion of Śiva! In my last moment, by your grace, may this much appear in my heart: this two-syllable Name, "Śiva, Śiva," your abode, the giver of Release, a Name that is auspicious to the whole universe (v. 101).

There are few in South India who have not heard of the Āyyāvāl Festival, which is still celebrated on Kārttika new-moon day in Tiruviśanallūr village, where Āyyāvāl spent so much of his life. Devotees continue to celebrate the episode in Āyyāvāl's life when he offered food to a starving untouchable, and then, ordered by offended Brahmans to bathe in the Ganges, saw the river goddess Gaṅgā arise from the well in his yard; devotees celebrate the event with a ritual bath at the well and with other festival ceremonies suitable to his memory.

There are many other interesting stories told about Āyyāvāl which show him as one who had attained great spiritual wisdom. He used to worship daily in a temple across the Kāverī river in Tiruvidaimarudur where Mahāliṅga Svāmī was the presiding deity. On two occasions floods obstructed this worship. Both times it is said that the Lord himself came to Āyyāvāl – once in the form of a priest, to deliver the divine offering (*prasād*) to him, and another time in the form of a boat-man to take Āyyāvāl across the river.

Notes

[1]The first two paragraphs and the last two paragraphs of this piece I have taken from V. Raghavan's introduction to the *Ākhyāṣaṣṭi* (Kumbakonam and Madras: Kāmakoṭi Kosasthānam, 1944), No. 15 in the series. The rest of the article (except for the translations from the *Ākhyāṣaṣṭi*) is from the introduction to *Śāhendravilāsa*, ed. V. Raghavan (Tiruchi: Tanjore Saraswati Mahal Library, 1952), pp. 60-74. I have had to omit some details because of space limitations.

[2]Among the donee names, we have one Veṅkaṭeśvara Vājapeyayājin (21st), one Veṅkaṭeśvara *Śāstrin* (24th), one Samavedi Veṅkaṭeśvara Śāstrin (39th), and one Veṅkaṭeśvara *Kavi* (42nd). Of these the Sāmavedi Veṅkaṭeśvara Śāstrin is evidently the same as the son of Ikkiri Appā Śāstrin alias Śrīnivasa, later Pūrṇānandayati, of Prayāga family, Kauśika gotra and Kaṇḍaramāṇikkam village. (*Ind. Ant.* 1904, pp. 127, 191.) The Vājapeyin and Kavi Veṅkateśvaras are not likely to be our author; the latter, mentioned as Kavi, is as shown above, the pupil of Rāmabhadra Dīkṣita and author of the *Patañjalicaritavyākhyā* and *Ūṇādinighaṇṭu*. There is also a Veṅkaṭeśvara Śāstrin found as one of the collaborators with our Śrīdhara Veṅkaṭeśvara in the compilation *Padamaṇimañjari*.

[3]Tāñjāvūr Ms. No. 3863.

[4]Madras Ms. R. 1843.

[5]It was published by the Vani Vilas Press in 1910 on the basis of two manuscripts from Mysore but neither of which contained the informing colophon in the Madras manuscript of that work (D. 15276). Two other works written by Ayyanna Dīkṣita are *Praṇavārthasudhodaya* and *Yajñaśāstrārthanirṇaya*. See New Catalogus Catalogorum, I, p. 271A.

[6]The Vaidika Vardhani Press at the same place started issuing with Tamil meaning the hymns of our author in a series called the Śrīdhara *Stutimaṇimāla*, and the most famous ones among these, the *Ākhyāṣaṣṭi* and *Dāyaśataka* appeared in 1900. In *Devanāgarī*, the Vani Vilas Press, Śrīrangam, began publishing them in their Stotra Booklet Series: The *Ākhyāṣaṣṭi* and the *Śivabhaktikalpalatikā* appeared in 1908; the *Dāyaśaṭaka* and the *Mātṛibhutaśataka* in 1911. Of the other hymns, the same Press published in Vol. V, No. 17 of the *Journal of the Śaṅkaragurukulam* (pp. 3-5) the *Kulīraṣṭaka*, the *Tārāvalīstuti*, and the *Ārtihara-Umeśastotra*. With English and Tamil translations, Tamil notes and Introductions, V. Raghavan

brought out the *Ākhyāṣaṣṭi* and the *Dāyaśataka* in the Kamakoti Granthavali. *Nāmāmṛitarasāyana* was published by Poornachandrodayam Press, Tanjore, 1926.

[7]The compilation, of which two manuscripts exist in the Sarasvati Mahal Library (Nos. 5011 and 5012).

[8]Tāñjāvūr Catalogue XIV, p. 6411.

[9]Editor's Note: I have omitted a detailed critique of Āyyāvāl's poetry, because it does not bear directly on our topic of Nāmasiddhānta.

[10]Editors note: I have selected these from V. Raghavan's translation of the *Ākhyāṣaṣṭi śatakam* of Śrīdhara Veṅkateśa Āyyāvāl (Kumbakoṇam and Madras: Kāmakoṭi Kosasthānam, 1944), No. 25 in the series. They are not in the original introduction to *Śāhendravilāsa*.

LEADERS OF KĀVERĪ DELTA NĀMASIDDHĀNTA

Three:

Sadāśiva Brahmendra: The Silent *Avadhūta*[1]

Who in Tamil Nadu has not heard the songs *Mānasa sañchara re* ("O mind, be occupied with Brahman"), *Brūhi mukundeti* ("Chant Mukunda, o my tongue") and *Piba re rāmarasam* ("Taste the nectar of Rāma's Name")? Their composer is no less renowned than the celebrated composer Tyāgarāja. While Tyāgarāja and Dīkṣitar sang of the personal divinity, *saguṇa* Brahman, "the Supreme Being with qualities," the *sannyāsin*-author of these songs sang of the Impersonal Absolute, the *nirguṇa* Brahman, "the Supreme Being without qualities." He sang in the fulness of his own realization of the one Godhead, beyond all names and forms and of the very nature of *sat-cit-ānanda*, ultimate Existence, Knowledge and Bliss. He was the bard of *advaita*, the philosophy of non-duality, divine oneness. Sadāśiva Brahmendra was his name.

Sadāśiva Brahmendra Sarasvatī, who was roaming as an *avadhūta*, one from whom worldly things have "fallen off," on the banks of the Kāverī river, is a memory still fresh in the minds of all truth seekers there; in the intellectual and devotional life of the Kāverī delta, he is still a force. Sadāśivendra, before he renounced life, was the native of the well known village, Tiruviśanallūr on the Kāverī near Kumbakoṇam, which Śahajī, the Mahratta king of Tāñjāvūr, A.D. 1684-1712, gave away as Śahajīrājapuram to 46 scholars. Among these was Mokṣam Somasundara Avadhani who was father of our saint whose civil name was Śivarāma. Śivarāma as a student was in the company of three outstanding personalities of the time, Rāmabhadra Dīkṣita, Śrīdhara Veṅkateṣa Āyyāvāl and Gopālakrishna Śāstri, the last of whom later became, at Sadāśivendra's instance, the preceptor of the Tondaman Chief of Pudukoṭṭai. A vexatious delay at his father-in-law's house on a festive occasion produced a sudden revulsion in the keen mind of young Śivarāma; an excuse, as it were, suddenly marked a predestined turn in life; the scales fell; awakening beamed forth, and Śivarāma renounced life, sought the feet of the *sannyāsin* Paramaśivendra Sarasvatī, and himself entered the order as Sadāśivendra Sarasvatī.

To Brahmendral, as South Indians now reverentially speak of him, success on the spiritual path came rapidly. A redoubtable dialectician, he used to submit every scholar-visitor to his guru to severe cross-examination. When reports reached the guru of Sadāśivendra's interrogation of scholars, the guru chided him "when are you going to control your tongue?" From that moment, Sadāśivendra gave up speech and became a silent sage (*mauna-yogi*). Another time, Sadāśivendra was lying down on an open field resting his uplifted head on air as it were; and a farmer passing across the field where Sadāśivendra was lying made a remark against him for demonstrating his yogic power. With this, the lingering infirmities of vanity of scholarship or yogic power were completely removed and his Brahmanhood reached its untainted fullness.

Mad with delight of Brahman, native of no roof, eating off his palm whatever fell there by chance, the Brahmendra roamed about, exemplifying the great state of one liberated while alive, *jīvanmukta*, which he himself later sang in the *Ātmavidyā vilāsa*, "The Play of the Knowledge of the Self."

Verily, the silent sage, ever engaged in inward

meditation, takes the alms placed in his hands as food and wanders along the street like an idiot (verse 39).

As the late Nrisimha Bharati Svāmī of Śrīngeri said in his hymn on Sadāśivendra, the guru of Sadāśivendra – Śrī Paramaśivendra Sarasvatī – heard of his pupil's high *siddhi* and "bemoaned his own failure to reach those heights."

Sadāśiva Brahmendra enjoyed the highest states of consciousness sought by yogis and *sādhakas*, and tasting sublime bliss he was oblivious to the world.

While wandering in this state, he got once buried in the sands of the river near Kodumudi and when four months later the floods subsided a digger's spade found him still in *samādhi*. According to another story, his arm was once severed but he went his way unconcerned! Is not the *ātman*, with which he had become one, incapable of being severed by sword?

His final disappearance was, according to an announcement made by himself, at Nerūr near Karūr, where even now his shrine and festival are kept up by the Pudukoṭṭai State whose then ruler received Sadāśivendra's blessings when the saint was wandering in his dominion. His *mahāsamādhi* was on *Jyestha-suddha-dasami*, coming in the later part of June.

Sadāśiva Brahmendra's Writings

Sadāśiva Brahmendra is an equally distingushed name in the literary history of *advaita*. He has left brief pointed glosses on some of the *Upaniṣads* and the *Brahmā Sūtras*. On the *Yoga Sūtras* of Patañjali, he commented, and the intricate and ramified material in Appayya Dīkṣhita's *Siddhāntalesasaṅgraha* he summarized in his *Siddhānta Kalpavalli*. His guru Paramasivendra made a valuable compilation of words expressive of Brahman found in the *Upaniṣads*, the *Vedānta-*

nāma-sahasra-vyakhya. Sadāśivendra abridged this in 36 verses under the title *Ātmanusandhāna*.[3]

Another interesting work by Sadāśivendra which I have been trying to piece together from scattered manuscript fragments is a compilation of all advaitic passages from the different *Purāṇas*.

Of the other philosophical minor works that he wrote, the most well-known is the *Ātmavidyāvilāsa*.[4] Indeed it is this text to which some historical importance also attaches, as can be gathered from the informing postscript in one of its manuscripts in the Tāñjāvūr Saraswati Mahal Library. Once when Brahmendra was sojourning in the village of Dipambapura, a *sarvamanya* village of the Tāñjāvūr Queen Mother, one Malhari Pandita, a friend of King Śahajī's next brother, Serfojī I, performed three *bhīkṣas* to Sadāśivendra and conveyed the King's request to bless him with progeny; Brahmendra sent to the King a copy of his *Ātmavidyāvilāsa* as his blessings, not long after which Serfojī was blessed with a son.

According to *advaita* on which the *Ātmavidyāvilāsa* is based, the only reality is the Brahman sung of in the *Upaniṣads* as being of the nature of *sat-cit-ānanda*, Being, Awareness and Bliss. The world of name and form, *nāma-rūpa*, is only its appearance, *māyā*, i.e., ultimately unreal but tentatively real; the various individual souls are only the reflections of the one Brahman. The perishable phenomenal realities of name and form are mere transfigurations (*vivartas*) of Brahman, even as waves are of the water of the sea. Owing to our ignorance, *avidyā*, we superimpose an erroneous reality, later sublated by correct knowledge, even as we imagine a snake in a rope and run away. The removal of this error (*bhrama*) is achieved by the help of a guru, the cultivation of the four kinds of requisite self-discipline (*sādhana catuṣṭaya*), and by listening to, ratiocinating about and contemplating upon, *śravaṇa*, *manana* and *nididhyāsana*, Brahman and its true nature.

When this knowledge of Brahman dawns, one becomes released though yet embodied and moving amidst us; he becomes *jīvan-mukta*, an ideal as glorious as that of the *bodhisāttva* of Buddhism. Texts of the *Upaniṣads* and the *Bhagavad Gītā* glorify this state in which the realised souls, owning to the remnants of the traces of the unburnt karmic legacy that has begun to fructify, still move amidst us and work for our salvation. There is controversy and diversity of opinion on the *jīvanmukta* doctrine among advaitic writers themselves but Śaṅkara definitely says in his *Sūtra Bhasya* that it is a matter of one's experience and is not to be questioned at all. The life and doings of Sadāśivendra form a further testimony on the *jīvanmukta*, one who is liberated while atill alive. The *Ātmavidyāvilāsa* is a poem on this great state.

After paying obeisance to the divine guru Dākṣinamūrti and his near guru Paramaśivendra, Sadāśivendra opens with a description of the Supreme Soul, pure and always enlightened, incomparable, eternal and devoid or parts, attributes or forms:

> The Supreme Soul shines pure and awake and devoid of all mutations (*vikalpas*); It is unique, eternal and free from passion; It is an indivisible whole untouched by *māyā* (ignorance) and free from the *guṇas* (the three-fold qualities: *sāttva*, *rājas* and *tāmas*) (verse 4.).[5]

The next two verses show how, involved in its own illusory extension, the soul begins to delude itself and act, but at the end, by the grace of a teacher realizes its delusion and regains its pristine state. Five verses which follow emphasize the important role played by guru in helping the bound soul to regain its lost freedom. On the attainment of this realisation, one is rid of the invidious distinction of you and I, and goes about care-free like a boy, immersed in the ocean of unalloyed bliss.

The *avadhūta* state in which the author himself was roaming is then described:

> Delighted in the *ātman* (the eternal Self which he has realized) and rid of the bondage of *karma* (action), the Prince of *sannyāsins* is wandering about in the outskirts of the jungle, like a deaf blind idiot (verse 15).[6]

The four directions are his garments; desirelessness his ornaments; palms, his vessels; the foot of trees his abode; as he lies on the soft sand-dunes of river beds, *vāyu* (the wind) fans him and the full moon holds the lamp.

> The sage shines supreme, silent and placid, with the ground under the tree as his nesting place and with his palm as the begging bowl, wearing no clothes but only the jewel of non-attachment (verse 35).[7]
>
> The great recluse who has awakened to the state of perfect Being-Awareness-Bliss rests in his house, which is the deserted bush on the river-bank, on the rare and very comfortable bed of soft sands (verse 36).[8]
>
> The recluse shines a king of kings, resting serenely on the soft bed of bare ground, with the cool breeze as his unique *cāmara*, the royal whisk, and with the full moon as his lamp in the royal chamber (verse 37).[9]

In a series of poetic fancies, the ecstatic state of Brahman-realization is then described, depicting the soul as a lover in spiritual nuptials with the spouse of peace, as the king ruling over the kingdom of *svārājya*, as the intellectual hero who has slain the foes of nescience, as the effulgent sun on the horizon of knowledge, as the cloud raining the nectar of immortality and removing all the heat of inner ills, as the refreshing breeze from the park of bliss, as the swan sporting in the lake of wisdom, as the cuckoo perched on the boughs of the *Upaniṣads* and warbling sweetest notes. He is beyond praise and blame; has transcended learning and left all activity behind, is full and shines like a steady flame:

> The yogi remains in a state of plenitude, like an unruffled lamp, having cast all injunctions (of the *Śāṣtras*) aside, and having completely rejected (even) acts of duty (verse 42).[10]

Unassailed by any sense-objects, he stands like a log, in his own incomparable plentitude. He makes no distinction between one living being and another, seeing everywhere the full Brahman. He rejects none, accepts none; knowing the play of *avidyā*, he is supremely indifferent to everything; in the fullness of his knowledge, there is no retrospection on a past nor a prospecting of the future; a great beggar, yet the king of all the passionless. A rhapsody of four verses on the Brahman, which now end the poem, sweeps us off our feet and deposits us on that summit of *sat-cit-ānanda*, infinite Being-Awareness-Bliss, that equanimity which has no limitation and where all fear is completely ended in that unequalled fearless Truth.

Not satisfied with these poems of his on the advaitic Brahman, Sadāśivendra, who pursued the time-honored *sādhana* of *nāda-vidyā* (the wisdom of divine sound) also, sang musical pieces on the same theme.

As already mentioned, contemporary with Sadāśiva Brahmendra were apostles of the path of adoring the *saguṇa*-forms of the Supreme Being through the recital of the Lord's Name, with or without music. Sadāśivendra who cherished *nāda-upāsana*, devotion through holy sound, as a spiritual discipline, sang several pieces which are even now heard on the music platforms. These songs are on different *saguṇa*-forms on the Absolute or Para-Brahman. Sadāśivendra thus holds a unique place as the bard of *advaita*. Even when he sings of Rāma, he takes the esoteric line and sees in the story the symbolism of the self as Rāma, of the tiny inner ether of the heart, *daharākāśa*, as the City of Ayodhyā and Sītā as Peace, *śānti*:

He plays in my heart –
Rāma – he plays in my heart . . .
He whose consort is Peace,
the daughter of Videha,
(Sītā), and who rejoices
in the city of Ayodhyā
("the Impregnable"),
which is the ethereal center
of the heart (*dahara*) –
He plays in my heart . . .[11]

The advaitic songs of Sadāśivendra teach the *sādhanas*, the spiritual disciplines. They elucidate the conception of ignorance, *avidyā*, and again and again sing of the advaitic state of realization. The felicity with which this state of realization, this state in which there is no care or thought, and nothing to be said or done and the soul is revelling in the plentitude of its bliss and knowledge, could not have come except from the lips of a *jīvanmukta*. These songs on the *ātman* in the state of its self-realization read like a musical version of his *Ātmavidyāvilāsa*: When Sadāśivendra sings –

He sports in the material world
of microcosm and macrocosm –
Bhagavan – He
sports in the material world
He sports, saying "I am that Swan,
I am that Swan,
I am That." He sports . . .

He sports, saying "I am the Soul Supreme,
I am all complete, I am
indeed Brahman, Brahman is my self."
He sports in the form of a Paramahaṃsa,
He who first created
Brahmā, Viṣṇu, Rudra and others.
He sports . . .[12]

He is singing only in tune with the *śruti*, the revelation which declares that the realized soul is the supreme poet of the Universe and the singer of Brahman –

This is the symphony of Brahman
that He is singing; Ah!
I am the enjoyed and the enjoyer;
I am the poet-author of
the whole universe; I am elder
to the world, I am earlier
than the very gods; I am the hub
of Immortality.[13]

Notes

[1] *Vedānta Keśari*, December 1950. Also published in *A Seminar on Saints*, ed. T.M.P. Mahadevan (Madras: Ganesh, 1960).

[2] āntaramekam kiñcit santatam
anusandhanmahāmaunī
karapuṭa bhikṣāmasnan
aṭati hi vīthyām jadakṛitiḥ kópi

[3] This, along with a homage to his guru called the *Navamaṇimala* the present speaker (V. Raghavan) had the good fortune to bring to light first.

[4] In fact, the Vani Vilas Press has published in the same booklet two minor works of Sadāśivendra of this name; the second is in 43 *vasantatilaka* verses, more scholastic in style and partly cast as a *Guru-śisya-samvada*; the first is in 65 *ārya* verses and is couched in a considerably more felicitous diction and forms a regular poem on

ātman and Brahman-realization. It is this text which is more famous as the *Ātmavidyāvilāsa.*

The Kāmakoṭi Kosasthānam Prakāśitam in 1951 published Sadāśiva Brahmendra's *Śivamanasikapūja kīrtanani* and *Ātmavidyāvilāsa*, with translations into Tamil and English by V. Narayanan. The translations in this article follow those renderings.

[5]nirūpamanityanirīho
niskalanirmāyanirguṇākāraḥ
vigalita sarva vikalpaḥ
śuddho buddhaśca kāsti paramātmā

[6]avadhūta karmajālah
jaḍabadhirandhopamaḥ kópi
ātmārāmo yatirāḍ
aṭavikoṇeṣvaṭannāste

[7]āśā vasano maunī
nairāśyālaṇkṛtah śāntah
karatala bhikśāapatraḥ
tarutalanilayo munirjayati

[8]vijananadī kuñjagṛihe mañjula pulinaika mañjutaratalpe
sete kopi yatindraḥ samarasasukha bodha vastunistandraḥ

[9]bhūtala mridutaraśayyaḥ
śītala vātaika cāmarah sāntaḥ
rākādimakaradīpo rājati
yatiraja sekharah kópi

[10]santyajaya śāstrajālam
saṁvyavahāraṁca sarvatastyaktvā
āśritya pūrṇa padavīmāste
niṣkaṁpa dīpavadyogī

[11]Pallavi: khelati mama hṛidaye rāmaḥ
khelati mama hṛidaye
Caranam 2: śāntividedasutārahacāri
daharayodhyanagaravihari

[12]Pallavi: khelati piṇḍānde bhagavān
khelati piṇḍānde
Caranam 1: haṁsah so'ham haṁsaḥ so'haṁ
haṁsah so'ham so hamiti

Caranam 2: paramātmāham paripūrno'haṁ
brahmaivāham ahaṁ brahmeti
Caranam 6: paramahaṁsa rūpeṇa vidartā
brahmāviṣṇu rudrādikakartā

[13]This verse is cited but not identified in the original article.

LEADERS OF KĀVERĪ DELTA NĀMASIDDHĀNTA

Four:

Nārāyaṇa Tīrtha: Lyricist of Krishna's Divine Play

Part One

In India there has been a continuous tradition of *advaitin sannyāsins*, renunciate yogis living by the philosophy of monism, cultivating both *bhakti* and *nadopāsana* (devotion through divine sound) as *sādhana* (spiritual exercise). In this line of *sannyāsins* whose names have illumined the pages of Karnāṭaka music history are Nārāyaṇa Tīrtha and Sadāśiva Brahmendra. Of these two, comparatively speaking, the latter is more renowned for his copious philosophical writings, while the former is more famous in music and in literary and devotional writing. From the biographical point of view, we have more abundant and precise data about Brahmendra than about Tīrtha.

Tīrtha Nārāyaṇa Svāmīgal, as he is referred to, is an integral part of the *bhajana sampradāya*, in which he is venerated with invocatory verses and his whole composition is sung in *bhajanas*; but a few of his songs also hold a place in the repertoire of concert musicians. These songs are popularly called *taraṅgas* ("waves") because they are taken from a long Sanskrit poem of his, composed for dance-drama, on the *līlās* of Krishna as a youth, depicting him up to the time of his marriage with Rukmiṇī.

The *Krishna-līlā-taraṅgiṇī* ("Waves of the Sports of Krishna") was evidently composed during a period of pilgrimage which extended from Puri in Orissa to Vahahūr in

Tāñjāvūr district in Tamil Nadu; for included in the poem are pieces on Jagannāth, Viṣṇu at Śrīkakulam and Narasimha at Sobhanadri and Vedagiri in Andhra. Evidently, Nārāyaṇa Tīrtha, who attained fame and is cherished and worshipped in Cola Deśa, hailed from Andhra like other celebrities in music and Sanskrit in the Kāverī delta, in the times of the Telugu and Maharatta rulers of Tāñjāvūr. There is a tradition of Taraṅgiṇī being sung, sometimes with dance, in Guntur, Krishna and Godāvari districts of Andhra Pradesh in *bhajana* groups.

There is a legend of how he reached Varahūr. He is said to have been suffering from chronic pain in the stomach and a boar (*varaha*) which appeared before him led him to the village of Varahūr or Varāhapura, previously known as Bhūpatirājapuram. Several legends have naturally grown, some recently, out of the modern pressure to historicize with incidents as against the traditional trend to absorb a personality in the current of the cultural and conceptual universal.

His Masterpiece: the *Taraṅgiṇī*

The *Krishna-līlā-taraṅgiṇī* is dedicated in its opening pieces to Lord Viṣṇu as Śrī Veṅkaṭeśa at Varahūr. There is a continuous *bhajana sampradāya* at Varahūr, initiated by Nārāyaṇa Tīrtha, and his poem is still sung there and all over Tamil Nadu wherever the *bhajana sampradāya* has taken root. At the beginning of the *bhajan*, verses on Nārāyaṇa Tīrtha are sung, as also on Bodhendra, Āyyāvāl and Sadgurusvāmī: these were the four "*ācāryas*" of this tradition which preserved, in the recent centuries, both *bhakti* and music in Tamil Nadu. Nārāyaṇa Tīrtha attained *samādhi* at Tirupponturutti between Tāñjāvūr and Tiruvaiyāru and recently a festival has been growing there in memory of the saint-composer.

In the signature lines of the songs in the *Krishna-līlā-taraṅgiṇī*, the composer calls himself sometimes more fully Śiva Nārāyaṇa Tīrtha and mentions his *vedānta* teacher as Śiva

Rama or Śiva Ramananda Tīrtha. In the fields of *vedānta*, *saṁkhya* and *bhakti*, there are some Sanskrit works appearing to be Nārāyaṇa Tīrtha's, but there is no conclusive evidence to identify their authorship with our composer. However, his scholarship and equipment in *vedānta* and *Śāstras* are fully born out in the *taraṅgiṅī* itself. A slightly greater possibility of authenticity may attach to a sister dance-drama composition in Telugu, found in two manuscripts as the work of Nārāyaṇa Tīrtha, and it is called *Pārijāta haraṇa*. Another work in Sanskrit definitely known as his relates to the *bhakta* tradition and akin in theme in the *taraṅgiṇī*, is the *Hari bhakti sudhārṇava*.

The *Krishna-līlā-taraṅgiṇī* is one of the numerous compositions that arose in the wake and on the model of Jayadeva's *Gīta Govinda* bearing the triune tradition of devotion, music and dance. Of the numerous compositions of this class, only a few have enjoyed or still enjoy vogue in music and dance, these being the *Krishna gīti* or *Krishnāttam* of Manaveda Zamorin of Calicut, still played at the Guruvayūr temple, the *Śiva gītimalika* of Chandraśekharendra Saraswathī of Kāñcīpuram Kāmakoṭi Pīṭha, which was being sung as part of the temple routine at Tiruvārūr.

The *Krishna-līlā-taraṅgiṇī* presents Śrī Krishna's *līlās*, his playful pastimes, closely following the *Bhāgavata purāṇa*, sometimes echoing the latter's expressions and going up to Rukmiṇī's marriage, after which it makes a brief reference to Śrī Krishna's other *mahiṣis* and his stay in all his divine glory in Dwāraka. The text, which is in 12 cantos, comprises narrative verses in diverse metres, *darus*, *gadyas* or prose passages and regular songs of varying length. The song sections are more akin to *Gīta Govinda* and the *padas* of the pre-Trinity (Tyāgarāja-Dīkṣitar-Śyāma Śāstri) period. The *rāgas* and *tāḷas* are given and in some of the songs, *jatis* are also to be found; for example, *taraṅga* III, Yajñapatnīs' songs, VII *Gopikā gītā*; the long *Rāga-tāḷa-mālika* song describing the *rāsa līla* and *Gopikā gītā* and is called a *sūlādī prabandha*.

Directions are given about the songs being rendered in gestures (*atha abhimyate*). In fact, each chapter is marked as *abhinaya* of such and such an episode.' In the *sūlādī* composition in the seven *sūlādī tālas*, the *tālas*, the *gatis*, the *abhinaya hastas* and the *aṅga* and *pratyaṅga abhinayas* are mentioned. There are thus over a hundred and fifty songs in the poem. About 40 *rāgas* are used including rare and *rakti rāgas* like *Malavi*, *Ahiri*, *Ghanta*, *Kurañji*, *Dvijavanti* and *Gaurī*. *Rāgas* which are frequently used are *Mohana*, *Saurāṣṭra*, *Nādanāmakrīya*, *Kedāragauḷa*, *Punnāgavarāḷi*, *Nilambari*, *Mukhāri*, *Bhairavī*, *Kāmbhōji*, *Pantuvarāḷi* and *Madhyamāvatī*. The work is couched in chaste Sanskrit and classic diction and is rich in poetic quality. For sheer grace and beauty of diction and free and mellifluous flow of words, which do not seem to stand apart from the music, we may note the *Bhairavī* song is *taraṇga* VII. *Govindam iha gopikān-andakandam*. While the style is elegant and generally easy to comprehend, by reason of the theme, if often waxes eloquent with *vedāntin* ideas. The author brings out often, by use of double-meaning words, the transcendent and metaphysical aspect of the Para Brahman while describing the *līlās* in the Krishna *avatāra*: for instance, the song in *Āva ranam mama dehi* in *taraṅga* V in the *gopī vastrāpakārana* episode in which Krishna steals the milkmaids' clothes, where *avarana* means the clothes as well as the obscuring cover of *māyā*, cosmic illusion. The teachings of Ch. VI of the *Chandogya Upaniṣad* are embodied in the songs of the *rasa līla* episode in *taraṅga* VII, in *Nāthanāmakrīya* and *Ghanta rāgas*. The songs of the *yajñapatnīs* in *taraṇga* III may also be mentioned as examples of philosophy turned into lyrics.

Taraṅgiṇī and the *bhajana sampradāya*

As the *Krishna-līlā-taraṇgiṇī* was an essential part of the *bhajana* tradition, the ears of Tyāgarāja (who was a flower that bloomed in this same tradition) were naturally filled with the music of the *taraṇgas* and his soul fed with the devotion and ideas of Nārāyaṇa Tīrtha. Upaniṣad Brahmendra of Kāñcīpuram, who invited Tyāgarāja to Kāñcī, composed his *Rāma taraṇgas* under the influence of Nārāyaṇa Tīrtha. There are indeed several echoes of the expressions of the Taraṇgiṇī in the *kṛitis* of Tyāgarāja. To give an instance, in *Dhyāname varamaine*, *Gaṇgasnāname* and *Koṭināḍulu*, Tyāgarāja emphasises that the real *snāna* and *tīrtha* (bath and holy waters of pilgrimage) are to be found in the contemplation of the Lord and in His devotion, and not in Gaṇgā or in other rivers; in the first *taraṇga*, in the song ushering Sānaka and other sages, Nārāyaṇa Tīrtha says: "One should bathe in the super Prayāga (river confluence) of the mingling of the divine names of Rāma, Krishna and Govinda; Rāma *nāma* is the Gaṇgā, Krishna *nāma* the Yamunā and Govinda *nāma* the Saraswatī river."[2]

Notes

[1]This article was first published in *The Hindu*, Jan. 4, 1970.

The earliest publication of *Krishna-līlā-taraṇgiṇī* was in *grantha* script in the district of its origin; one of these from Kumbakoṇam (1920) was carefully done with brief explanatory notes and variant readings. Two *devanāgarī* editions, including a recent one from Repalle in Andhra have appeared. There is also an incomplete ms. of a commentary on the *Taraṇgiṇī*, but a critical annotated edition of it is a desideratum. The Music Academy, Madras, has on hand an edition with notations of select Taraṇgas by Śrī T.S. Vasudevan, son of the late Sitarama Iyer, Librarian of the Hindu High School, Triplicane, who was a votary of the *bhajana paddhati* and a repository of its authentic and unbroken tradition of songs and their *varṇa mettus*.

(Editor's note: Since V. Raghavan wrote this a translation and study of the *Krishna-līlā-taraṅgiṇī* has been published. B. Nataraja (assisted by his brothers, B. Venkataraman and B. Ramachandran), *Śrī Krishna Leela Taraṅgiṇī*, Vol. I (Madras: Mudgala Trust, 1988). The second volume was published in 1990.

[2]The passage recommending devotees to bathe in the Name-waters is:

Rāmakrishna Govinda Nāma samprayoge
Kāmamiha snatavyam sarvottama Prayāge . . .
Rāma Nāma Gaṅgā ya milita krishna nāma
Yamune Govinda nāma Sarasvatī prathite

Nārāyana Tīrtha: Singer of Krishna's Play[1]

Part Two

Nārāyana Tīrtha is remembered most today by the adherents of the *Bhajana-sampradāya*, and to some extent by Karṇāṭaka musicians who reverentially refer to him as Tīrtha Nārāyaṇa Svāmī or Tīrtha Nārāyaṇa Yati. Indeed a few of his compositions may still be heard in concerts and are mentioned as *Taraṅgas*. The better informed know that his Sanskrit songs are taken from a musical poem on Krishna composed by him, called the *Krishna-līlā-taraṅgini* and that the composer was a *sannyāsin* worthy of the highest respect.

Nārāyaṇa Tīrtha, as his suffix Tīrtha shows, was a *sannyāsin*; he was of *advaitic* persuasion. The use of music as a yogic *sādhana* is known from the times of sage Yajñavalkya, and the singing of God's names, praises and glory, *bhajana*, as part of devotional exercises is also well-known. There was a line of *advaitin sannyāsins* among whom this tradition of cultivation of music and *bhajana* as a spiritual aid and a devotional adoration of God was prevalent. We have the illustrious example of Sadāśiva Brahman, a great *advaitin siddha*, and author of not only Sanskrit philosophical treatises but also of songs on the supreme Brahman, and the various forms of the Godhead. Of equal greatness is Nārāyana Tīrtha, less celebrated as a writer of Sanskrit treatises but occupying a far more important place in the history of Karṇāṭaka music and the *bhajana-sampradāya.* We had also Upaniṣad Brahman of Kāñcīpuram, elder contemporary and inspirer of Muthusvāmī Dīkṣitar and Tyāgarāja and also an incumbent of the Kāñcīpuram *Śaṅkaracarya Pītha* itself who composed a musical poem called *Śivagīti malika.* It is in conformity with this tradition that the celebrated Tyāgarāja also took to *sannyāsa* towards the end of his career.

Like Sadāśiva Brahman and the later Tyāgarāja, Nārāyaṅa Tīrtha was a Telugu Brahman. When Vijayanagar declined and the kingdom of Tāñjāvūr became, first under the Telugu Nāyaks and then under the Mahrāttas, a center of patronage for art and letters, many families of talent and attainment, authors, poets, musicians, dancers and dance-masters, left the banks of the Krishna and the Godāvarī and sought the banks of the Kāverī. Nārāyaṅa Tīrtha was one of these and it is in the Tāñjāvūr District that he became famous, that he lived and worked and finally attained *samādhi.* The village hallowed by his stay is Varahūr and the village sanctified by his *samādhi* is Tiruppunturutti.

As to how Nārāyaṅa Tīrtha came to the Tāñjāvūr area, we do not have any authentic information. But we have a traditional story told about this. One night, in the village called Nadukkaveri, in an empty *maṇḍapa*, a *sannyāsin* afflicted with severe stomach ache was undergoing acute pain. As a little drowsiness came on him, he had a dream in which he was told: "Early morning when you wake up, you will see an animal; keep following it and at the place to which it brings you and vanishes, you will be rid of this stomach-ache." When it dawned and the recluse opened his eyes, they fell on a boar which was standing in front of him. The animal began to move and the recluse followed it. They went three miles along the banks of the river *Kodamurutti*, a branch of the Kāverī, and reached the village Varahūr otherwise called Bhūpatirājapuram after a Tāñjāvūr King. In that village was a temple dedicated to Lord Veṅkaṭeśvara and the boar that was leading the *sannyāsin* vanished into that temple. It then struck the recluse that it was the Lord Hari once incarnated as the great boar who had again, out of his compassion for him, showed himself as the boar and brought him to that temple of Veṅkaṭeśvara and that if he stayed on and worshipped Lord Veṅkaṭeśvara in the shrine, he would be rid of his malady. The story is narrated in more or less these details in the opening part (ch. I, verses 70-96) of the poetical work *Śikyotsava Prabandha* by Nārāyana Kavi of Varahūr (1868-1935 A.D.). There is also a Sanskrit *stotra* about Lord Veṅkaṭeśa at Varahūr, available in print, where again the above mentioned episode is touched upon.

The *sannyāsin* was Nārāyaṇa Tīrtha. Because a boar (*varaha*) had brought him there, it is said, the village Bhūpatirājapuram acquired the name Varahūr. Nārāyaṇa Tīrtha stayed on and became freed of his ailment. Consequently, the sancitity of the shrine and the village increased. It was here, as an act of grateful homage to the deity here, that Nārāyaṇa Tīrtha completed and dedicated his musical play on the story of Lord Krishna, from birth up to the marriage of Rukminī, the *Krishna-līlā-taraṅgiṇī* or the "River of the Sports of Lord Krishna." The dedicatory song at the beginning mentions "Śrī Varahapura Veṅkaṭeśa."

That this village of Varahūr was a center of music and dance in the times of the Nāyak Kings of Tāñjāvūr (17th century) is attested by the fact that the celebrated composer of dance-*padas* Kṣetrayya, visited it and has mentioned it in his *padas*.

In Varahūr, Nārāyana Tīrtha established a *bhajana sampradāya*, of followers of his who sang, danced and rendered into gesture his musical play on the Lord and celebrated the festival of Krishna every year at the time of *Janmāṣṭami* or *Gokulāṣṭami* as we call it here. The performance of *uriyadi* (the enactment of Krishna stealing butter placed on top of a pole) as part of this festival attracted a large concourse of people.

Nārāyaṇa Kavi of this village composed a *campu kāvya* or poem describing this festival.

Thus Nārāyana Tīrtha was one of those who augmented the *bhāgavata* tradition in the Tāñjāvūr District and spread the cult of adoring the Lord with song and dance. There are three verses of praise on Nārāyaṇa Tīrtha that are sung at the outset in *bhajanas*. Followers of this *bhajana* tradition would, with *tambura* (stringed drone instrument) and *chiplas* (jingling clappers) in hand and bells (*gajjai*) on feet, go about singing the Lord's praise and dancing. Of the celebrated *bhāgavatars* of Varahūr were Varahūr Pañju Bhagavatar and Varahūr Gopāla Bhagavatar and a portrait of the latter, in typical costume, is still venerated by the votaries of *bhajana*.

In addition to the musical and dramatic treatment of the story of Krishna, Nārāyaṇa Tīrtha, as a Sanskrit writer, has given us a devotional poem on the same theme, *Haribhaktisudhārṇava*. One of the prayer-verses at the opening of this poem forms part of the preliminary songs sung at the beginning of *Hari kathās* (musical; discourses). As an exponent of the school of *bhakti*, he wrote a commentary also on the *Bhakti mīmāṃsā sūtras* of Sandilya. Both these works are yet in manuscript. On his *Krishna līlā taraṅgini* which has so far been printed only in *grantha* and Telugu scripts, there is an unpublished Sanskrit commentary also written by one Veṅkaṭeśa, assisted by a Govinda Dīkshita, and recently, I was surprised to find manuscript copies of both the text and the commentary in far away Banāras.

In some of the songs in his *Krishna līlā taraṇgini*, the author calls himself also *Śiva* Nārāyana Tīrtha. His guru was *Śiva* Rāmānanda Tīrtha.

Nārāyaṇa Tīrtha attained *siddhi* at the village of Tiruppunturutti, seven miles to the east of Varahūr, where at his Samadhi, an annual festival is still held.

The same *bhāgavata* tradition was responsible also for the cultivation of a dramatic art, in which devotional stories composed in the form of songs and set to dance were sung and danced and interpreted in gesture by Brahman devotees. This is the tradition maintained in *Kuchupudi* in Andhra and in some of the *agrahara* (Brahman) villages of Tāñjāvūr, Merattur, and elsewhere. In Merattur and the Saraswati Mahal Library, Tāñjāvūr, there is a Telugu play intended for such enactment composed by one Nārāyaṇa Tīrtha. This play called *Parijataharaṇa nāṭaka* has the *mūdra* or signature of Nārāyaṇa Tīrtha in some of its pieces and from its concluding piece, appears to have been composed at Merattur village and dedicated to Lord Acyuta Varadarāja there.[2]

I started by saying that it was his music that is still best remembered and that of his works, the *Taraṅgiṇī* is most widely known. Under its inspiration Upaniṣad Brahman of Kāñcīpuram, as I have shown in my account of his life and works[3] composed songs on Rāma called *taraṅgas*. It was, as I already said, the example of *sannyāsins* of his type that induced Tyāgarāja also to enter the fourth asrāma at the end of his life. The influence of Nārāyaṇa Tīrtha on Tyāgarāja was more than this. The two musical plays of Tyāgarāja took inspiration from Nārāyaṇa Tīrtha's *Taraṅgiṇī*. Also the fact that Nārāyaṇa Tīrtha's pieces, from his *Taraṅgiṇī*, were widely sung, is borne out by the influence they had on the mind of Tyāgarāja, the great composer, who echoed phrases from Nārāyaṇa Tīrtha's compositions as I have shown.[4]

The *Krishna līlā taraṅgiṇī* was evidently composed over a period of time when the composer was on pilgrimages, and finally completed and dedicated at Varahūr. For, included in this composition are songs on Viṣṇu at Srikakulam, Narasimha at Sobhanādri and Vedādri, all in Andhra, and one sung at Puri.

The *Krishna līlā taraṅgiṇī* is one of the numerous works that rose in the wake of the *Gītagovinda* of Jayadeva and may be acclaimed as the only one among such works to have gained or maintained a comparable musical status. It is written in perfect literary Sanskrit, a fact to be specially noted because, in the next age, though Sanskrit was handled for music compositions and though even while Telugu was handled, it was a style dominated by Sanskrit, the grammatical and literary equipment of composers became a secondary qualification. The diction in the *Taraṅgiṇī* is fine, figures of speech including *śleṣa* are employed, and the songs are replete with ideas from the Upaniṣads. The composition is in twelve *taraṅgas* and the songs are linked with verses and varied by prose, *gadya*, passages. It is composed as a regular dance-drama and there are directions that such and such a context is being sung and gesticulated in the coming piece and so on. There are also set rhythm-syllables or *jatis* for dance, fitted to some of the pieces, e.g. the long prayer of the Yajñapatnis in the third *taraṅga*, and the composition on *rasakrida* in *Nāṭa* and *Dhruva tāḷa* in the seventh *taraṅga*. There is also a *suladi* composition.

The rehabilitation of the *bhajana* and *bhāgavata* tradition which put forth these blossoms of the arts of music, dance and composition would be the renaissance of a cultural heritage whose unity could be seen from the Kāverī to Kāmarūpa.

Notes

[1] First published in a booklet by the Śrī Nārāyaṇa Tīrtha Festival Celebration Committee, Tiruppunturutti, Tāñjāvūr District, (M.W.N. Press, Madras) undated.

[2]V. Raghavan writes: It was my good fortune to bring to light this composition in the pages of the *Journal of the Madras Music Academy* (Volume XIII, pp.74-76), but students of Telugu literature who had later occasion to examine this are not unanimous in their opinion about this play being the work of the great Nārāyaṇa Tīrtha himself. If it is a genuine work of his, it would give us some historical data: Merattur was gifted to families of musicians, dancers etc, by King Acyutāppa Nāyak of Tāñjāvūr (A.C. 1561-1614), and renamed after himself as Acyutābdhi. It would show also that Nārāyana Tīrtha had something to do with the dance-drama tradition at Merattur, which is a thing to be expected. (V. Raghavan)

[3]*Journal of the Music Academy*, Madras, Vol. XXVII, pp. 125-6.

[4]This is discussed in a special article in the Tyāgarāja Centenary volume issued by the Andhra Gana Kala Parishad, Rajahmundry (pp. 84-88).

IV

Creative Exponents of the Name, and Related Studies

Vāk Devatā[1]

The *Rigveda*[2] says Vāk (Speech) is a divine gift, and in a whole hymn (X. 125) of which *Vāk* Herself is the speaker, *ṛisi* and deity, She declares that whomsoever She likes, She makes into a Seer and a man of fine intellect. "I make the man I love exceedingly mighty, I make him into a sage, a *ṛisi* and a brahman."

Rigveda hymn X.71.2 says that the wise ones sift and purify *Vāk* in the sieve of their minds and thereby She becomes auspicious and beautiful. The Seers of the hymns, the *ṛisis*, are called *kavis* or men of far-reaching vision (*krantadarśins*) and later, not only did this word *kavi* become the normal name of the poet but according to the Kashmirian aesthete of the 10th Century, Bhaṭṭa Tota, the *ṛisi* and the *kavi* were inseparable and represented but the two phases of the same genius, the former signifying the vision and the latter the verbal incarnation of it.[3]

The *Brāhmaṇas* have a high conception of *Vāk* and its role. The *Taittirīya Upaniṣad* says: "Speech, the imperishable, is the first born of Truth, mother of the *Vedas*, the hub of immortality; may She in happiness, come to us, in the sacrifice; our protecting Goddess, may She be easy of invocation for us." (VIII.8.5)

The *Upaniṣads* also assign a high place for *Vāk*. The *Chandogya Upaniṣad* says: "It is *Vāk* which makes us know not only the *Vedas* and the ancillary literature, but also heaven and earth, gods and men, *dharma* and *adharma*, truth and untruth, good and bad; it is *Vāk* that informs us of these; therefore adore *Vāk*" (VII.2.1).

As *Praṇava* or *Oṃkāra*, Vāk's place is close to the Supreme Being, Brahman itself, as its nearest symbol (*nedistha-abhidhāna* and *pratika* as Śaṅkara says in his *bhāṣya* on the *Bṛihadaraṇyaka Upaniṣad* (V.i). The whole *Maṇḍukya Upaniṣad* is based on this conception. This Sound (Om), the *Śabda Brahman*, and the Supreme One (*Para Brahman*) are the two Brahmans to be known and it is after realizing the former that the man of knowledge passes on to the latter. The philosophy of *Śabda Brahman* in the form of *sphota* lying at the basis of all sounds which grammarians latter evolved and of which Bhartṛihari gave the classic exposition, developed from this *Vedic* doctrine of *Vāk* and *Praṇava*. The sacred character and the spiritual role of all manifestations of Sound in the form of literature, were stated by the *Bṛihadaraṇyaka Upaniṣad* when it declared that *Ṛik* and other *Vedas*, the Epics and other scriptures were the "breath" of the Supreme Being itself. "Just as smoke and sparks pour out of a fire made of damp wood, the *Atharvāṅgirasa*, *Itihāsa* narratives, *Purāṇas*, *Vidyas*, *Upaniṣads*, *ślokas*, *sūtras*, *Anuvyākhyānas* (explanantions of mantras) – all these are the breathing of the Supreme Being." (II.4.10)

And it is this philosophy of literature (as emanation) that the *purāṇas* express and the later votaries of the Muse had before them in their creative work. The *Viṣṇu Purāṇa* says: "Whatever poetry there is, and whatever song there is, all that is an aspect of the all pervasive Supreme Being in His verbal and sonant form."

The Supreme principle of Speech, in its subtlest for (*para vāk*) was considered as the first *spanda* or *'throb'* or *'heaving'* of the Supreme Śiva by the Kashmirian philosophers. The great poet Kalidāsa gave expression to this concept in the opening verse of his long poem the *Raghuvaṃsa*, thereby giving us his basic faith and inspiration in his approach to the Supreme Spirit through the path and medium of poetry.

It is the marriage of word and meaning that the poet celebrates in his other long poem, the *Kumārasambhava*, where the seven sages who go to Himavan as messengers to ask the hand of Pārvatī for Śiva tell Himavan that he should unite Śiva with Umā, as Meaning with Word.[4]

That Kalidāsa adored the Divine Speech as a blessing and its manifestation in one as being at once the means of sanctity and beauty for one, is seen in his description of Pārvatī's manifestation as the daughter of the Himalayas.[5]

Bhavabhuti, next in rank to Kalidāsa as a poet, was equally an adorer of this *Vāk*; in the concluding verse of his masterpiece, the drama *Uttararāmacarita*, he calls himself not only one of matured intellect but also a knower of the *Śabda-Brahman*, a *kavi* in the true and full sense of the term. And in the opening verse of the same drama, he pays his obeisance to this *Vāk* and describes Her as the immortal digit or sprout of the Self.

The gifted 17th century poet of the Madurai Nāyak court Nilakantha Dīkṣita draws out in fuller form the same idea in the pregnant lines of Kalidāsa, of Śiva as Ardhanarīśvara, the Devī forming the left half of Śiva's form being *Śabda*, and Śiva the right half being *Artha*; and says that it is the blessed ones among men who deserve this Poetry which is thus the embodiment of God.[6] Poetry, the same poet says, is not only the goal but also the path to that goal; a *yoga* not of severe austerities and exacting exercises, but of beauty and bliss.

To compose is to gain composure; to be engrossed in right idea and choice word is to be in concentration on a perfect union and harmony; to be thrilled with the fine poetry that is born thus is to be absorbed in the very bliss of Brahman, the *rasa*. The aesthetic theory of Indian poetics, in the hands of its best exponents, bases itself on this philosophy of the relish of poetic beauty being of the same category as the relish of spiritual bliss, *Brāhmānanda*; the very word *rasa* goes back to the *Taittirīya Upaniṣad* which states "whatever is done well, that is beauty and bliss."[7]

Notes

[1] First published in *Dilip*, May-June, 1975.

[2] Ṛg Veda VIII.100.11.

[3] nānṛiṣiḥ kavirityuktaḥ ṛiṣiśca kila darśanāt.

[4] tāmarthamiva bhāratyā sutayā yoktumarhasi "Śiva, who witnesses all activities in the world and fulfils desires, sending his word through us requests your daughter's hand; just as if wedding sound and meaning together, please marry him to your dear child." *Kumārasambhava,* VI 78-79.

[5] samskāravatyeva girā manīṣī tayā sa pūtaścavibhūṣitaśca

[6] *Śivalīlārṇava,* I.15.

[7] yadvai tatsukṛitam / raso vai saḥ.

Creative Exponents of the Name, and Related Studies

The Bhāgavata Purāṇa[1]

"O ye men of taste in this world! A fruit has dropped from the celestial wish-fulfilling tree of the Vedās. The parrot (Sage Suka) has had a peck at it, and found it dripping with the juice of immortality. It is the *Bhāgavata*! Go on drinking its juice till you become liberated completely."

"Unadulterated Dharma is its theme; it is for those good souls free from intolerance. What is to be known here is the supreme Truth, the bestower of supreme welfare which is the end of all misery; the Lord is captured immediately in the hearts of those who listen to this *Bhāgavata* composed by the great sage."

Although the latest of the *purāṇas*, the *Bhāgavata* became the greatest, and indeed eclipsed all the other *purānas* including the *Visnu Purāṇa* on which it is mostly modelled. A book of devout reading and exposition, *parayana* and *pravacana*, it ranks with and even contends with the *Rāmāyaṇa* in popularity and appeal. Like the works of the three great Āchāryas, the *Bhāgavata*, a product of the South, gained wide sway all over North India where it became the inspiration and the Bible of schools of ecstatic devotion to Krishna, from Maharashtra and Gujarat, across Mathura, to Bengal and Assam, of the *bhaktimārgas* (devotional paths) of Vallabha, Nimbarka, Śaṅkaradeva and Caitanya. It gave birth to an efflorescence of the music of devotion, in Narasimha Mehtā, Mīrabāi, Surdās and others, and to the birth of a vernacular literature and drama in Assam and a similar literature of Krishna *bhakti* in Sanskrit and the local languages–hymn, song, poem, drama and treatises on the doctrines of devotion in Bengal and Orissa. Several commmentaries were written on the *Bhāgavata* to explain its meaning, including the esoteric, adopting the ideologies of the different schools of thought, not excluding the advaitic. In fact, the *advaitins*, who practiced devotion as an accessory to their path of knowledge, contributed perhaps the most important exegesis of the *Bhāgavata*–for example the great commentator Śrīdhara, as also Bopadeva in Maharashtra, the pioneer to analyze, index, and work out a scheme for understanding the unity, plan and purpose of the *Bhāgavata*. Bopadeva's *Bhāgavata-mukta-phala* is an invaluable aid to the study and enjoyment of this *purāṇa*.

For the *Bhāgavata*, we have a *mahātmya* in 6 chapters given in the *Padma Purāṇa*, which furnishes us with the key to the *purāṇa*. *Bhakti* or *devotion* is introduced here as a young wandering lady, accompanied by two old sons, *jñāna* and *vairāgya*, knowledge and detachment. She tells Nārada that she was born in Tamil country, grown in Karṇāṭaka, and in a few places in Maharashtra and became shattered in Gujarat. Unbelievers had attacked her there, but on reaching Brindavana (Mathura), she gained her youth but her two sons continued to be in their shrivelled up condition. On behalf of these three, Nārada asks of the four eternally young divine sages, Sanatkumāra and others the way and they assure him: "Let the *Bhāgavata* be read aloud to them; that great book will revive all the three of them." Nārada submits: "But the Vedās, the *vedanta* and the *Bhagavad Gītā* has already been blown loudly to their ears, and all that has not been able to rouse them from their prostrate condition." The four Kumaras explain: "Well, the *Bhāgavata* is born of the essence of the Vedās and Upaniṣads. In a tree, no doubt, the juice is present all over, but cannot be relished; when it gets concentrated into the fruit, it is enjoyed. It is even as butter which has to be churned out of milk and sugar from the cane. Such is the *Bhāgavata*, composed by Vyāsa, especially for the resuscitation of *bhakti*, *jñāna* and *vairāgya*."

In the opening chapters of the *Bhāgavata*, we are told of how Vyāsa came to compose this *purāṇa*, *par excellence*, of the Lord, as it is called. Vyāsa had already codified the Vedās, distilled the Upaniṣads into the *Vedānta Sūtra*s, composed the *Mahābhārata* together with the *Bhagavad Gītā*, and several other treatises including all the other *purāṇas*. Yet in his inner heart there was a dejection and an emptiness and when none could give him any consolation and explanation, Nārada came and enlightened him. This initial chapter of the *Bhāgavata*, forming an exordium, is also an essay in criticism and a comparative estimate of the great sacred books, the Vedās and Vedānta and the *Mahābhārata*. "The impersonal principles of *dharma* and Brahman have been presented in the former; but for attracting and holding the human heart, the emphasis should be on the personality, particularly in the present age. You no doubt shifted to the personality in the epic, but you lost yourself in the fineries of poetry and expression and in the passions and violence of unseemly story and mess of episodes. Indeed, the people missed your message in it. Do not hide your mission; let not expression nor interesting story divert your attention or that of the readers. Declare your subject, the Lord and the singing of His Name and Glory, as your sole objective and compose a new purāṇa to this end.' Vyāsa obeyed, sang this *purāṇa* of Bhagavan, the *Bhāgavata*, and found his complete satisfaction.

The *Bhāgavata* achieved the above purpose by its own reorientation of the conception of *purāṇa*. The *purāṇa* is defined by five topics, *Pañcalakṣaṇas*, comprising the following: primary and secondary creations, the genealogies of gods and sages, periods of time and the dynasties of kings. Through these, it was intended to reinforce the supremacy of the Lord and *dharma*. This again, the *Bhāgavata* felt was overlaying the essential teaching with too much of other material and in a scheme in which it obviously doubled the topics to ten, *dāsalakṣaṇas*, it yet unmistakably declared that the tenth is the highest, viz. the Lord Himself, and that it is to clarify the tenth that the other nine were used (*daśamasya viśuddhyartham navamam iha lakṣaṇam*). And it also declares in the beginning that this tenth subject, the Lord, is brought out in a most emphatic manner in the tenth of the twelve books of the *purāṇa*, by which it means that although the pronounced theme of the *purāṇa* is to speak of all the major incarnations and the partial manifestations of the Lord for the redress of the imbalance in the reign of *dharma*, the appearance as Krishna is the greatest, the crown and culmination.

The accounts of creation, of deluge, of the different *yugas* and *manvantaras* are all here, but the treatment is such that in every narrative it is the greatness of the Supreme Being that is again and again brought home to us. As part of this endeavour, the *Bhāgavata* gives in abundance *stotras*, hymns to the Lord, strewn all over the work, embodying Upaniṣadic ideas and feelings of devotion. If one should attempt the difficult task of choosing among these, one many mention the hymns of Kuntī, Parikṣit, Bhīṣma, Dhruva, Vṛitra, Prahlāda, Gajendra, Brahmā, Vasudeva and Devakī, Akrura and the Veda-stuti. To the same end are addressed the several exalted discourses in the *Bhāgavata* of which again mention may be made of those of the Lord to Brahmā (II), Kapila's to Devahūti (III), the Lord's to King Pṛithu (IV), those in the story of Pracinabarhis (IV), Brahmā's to Priyavrata (V), Ṛiṣabha's (V), Jaḍabharata's to King Rahūgaṇa (V), to Citraketu (VI), Prahlāda's to his class-mates and his father (VII), Ajagara's (VII), Krishna's to the *gopīs* (X) and above all Krishna's discourses to his friend

Uddhava in Book XI which form a veritable *Bhagavad Gītā* it themselves.

The *Bhāgavata*'s exhortation is for *bhakti*. In fact, what it has said on *bhakti* and its forms and phases, on the recital of the Lord's Name, *nāmam*, all this has become the basic tenets of the *bhakti* school expounded in many later treatises. The adoration of Krishna, expecially as the child, and the love of the *gopīs* as the prototype of *bhakti* at its height, all this again we owe to the *Bhāgavata*. But the *Bhāgavata* deals with all the three *yogas* – *jñāna*, *karma* and *bhakti*, and the *bhakti* that it emphasizes is a synthesis of all the three yogas, as the one naturally involves the other. To love God is to know and realize His true nature, as also to serve Him in all manner possible. Hence it is said in a verse setting forth the theme of the *Bhāgavata* that it expounds *naiskarmya*, cessation from all mundane activity, informed by knowledge, detachment and devotion: *jñāna*, *viraga* and *bhakti*: *yatra jñāna-virāga-bhakti-sahitam naiṣkarmyaṁ āviṣkṛitam*. Kapila who teaches the *samkhya* path of knowledge calls it *bhakti yoga*; and explains highest *bhakti* as the realization of oneself and the Lord in every being around one. The *mukta*, the *bhakta*, the *sadhu*, the *bhāgavata*, the *jñānin* and the *muni* are all described in different contexts but their characteristics are mostly in identical terms. In his summing up to Uddhava, the Lord says: "Of the three yogas, those who have desires and projects and programmes in the world should take to *karma yoga*; those who can detach themselves and are given to stoic nature, may take to *jñāna yoga*; but those who are in the middle, who have desires and yet can think of the Lord, let them cultivate the path of devotion to Me, surrender unto Me themselves and the fruits of their acts, and do their appointed duties as an adoration and offering to Me."

From what was said at the beginning, it should not be

supposed that the *Bhāgavata* has no appeal of language. It no doubt rides rough-shod over classical grammar and lexicon but only as a master of both; this it does consciously, to elevate its diction to the Vedic plane. It can pour forth exquisite poetry as in the description of the seasons and of moonlight and the *rasa-līlā* dance of the *gopīs* with Krishna in Book X. By its compounds it imparts a vigour and rhythm to its *anushtubh* and *upajati* verses which make it a delight to read them aloud and get them by heart.

In putting across ideas, in denunciation of the small things of material life, the *Bhāgavata* does not mince matters, it speaks forthright and as the Tamil saying goes, drives in its ideas like nails into green wood. It rises to heights sometimes and expresses its ideas in an astounding manner, with an intellectual and modern ring. "He who wants more for himself and accumulates is a thief, he is to be punished," it declares in one place. "Let us have adversities more often, so that we may remember the Lord more incessantly," prays Kuntī. "The Lord is in the form of Dharma which is a means to self-purification." The Lord says through Kapila: "I am not pleased with all the pomp of worship if one insults the living beings in whom I am immanent." "Leave off pride and shame and prostrate before all creatures, including the dog and the ass," says Krishna to Uddhava. Prahlāda says out of compassion for the suffering beings: "There are sages retired in forests striving for their own lonely salvation; but I do not want to leave behind these wretched folk in suffering and seek salvation, for myself alone." King Rantideva prays: "I do not aspire for divine status or miraculous powers; no, not even salvation; I want to enter into fellow beings in suffering and see that they are rid of their misery." In another place, Manu defines the Lord "as the exemplar of Man, one who works but is selfless; being full, wishes for nothing; acts without being urged by anybody; and teaches, by himself following the proper path and thus promulgates all *dharmas*." Lastly, listen to the universal prayer in the *Bhāgavata*'s own characteristic language: "May there be welfare for the world; may the wicked become tranquil; may beings contemplate each other's good; may the mind take to the good; and our thought become naturally possessed of the Lord."

Note

[1]Originally published in *Vedānta Kesari*, October 1965.

Creative Exponents of the Name, and Related Studies

Encountering Tulasidās: The Rāma Story in Translation[1]

In 1948, I was travelling by Rail to Darbhanga for the 14th session of the All-India Oriental Conference. On the platform of one of the larger stations, where the train stopped at daybreak, I suddenly heard some song on Rāma that set a thrill through my whole body. I looked out and saw a poor man in a rag of a cloth, just bathed at the water-tap on the platform and with his bare frail frame walking in the cold with a bucket of water in hand. He continued to sing and I to listen; and in a short while, I realized that it was from Tulasi's *Rāmāyaṇa* that he was singing. The impression has remained indelible; it was not only the magic of Tulasi's words but also the miracle of how all this heritage has had its hold over the people, even the very humblest of them.

The Rāmāyaṇa (Rāmacarita mānasa) of Tulasidās (1532-1574 A.D.) is, in the words of Sir George Grierson, the great linguist, the universally accepted Bible of all classes from the Himalayas to the Narmada, "the perfect example of a perfect book," exercising its spell over the unlettered millions to whom it brought in their language the entrancing and elevating personality of Vālmīki's Rāmacandra, the incarnation of *Satya* and *Dharma*, the saving grace of Rāma *nāma* and the ideal of Rāma *rājya* as the kingdom of God on earth. The Muslim-Hindi poets Abdur Rahim Khani Khan and Raskhan adored it as the "very lifebreath of saints" and "endearing as the stream of milk flowing from the udders of the celestial cow." Grierson hails Tulasidās as "one of the half-dozen great writers that Asia has produced" and "a saviour of Hindustan."

It is through Tulasi that Rāma *bhakti* and Rāma *nāma* gained their sovereign sway over the whole of North India. It is through Tulasi that Gandhiji came to prize Rāma *nāma* as the most potent medicine and cherish Rāma *rājya* as his ideal of *svarāj* – spiritually empowered self-rule.

Long before any of the recent organizations or movements started their efforts to make the literary treasures in one Indian language known to the poeple of other languages, the name and work of Tulasi had spread to South India. The tradition of the Saint-singers, the *Bhāgavata* and *Bhajana-kīrtana sampradāya* and the movement of the votaries of this tradition from one part of the country to the other had brought the life story of Tulasidās and his songs and his *Rāmāyaṇa* to the devout Tamil people. To the Tamils who get so deeply involved in music and devotion, the *Mahātmas* of Mahārāṣṭra, of the Hindi areas and of Bengal are all objects of veneration and their *abhangs*, *chaupais* and *padas* are part of the repertoire of Tamil *Harikathā* performers. Our great singer of Rāma-songs, Tyāgarāja, pays his homage to Tulasi as one of those who had blazed the path of Rāma *bhakti* and Rāma *kīrtana* before him.

Outside of this religious milieu, it is but proper that an outstanding classic of the kind of the *Rāmacaritamānasa* should be made available to the literary world of Tamil Nadu. This service, Śrī S. Jagannarayanan has done in his Tamil rendering which he did together with comparative notes from Vālmīki, the Tamil Rāmāyaṇa of Kambar and the songs of Tyāgarāja. The translator, along with his late talented wife, has been for long a worshipper at the altar of music and devotion and has naturally brought to his translation his dedicated spirit. This is seen prominently in the *dhyānas* or preludes for helping contemplation of Rāma that he has put in all through the narrative. The knowledge of the Hindi that he had gained through his long stay in the north has had its best fruit in this sacred task he had set for himself and has accomplished.

Although each of the books of the *Rāmāyaṇa* has its own importance and projects a prominent phase of the scintillating prismatic personality of Rāma, it is the *Ayodhyā Kāṇḍa* that narrates the great giving up of the kingdom and the greater thing, namely Rāma not being affected in the least by this apparently serious loss and continuing to have the wonted and excelling cheer on his face, and in the midst of everyone else in a disturbed state at the sudden turn of events, he alone, standing like a rock of *Dharma* and *Satya*, as one towering above all others, the veritable God among men that indeed he was. In his memorable lines on this, Vālmīki said: "Losing his kingship diminished his great majesty no more than night lessens the radiance of the moon's cool light, which charms the world. Although Rāma was about to leave his own land and journey in the forest, his composure was that of a man who has transcended all worldly things."

It is this idea that Tulasi seizes as most significant and embodies in one of the three opening Sanskrit verses of his *Ayodhyā Kāṇḍa*: "That which did not wax more gracious because of the (proposed) coronation nor wane because of the (impending) difficulties of forest life, may that charm of the lotus-face of Rāma be for all time the bestower on me of things pleasing and auspicious." No image of Rāma in the epic could be more inspiring and thrilling than the one at this moment as he strode out of the chamber of Kaikeyī, having promised her that he was going to the forest and with the charm of his face not diminishing even by the slightest shade!"

Note

[1]Originally published as a foreward to S. Jagannarayana's Tamil translation of the *Rāmacaritamānasa* of Tulasidās.

Creative Exponents of the Name, and Related Studies

The Bhakti of Guru Nānak[1]

Motto: Let me be a sacrifice unto that song
By which we attain immortality.

Guru Nānak, Singer-Saint

Guru Nānak appeared as one of the high billows in the great popular upsurges of religion and devotion, which began in the 7th century with the Tamil Śaiva and Vaiṣṇava saints, *nāyanmār*s and *āḷvār*s, and spread all over the country, a movement which had been active till very recently. This was, so far as this country was concerned, universal and comprehensive of all the faiths and sects and schools of thought, orthodox and heterodox, the Jain and Buddhist mystics having also participated in this movement with their own output, in verse and song, of religious and devotional mysticism. The adoption of the popular languages as the medium of expression and the harnessing of the art of music as effective means of reaching the masses, the compositions being mostly of the form of songs, the employment of homely diction, telling parables and suggestive similes and analogies—all these form on the external side common features of this vast literature of the popular saints, which forms in the history of almost all the regional languages the foremost if not the first creative work. On the more substantial side, leaning towards the practical aspects of the spiritual and religious pursuit, there were ideas which were common to all these saint-singers, the most prominent of which are the emphasis on the *name* of the Lord and its recitation and contemplation, and the *guru*, and its extension the *satsang*.[2] While all these common features were there, it should not be forgotten that those who participated in this great religious creative activity belonged to different traditions and schools of thought and their ultimate literary and philosophical background or affiliation varied. There is, no doubt, a large part of their musical, religious and devotional outpourings which disclose universality and a synthetic trend but behind this patent unity there are the basic ideas of the schools of thought or tradition from which each one of them emerged. While it is useful to emphasize the great integrating role which they played, it is also necessary, in the interests of complete and scholarly understanding of the thought-content of this song-literature to examine the underlying philosophical ideas which have gone into the making of the songs of each school or succession of these saint-singers.

Ideas Symbolized in Lyrics

Among these saint-singers there are those who sought the Personal God, the *saguṇa* Brahman, God with form; among these again, those who sang of one form or the other, Śaiva or Vaiṣṇava; of these last again, those who loved Rāma or Krishna, the latter in larger number. On the other hand, there were those who sought the Impersonal, the *nirguṇa* Brahman, God without form. Looking at them from the standpoint of philosophies, we had dualists, monotheists, qualified monists and monists. These affiliations are known from history more than from views expressly or clearly found in the songs. The saints had intuitions and mystic experiences and ecstatic communions and trances and what flowed out of them in songs and through parables, analogies, and metaphors is too artistic a medium to allow of systematic analysis and tracing of self-contained logical systems of thought. But many schools and sects have grown, developed theologies and metaphysical systems just from out of these songs. The Ṛig Vedic hymns themselves form the foremost and earliest examples in this respect. We may therefore legitimately study in depth the songs and trace the thought-pattern as closely as possible.

That song-poetry could be interpreted so as to yield phases of thought may be illustrated from one of Nānak's compositions, in *Śrī rāga: re man aisi sion prit kar*[3] in which Nānak uses a series of five similes for the love of man for God; the love of the lotus for the water, that of the fish for water, that of the *cātaka* bird for water—these three in one set, and two more, that of the water for the milk with which it is mixed and that of the *cakravaka* bird for the sun and its beloved one. The first series of three illumines three stages of the condition of the devotee: In the first the lotus is tossed and tormented by the waves of the water, bears all the trials and tribulations to which it is submitted and without getting uprooted, sticks on to the water in which it is born and has its being. In the second, whatever the flow and surge and depth of the water, the fish buoys itself up and swims through; this is a higher stage in which the devotee has achieved an inner capacity and poise and can never get sunk. The third is a still higher stage in which, although there is a flood of water all round, the *cātaka* thirsts only for the drop of water from the cloud above; that is, the devotee, a master of the situation around, is not satisfied with any affluence, power or plenitude here, unless he has at least a drop of divine grace, which outweighs all else. The next two similes, the fourth and fifth, refer to conditions of union and separation; man and God are united like water and milk; the comparative nature and position of the two are no doubt clearly brought out by the two subjects chosen, but what is more significant is the idea that for the sake of the latter, the Lord (the milk), the former (water), the self of man, has to efface or annihilate itself completely. The last simile of the *cakravaka* bird and its beloved partner and the sun brings out effectively the ideas of how the beloved partner is all the time near at hand, but because of the darkness of ignorance, it is not able to see the beloved, and pines and pines, till on the rise of the sun and knowledge in the morning, the discovery and union take place automatically.

Following this method of intensive study of the songs, we can cull together the ideas which could build up to a thought-pattern with contours more or less clear. The first question will of course be: What is the nature of the God or Godhead adored by Nānak?

The Nature of God

Bhakti is advocated at every step in the songs of Nānak. There is reference to God as a storehouse of qualities, *Guṇa nidhāna*[4] and an ocean of virtues.[5] Stress is laid on the Lord's grace as necessary for release. "By God's Grace alone," says Nānak, "is God to be grasped" says *Japji*[6] echoing the Upaniṣad's *Yam evaiṣa vriṇute tena labhyaḥ*. Again : 'In the realm of Grace, spiritual power is supreme, nothing else avails.'[7] In a *Śrīrāga* song, we find: "Those on whom descends the Grace of God are his favourites."[8] Nānak points out that the law of karma, of one reaping the fruits of one's action, as inexorable, but observes that the Lord can always forgive and save: "When the balance of deeds is struck, Yama strikes us on our head. Then we have to render the account when he asks for it. It is on the mediation of the True One (i.e. the Lord) that we are all saved and the Lord forgives us.

This Being of grace, whom one must adore with love and devotion, is however not any *avatāra* like Rāma or Krishna, nor any of the three Gods: Brahmā, Viṣṇu or Hari and Śiva. Nānak may refer to Harinām but Hari of Nānak is just God, like Rām of Kābīr. For according to *Japji* 30[9] the *Trimūrtis* (three forms of God) are just three acceptable disciples brought forth from the one God, by *māyā*. In the same text[10] in which God is mentioned as "treasury of qualities," he is also called *Nirañjana* (pure, free from passion) and it is said that he cannot be installed anywhere nor is He in a form that could be installed. The *Japji* adds: "If anyone thinks he knows Him (that Lord), one does not speak the truth, as such an utterance is not possible," recalling the *Kena Upaniṣad*:

Yasyāmatam tasya matam matam yasya na veda sah
Avijñātam vijānatām vijñātam avijānatām
"He has neither form (*rūpa*) nor material sign."[11]

In a *Rāmakali* song, he says: "Our creator the Lord Himself creates all; Brahmā, Viṣṇu, Śiva too are contained in Him, the One Alone.'" The *Mūla mantra* itself declares the Lord as the One, the True, Timeless, Formless, Unborn, Self-luminous *sat* (eternal being), *akāla* (beyond time), *amūrta* (formless), *ayoni* (without womb), *svayambhu* (self-dependent). In *Japji* 4, he is called the Lord who is Truth, having Truth as his Name. In *Japji* 29, the following terms are used to designate Him: the beginning, colorless, the beginningless, the subtle Sound: *ādi*, *anīla*, *anādi*, *anāhata*.

All the forms into which It spreads out, all the diverse forms which different schools speak of, are only the many aspects of the one Lord. Says Nānak with a telling simile:

Six the systems, six their teachers,
And six their different teachings,
The Lord of them all is the One Lord
However various His aspects are:
O, brother, follow that system
That sings the Lord's praises:
There thy true glory lies.

Seconds, minutes, hours, quarters of a day;
Lunar and solar days make up a month.
Yet there are many times and many seasons;

One single sun runs through them all.
O Nānak, Thy Lord is likewise One,
However various His aspects are.

The One Lord is not only of the form of the many but He is also above all forms. In a *Dhansari rāga* song, Nānak says: "Thou hast a thousand forms and yet not one form," and in a *Pauri rāga* song, "Thy Name is Formless."

Contrary to some opinions held,[12] it is only on the basis of the *advaita* of the *Upaniṣads* and Śaṅkara that we can explain the above statements of Nānak. The *nirguṇa sampradāya* (or tradition of the Supreme as formless) in which Nānak emerged and the well-known epithet *Nānak Nirankār* cannot be explained otherwise. The ultimate disappearance of duality and realization of unity are both voiced forth in the songs. "Then the *ātman* becomes one with the *paramātman* and duality is destroyed."[13]

In a *Bhairava rāga* song: "Without the Name the disease of duality has spread throughout the world.'" Elsewhere, "Thou the Formless One, beyond fear and enmity, I blend in Thy pure light."[14] In a song in *Śrī rāga*, Nānak says: "Through the guru's words alone there comes the moment of knowing 'Myself is that Self.'"[15] And in another in *Maru rāga*, "I am that, that is I; the three worlds are included in that formula."[16] Thus in the words of a recent Sikh writer on this subject,[17] "*Bhakti* of the Guru-poets is of absolute monistic nature and of the formless and everliving God."

The Self and the Infinite

In an advaitic poem called *Prabodhasudhākāra*, the aspirant after union with the supreme exclaims to the Lord: "Even if our difference ends, I am yours, not you, mine; the wave is the ocean, not vice versa."

Satyapi bhedāpagame Nātha tavāham na māmakīnastvam
Samudro hi taraṅgaḥ kvacana samudro na taraṅgaḥ

On this question of the relationship between the supreme Self and the finite self, Nānak has a riddle, in a song of riddles in *Rāmakali rāga*. The intriguing nature of the question is well answered by propounding the things as a riddle, the secret of which, is, Nānak says, known only to the Lord; but his answer is clear, viz., the unity of the two. Using almost the same analogy of the sea and a part of it, Nānak asks:

> The drop of water is in the sea,
> And the sea is in the drop of water;
> Who shall solve this riddle?
> Who knoweth the secret?
> He from whom all creation came,
> He surveyeth that which He hath created,
> He, the Lord, is the One knower of the secret;
> And the man who understandeth this in his heart
> Is freed from human bondage,
> Is made at one with the Lord.

Māyā

For the process of the One Absolute becoming diversified and dynamic and creative, Nānak uses the Vedantic concept of *māyā*, the primal potency conceived as the Goddess and Mother of all creation. The *Japji* (30) states: "The Lord of Māyā, through Her union becomes manifold into the Creator, Sustainer, and Destroyer; and as He directs they obey and do their duties." In a song in *Maru rāga*, it is stated that *Māyā*, the Goddess is the veil of illusion which obscures the Truth and increases worldly attachment. It is the cause of duality, falsity, ignorance, attachments to mundane things and eventual transmigration and bondage. In these roles it is repeatedly denounced: "Māyā's disciple is false; he abhors truth. Bound up in duality, he transmigrates,'[18] "the fool is entangled in duality and forgets the divine Name."[19]

All this is quite in conformity with the Vedāntic ontology and creative process. If the one timeless absolute alone is truth, it follows that the manifold that has arisen therefrom is the opposite of truth. It may, for the time being and for practical purposes, be real but is not really real. It has been accepted in the monistic tradition that all teachings and endeavours on the spiritual path are only the means to reach the goal, effective for the duration of their agency, and transcended or sublated when the Truth is reached. It is this ultimate falsity that Nānak speaks of:

> False is the king, false are the subjects, false is the
> whole world.
> False is the palace, false are the skyscrapers,
> false the indwellers.
> False is gold, false is silver, false is the wearer.
> False is the body, false the garments,
> false the infinite beauty.
> False is the groom, false the bride,
> they are wasted away
>
> * * *
>
> O Lord, without Thee all is false.

Nānak and the Name

Like the other members of the galaxy of Saint-Singers of India, Nānak also assigns a high place to the Lord's Name, *nāma*, and gives the three requisites or *sādhanas* of *śravaṇa*, *kīrtana* and *smaraṇa*, listening to the Name, its recitation and its uninterrupted remembrance. The lines referring to these ideas are too numerous and too well-known to need any quotation. We should rather linger to consider what this Name is. *Nāma* occurs along with the related concept of *śabda* which we are coming to shortly. It is not the Name like Rāma,

Krishna etc. which are well-known to adherents of other paths of devotion centering round particular personal deities; they are rather on a par with the attributes or terms applied to the Supreme Being in the *Upaniṣads*, in its *nirguṇa* aspect, as also in its primary *saguṇa* aspect; *akāla*, *nirañjana*, and so on, in the *nirguṇa*; and *karta*, *puruṣa* and so on in the latter primary *saguṇa* aspect as Creator, Sustainer, Destroyer, the immanent indwelling Self (*antaryāmī*), and so on. A *Rāmakali rāga* song says: "From the Absolute He of Himself became manifest the Pure One; from being attributeless (*nirguṇa*), He was endowed with attributes (*saguṇa*)." Again "He the Lord Himself created Himself and assumed Himself the Name and then He created Nature, and abiding within it, He revelled in His wonder." In a song in *Sorath rāga*, "In all hearts is hid the Lord, all hearts are illumined by the light of the Lord." It is these terms by which the Supreme Being is characterised in its absolute aspect or its creative and primary *saguṇa* aspect that constitute the Names to be meditated upon constantly. This is quite germane to the advaitic tradition and indeed there is a collection and exposition by a South Indian *sannyāsin* scholar, Paramaśivendra Sarasvatī, of these epithets of the *nirguṇa* and *saguṇa Brahman* as the "One thousand Names of the Supreme from the Upaniṣads" – *Upaniṣan-nāma-sahasra-vyākhyā*. It is in this sense again that Islam also cherishes the Names of the Lord: "The Divine Names are either names of the Essence e.g. the One, or name of attributes e.g. the Merciful, the Knowing"[20] and so on.

Śabda

One with the idea of *Nāma* is that of Word, *Śabda*. As often as *Nāma*, *Śabda* also occurs in the songs. It is also one of the concepts whose correct understanding and identification are not easy. It is used both as being one with God and also as a means of gaining that state. On the other side, it occurs as a compound with *Guru*, *Guru-Śabda*, and sometimes as Guru's *Śabda*, the former signifying an identity. In answer to the question of a yogi, as to who his guru was, Nānak replied: "The true Guru is the Word."[21] Thus *Śabda* is something which is almost identical with the highest, the highest means of attaining that, and the words of Teacher, e.g. the scriptures and the songs themselves. It has been recorded by Nānak that whenever he heard the "Word," he immediately sang,[22] and that he once exclaimed when he was in meditation: "Mardan! Touch the chords, the Word is descending," but Mardana who played the Rabab for him replied: "But, Master, the horse is grazing and my hands are occupied holding the reins, lest the animal run away." Nānak said: "Let go the horse." As already mentioned Nānak was asked by the yogis and *siddhas* as to who his guru was and Nānak replied that *Śabda* was his Guru; "The Word is the Guru and the mind attuned to the Word is the disciple."[23]

In *Var-malar*, he says: "He who meditates on Thy true *Śabda* is joined in union with Thee . . . The Guru's *Śabda* is like a gem which reveals Thee by its light." In a song of his in *Sorathi rāga*, we read: "God has neither form nor color nor material sign but he is revealed through true *Śabda*." In another in *Gowri rāga*: "Meditating on *Śabda* and repeating the Name of the Lord, man is released." In a third in *Śrī rāga*: "Without the *Śabda* one is condemned to wander." In a further one in *Śrī rāga*, we read: "In the contemplation of the Word is bliss" and " . . . release from bondage comes from contemplating the Word."[24]

From some other utterances, *Śabda* is seen to be all-comprehensive. "The Word is my meditation, divine instruction, the music of my horn for me to hear."[25] "All acts of purification, austerities, devotion, penance and pilgrimages abide in the Word." A piece in the *Japji* describes *Śabda* as something to be realized through the virtues of chastity, patience, understanding, knowledge, austerity, fear and devotion.[26]

> In the forge of continence,
> Let patience be the goldsmith,
> On the anvil of understanding
> Let him strike with the hammer of knowledge:
> Let the fear of God be the bellows,
> Let austerities be the fire,
> Let the love of God be the crucible,
> Let the nectar of life be melted in it;
> Thus in the mint of Truth,
> A man may coin the *Word*.

A song in *Bilaval rāga* says: "The Lord himself is the Word; Himself stamps it with his approval."

From all this it is clear that the concept of *Śabda* is both intriguing and interesting and deserves some examination, particularly because it has a fundamental place in Nānak's thought. It is well-known that part of the heritage of Nānak lay in the tradition of the *nāth yogis* and according to the tradition of the yoga, a stage is reached at the heights of perfection when the yogin is able to hear the subtle Sound pervading the universe. This is the unmanifest or unstruck Sound, *avyakta, anāhata nāda*. Nānak has of course denounced the mere physical practice of the yogic exercises, without real spiritual attunement, but it is clear that he had some esoteric practices of his own. When he was asked by the yogi Loharipa to adopt his system, Nānak replied, "My own system is the constant contemplation of the Word,"[27] and we find references to the *anāhata nāda* in the *Japji*[28] and his songs.

In a piece in the *Asa* we find the following: "One loves one's Lord, ever attuned to him, imbibes the *unstruck music of the Word* in the mind." In *Japji* 29 the Lord is described as the Primary Being, one devoid of all colour, beginningless and *Anāhata.* In the beautiful cosmic *Ārti* song, the first part ends: "Unstruck music is the sound of Thy temple drums."[29] Elsewhere[30] I have drawn attention to the text *Haṭhayogapradīpikā* and what it says about this subtle inner *Nāda* in which the mind gets dissolved and beyond the state of *Manolaya* is the soundless state of the Supreme Being. This *anāhata śabda* or *nāda* has unfortunately not come out in its correct form in the translations of or commentaries on the songs that we have. There is however no doubt about this *Śabda* being, in its ultimate sense, the *anāhata nāda.* This will be clear from the universality of the concept of the Primordial Sound which all the scriptures of the world mention: for example, in the Bible, John: "In the beginning was the *Word* and the *Word* was with the God and the *Word* was God." In the further interpretation of this word the philosophy of the *Logos* developed and the *Logos* was identified with Sophia, Thought and Idea. The Hermetic tradition of the hellenized cities of Egypt identified that Logos was first-born of the Lord: "With Logos, not with hands, did the Creator make Universal cosmos." It would not be difficult to see the parallel in the Upaniṣads where the one Brahman, which becomes two and creates the Universe, is said to be in *tapas* or in brooking, contemplation or thought, *ālochana.* In other schools of thought, this is termed *vimarśa* and identified with *Devī* or *Śakti* and *Śabda.* We see this also in the Islamic and Sufic background which was the part of the heritage of Nānak. We can go to no better authority for this than the pioneer student of comparative religion, Prince Dara Shikoh and his work *Majma-ul-Bahrain* or "The Mingling of the Two Oceans (of Islam and Hinduism)" where he says in section 8 on Sound:

> Sound emanates from the same breath of the Merciful which came out with the word *Kun*, at the

> time of the creation. The Indian divines call that Sound *Sarasvatī*, which they say is the source of all sounds, voices and vibrations. According to the Indian monotheists, this Sound, which is called *Nāda* is of three kinds. First *Anāhata*, which has been in Eternity Past, is so at Present, and will be so in Future. The Sufis name this sound *Swaz-i-Mutlak* (The sound of the Absolute) or *Sultan-ul-Adhkar* (king of all devotional exercises). This sound is eternal and is the source of the perception of *mahākāśa*; but this Sound is inaudible to all except the great saints of both the communities. Secondly *Āhata* . . . Thirdly *Śabda* . . . *Śabda* possesses an affinity with Sarasvatī and is the source of *Ism-i-Azam* (the Great Name) of the Musalmans and the *Veda-mukha* or OM of the Hindu divines. *Ism-i-Azam* means that He is the possessor of the three attributes of Creation, Preservation, and Destruction; and *Fatha, Dhamma* and *Kasra* which correspond with *a-kāra*, *u-kāra* and *ma-kāra* have also originated from this. They (the Indian divines) assign a special symbol to this Sound which bears a close resemblance to our *Ism-i-Azam* and in which traces of the elements of water, fire, air, dust and of the Pure Self are manifest.

As in the philosophical interpretation of the Biblical concept of Word, in respect of this Word *Kun* it has been said: "According to Muhammaden belief the word owes its origin to the Will of God which was expressed by the word *Kun* or 'Be'."[31] In his *Studies in Islamic Mysticism*,[32] R.N. Nicholson says "Mohammed is the Logos who unites the Essence, the Attributes and the Names in a single nature. The Perfect Man is neither Absolute Being nor contingent Being, but the third metaphysical entity i.e. the Logos." The relation of the will of God to create and the Word is seen in a long song on creation in *Maru rāga*, where Nānak says: "When He so *Willed*, He shaped the Universe . . . To some, chosen few, the Guru revealeth the Lord's Word."[33] The will of the Lord such as that "Let the worlds be" is also called the *saṅkalpa* of Īśvara. Nānak calls it the *hukam* or *ājñā* or Order in *Japji* 2: "Through His Will He creates all the forms of things" and adds that this will of the Lord is inscrutible.

Śabda is therefore the same highest symbol of the Supreme Being that the Upaniṣads speak of as *Om* or *praṇava*. That this is so is borne out by a song in *Rāmakali*[34]

> Oṃkār is He who created Brahmā,
> Brahmā who treasured God in his mind.
> Oṃkār is He who created the mountains
> and the *yugas*.
> Oṃkār is He who created the Vedās.
> Oṃkār is He who, through the Word,
> emancipated all.
> Oṃkār is He through whom the God-conscious
> beings were saved.
> Hear ye, the meanding of the Word OM,
> Which indeed is the essence of the three worlds.

In fact, at the very opening, the *Mūla mantra* begins with this highest mystic syllable. *Oṃkār Sat-Nām kartā puruṣa* and so on.

Nānak's Ideal Way of Life

The monistic view is not inconsistent on the empirical plane where ethics based on duality has its fruitful role to play. *Jñāna* and *dhyāna yogas*, rarefied *bhakti yoga*, and *karma yoga*, as taught by the *Bhagavad Gītā* as submission to the will of God and discharging one's duty with detachment – all these form an amalgam in the approach of the mystic, such as Nānak was. "True yoga," says Nānak, "lies in living a detached life amidst attachments."[35] "One liveth detached, enshrining the One Lord in the mind . . . "[36] The ideal of such a God-centered life of contentment, dedicated work and service is the message that Nānak gives all men, whatever their walk of life or opportunity to play their part: "Serve others and dwell on the Word; practice contemplation and self-control and overcome the ego."[37] "Dedicate thyself to service in the world and thou gettest a seat in the Lord's Court."[38] "The man who earns his bread by sweat of his brow and gives some of his gains in charity knows, Nānak, the true way of life.[39]

> Man set in authority,
> Let devotion to God be thy service,
> Let thy toil be faith in the Name.
> Check thy mind from wandering
> after temptation
> Stand alert on guard against all evil,
> So from all men thou shalt earn the praise,
> And the Lord, thy Kind, will delight in thee
> With a four-fold increase of His Love.[40]

The following universal message of his may be the fitting finale to his homage to the Guru:

"Let there be brotherhood with all men. To subdue the mind is to subdue the world."[41]

Notes

[1] First published in *Guru Nakak – A Homage*, ed. K.R. Srinivasa Iyengar. (New Delhi: Sahitya Akademi, 1973). I have left the information in the footnotes as they are found in the text, when unable to add further information to them. See also V. Raghavan's Patel Memorial Lectures of 1964, published as *The Great Integrators–The Saint-Singers of India* (New Delhi: Publications Division, 1966; 1979, 4th ed.)

[2]Maṅgala Śloka: Raghavan's Sanskrit version of the Mūlmantra was placed next to the motto in the original publication:

Eka Oṃkāra-San-Nāmā kartā Nirbhyapūruṣaḥ
Nirvairo'kāla-mūrtaś ca'pyayoniśca-svaykamprabhaḥ
Guruprasādo jayati yenaivam jñāyate Prabhuḥ

[3]*Japji* (UNESCO edition) entitled *The Sacred Writings of the Sikhs*, tr T. Singh and others. (India: National Academy of Representative Works of India Series, 1960), pp. 71-73.

[4]*The Sacred Writings of the Sikhs*, p. 31.

[5]Ibid. p. 52.

[6]Ibid. p. 32.

[7]Ibid. p. 37.

[8]Ibid. p. 68.

[9]Ibid, p. 46.

[10]Ibid, p. 5.

[11]*Kena Upaniṣad, Suhi Ast.*, 1.3.

[12]See *Guru Nānak and the Sikh Tradition*, W.H. Mcleod (London: Oxford, 1968), pp. 165, 185.

[13]Jogendra Singh, *Thus Spoke Guru Nānak* (London: Oxford University Press, 1934), p. 61.

[14]*Asa Ast.*, 8.7.

[15]*The Sacred Writings of the Sikhs*, p. 73.

[16]Ibid, p. 106.

[17]*Bhakti of the Sikh Guru*, Dr. Darshan Singh, *Parkh*, A Research Bulletin in Punjabi Language and Literature, Chandigarh, II, 1967, p. 105.

[18]*Majh Ast.*, I. 5.

[19]*Asa Ast.*, 9 (2).

[20]P. 93, *Studies in Islamic Mysticism*, R.N. Nicholson.

[21]*The Sacred Writings of the Sikhs*, p. 102.

[22]Cf. song in *Tilang rāga, The Sacred Writings of the Sikhs*, p. 69.

[23]Song in *Rāmakali rāga.*

[24]*The Sacred Writings of the Sikhs*, pp. 74-5.

[25]M.A. Macauliffe, *The Sikh Religion, Its Gurus, Sacred Writings and Authors* (London: Oxford, 1909), p. 172.

[26]Ibid, p. 378.

[27]*The Sacred Writings of the Sikhs*, p. 101.

[28]In a learned Sanskrit commentary on the *Japji*, this is rendered as *avrara*, un-injured, according to a description in the Upaniṣad. In a well-known English translation, it is just rendered as "changeless."

[29] *The Sacred Writings of the Sikhs*, p. 61.

[30] In my article "Nānak–Tradition and Thought" in the volume *Guru Nānak* (New Delhi: Publications Division, 1969), pp. 18-32.

[31] M.M. Huq, in his translation of *Majma*.

[32] R.N. Nicholson, *Studies in In Islamic Mysticism* p. 157.

[33] *The Sacred Writings of the Sikhs*, p. 105.

[34] *The Sacred Writings of the Sikhs*, p. 93.

[35] Suhi, M.1.

[36] Rāmkali.

[37] Pārbhatī, M. 1.

[38] Śrī rāga, M. 1.

[39] Var Sarang, *The Sacred Writings of the Sikhs*, p. 116.

[40] *The Sacred Writings of the Sikhs*, p. 96.

[41] *Japji* 28.

Creative Exponents of the Name, and Related Studies

Bhadrācalam Rāmadās[1] The Singer-Saint Whom Rāma Sprang from Jail

The Era in Which Rāmadās Lived

It was the time when the Qutub Shāhis were ruling in Golconda. Although these rulers were Muslims, they were great patrons of the local language, Telugu, and the local arts of music and dance. The best of them, Malik Ibrahim patronized Telugu writers and the 'Iburamu' figuring in many Telugu songs is this Malik Ibrahim. His son Muhammad Quli Qutub Shāh became attracted to a temple dancer, a *devadāsi* proficient in music and dance, named Bhāgamatī, and named the city Bhāgnagar after her; the city later came to be known as Hyderabad.

Later, Kṣetrayya, a devotee of Krishna as Muvva Gopāla, came to the court of Abdulla Qutub Shāh. Kṣetrayya, a Telugu poet, music-composer and authority on *rasa* and *Alaṁkāra śāstra* had a contest in the Golconda court on the subject of *nāyika-nāyaka-bhāva* with another scholar Tulasimūrti and in this connection composed under the patronage of the Padshāh and by the grace of Krishna in the form of Muvva Gopāla, 1100 *padas*. Evidently at this time the *nāyaka-bhava* (the mood of longing for the beloved) which had also much to do with the phase of devotion called *madhura-bhakti* ("the sweetness of spiritual love") and music compositions based on it inspired much interest. One of the divines, connected with the court as preceptors, at the royal school or *dargah* at

Gulbarga of Gezu Daraz, Shāhrāja or Bada Akbar Shāh, also evinced keen interest in the subject and a text entitled Śṛingarāmañjari in Telugu and Sanskrit versions was produced on this subject.[2]

In the time of the successor to these rulers, Abud Hasan known as Tani Shāh, Hindu-Muslim unity had grown further. Not only were his ministers, the two brothers Akkanna and Madanna, Hindu, but many Muslim officials freely participated in Hindu festival.

It is this Muslim ruler Abul Hasan Tani Shāh who figures in the story of Śrī Bhadrācalam Rāmadās. It is necessary to know something about the history of Abul Hasan to understand the background of this ruler in proper perspective.

Abdulla Qutab Shāh was thinking of giving his daughter in marriage and naturally his thoughts went to the *dargah* (royal school) of Gezu Daraz at Gulbarga whose divines had always advised the rulers. Shārāja or Bade Akbar Shāh was in charge of the *dargah* at that time. Abul Hasan, a young boy, who descended on the side of the mother of Abdulla, was studying at the royal school. The boy had been under Shārāja's tuition for twelve years. Abdulla took a sudden decision to give his daughter to him and later to give him the kingdom as well.

Abul Hasan was more popularly known as Tani Shāh, which means "jovial king." But deep below his gaiety, there was all that he had imbibed during his youthful stay in the religious atmosphere of Gulbarga. His maturity of spirit was due also to the rare experience he had in his contact with Rāmadās, in the sight of Śrī Rāmacandra with which he was blessed. It is not a matter of wonder that through his *bhakti* to Rāma, Rāmadās attained salvation. The wonder is that Rāmadās took with him the Muslim ruler.

"O you are a more fortunate man than I am—

You saw with your own eyes the feet of Rāma my father!"[3]

Thus did Rāmadās himself exclaim and felicitate Tani Shāh on the divine *darśan*, the vision of Rāma, with which he was blessed.

The time of Tani Shāh is 1674-1699 A.D. Traditionally Kabīrdās of Banāras is said, by Harikathā performers, to have been the guru of Rāmadās but this is not possible as Kābīr, a disciple of Rāmānanda, flourished between 1440 and 1518 A.D. further there is nothing hazy about the figure of Rāmadās who is a well known name in Telugu history and literature. All that he wrote, his time, his life, – all these are known to us authoritatively, more authoritatively than the life and career of Tyāgarāja who lived much nearer our time. We can visit Golconda and see the hill and the place where Rāmadās was imprisoned and the hole through which food is said to have been dropped for him.

In 1832 A.D. one Varada Rāmadās who described himself as a descendant of Bhadrācalam Rāmadās, made a representation to Chandulal, Dewan of the Nizam of Hyderabad that he should be appointed to look after the Rāma temple at Bhadrācalam and got his request granted. In confirmation of the historicity of the whole story of Rāmadās and the Muslim Ruler, we have had the continuing practice of the Nizam of Hyderabad making a grant for the conduct of the festival of the temple of Rāma at Bhadrācalam. It was reported in the papers that during the anti-Hindu agitations and activities of Razakars and their leader Kasim Rizvi, the Nizam stopped the grant to the Bhadrācalam temple, but soon realized that this was a wrong action and restored the grant.

Biographical Background

Tani Shāh had a Brahman Minister named Madanna. Madanna had a sister Kāmāmbā who was given in marriage to Liṅganna Mantri. Rāmadās was the son of Liṅganna. His real name was Gopanna. They belonged to the family surnamed Kañcharla whose members were spread all over South India. One of the *stotras* or (hymns) written by Rāmadās is the *Bhadrācala Daśarathī Śatakam* and in this Rāmadās gives at the beginning biographical details about himself. They belonged to the place called Nelakondapalli in the former Nizam's dominions. His gotra was Atri, his Veda *Śuklayajus* and as stated above, his house-name was Kañcharla.

His father was Allana Liṅga Mantri
He belonged to Atrigotra Adi-sakha
His family name was Kañcharla
The family composed songs in praise of Bhagavan
And I myself composed one hundred verses
on Rāma who is the ocean of mercy.[4]

In this same text, the *Daśarathi śatakam*, he mentions his guru, Raghunātha Bhattāchārya:

With body bent I bow to all gurus
I bow to my guru Raghunātha Bhattar Añjaletti.[5]

This guru was a Śrīvaiṣṇava who belonged to the "Sesha" family.

Because of his Rāma-*bhakti*, the boy named Gopanna came to be known as Rāmadās, "the servant of Rāma." The whole family was devoted to *bhakti* and its propagation. According to an unpublished document, his uncle the Minister Madanna arranged for a *yakṣagana* or musical dance-drama troupe to tour from village to village, enacting puranic stories and spreading *bhakti*. Rāmadās continued this tradition, courting the company of *bhaktas*, and arranging for *bhajanas* and festivals. Rāmadās must have had initiation and *mantropadeśa* (instruction in the mantra) from some great soul and progressed in the spiritual path to such an extent that he saw Rāma in all beings and things, a state which he himself expressed in one of his songs: "The whole universe of full of Rāma."[6]

By constantly inviting *bhāgavatas*, devoted singers and expounders, to his home, and entertaining and attending upon them, Rāmadās spent much wealth and gradually became reduced to poverty. Thereupon, through the good offices of his uncle Madanna, he got from the Nawab the Tahsildarship (the position of revenue officer) of the *firka* or area of Bhadrācalam. He was discharging his duties well in this office for some time.

The Story of Rāmadās' Imprisonment

The Rāma shrine for which Bhadrācalam was well-known was in a damaged state. Rāmadās felt that he should repair the temple and provide the Rāma image there with new jewels. Until that time Rāmadās, responsible for revenue collection, was prompt in remitting the revenues of his division to the Central Treasury but after his mind turned to the renovation of the Rāma shrine, the collections came to be directed towards the Rāma shrine and not to the Padshāh's exchequer. In one of his songs on Bhadrācalam, Rāma and His temple there, Rāmadās describes the golden pinnacles of the towers of this temple, the bejewelled flagstaff, the tank, the garden, the surrounding shrines, the *agrahara* (Brahman's settlement) and so on. From this song which refers to Bhadrācalam as "Vaikuntha, Viṣṇu's heaven on earth in this Kali age," we may see the nature and extent of improvement that Rāmadās had effected in the temple. In a further song of lament which he sang in prison (*Sītā Rāmasvāmī nā jesina neramuleni*), he asks "What wrong did I do? did I make the earrings, the rings for all the ten fingers, the diadem, for myself? It is to give honor to you, Oh Sītā-Rāma, that I did all this!" From this again we see that he spent large sums of money on the decorations of the image of Rāma at Bhadrācalam.

The revenues had not been remitted for a long time and notices sent from time to time produced no response. Then the State officials had Rāmadās arrested and thrown into the prison in Golconda. That he suffered in the prison for twelve years is mentioned by him in a song of his:

> Why has your compassion not come, O Rāma,
> Why are you not saving me?
> I shall not request any other deity's help
> I am forever attached to you
> I have been languishing in this jail
> twelve years now.[7]

It was during this twelve years of prison-life to which he had been condemned by the Padshāh that Rāmadās sang most of his moving songs. Why had Rāmadās to suffer so long in this manner, when his own uncle was Minister? Firstly, Minister Madanna could not go out of the way and do anything to save his nephew who had spent state money excessively on the Temple; nor could the uncle have had that large amount of money that his nephew had spent, to be paid to the State and release his nephew.

Songs Reflecting Rāmadās' Sufferings

The State officials must have from time to time beaten Rāmadās for the payment of dues. This is clear from the cries of pain that we hear in the *Asāveri rāga* song:

> O my father,
> I cannot bear
> these beatings –
> They are lashing me with whips,
> So please
> come and save me![8]

Gopanna believed that whatever the treatment he received, Rāma always stood by his side armed with the discus of Viṣṇu, and therefore that he had nothing to be afraid of: "There is no lack of anything as long as my Rāma is there with me, standing at my side like a friend, *cakra* in hand."[9]

Rāma alone constituted Rāmadās' wealth and strength; in happiness or misery he was always with Rāma. "As long as I have no famine, as long as I surrender to you you may drown me in milk or in water, and now it's left to you to drown me or save me, so don't try to cheat me."[10]

Recalling how, in their times of distress, He appeared before Gajendra and Pañchali, he asks Rāma in a song in *Natakurañji rāga* where He was and why He was not coming to him when he was suffering like that:

Where is my Lord
the one who dwells
in Bhadrādri?
Where is my Rāma,
Protector,
and Shelter?[11]

In another song he asks what he will do if Rāma does not protect him:

To people who have said "O Lord protect me!"
You are the refuge, you have been saving them all along.
You have the reputation of sheltering all souls
who take refuge in you, but when I keep shouting
now, and crying in different ways
you do not show your mercy, so how shall I call you?[12]

At one moment he lays all his burden on Rāma, declaring in a mood of strength, "I belong to Rāma, why should I be afraid? All my burden is His."[13] Elsewhere he remarks,

Although we suffer at this point
in the turn of fortune's wheel
we always have faith in Rāma;

why should we ever
resort to anyone else
for any reason?[14]

And: "Rāma, why do you not speak? Are words pieces of gold? Would you be casting away pearls by uttering a few words? I have never lost the thought of your Name – not even when I am dreaming."[15]

Finding Rāma silent, he calls upon Sītā to speak to Rāma on his behalf, in *Nannu brova* and *Rāmacandrulu*. In the latter he pleads "O Sītā, Rāma is angry with me – please put in a good word for me."[16]

Finding no improvement in his situation, for a moment he appears in his wailings as if his faith was slipping, as he demands to know if Rāma cannot respond with pity why then should devotees pray: "Are you so devoid of grace? Why is Goddess Pārvatī doing *japa* of your Name? Why do Prahlāda and other devotees have faith in you?"[17]

In another mood, he regrets that, being in prison, he is not able to perform the worship of Rāma in proper form and goes through its required details mentally instead, doing what is called *manāsika-pūjā*, in his song beginning *Rāma Rāma manasā*.

The Story of Rāmadās' Rescue

The moment of succor from Rāma finally arrives when Rāma and Lakṣhmana put on the guise of two employees of Rāmadās, enter one night the apartment of Tani Shāh, pay him the entire dues that Rāmadās owed and ask for a receipt. Tani Shāh is stunned. The extra-ordinary effulgence and charm of the two servants overpower Tani Shāh. All of a sudden, the dues of several years being paid together, all in gold, at that time of night, the appearance of the two who brought the money, and their disappearance, –all these revolve in Tani Shāh's mind and make him decide that two servants are none else than Rāma and Lakṣmana whom Rāmadās had been worshipping. Tani Shāh then ran to where Rāmadās was imprisoned and reported to him the miraculous darshan he had. Rāmadās congratulated the King: "Tani Shāh! You are blessed, you have seen face to face Rāma whom I am yet to see."[18]

Tani Shāh, for his part, expressed his gratitude to Rāmadās, loaded him up with an enormous amount of money, put him on a palanquin and sent him to Bhadrācalam to continue his devotion and service to Rāma. To keep guard over his devotee and the riches he was taking, Rāma and Lakṣmana walked, bows in hands, on either side of the palanquin. So says Rāmadās in his song *Rāmuḍu galadu.*

Rāmadās' Vision and Lyrics

Rāma blessed Rāmadās too with darshan for which Rāmadās had been yearning: "Rāma, your sweet face I have seen!" (*Rāma nī muddu momu jupara*). In the ecstacy of the sight of Rāma, Rāmadās sang, "O Rāma I gaze upon your lustrous face!" (*Kanti nīḍu Rāmula kanukoṇṭi nīḍu*). Taking humiliation and honour as equal, deeming as friends even those who subjected him to suffering, Rāmadās, exemplifying the Gītā-ideal of equanimity– being alike in praise and blame, and being serene under all conditions, treating friends and foes the same (*Tulya-ninda stutiḥ, Talyo manapamanayoḥ . . . Tulyo mitraripakṣayoḥ*), he became the recipient of the grace of the Lord in full.

What does it matter
if someone abuses me?
What does it matter
if someone praises me?
Probably those who want to harm me
are really doing me some good.[19]

In addition to these songs, as already noted, Rāmadās wrote on Śrī Rāma at Bhadrācala. His *śataka stotra* in Telugu entitled Daśarathī Śataka, is considered as one of the best compositions in this class. Rāmadās has shown his literary gifts here and worked in many sound effects. "To me Rāma alone is God; there is none to equal Him – this I can proclaim by beating the drum placed on the back of the elephant." When he says this in one of the verses here, Rāmadās produces the verbal sound effect of a tom-tom by repetition of the syllables *ndu* and *du*:

> Pa*nda*na bhimu*ḍu* artajana ba*ndhavuḍu*
> Ujjavala-bana-tuna Koda*nda*kalaprocha*nda* . . .
> Kadakatti bherika *tanta-tatanta tanta*

"My poetry is fit for dedication to God alone, I will not let myself down by employing it for the flattering of man." He says in another verse of the *Daśarathī Śataka* that his lyrics are not composed with human listeners in mind: "How can I throw pearls before swine? I suffered and offered my poetry to evil men and I was cheated in doing that. My poetry is fit for dedication to God alone. I will not let myself down by employing it for the flattery of men. So, O Rāma, ocean of mercy, please listen to my lyrics and respond accordingly."[20]

Rāmadās and Tyāgarāja

Rāmadās was well versed in Sanskrit also and using twenty-four names of the Lord-Keśava, Nārāyana etc., he has summarily set forth the whole Rāmāyaṇa story in the form of a prose-poem, a *churṇika.*

Rāmadās gained a noteworthy place in the tradition of the galaxy of Rāma-*bhaktas.* His songs on Rāma spread all over the country. His life, his sufferings and his obtaining in the end the blessing of Rāma became a common story among the people. His songs on Rāma showed the way to the other great

Telugu Rāma-*bhakta* who was born in the South land, in Tamil Nadu – Śrī Tyāgarāja. Tyāgarāja salutes Rāmadās at the very outset of his long narrative with songs entitled the *Prahlāda bhakti-vijaya*. In two of his pieces Tyāgarāja has made a special reference to Rāmadās, his sufferings and the blessings of Rāma that he eventually received. In the song *Kṣirasāgara sayana* in *Devagandhāri rāga*, Tyāgarāja says "I have heard you saved the brave Rāmadās from the prison." (*Dhīruḍu Rāmadāsuni bandhanamu/Tirchinadi vinnanura*)

In the song *Emitova* Tyāgarāja says "Had I been Rāmadās, Sītā would have come forward to speak to you on my behalf." The ideas and expressions in Rāmadās' songs are echoed by Tyāgarāja in several songs. It is to be noted that, apart from the vogue the songs of Rāmadās enjoy in devotional congregations where *bhajans* are sung, some of them continue to be sung in Karṇāṭaka music recitals. Portions from several of his songs have already been quoted above.

A Song by Rāmadās on the Power of the Name

The following song shows the style of Rāmadās and his treatment of the subject of devotion to Rāma.

O all you people of the world!
Why not buy the Rāma-jogi's medicine?[21]

When, with love, you take this remedy
of the Rāma-mendicant,
it completely destroys pride, jealousy, avarice,
and the accumulation of *karmas*.

The remedy of Rāma-*jogi*,
which is unequalled in the world
and destroys the formidable fetters of life,
the remedy which cannot be obtained
even by spending crores of rupees
and is always remembered
by the unequalled devotees of the Lord;

it is the remedy at Bhadrādri[22]
which helps attainment of salvation
and which is ever worshipped
with devotion by Rāmadāsa."

Notes

[1]This piece was first published in *Devotional Poets and Mystics, Part II* (New Delhi: Pub. Div. Ministry of Information and Broadcasting, Government of India, 1978).

[2]This very erudite work on *nāyika-nāyaka-bhāva*, in its Sanskrit version, was discovered and edited by V. Raghavan for the Archaeological Department of Andhra Pradesh, 1951. See also V. Raghavan's article 'Hyderabad as Centre of Sangita, Journal of the Music Academy, Madras, XVI, 1945, pp. 116-20.

[3]Dhanyuḍavu Tanīsā nīvu/ nannu kannayya padamulu kanula/ kannāvu

[4]Allana Liṅga mantri sutuḍa
Atrigotrajuḍa Ādi-sākha
Kañcharla Kulodbhavundanu
Prasiddhudanai Bhavamdankitamuga-
yella kavul nutiyimpa rachiyiñchithi
Gopa-Kavinḍrudan Jagadvallabha
nīku dāsuḍanu Daśarthi Karuṇāpayōnidhi

[5]Ācāryula kella mrokki vinatāngudanai
Raghunāthabhattārācāryulaku añjaletti

[6]Anta Rāmamayam, ī jagad anta Rāmamayam.

[7]Emitiki dayarādu Śrī Rāmulu nannu
Emiṭiki rakṣhimpavu Śrī Rāmulu
Parulanu ne vēdabonu Śrī Rāmulu
niḳe karamula sāchi yunnanu
pannendēnḍlu āye nēdu
bandikhānalōna yundinānu

[8]Abbabbā debbalaku tālalera
Rāmappa Gobbuna nannādukōra

[9]Takku vēmi manaku Rāmuḍu Okkadu undvaraku
Prakka toduga Bhagavantuḍu munu
Chakradhāriyai sagucu nunḍaga (Nādanāmakriya)

[10] Kalimi balami nāku ilalō nī vani . . .

varinchiti nī
pālamunchinanu nīlamunchinna nī
Pāla paditi-nika jalamu chēyaka.

[11]Ēḍannāḍo Bhadrādrivāsuḍu
ēḍannāḍo nāpāli Rāmuḍu ēḍannaḍo

[12]Sarananna janamula birabira brōcheḍu
Birudu galgina dorave Ō Rāma
Paripari vidhamula moralida vinaka
Nannaramarachēsina Harininnē mandu

[13]Rāmuni vāramu mākemi vichāramu
Svāmī nīdē bhāramu Dāśarathē jīvādharamu

[14]Rāmuni vāramaināmu
Itarādryula ganana chēyamu
Graha gatulaku verava bōmu
Maku kaladu Daivānugrahamu

[15]Palukē bangāra māyena kodaṇḍapāni
Kalalō nī nāmasmarana maravā chakkani Tanḍri

[16]Rāmacandrulu nāpai calamu
Cēsinaru Sītāmmā ceppavammā

[17]Ādaraṇaleni nī Nāma-mantra-japam
Adn, emani jesera Rāma?

[18]Dhanyuḍavu Tānīśa nīvu nannu
Kannayya padamulu kanula
Kannāvu

[19]Evaru dūshiñchinanēmi, mecchi
Evaru bhūṣiñchinanemi. . . .
Aparādha mula neñchuvāru māku
upakārulai yunnavāru (Bilahari)

[20]Masakoni rēgu pandlakoni mauktikamul
Vela pōsinatlu dur-
Vyāsanumu jendi kāvyamu durāthmula-
Kicchiti mosamayye
Nā racanaku Pūta-vṛitti sukarambuga chekūrunaṭlu
Vāk-sudhārasamulu olukan
Madīya mukha raṅgamunandu naṭimpa vaiya
Santasamunu jendi Bhadrāgiri Dāśarathī
Karuṇapayōnidhī

[21]The "Rāma-jogi" mentioned is the mendicant from whom medicines and antidotes could be had; the prescription meant here, as given by God Rāma is himself, His name and worship.

[22]Bhadrādri is the shrine in Andhra. For renovating this temple with state funds, the saint was imprisoned.

Creative Exponents of the Name, and Related Studies

Upaniṣad Brahmayogin:

Maṭha-founder, Commentator, Composer

From V. Raghavan's Introduction to *Upeya-nāma-viveka*[1]

Upaniṣad Brahman's Contributions

Upaniṣad Brahmayogin occupies a noteworthy place in the school of *advaita-vedānta* as well as in that of *nāma-bhajana*, the tradition of *bhakti* in which the Lord's Name is recited and adored with the aid of the art of music. With his *maṭha* (monastery) at Kāñcīpuram, his works, long and short, with which he was ceaselessly engaged, and his bhajanas, he played a dominant part in molding the devotional spirit and musical activity of the Tamil country in the middle of the eighteenth century.

The author was first known, after taking *sannyāsa* vows, as Rāmacandrendra, but because of the special efforts made by him to collect together and present all the major and minor *Upaniṣads* with his own commentaries, he came to be called Upaniṣad Brahmendra, which became his more popular name.[2]

So far as his contribution to *advaita* is concerned, it suffices for the present to mention that although a follower of classical *advaita*, he made several innovations in minutiae and introduced a fresh orientation, classification and terminology in which he seems to have revelled. This last-mentioned aspect remains to be studied fully and presented to the world of scholars.

His *Upeya-nāma-viveka* ("Discernment of the Name as

the Goal") appertains to the other side of his personality and activity, the *bhakti* tradition based on the recital of the Lord's Name and its glory and efficacy, *nāma-māhātmya.*[3]

Nāmasiddhānta Leaders in the Kāverī Delta

It was, as we have seen, the two contemporaries, Śrīdhara Veṅkaṭeśa Āyyāvāl and Bodhendra, who gave a great stimulus to this devotional movement of repeating and chanting the Lord's Name, particularly in the Cola regions, at the end of the seventeenth and the beginning of the eighteenth centuries. The latter founded a *maṭha* at Govindapuram in Tāñjāvūr District with a succession of teachers of that *maṭha* to carry on the teachings of the Nāmasiddhānta school and propagate the *bhajana-paddhati.* Even now in numerous *bhajana-maṭhas* all over Tamil Nadu devotees venerate portraits of Śrīdhara Veṅkaṭeśa Āyyāvāl, Bodhendra and another saint, Sadgurusvāmī, and in all *bhajana* recitals which have been codified, songs and verses paying homage to these pioneer gurus of this school are sung at the outset.

The school of thought referred to as *Nāmasiddhānta*, according to which the repetition or singing of the Lord's Name, *nāmajapa* or *nāma-kīrtana*, is the easiest and most efficacious path for liberation in the present age, has a great bearing on the art of South Indian music. The greatest South Indian music composer, Tyāgarāja (A.D. 1767-1847), was a follower of this tradition and it is believed that he recited the Rāma-*nāma* nine hundred and sixty million times as enjoined by the scriptures and thereby attained his great creative powers. In the large corpus of his songs are some on the greatness of the Lord's Name, and the doctrines relating to it and its recitation. A proper understanding of the import of these musical compositions requires an adequate knowledge of the tenets of the *Nāmasiddhānta* school of thought. Tyāgarāja appeared in an area and at a time surcharged with the fervor of these religious movements, and for his inspiration and background he had the tradition handed down not only from Śrīdhara Veṅkaṭeśa and Bodhendra, but also from one who was an older contemporary of his and most active at that time in this devotional movement, namely Upaniṣad Brahmendra. Although according to a basic tenet of this school, no distinction is to be made between one kind of divine Name and another, e.g. Śiva, Hari or Rāma, the cultivation of any one Name as the favorite of the devotee is permitted, according to the doctrine of *iṣṭadevatā*; and in respect of the *iṣṭadevatā*, again Tyāgarāja and Upaniṣad Brahman had a special bond as co-worshippers of Rāma-*nāma*. Indeed there is a *śrīmukha* (letter) from our author to Tyāgarāja, asking the latter to visit Kāñcīpuram which has been preserved by the latter's pupils.

Having considered these aspects of Upaniṣad Brahmayogin's background we may now devote some attention to the ideas expounded by him and discuss them in relation to earlier literature and thought which might be taken to have some significance in the growth of the ideas on *nāma* and in our attempt to understand the views of our author on that subject.

The Nature of the Name and *Advaita* Oneness Via *Nāma*

The special feature of the *advaitin*'s adoration of the Lord's Name, whichever name it is, is the contemplation of that Name and the deity for whom it stands as being the Brahman which is identical with one's self, i.e. the *advaita-bhāvanā*, or contemplation of oneness, in which *bhakti* is cultivated.

This realization of oneness is declared as the main theme of the present work. The idea is first reinforced by the author with quotations from the *Rāmatāpinī Upaniṣad*. In the lower rungs of spiritual effort, the recitation of the *nāma* functions as a means, *upāya*, for attaining the Ultimate, the non-differentiated Bliss of Brahman; but the same *nāma*, as meaning the supreme Brahman itself, becomes the ultimate Reality gained, i.e. it is itself the end, the *upeya*. In the latter aspect, it is not the name of something, a deity, but it is itself the supreme Being, Knowledge and Effulgence.[4]

Rāma is no longer a *nāma* of a *rūpa* (form), but the *rūpa* itself. Quoting Śaṅkara's words, when he elucidates at the beginning of the commentary on the *Maṇḍukya Upaniṣad* the nature of OṂ as a symbol of Brahman, our author affirms the identity of the *abhidhāna* and the *abhidheya*.

The two-fold nature of *nāma* or *nāma-cit*, *nirviśeṣa* and *saviśeṣa*, the Absolute Being and the Name of a personal form of that Being, *upeya* and *upāya*, is then set forth in clear terms in verses 12-15 and the gloss thereon: *nāma* is the *upāya* when it is cultivated as the means to attain the possesser of the *nāma*, the *nāmin* or deity; although fundamentally, owing to their interdependence, the two do not differ, the notion of duality, in the earlier stages, makes the *nāma*, *upāya*. By constant cultivation on this plane, a stage is reached when in the final birth or the last embodied state, the soul knows the *nāma* as none else than the Supreme Being itself.

The *nāma*, in its *upāya* stage is of four forms, each one higher and more refined and subtle than the previous. By contemplation of it in its *sthūlāṃśa*, the annihilation of sins caused by bad deeds is achieved; by contemplation of its *sūkṣmāṃśa* (subtle aspect), one is freed of the effects of the good deeds done; through its *bījāṃśa* (seed aspect), the four kinds of liberation, *sālokya* (residing in the same heaven or world), *sāmīpya* (being near to the deity), *sārūpya* (being assimilated to the deity) and *sāyujya* (being absorbed into the divine essence), are gained; as a result of the meditation of its *turīya*, fourth or transcendent aspect, union with the Brahman is attained. These four aspects of the *upāya-nāman* are further elucidated with reference to the specific ends gained from the cultivation of each and the four ascending grades of aspirants who are fit for each of these four aspects.

It is well known how in the *Maṇḍukya Upaniṣad* the Praṇava, Om, is set forth in its four phases: *sthūlabhug vaiśvānara* (the waking state conscious of external objects), *praviviktabhuk-taijasa* (the dream state conscious of internal objects), *ānandabhuk-prājña* (deep sleep state conscious of vast blissful peace) and the *advaita* (transcendent consciousness, unthinkable and indescribable), the fourth. Upaniṣad Brahman equates the four phases of *upāya-nāman* with these four phases, *Vaiśvānara*, etc. He also explains here the nature of the three *guṇas* – *sattva*, *rājas* and *tāmas* – in these four states and refers briefly, to the classification of the *guṇa*-complex and the nature and proportion of the admixture of these in each state, as worked out in the text called *Guṇatrayaviveka* ("Discernment of the Three Strands of Nature.")

Rules for Name Reciters

Incidentally, Upaniṣad Brahman points out that the *adhikārins*, those fit to cultivate this form of *nāma*, are the whole humanity, irrespective of *varṇa* or *asrāma*. *Nāma* is the universal redeemer from sin. In connection with the mention of sins which *nāma* is capable of destroying, the author refers to the ten sins likely to be committed by a *nāma*-reciter; these, referred to as *nāma-aparādha*-s, may be explained:

1. San-nindā	Reviling pious souls.
2. Śrīśa-īśa-bheda-dhiḥ	Making a distinction between one Name and another (Śiva and Viṣṇu).
3,4,5. Aśraddha śruti-śāstra-deśika-girām	Lack of faith in scriptures, in sacred writings and in the words of the teachers.

6.	Namni arthavadabhrāmah	Mistaking the greatness of Name.
7,8.	Nāma astīti niṣiddha niṣiddha-vṛitti-vihitai-yāgau	Taking cover under the greatness of the Name and doing prohibited things and failing to do prescribed things.
9.	Karmāntaraiḥ sāmyam	Taking the Name to be just on a par with other prescribed duties (helpful to mental purification)
10.	Asati vaibhavāntara-kathā, or Asati nāma-vaibava-kathā	

The tenth *nāma*-offense is taken up separately as it involves some discussion; in the *Upeya-nāma-viveka*, it is listed as the second offense, and has not been set forth above. It is given as *asati vaibhavāntara-kathā*. In the version of this same verse quoted by Bodhendra in his *Nāmāmṛita-rasāyana*, a better reading is found: *asati nāma-vaibhava-kathā*. That this offense, whatever the reading of the verse here, means expatiating upon the glory of the Name before a wicked person or an unbeliever (*asat*) is clear from the description of these *nāma-aparādha*-s in the *Padma Purāṇa*, quoted by Bodhendra; there this offense is set forth as trying to impart the Name to the faithless, to the indifferent and the heedless.[5]

Significance of Rāma's Name

The next section is devoted to the special importance and glory of the Name of Rāma. Although all Names are equal, Rāma's name has a special status as the *tāraka* or redeemer par excellence; and on this Upaniṣad Brahman quotes the *Rāmatāpinī-* and the *Rāma-rahasya Upaniṣads* (verses 26 ff.). The word "Rāma" really means Brahman: "By the name Rāma the sole undivided supreme reality is indicated."[6]

This speciality of Rāma-*nāma* is sought to be brought out by a traditionally handed down explanation that RĀ-MA embodies the vital syllables of the eight-syllabled (*aṣṭākṣara*) Nārāyaṇa-mantra and the five-syllabled (*pañcākṣara*) Śiva-mantra.In the former, *om namo nārāyaṇāya*, the fifth syllable *rā* is the life, for if we take out that syllable, the mantra would become *nāyanāya*, meaning "not for salvation." Similarly, if we take out the syllable *ma* from the *Śivapañcākṣari*, that mantra becomes *na śivāya*, "not for good." Thus *RĀMA* stands really for both the Nārāyaṇa-mantra and the Śiva-mantra of which it is the vital essence (verses 28 ff.).

When and how many times Rāma-*nāma* is to be recited is the next question dealt with, and the author quotes here his text titled *Rāmataraṅgacandrikā*. On this and the efficacy of Rāma-*nāma*, the author quotes *Śruti* and *Smṛiti*, the *Rāmottaratāpinī Upaniṣad* and the *Bhagavad Gītā*; on the requisite qualities of the devotees of God, the *Bhāgavata Purāṇa* is quoted, and on the need for faith in the Lord, the *Bhagavad Gītā* again.

Up to this point, Upaniṣad Brahman has dealt with the first stage of adoring Rāma-*nāma*, contemplating Rāma as *Vaiśvānara* or *Vairāja*, in the *sthūlāmśa* (objectified portion) of the *nāma*. He now proceeds to explain how, after success in the first plane, the devotee proceeds to the next higher stage of *nāma* in the *sūkṣmāṃśa* (verses 58 ff.). In this phase, the *nāma* represents *Hiraṇyagarbha* consciousness; it comprehends the subtle *liṅga-sarīra* (the subtle body accompanying the soul in its transmigrations enduring from one life to the next). The aspirant reaches then the third rung of the ladder when he concentrates on the further subtle aspect, *bījāṃśa* of the *nāma* (verses 63 ff.). In this phase, the *nāma-cit* that is adored shines just in the form of the one seed, the cause of everything, *bījamātra*. The last realm is then reached where it is the one impartite consciousness, *pratyag-brahmaikya*, the ultimate meaning of the Name, the *nāmārtha*. In this connection, the very word RĀ-MA is given the esoteric explanation that its two syllables stand respectively for the two words of the *mahāvākya*, Tat (That, the transcendent) and *tvam* (thou, the individual soul) (verse 68). By their primary and secondary meanings (*vācya* and *lakṣya*), the syllable *rā* signifies respectively the God-consciousness (primary) and pure Existence Consciousness and Bliss (secondary); similarly, the syllable *ma* means the consciousness in the form of the embodied being (*jīva*, primary) and the consciousness of the inner soul (*pratyak*, secondary) (verse 69). It is the identification of the two in their secondary meanings that gives the unity of Tat and tvam. All this is based on the statement in the *Rāmarahasya Upaniṣad* (XII.14). With this understanding, one should contemplate nāman in its fourth, transcendent aspect, *turīyāṃśa* (verses 73 ff.). The sovereign glory of Rāma-*nāma* must be cherished in *abheda-bhāvanā*, in a non-dualistic contemplation, and this should be done till one firmly establishes oneself as the substratum and onlooker of everything.[7]

According to the stage of spiritual evolution one reached, one may even go straight to the final target and in one's desire for immediate release, *sadyo-mukti*, start cultivating the *upeya-nāma* of the final phase.[8]

Tracing Traditional Precedents for Teachings About the Name

Some ideas available in the earlier writings may now be considered for the purpose of tracing possible connections between them and the special ideas expounded in the *Upeyanāmaviveka* by Upaniṣad Brahman.

The *nāma*-reciters invoke as their Vedic authority the

passage found in Ṛg Veda, I. 156. 3: (*āsya jānanto nāma cid viviktana* . . .) ("Him have you satisfied, singers, as well as ye know, primeval germ of Order from his birth. Ye, knowing even his name, have told it forth; may we, Viṣṇu, enjoy the grace of the Mighty One."[9] There are indeed some hymns in the Ṛg Veda referring to *nāma* (e.g. Ṛg Veda I.164.46: "To what is one the poets give many a name.") but there is no indication of any special stress laid on the superiority of *nāma*-recital.

The *mīmāṃsā* philosophy of ritual developed the doctrine that when deities were invoked in sacrifices and other rites, it was the name of the deity, i.e. the word, *śabda*, which mattered and there was no other form of the deities behind those names (Jaimini IX. l. 4. 6-10). In this emphasis in *mīmāṃsā* on the Name, we may see an early forerunner of our present theme of *nāma-māhātmya*, praise of the name, but the point of view from which the emphasis is laid by Jaimini is different, as it is a corollary there of the primary importance of *karman*, efficacious ritual acts.

It would be more legitimate for us to look to the concept of *praṇava*, the syllable OM, and the ideas associated with its cultivation as a practice of chanting, for a precursor of the views of the later *Nāmasiddhāntins*. The *Maṇḍukya Upaniṣad*, from Śaṅkara's commentary on which our author makes a quotation in the present work, may be especially mentioned in this connection. Although Śaṅkara says more than once, in strict accordance with his school of thought, that Oṃkāra is the only means of knowing the *ātman*,[10] he states in the same context that OM which is the *abhidhāna* (name, appellation, title) of Brahman is identical with Brahman, its *abhidheya* (*abhidhānābhidheyayor ekatve*, etc.), an observation of which Upaniṣad Brahman takes hold.

In his commentary on *Kaṭha Upaniṣad* (I. 2. I 6), Śaṅkara

calls OM the symbol (*pratīka*) of Brahman. In his *Brahmā Sūtra* commentary (I. 3. 10) he states clearly that the *praṇava* is the means of attaining Brahman and the *śruti* texts speaking of it as being everything are to be taken only in a laudatory sense.[11]

Śaṅkara's *Bhagavad Gītā Bhasya*, VIII. 13, commenting on the words of the *Bhagavad Gītā, om iṭi ekākṣaraṃ brahma*, gives expression to the same standard *advaitic* tenet of *praṇava* being the *abhidhāna* or name of Brahman.[12] In the comments on the first name, Viśva, in the *Viṣṇu sahasranāma* commentary ascribed to him, Śaṅkara equates Viśva with OM and quoting several Upaniṣadic texts, as also the *Maṇḍukyakārikās*, observes again in the following words the non-difference of Brahman and Oṃkāra, for essentially the Name and its meaning are not different.[13]

The *Viṣṇu sahasranāma* commentary by Śaṅkara, particularly its introductory portion, occupies an important place among the authoritative texts of the school of *Nāmasiddhānta*.

Maṇḍana, the elder contemporary of Śaṅkara, and a subscriber to the theory of *sphoṭa* (vibration), salutes the Supreme Being as *akṣara* in the opening verse of his *Brahmasiddhi* and, while explaining this in his gloss, says that the Supreme is so called because it is of the form of Śabda, i.e. Praṇava; although the suffix *-kāra* is added to OM (Om-kāra), it does not mean that it implies something else which is its meaning (*abhidheya*); as *-kāra* occurs with letters in expressions like *a-kāra* and refers to those letters themselves, Oṃkāra refers to *śabda*, primal sound, or *praṇava* being Brahman itself:

Maṇḍana does not countenance the view that the *śruti* texts speaking of *praṇava* refer to *pratīkopāsanā*, worship of the abstract Brahman in a symbol or support (*ālambana*) for contemplation, Praṇava being the Name or *abhidhāna* of

Brahman. Quoting profusely from the *Upaniṣads* on OM and from the *Ṛg Vedic sūktas* relating to Vāk, Mandana argues that the whole manifest universe is merged in *Vāk*, and as OM is the truth of all *Vāk*, *vāk-śakti* itself is *citi* or Knowledge. Therefore the *ākṣara* is itself the Brahman.

In the *Brahmā sūtras* (I.3.10-12, *akṣaradhikaraṇa*), the question is discussed whether *akṣara* as it occurs in some Upaniṣadic texts refers to *vāk*, *sphoṭa* and OM or to the imperishable Brahman; as *prasāsana* associated with *akṣara* could only be possible in the case of a sentient entity, *Vāk*, it is contended, is ruled out; but introducing the third sūtra of the *adhikaraṇa*, Appayya Dīkṣita says, in the *Nyāyarakṣamani*, that according to *śabdādvaitins*, *sphoṭa* is endowed with *caitanya*, sound has consciousness; and on this view, Brahman and *sphoṭa* (*akṣara*) are not different.

Maṇḍana's ideas form a more complete articulation of the *śabda* philosophy of Bhartṛihari, which has been repeatedly stated in the first book of his *Vākyapadīya*. But it has not been clearly shown as to how it leads to *mokṣa*. Bhartṛihari no doubt refers to it as the indestructible Brahman without beginning and end (*Vākyapadīya*, I. 1), the inner light, the great *ṛiṣabha* with which one attains oneness, *sāyujya* (*Vākyapadīya*, I. I.30 especially).[14]

In his own commentary on this, Bhartṛihari waxes eloquent and describes this inner *śabda* as *ātman* (Self), as *mahān vṛiṣabha* (great might), as *prabodha* (knowledge) and as *sarveśvara*, Lord of all. In the *āntaraślokas* in *Vākyapadīya*, I. 142, he identifies this inner light with the subtle imperishable sound, *sūkṣmā vāk.*[15] It is the immortal end of the entirety of Being.[16]

In the complex of thought referred to collectively as Kashmir Śaivism as it crystallized with all its facets in the hands of Abhinavagupta, the stage beyond *paśyanti* the fourth, *parā vāk*, was identified as the *hṛidaya* or heart of the Lord and with His *vimarśa* aspect, and the Lord was referred to as *vācya* (to be spoken) and His reflective *citi* as *vācaka* (speaking).[17]

All these ideas, as they came over to the post-Śaṅkara *advaitins*, were integrated in the framework of Advaita proper. The *Śabda Brahman* was accepted as the penultimate step to *Para Brahman* and the formulation of this adjustment is seen in clear terms in some of the minor Upaniṣads which mention two Brahmans, the *Śabda Brahman* and the *Para Brahman*, the former being a step to attain the latter.[18]

Whether as *praṇava* or as *nāda*, the *Śabda Brahman* was considered to be the final door or the Supreme means of Brahman-realization or as the philosophy of music would say, the easier path through delectation to the final Beatitude.

In the *Yoga sūtras* of Patañjali, *praṇava*, the mantra Om is the Name of Iśvara and the support of contemplation.

In the path of *bhakti*, in the *Purāṇas*, the contemplation of God through the repetition of a mantra embodying the holy Name, and through the repetition of the divine Name, was emphasized. The *Bhāgavata Purāṇa* made emphatic declarations on it, particularly in the Ajāmila and Prahlāda episodes and the statements in this *Purāṇa* became the basic texts on the doctrine of the efficacy of *kīrtana*, one of the nine kinds of *bhakti*. The entire further growth of the schools of devotion, laying increased emphasis on the Lord's Name and its recital and singing, stemmed from this, nourishing the twin movements of devotion and song. While the *Bhāgavata Purāṇa* extols the Name as most efficacious, it does not exalt it beyond its status as the Name of the Lord and as an instrument of invoking Him or establishing His thought in one's mind. "The articulation of a name of Lord Viṣṇu is the only thorough atonement for the sins of all classes of sinners . . . for thereby the Lord's own mind is directed towards the utterer . . . "[19]

Three of the minor *Upaniṣads* are particularly related to the school of thought we are considering, the *Kalisaṃtarana*, the *Rāmatāpinī* and the *Rāmarahasya Upaniṣads*. The *Rāmatāpinī* is especially relevant as it is intimately related to our text which deals with devotion to Rāma and the potency of His Name. In fact, our text follows the *Rāmatāpinī* in the identification of *praṇava* and Rāma and the elaboration of the four states, wakefulness, dream, deep sleep and "the fourth," which the *Rāmatāpinī* also gives by making the *Maṇḍukya* part of itself.

The explanation in our text as to how the Rāma-*nāma* is the Name or mantra par excellence, being made up of the vital syllables of the mantras of Nārāyana and Śiva is also found, in some manuscripts of the *Rāmarahasya Upaniṣad*.

But in none of these *Upaniṣads* devoted *nāma* or Rāma is there the mention of the idea of the Name itself being the ultimate thing or of the idea of the two phases of the Name as means and end, *upāya* and *upeya*, as stated in our text.

Bhakti, in the literature on it according to the different schools, has been spoken of in two forms: the means and the end, the *sādhana* and the *sādhya* or *para*, the former also called *gauṇa* and the latter *mukhya*. In the former aspect, through different further means, *bhakti* grows towards stabilizing itself; also, in this stage, it is practiced not for its own sake, but for some desired objective like relief from suffering and expectation of gain (compare the *Bhagavad Gītā*, VII. 16-19, where the Lord speaks of four kinds of persons who worship Him including the *ārtha* and *arthārthin*). In the latter form, love of God has become complete and constant, and an end in itself with nothing extraneous to seek. Also, like *bhakti*, the Lord Himself has been spoken of as the way and the goal, *upāya* and *upeya*.

In the great development of the doctrines of the path of Bhakti in the Caitanya school, Rūpa (c. 1495-1550) the great and prolific writer of the school, his brother Sanatana and nephew Jīva put forth some ideas on *nāma* to which attention may be drawn here. Rūpa and Jīva said that there is no difference between the Name and the Lord, the two being identical (*nāmanāminor abhedaḥ*). In his *Bhagavatsaṃdarbha*, Jīva observed that the Name itself was the essence of the Lord (*bhagavatsvarūpam eva nāma*). Just like the *avatāras* of the Lord, this *nāman* is a kind of *varṇa-avatāra.*[20]

In his work entitled *Nāmaṣṭaka*, Rūpa says (verse 6) that *nāman* has two forms, the *vācaka* and the *vācya*, the latter being the Lord Himself:

Sanātana, in his *Bṛihadbhāgavatāmṛita* describes the two phases of *nāma-kīrtana* as *sādhana* and *phala*, practice and result.[22]

Earlier, Gopāla Bhaṭṭa had declared the identity of *nāman* and *nāmin* in his *Haribhaktivilāsa.*

The Kāverī Delta *Nāmasiddhānta* Renewal

In the fresh upsurge of the movement of *nāma*-recital in the region of the Kāverī delta, at the end of the seventeenth and beginning of the eighteenth centuries, several works on nāman were written by Bodhendra, Śrīdhara Veṅkaṭeśa Āyyāvāl and others. Āyyāvāl wrote a poem of sixty verses on the efficacy of *nāma* called *Ākhyāṣaṣti*, but in none of these writings where the role of the Name of the Lord is exalted even above the Lord Himself, by reason of special emphasis, is there any description of the two phases of the Name or the *nāma* as *upāya* and *upeya.*

We have noted how Upaniṣad Brahman is given to adding new orientations and classifications in the existent body of thought in the school. The *Upeya-nāma-viveka*, his text on the Lord's Name is an example of this characteristic of

Upaniṣad Brahman. Apart from the *advaitic* background with which devotion cultivated through the recital of the Lord's Name is synthesized by holding the highest form of the latter as the contemplation of oneself as Rāma with the *bhāvanā "rāmo 'ham"* and the pressing into service of the doctrine of OM, the *praṇava* with which the Lord's Name is integrated, Upaniṣad Brahman introduces also the idea of the Name functioning at two levels, as means and as end. As we have seen, although not directly, the trend of several old ideas on *nāma*, on OM, on *Śabda Brahman*, on *bhakti*, and on the efficacy of the Lord's Name inspired Upaniṣad Brahman to the formation of the leading idea of the present text, the *nāman* as *upāya* and *upeya*. It is in the nature of things that what is, at the earlier stages of endeavour, the means becomes in the end the very substance of the thing or the very character of its being. Śaṅkara says in his commentary on the *Bhagavad Gītā* when dealing with the characteristics of the *sthitaprajña* (II. 55): and the *Bhāgavata Purāṇa* emphasizes, in its own eloquent manner, how even in the supreme state of self-realization, liberated souls for ever love God, serving Him and singing of Him, without any purpose (*ahaituka*), involuntarily – the the most natural form of their free activity in that state. It is in this state and in this form that *bhakti* and the recital or contemplation (*kīrtana*, *anusaṃdhāna* or *bhāvanā*) of the Lord's Name is the end, *upeya*. The Name itself which is identified with Brahman and one's own self, in this state, is endowed with consciousness, as the *śabda* is for the *Śabda-Brahmā-vādins*; Upaniṣad Brahman thus refers to *nāma* as *nāma-cit*, name-consciousness.

Notes

[1]The *Upeya-nāma-viveka* was first edited and published with a more complete version of this introduction by V. Raghavan in *The Adyar Library Bulletin*, vol. XXIX, parts 1-4, 1967. For the sake of easier reading I have placed some parts of the text in footnotes and omitted

other parts because of considerations of space. I have also added sub-headings.

[2] These commentaries of his on the *Upaniṣads*, and his gloss on the *Bhagavad Gītā*, as also his short treatise on the *Brahmā sūtras* and some other minor Vedāntic tracts have been published by the Adyar Library, as independent works or as reprints from *The Adyar Library Bulletin*.

[3] The *Nāmārtha-viveka* with the gloss *Upeya-nāma-viveka* of Upaniṣad Brahmendra falls in line with works like the *Bhagavannāma-kaumudi* of Lakṣmīdhara, the *Bhagavannāma-māhātmya* of Puruṣottāma, the *Bhagavannāma-mahātmya* of Raghunāthendra Yati and the *Bhagavannāma-darpaṇa* and the *Bhagavannāma-vaibhava* of Muralīdharadāsa written in the North; and in the South, the *Bhagavannāma-bhūṣana* of Śrīdhara Veṅkaṭeśa Āyyāvāl, the *Nāmāmṛitarṇava*, the *Nāmāmṛita-rasayana*, the *Nāmāmṛita-sūryodaya* and the *Nāmāmṛita-rasodaya* of Bodhendra Yati, the *Nāmātaraṅga* in the *Puruṣārtha-ratnākara* of Bālakrishnānanda, and the *Bhagavannāma-cintāmani* of Veṅkaṭakrishna.

[4]tasyā videhamukteh svarūpatah sarvatra yan maho rājamānam,
tadeva śrīrāma śabdeneritam /
śrī rāma eva nāma syāt, nābhidhānam, upeyatah /
upeyarūpavasthānam nāmārtha iti viśrutam //

[5]aśraddadhāne vimukha 'py aśriṇvati yaś copadeśah.

[6]iti rāmaśabdena pratyag-abhinnaṃ brahma ucyate.

[7]Śrīrāmabhakti sāmrājyam svābhedenaiva bhāvayet /
yāvatsamastādhiṣṭhānasākṣysmīti dṛidhā matiḥ //
"rāmo'hamahameva rāmaḥ" iti bhāvayet
(verse 77 f. and the commentary thereon)

[8]vikalebarakaivalyopeyanāmasvarūpatah /
paramādvaitarūpena śisyase nātra samśayaḥ //
he vidvan
commentary: idānīm te yadi sadyomukti prāpakopeyanāma brahmamātrāvaśeṣadhiḥ bhavet tadā (verse 83

[9]Translated by Ralph T.H. Griffiths, *Hymns of the Ṛg Veda* (Delhi: Motilal Banarsidass, 1986 reprint), p. 104. [Editor's note: I have given another translation of this passage earlier in this book.]

[10]e.g. katham punar oṃkāranirṇaya ātmatattva-pratipatty-upāyatvaṃ pratipadyata iti –introductory *bhāsya*.)

[11]Editor's Note: This paragraph has been incorporated into the text from the footnotes of the original.

yadapi "oṃkāra evedam sarvam" iti, tadapi brahmpratipattisādhanatvat stutyartham draṣṭavyam /

[12]brahmaṇo abhidhānabhūtam omkāram vyāharan uccārayan tadarthabhūtam mām īśvaram, etc. Madhusūdana Sarasvatī clarifies further the correct *advaitic* stand that Om is the *vācaka* or symbol (*pratīka*) of Brahman (brahmavacākatvāt pratimāvad brahmapratīkatvād vā).

[13]vācyavācakayor atyantabhedābhāvād viśvam ity oṃkāra eva brahmety arthaḥ.

[14]api prayakturātmānam śabdamantaravasthitam
prāhurmahāntamṛiṣabham yena sāyujyamiṣyate

[15]svarūpajyotirevāntaḥ sūkṣmā vāganapāyinī

[16]puruṣe ṣoḍaśakale tāmāhuramṛitam kalām

[17]See *Paryantapantapañcāśikā* of Abhinavagupta, edited by V. Raghavan, *Annals of Oriental Research*, Univ. of Madras, vol. 8, 1950.

[18]dve brahmaṇī veditavye śabdabrahma param ca yet /
śabdabrahmaṇi niṣṇātaḥ param brahmādhigacchati // Maitrāyaṇī VI.22.

See also *Tripurātāpanī*, v. 17; *Brahmabindu*, 17.

[19]See especially VI.2.10 in *Ajāmilopākhyāna*:
nāmavyāharaṇam viṣṇoryataṣṭadviṣayā matiḥ /

[20]avatārāntaravat parameśvarasyo varṇarūpeṇa avatāro 'yam.

[21]vācyam vācakamityudeti bhavato nāma svarūpadvayam

[22]Nāmasaṇkīrtanam proktam kṛiṣṇasya premasampadi
baliṣṭham sādhanam, śreṣṭham paramākarṣamantravat //
tadeva manyate bhakteḥ phalam tadrasikairjanaiḥ
bhagavatpremasampattau sadaivāvyabhicārataḥ //

Creative Exponents of the Name, and Related Studies

Tyāgarāja: The Singer-Saint[1]

In several respects, the genius of Karṇāṭaka or South Indian classical music may be said to touch its high water-mark in Tyāgarāja. The infinite play of imagination and originality is evident in him more than in other composers. In fashioning a variety of expressive forms in well-known melodies or in newly invented melodies, in the perfecting of the form of composition called *kṛiti* and enriching it with inventive elements, in the poetry and philosophy of the text of the songs,–in all these, he stands out as the foremost tone-poet and as the single complete example of the genius of Karṇāṭaka music at its best and highest.

It is no wonder that in the last half a century and more, his songs have come to dominate the concerts of Karṇāṭaka music. Even among the three great composers–the celebrated "trinity"–himself, Muttusvāmī Dīkṣitar and Śyāma Śāstri whose compositions threw into the background the earlier works, Tyāgarāja enjoys a special popularity with musicians and lovers of music alike. His name, sometimes mentioned only as "Āyyārvāl" or "Svāmīgal," evokes a special sense of veneration among the votaries, active as well as passive, of the art. His anniversary is an annual festival wherever, in India or now in foreign countries too, there are South Indians.

Tyāgarāja appeared in a period which was thronged with giants in the arts, performers, theorists, composers, makers of dance-music, dance-drama and authors of compositions of grammatical and scientific value (*lakṣanagītas*, *thayas*, *varṇas*).

Girirājakavi, perhaps his maternal grandfather, was a poet and composer. His guru was one of the great masters of the time, Śoṇṭhi Veṅkaṭarāmanayya, son of Śonthi Subbayya. With all the roads for the artists leading at that time to Tāñjāvūr, Karṇāṭaka music was getting enriched from all sides and shaping itself through a ferment of theory and the formulation of its grammar and crystallization of the forms of its creative expression. To have appeared amidst this throng of talent and to have outshone the others with his creations is indeed the greatest testimony to his genius.

Tyāgarāja was born in 1767 at Tiruvārūr in Tāñjāvūr district of Tamil Nadu. Tiruvārūr is not only a renowned place in the religious history from the times of the *nāyanār* saints but was also the religious headquarters, in a manner of speaking, for the Mahrātta rulers of Tāñjāvūr. Tiruvārūr was also famous for the arts of music and dance centering round the great temple of Tyāgarāja, the dancing Śiva deity at this place. Scholars and artists attached to the Telugu and Mahrātta courts of Tāñjāvūr were living at Tiruvārūr. A leading Telugu writer and composer among them was Girirājakavi and it is to his daughter that Tyāgarāja was born. It was after the presiding deity at Tiruvārūr that the child was named Tyāgarāja.

Tyāgarāja's family, on the side of his father, Rāma Brahmam, was living in Tiruvaiyāru or Pañcanada, a sacred place on the Kāverī river, about 11 kilometers from Tāñjāvūr, the seat of the ruling Mahrātta dynasty. Tyāgarāja came of a Telugu Vaidika Muriginādu family named Kākarla, and his ancestors must have come from the Telugu area and settled here during the Nāyak rule of Tāñjāvūr. The name Tiruvaiyāru or Pañcanada refers to "five rivers" which flow through and near this place, a center of pilgrimage and festivals. Of the holy and beautiful Kāverī river flowing here, Tyāgarāja draws a fine picture in two of his songs, *Muripemu* and *Sarivedalina.*

Tyāgarāja loved the Chola country as he says in the first of the two songs referred to above: "The Chola-sima, most beautiful land in this world."

Tyāgarāja's Life

Details of Tyāgarāja's life are known only from tradition, some of which could be verified from references in his songs, e.g., the names of his family and father which he mentions. Tyāgarāja is said to have married twice, the first wife having died early without any issue. To the second wife was born a daughter named Sītālakṣmī, and a son named Tyāgarāja was born to her. When this grandson died issueless, the main line of Tyāgarāja ended.

Tradition speaks of an elder brother of Tyāgarāja named Japyeśa. To glorify Tyāgarāja and provide background for some songs of the composer, Japyeśa is made into a villain, who ill-treated Tyāgarāja, disapproved of Tyāgarāja's devotional activities, pressed him to seek royal patronage, threw into the Kāverī river the Rāma image worshipped by him, partitioned the ancestral house and so on.

There must be some basis for these stories to grow; actually in two of his songs, Tyāgarāja speaks of his elder brother: in the piece *Anyāyamu sēyakurā*, he prays to God to free him from the troubles given by his elder brother and in *Nadupai* he refers to accusations against himself as being responsible for the partition of the ancestral house to enable him to celebrate his festivals for Rāma. In two other pieces (*Nāyeḍa vañcana* and *Eṭula gāpāḍutuvō*), Tyāgarāja mentions confrontations with his relatives (*dāyāḍis*).

Tyāgarāja had to face many detractors even outside his family. The single largest group of his songs–which are high-strung on the emotional side–represents what he sang in anguish of this hostile atmosphere in which he had to live. In the song *Prārabdhamiṭṭunḍagā*, he bemoans his fate: "Those whom I help turn against me; those whom I treat charitably level baseless charges against me." The detractors around him reviled his devotional activities as well as his music compositions. In a number of songs, he prays to Rāma to protect him from these revilers; in *Sarivārilōna*, he asks Rāma: "Have I not been sufficiently ridiculed among my compeers? . . . Is it fair on your part to be passive while seeing me agonize in the midst of these wild prattlers?" All these trials, like fire, made the gold of his faith in Rāma glow brighter and drew from him more and more masterpieces of moving music.

Tyāgarāja had vowed to lead the life of voluntary poverty. According to the tradition of the *bhāgavatas*, he adopted for his livelihood *uñchavṛitti*, going out every day singing the Lord's songs and receiving handfuls of rice from householders who might feel like giving. He sang of the Lord alone and avoided *nara-stuti*, the praising of mere man for obtaining rewards, which was prohibited according to the practice of the devotees of the Lord.

Tyāgarāja and Devotion to the Name

In the practice of devotion, Tyāgarāja followed the tradition of reciting Rāma's saving name, *tāraka nāma*, for the prescribed number of times. Rāma-worship came down in his family as mentioned by him in several songs and was strengthened by contacts with the active promoters of that path at that time like Upaniṣad Brahmendra of Kāñcī who was a friend of Tyāgarāja's father and the invitation from whom is preserved in the Tyāgarāja-manuscripts handed down in the Walājapet School of Tyāgarāja's pupils. Tyāgarāja himself mentions one Rāmakrishnānanda, a *sannyāsin* of his times, as his guru. Tyāgarāja is said to have successfully completed the repetition of Rāma-*nāma* 960 million times as prescribed, and succeeded in gaining the vision of Rāma.

Tyāgarāja's songs embody many doctrinal ideas of this

school of reciting the divine Name (*Nāmasiddhānta*) and of the larger path of devotion, *bhakti-mārga*, songs which appear to have been specially composed for use in religious-musical discourses in *bhajanas*, *kīrtanas* or *harikathās*. Not only on the efficacy of the Lord's Name but also on how best to recite it, Tyāgarāja speaks in his songs. In the well-known song in *Pūrṇacandrika*, *Telisi Rāma*, Tyāgarāja emphasizes that the recitation of Rāma's Name is no mechanical muttering but should be based on a full realization of the significance that Rāma is the Supreme Being; and in another equally well-known song, *Rāma niyeda prema*, he stresses that the uttering of Rāma-*nāma* should be accompanied by real love for Rāma.

The *iṣṭa-devata* or favorite form of God whom Tyāgarāja sought through the *Name* and whose glory he celebrated most in his songs is Rāma. He repeatedly declared that Rāma was his favorite deity (*Iṣṭadaivamu nive*–in a very appealing song – *Śyāma sundarāṅga*); "Rāma alone is my God" (*Rāma eva daivatam . . . me*); "Who is there to equal you, O Rāma" (*Rāma nī samanam evaru*); "Rāma alone is God" (*Vāḍēra Daivamu*); and so on. This Rāma is not only the avatāra endowed with infinite excellences sung of by Vālmīki. Tyāgarāja has gone over, in his songs, the whole epic and the episodes and exploits of Rāma described there; but behind all this there is the faith that Rāma is the Supreme God beyond the Trinity (see his song–*Manasā śrī Rāmachandruni*), indeed the Para Brahman itself. In his well-known song *Telisi Rāma*, Tyāgarāja declares that the word "Rāma" is a name of *Para Brahman*, recalling the well known elucidation "*Rāma-padena asau param Brahmā abhidhiyate.*" As a minstrel of Rāma, by the quality and quantity of his songs on Rāma, Tyāgarāja takes his place in the galaxy of the great Rāma-poets of India, who followed in the wake of Vālmīki. Tyāgarāja came of a *smārta* family of *advaitin* tradition and according to the universalistic outlook of this tradition, he sang of other deities too, Śiva, Devī, and others. In his song *Itara daivamula* he says that his mind is passionately in love with Rāma without harbouring any prejudice towards other deities and faiths. He believed in a *bhakti* which had its consummation in the undifferentiated union with Godhead, (*So'ham* – "I am Him"), as he says in his song *Intakanna.*

In a large number of songs Tyāgarāja expatiates on the character of true devotion and of a true devotee, on the futility of observing mere rites and rituals and other formalities and accessories like baths in sacred waters, long *pūjās*, etc., on the necessity for ethical and moral qualities rather than for conformity to mere orthodox habits, etc. These songs, in which Tyāgarāja is eloquent follow the line of the exhortations of all the earlier saint-singers. In the song *Dhyāname*, for example, he points out that the best bath in Gaṅgā is the contemplation of the Lord. He refers in *Naḍaci naḍaci* and *Balamu kulamu* to pretenders who bathe, fast, close their eyes, and roll the rosary. The picture of a true devotee is given in the song *Bhaktuni cāritramu*:

> O Mind! Listen to the conduct of a devotee of Sri Rāma! The devotee who, without attachment to sense-pleasures, seeks Him, becomes a *jīvanmukta* and enjoys supreme bliss. Such a devotee should not boast of his having done *japa* and *tapas*; he should not behave or speak like a hypocrite; should not be weak, fickle-minded and lost in attachments; should not regard material prosperity as real; should never make distinction between Śiva and Mādhava; should make no profession out of his qualifications; should not allow the sway of *rājas* (passion) and *tāmas* (ignorance and inertia); should not desist from yogic practice and should never forget Śrī Rāma.

Similarly real *pūjā* is that which is done, not with a lot of external accessories but with a complete inner dedication, an internal worship, a *bhavapūjā*. He sings in *Paripālaya*:

> My body is your favourite abode (*pūjā-gṛiha*); my steadfast mind, your golden throne (cf. also his *Manasu nilpa*); my meditation of your beautiful feet is the Ganga-water; my attachment to you is your beautiful dress; my praise of your glory, your sandal-fragrance; my remembrance and recital of your Name, the full-blown lotus for you; the fruits of all my past misdeeds is the incense to be burnt before you; my devotion to your feet is the all-day lamp to you; the very fruit of this kind of superior worship that I do is the food-offering to you; the lasting bliss that I derive is the pan (*tambula*) for you; my seeing you (*darśana*) is the waving of light before you.

Mere scholarship is of no use he says in *Kṣīṇamai*, and faith in astrology leads one nowhere he says in *Graha-balamēmi*. Real *bhakti* alone saves and nothing else can be a substitute for it. Gēnuine devotion is the great royal road (*Cakkani rājamārga*). In many of these songs in which he exposes the prevailing shams and hypocrisies and emphasizes the essential things as against the accessories, Tyāgarāja's literary gifts, imagination, ability to develop an idea and stinging similes and gift for wit and satire come out prominently.

Songs on the Sacredness of Music

Tyāgarāja is also remarkable, and singularly so, for a good number of songs in which he has expatiated on *nadopāsana*, on the art of music as an aid to devotion and contemplation, on God being the embodiment of *nāda*, subtle sacred vibration, and the absorption in the joy of melody as itself constituting spiritual liberation, *mokṣa*. In the exhortations in his songs, he holds up this high spiritual ideal for the musicians and condemns music devoid of devotion. For example, *Saṅgītajñānamu*, *Nādatanum*, *Gītārthamu*, *Nādopāsanacē*, *Nādalōluḍai*, *Mokṣamugaladā*; *Svara-rāga* are songs on these topics. In *Nādatanum*, he describes Śiva as the embodiment of Nāda (sacred sound), as constituting the essence of Sāmaveda and as delighting in the seven *svaras* (musical notes) born of His own five faces. In *Nādasudhārasambilanu*, he similarly portrays Rāma as the ambrosial *rasa*, the "essential juice" of *nāda* itself taken human form. "Devotion associated with the nectar of *svara* and *rāga* is verily paradise and salvation," he declares in his well-known song *Svara-rāgasudhārasa*. The burden of another well-known song, in *Dhanyāsi rāga*, is "Knowledge of music without *bhakti* will not lead to salvation." A third well-known piece, *Mokṣamugaladā*, shows the idea that Realization and Release (*sakṣatkara* and *mokṣa*) are not possible for those who are devoid of knowledge of music coupled with true devotion to the Lord; and the seven notes of music are manifested out of the *nāda* of the mystic syllable OM. "The joy of music is itself the bliss of Brahman that *vedānta* speaks of," declares Tyāgarāja in three songs: "O Mind! drink and delight in the immortal elixir of melody and attain the fruit of *yāga*, *yoga*, *tyāga* and *bhoga*; those who understand that *Nāda*, *Oṃkāra* and *svara* are nothing but Śiva are verily Jivanmuktas, those who have realized liberation here itself." (*Rāgasudhārasa*). "O Mind! He who delights in *nāda* attains the bliss of Brahman." (*Nādaloluḍai*). "The body that does not float on the ocean of the ineffable bliss of Brahman called music is a burden to the earth." (*Ānandasāgara*).

Tyāgarāja and Traditions of the Name

Mention of Vālmīki having been a hunter, of Rāma's Name being imparted to Śiva to all persons dying in Varanāsi, of Rāma's greatness being told by Śiva to Pārvatī, of the Name Rāma meaning Supreme Brahman, of Hānumān under the Parijata tree treading *Purāṇa*, these and several other details of this kind show that the whole literature of the Rāma tradition from the *Rāma tāpinī Upaniṣad* to different *Purāṇa* and *Samhita* texts and the different *Rāmāyaṇa*s in Sanskrit, as well as the version of Tulasidās whom he mentions and salutes, were quite familiar to Tyāgarāja. Similarly he must have read the *Bhāgavata Purāṇa*, the Bible of the *bhakti-mārga*. A manuscript of the Telugu *Bhāgavata* of Poṭana is among the Tyāgarāja manuscripts preserved by the Walājapet school. Upaniṣad Brahmendra's writings on the Lord's Name and its recitation, the idea that the Name "Rāma" is the vital essence of the five-lettered Śiva-mantra and the eight-syllabled Nārāyana-mantra – mentioned in his song *Evarani* – is explained in detail by Upaniṣad Brahmendra in his *Upeyanāmaviveka.* Composers who came before Tyāgarāja who sang on Rāma and doctrines of *bhakti* and *nāma* and on music as a *sādhana* – Annamācārya, Purandaradāsa, Rāmadāsa–were also part of the heritage reflected in Tyāgarāja's songs.[2] Rāmadāsa of Bhadrācalam with his Rāma-devotion and suffering stood in a special relation to Tyāgarāja and is mentioned by name by Tyāgarāja in his *kīrtanas.*

Festival Songs

As already observed, Tyāgarāja belonged to the *Bhajana-sampradāya*, the codified devotional song program tradition, which was at its height in the Kāverī delta at that time. In the *bhajas* conducted by groups at homes or in special halls, *bhajana maṭhas*, they celebrated special festivals, the marriage of Rāma and Sītā or Krishna and Rukminī and held congregational singing of devotional songs, for all of which a pattern, *paddhati*, had evolved, starting with the announcement of the Lord's arrival (*Heccharikagā*), his taking the seat in the court hall (*Kolu*), the marriage which includes Gaurī *Kalyānam* or the actual marriage, *Nalaṅgu* or the divine couple in play, *Hārati* or waving of light, *Lali* or enjoying the swing; laying the Lord to bed (*Pavvalimpu*) and the waking Him up next morning (*Suprabhatam* song). For use in the *pūjā* of the Deity, as part of such celebrations, there were songs for the offering of the different *upacāras* to the Deity. A set of songs was composed by Tyāgarāja for use in such congregations and festivals. These songs, called *Utsava-sampradāya-kīrtanas* numbering about twenty-seven, are simpler in setting but rich in ideas and literary quality. Of the same type and for similar congregational singing by devotees, Tyāgarāja composed many other songs, about seventy-eight in number, which go by the name *Divya-nāma-samkīrtanas*. Many songs from these two groups figure now in concerts where musicians render them in the closing part of their performances.

Tyāgarāja's Contributions

Tyāgarāja's chief contribution to Karṇāṭaka music is the perfection of the composition form called *kṛiti* or *kīrtana* which was evolving at this time out of the older *prabandha* and the immediate predecessor *pada* and which comprised in itself all the aspects of music and displaced earlier and more ponderous media of rendering or preserving the *ragas* in unbound or bound forms. In one of his *kṛitis*, he describes what a *kṛiti* should be like in form and content. In this song *Sogasugā* he says that the *kṛiti* should be couched in words conveying the true spirit of the *Upaniṣads*, should have correctness of the musical notes of the *rāgas* in which they are set, should be marked by beauties of alliterations and successive increases and decreases of notes or syllables, should be conducive to the cultivation of true devotion and dispassion and as literary expression, they should possess grace and simplicity and embody all the nine *rasas* or esthetic moods. He had distinguished contemporaries specializing in the same line – Muttusvāmī Dīkṣitar and Śyāma Śāstri, but he excelled them by the all-round excellence of his creations.

The most remarkable feature of Tyāgarāja's compositions is the "variations" or *saṅgatis* which they embody in the very opening of the *pallavi*. These *saṅgatis* synthesize, one could say, the bound and unbound forms by providing for improvization within the framework of a fixed tune and setting. This Tyāgarāja took no doubt from *pallavi*-singing on the one hand and the improvizations in dance-music where variations are done for *abhinaya* and the bringing out of different phases of the basic feeling. By grafting it on to his *kṛitis*, Tyāgarāja gave scope for the singer to bring out not only the total phases of the *rāga* of the song but also the emotional phases of the meaning of the prominent idea of the text of the song as given in the *pallavi*. Some well-known and oft-sung masterpieces of his, which open with this cascade of *saṅgatis* may be recalled: *Sakkani rāja mārga*, *Rāma nī samana*, *O Raṅgasayi*, *Nā jīvadhara*. But the *saṅgatis* form a part of all his songs, so much so that they have come to stay as part of Karṇāṭaka music itself and even the *kṛitis* of other masters like Dīkṣitar which belong to a different style and aesthetics are rendered by musicians in the same *saṅgati*-ized" style. Although Tyāgarāja has some songs in the slow tempo, the medium one is his chief characteristic tempo. The medium tempo (*madhyama*) is also an adjunct of this *saṅgati*-style and that tempo has also become the prevailing one for Karṇāṭaka singing and even Dīkṣitar's music which is in the *vainika* style in slow tempo, with *gamakas* as its life, is also spurred up to the middle and fast tempo. In fact, all *kṛiti*-composition of the post-Tyāgarāja composers, like Pattanam Subrahmanya Iyer, is after Tyāgarāja's model. Thus, as is the case of Kalidāsa, we may say of Tyāgarāja too: "All that was before him was thrown into the background; all that came after has been on his model."

In keeping with his *advaitin* tradition and following several of his predecessors who illumined, in his part of the country, the three paths of *advaitic jñāna*, *bhakti* and music – Nārāyaṇa Tīrtha, Sadāśiva Brahmendra, his elder contemporary Upaniṣad Brahmendra and his own teacher Rāmakrishnānanda, Tyāgarāja took to *sannyāsa* vows towards the end of his life. In two of his songs (*Giripai* and *Paritāpamu*), he refers to Rāma's promise to him to bestow *mokṣa* on him. His *sannyāsa* is certainly one of the elements that added to the halo of his personality and responsible for the annual observance of the day of his *samādhi*. Tyāgarāja attained *samādhi* on January 6, 1847 (*Puṣya bahula pañcami*). At his *samādhi* in Tiruvaiyāru where a shrine has been built by his devotees, his anniversary is a sacred day for all musicians who make their pilgrimage every year to this place and pay their homage to the master by singing his songs there. In fact, there are several ardent followers of his, who observe his day, wherever they are, every month on this fifth day of the dark fortnight (*Bahula pañcami*) on which he passed away, assemble and sing his songs before his portrait.

The Enduring Quality of His Work

Through his direct disciples, three schools, traditions or styles of rendering his *kṛitis* became established, the Umayālpuram school which is the best and most widely represented, the Tillaisthānam school and the Walājapet school. The last-mentioned played a part on the eve and the turn of the present century in bringing to light Tyāgarāja's compositions and leading to their increasing vogue in the concerts. But for the emergence of Tyāgarāja, and along with him, of his two contemporaries, Muttusvāmī Dīkṣitar and Śyāma Śāstri, Karṇāṭaka musical heritage might not have been consolidated in the recent past and handed down to us. Taking their stand on the tradition, these men of genius saw into the future, and therefore, although two centuries have rolled by since Tyāgarāja appeared he continues to be, to this day, the mainstay of Karṇāṭaka music. The *Dūra-deśa*, distant parts of the country, where, according to his own song (*Daśarathi*), his music had been made famous, is today a continuously expanding world.

How can I ever repay you, O Rāma,
You have made me known in faroff lands!

Notes

[1] This essay first appeared in *Composers*, Cultural Leaders of India Series, edited by V. Raghavan, Publications Division, Government of India, New Delhi, 1979, pp. 20-39. I have omitted some passages because of considerations of space.

[2] There are three complete songs of Annamācarya singing the glory of the Lord's name, *Sakalasaṁgrahamu*, *Tatigoniyemaraka* and *Japiyiñcare sarvajanula yi nāmamu*, the last one of Rāma-*nāma* itself. These may be compared with the several *kṛitis* of Tyāgarāja on *nāma*. In the first Annamācārya describes Hari-*nāma* as the essence of all Vedas, *Śāstras* and *Purāṇas* and as the king of all mantras, *mantrarāja*. In the second one in *Dhanyasi rāga*, Annamācārya has a precious idea which Tyāgarāja also has in a song of his. In the first *caraṇa* (lyrical "foot" or quatrain) of this piece, Annamācārya says that the Lord's name is to the devotee what the *maṅgala-sūtra* is to a Pativrata, a good wife who has taken marriage vows. (*Kappi pativrataku maṅgalasūtramuvale.*) Pressing before Rāma that although there are several Gods, Rāma was his *iṣṭa-devatā*, Tyāgarāja compares the former to different kinds of ornaments that a woman wears and Rāma to her *maṅgala-sūtra* wedding necklace.

The song *Śrī Rāma padama* of Tyāgarāja in which Ahalyā figures prominently may be considered an offspring of Annamācārya's *saṅkīrtana* on the Lord's feet in (*Mukhari rāga*) which begins *Brahmā gadikina padamu* where Ahalyā's purification occurs as one of several wonders.

Not only does Annamācārya frequently speak of Rāma in his

songs, although they are mainly addressed to Lord Veṅkaṭeśvara, he has also songs on Rāma specifically, on Rāma-*nāma*, on Sītā, Añjaneya etc. in all of which the leading ideas of Rāma *bhakti*, such as the belief in Śiva imparting Rāma-*nāma*, which are met with at every step in Tyāgarāja, are seen also in Annmācārya; in these songs, Annāmācārya too, like Tyāgarāja later, used the entire Rāma-milieu as found in the different *Rāmāyaṇas* in addition to that of Vālmīki.

(The text of this footnote is taken from V. Raghavan's article entitled "Tyāgarāja and Annamācārya," in the *Souvenir* of the Forty-first Conference of the Music Academy, Madras, 1967. Pages unnumbered.)

Creative Exponents of the Name, and Related Studies

Mahatma Gandhi: Bhajans, Prayer and the Name[1]

[Though he was not from the Kāveri delta region, Mohandas K. Gandhi was a well known Hindu of our times to whom the Name was very important.]

One of the most popular expressions of Gandhiji's religious activity was his prayer meetings, recitations of hymns, *bhajans*, *Rāmdhun*, recitation of Rāma-*nāma*. This one thing of all, put him in tune with the saints, *sadhus* and *bhaktas* ranging from Vālmīki to the latest singer of *Rāma-kirtanas*. In his article "Nothing without Grace" Gandhi said that God's grace could be obtained by repeating the divine name all the twenty-four hours of the day and by realizing that God resides within us. Along with Rāma-*nāma*, he mentioned also the *dvadasākṣara* "twelve syllable" mantra as being equally efficacious but it was Rāma-*nāma* that was his favorite.

In agreement with all devout Hindus, Gandhi believed in carrying *mantras* which one should repeat. He said "The mantra becomes one's staff of life." Quoting the great medical authority Charaka, he believed that the recitation of God's name was an aid to cure oneself of illness. He called Rāma-*nāma* "a sovereign remedy" and "an unfailing panacea of all ills." "Repetition of Rāma-*nāma*," he said, "has been a second nature with me with growing knowledge and advancing years." He was well-versed in the tradition and literature of the doctrine of recitation of God's name, for he says in one place, "But more potent than Rāma is the Name" – which has reference to a tenet of this school of Nāma-reciters that God had two real forms, the sound-form or Name, and his appearance (*rūpa*), and that of these two, the former is superior. In fact, we can compare some of his expositions on this subject to those of a traditional expounder of the greatness of the divine Name – *Nāma-mahātmya* – like Tyāgarāja. How the recitation of the Name should come from the heart, how Rāma means the Supreme Godhead and so on, – Gandhi's teachings on these topics can be compared to similar statements found in Tyāgarāja's songs.[2]

He repeated the name Rāma, but held that this, as also the thousand Names in the *Viṣṇu sahasranāma* hymn do not exhaust the names of God. "You may give Him as many names as you like, provided it is one God without a second whose Name you are invoking. That also means that He is Nameless too."[3] Many asked him "Who is the Rām of the *Rāmdhun*?" and he had no hesitation in saying "I have accepted all the names and forms attributed to God, as symbols connoting one formless omnipresent Rāma." Gandhi had evidently in his mind what all devotees of Rāma had in mind, what the *Rāma pūrva tāpinī Upaniṣad* had said: "This name of Rāma delights the world, and for that reason shall really continue to be treasured up in the memory of the world for ever and ever. This (Rāma), the *Paramātman* (Supreme Being) is known by the name of Rāma [meaning "that which delights"], for the reason that yogins delight in this infinite existence, in this eternal bliss of the character of the *Ātman* of sentience."[4]

To the question could non-Hindus join in *Rāmdhun*, Gandhi gave an answer which he said was not his own but was that of Tulsidās himself. He replied, "My Rāma, the Rāma, of our prayers, is not the historical Rāma the son of Daśaratha and King of Āyodhyā. He is the eternal, the unborn, the one without a second."[5]

Notes

[1] First published in *Swarājya* journal. (Editor's note: I have not been able to trace the issue number or date.)

[2] See for example songs like "Rāmaniyeda permarahitulaku nāma-ruci telusuna," "Telisi Rāma cintanato Nāmamu – Rāma yani parabrahmamunaku peru and so on."

[3] *Harijan*, Dec. 21, 1936.

[4] Rāmānte Yogino'nante nityanande chidātmani iti Rām-padena asau param Brahmā abhidhiyate (1,6). Translation from *Vaiṣṇopaniṣads* (Adyar, Madras: Theosophical Publishing House, 1953), p. 381.

[5] *Harijan*, April 28, 1946.

V

Viṣṇu-Sahasra-Nāma: The Thousand Names of Lord Viṣṇu

Translated by V. Raghavan[1]

From the *Mahābhārata*, *Anuśāsana pārvaṇ*, Chapter 254.

Having listened to all the *dharmas*, sanctifying in every way, Yudhishṭhira again addressed Bhīṣma: "Which is the sole divinity in the world? What is the one supreme path? By praising and worshipping Whom will men attain weal? What *dharma*, according to you, is supreme among all *dharmas*? And by reciting which, will a being born here be released from the fetters of birth and rebirth?"

Bhīṣma replied: "If man, with constant endeavor, praises the Lord of the universe, the unlimited Supreme Being, with His Thousand Names, if he worships daily and with devotion the same imperishable Being, meditating on Him, praising Him, bowing to Him, and making offerings to Him, if he sings daily the praise of that Great Lord of the whole universe, Viṣṇu, who has neither beginning nor end and presides over the world, he overcomes all unhappiness. *** If man should constantly adore in devotion the lotus-eyed Lord with hymns, that according to me, is supreme over all the *dharmas*. *** The God of gods, He who is the eternal Father of all living beings, from whom all beings proceed on the advent of the primary aeon and into whom they disappear again when the aeon comes to an end, of that Lord of the whole world, the Chief of all beings, hear from me, O King, these Thousand Names which drive away sin and fear! The celebrated names of the great Lord which are based on His qualities, and which the sages have sung, I shall proclaim for the weal (of the world):

"He who is of the form of the Universe and is All-pervasive, who is of the form of Sacrifice, who is the Lord of the past, future and present, the Creator of all living beings, their Sustainer and their existence, their Indweller and Well-wisher; the Pure and Supreme Being, the highest goal of the liberated, the imperishable Spirit that is the Onlooker and the eternal Knower of the body; who is the Path and the Leader among those that know the path, Himself Matter, Spirit and God, the Supreme Being who took the form of the Man-lion, who has rays of light as hair, and possesses the Goddess of Fortune; the All, the Destroyer, the Beneficent, the Steadfast, the Prime Source of beings, the Inexhaustible Repository; one who comes into being as He pleases, the Benefactor, the Protector, One whose birth is unique, the Capable, the Master; the Self-born, the Giver of happiness, the Solar deity, the Lotus-eyed, the Speaker of the sublime sound named Veda, One without birth or death, the Primary Creator and the Subsidiary Creator (Brahmā) and One beyond even the Primary Creator; the Inscrutable, the Lord of the senses, He who has the Lotus (with Brahmā) in his navel, the God of the gods, the Divine Architect, the Thinker or the Sage-lawgiver Manu, the heavenly Architect Tvaṣṭar, the Huge, the Aged, the Firm; the Incomprehensible, the Permanent, the Attractive Krishna, the bright-eyed, the Destroyer, the Ample; existing above, below and in the middle; the Supreme Sanctifier and Auspiciousness; the Controller, the Life-giver, the Life-breath, the Eldest, the Best, the Lord of beings, the primordial Creator, He who has the whole Earth within Himself, the Scion of the Medhu race and Killer of the demon Madhu; the Powerful Lord, wielder of the bow; the Intelligent; Power and Order; the Unexcelled, the Unassailable, the Grateful, the

Act, the Self-possessed; the God of gods, the Refuge, Happiness, the Author of the universe, the Source of all Beings, the Day, the Year, the Great Serpent (of the form of Time), Understanding, All-seeing; the Unborn, the Lord of all Endowed with miraculous powers, Himself those miraculous powers, the First of all, the Stable, He who took the form of the Boar of Dharma, the Immeasurable, One who has transcended all associations; Wealth, Endowed with an excellent heart, Truth, Serene, Equal, the Unfailing, the Lotus-eyed, the Righteously Active, the Embodiment of Righteousness; the Terrible, the Multi-headed, the Tawny One, the Origin of the universe, of Unstained Fame, Immortal, Eternal, Steadfast, of Excellent limbs and severe penance; Omnipotent, Omniscient, the Shining One whose hosts are everywhere, the chastiser of the erring folk, the Veda, the Expounder of the Veda, the Full, the Ancillary Lore of the Veda, the Inquirer into the Veda and One of far-reaching vision; One who presides over the world, the gods and law; the created Effect as well as the uncreated Cause, Who takes four forms for creation, maintenance and dissolution, Who has four tusks (as the man-lion) and four arms; the Brilliant, the Food as well as the eater, the Forbearing, First-born of the world, the Sinless, the Victory and the Victorious, the Source of the universe and One who repeatedly comes to dwell within beings; Indra's brother and yet above him, the Dwarf as well as the Colossus, the Successful, the Pure, the Strong, the Epitome of (all) Creation, Self-possessed, Regulation and Restraint; the Object of Knowledge, the Learned, ever a Yogin, the Slayer of heroic fighters, the Lord of spiritual learning, the Sweet, One who transcends the senses and is endowed with mysterious power, of high endeavour and mighty strength; endowed with supreme Intellect, Potency, Power and Lustre; of Indescribable Form, the Beautiful, the Vast, the Supporter of the great mountain; the Great Archer, the Lord of Earth, the Abode of Fortune, the Refuge of the good, the Irrepressible, the Delight of the good, the Saviour of the earth, the Chief of those that understand Speech; the Ray of Light (or sage Marīchi), the Controller, the Swan of the Spirit, the fleet divine Bird (Garuḍa), the Chief Serpent (Sesha), of golden navel, of excellent austerities, the Lotus on His navel and Brahmā (thereon); Immortal, Spectator of everything, the Fierce, the Link, Linked (with all), the Enduring, the Unborn, the Unbearable, the Ruler, the Celebrated, the Slayer of the enemies of the gods, the Teacher, the Most Weighty One, Light, Truth, One who displays His valour on behalf of Truth, the Moment, the Vigilant, the Garlanded, the Lord of Speech and One of Sublime Intellect; the Foremost, the Chief, the Rich, the Right Path, the Leader, the Inspirer; the Thousand-headed, Thousand-eyed, Thousand-footed, Embodiment of the universe; He who rotates the whole world, yet keeping Himself aloof from it; the Hidden one Overriding all, the Day, the Deluge, Fire, Wind and Mountain; the Supremely Gracious, the Tranquil, the Prop as well as the Consumer of the Universe, the All-pervading; the Bestower of honour, the Honored and the Good: Who draws and hides within Himself the whole Universe, the God who is the Goal of man and the Man himself; the Innumerable, the Unknowable, the Unique, the Patron of disciplined souls, the Spotless, One whose objects and wishes are fulfilled, One who gives success and is also the means of success; One for whom Righteousness constitutes the day, Who showers the desired objects, of giant stride, One who is to be reached by the steps of *dharma* and who is within *dharma*; the Promoter of growth and the Growing, Who is far apart, Who is the ocean of revealed wisdom; of beautiful arms (that protect), whose thought is too difficult to be retained, the Eloquent, the Great Indra, the Bestower of Riches; of manifold and huge form, the Sacrifice and the Revealer; Bearer of Force, Power and Effulgence, Embodiment of Light, the Scorcher, Rich (in everything), the

Manifester of syllables and the Sacred Syllables themselves, Moonlike as well as Sunlike in splendour; the Source of ambrosial rays, Himself both the Sun and the Moon, the King of gods, the Medicine, the Protective Embankment of the world, One whose valor is exercized for Truth and Righteousness; the Lord of the past, present and future, the Wind, the Purifier, the Fire, the Destroyer of lust, the Promoter of noble love, the Loveable, the Lover that gratifies with love; the Promulgator of aeons, the Conductor of aeonic cycles, of manifold mystic powers, that All-devouring, the Unseen, of Unmanifest form, Victor over thousands and the Endlessly Victorious; the Desirable, the Remarkable, Dear to those that conform to His commandments, Krishna who wears the peacock-feather on His crest (or the Śikhāndin who has come as my Death), the Encircler, Dharma, the Destroyer of anger, at the same time its Employer, and the Doer, with a thousand arms, and Bearer of the earth; the Unflinching, the Famous, the Life and Life-giver, Indra's brother, the Ocean, the Substratum, the Vigilant one who is firmly established; the Destroyer (of enemies), the Supporter of such destroyers and Himself the Bearer of the brunt; the Bestower of boons; the Mover of Wind; the Lord in whom all dwell and who dwells in all; the Bigger Sun, the Prime God, and the Destroyer of enemy cities; the Sorrowless, He who helps to cross over, the Crossing over (or the Mystic syllable OM), the Valorous, the Scion of the Sūrasenas (Krishna), the King, the Favorable, Who returns to us innumerable times, the God with the lotus and the lotus-eyes; Who is seated at the centre of the lotus, the Lotus-eyed Lord who is within the lotus of one's heart, who takes corporeal forms, the greatly Affluent, the Full, the Old, the Large-eyed, the God with the kite-banner; the Incomparable, the Fierce Being that excels even the lion; the Knower of the esoteric practices (or Knower of propriety), the Offering, the Lord who strips one and tests him, Marked with all features of beauty, Bearing the Goddess of Beauty, the Victor in battles; the Imperishable, He who took the Fish)incarnation, the Path, the Cause, One in whom all Names are included, Endowed with endurance, Bearer of earth, of great fortune, the Swift, the limitless Consumer; the Origin, One that stirs up the Creative Activity, the Sportive, Bearer of Prosperity, the Lord Supreme, the Instrument and the Cause, the Doer and the Undoer, the Dense and the Secret; Determination, the Regulator, the End, the Bestower of rank, the Stable, Supreme Prosperity, the Absolutely obvious, the Contented, the Well-nourished, having auspicious looks; the Delighter, the Final end (of all), Free from passion, the Path and the Goal, the Right Policy, and at the same time Himself the Sovereign, not subject to any; the Hero, Best of all the powerful, Dharma, and Foremost of the knowers of *dharma*; the Unimpeded Heavenly State, the Supreme Spirit, Life and Life-giver, the Mystic OM, the Vast, the Creator (Brahmā), Slayer of enemies, the All-pervading, the Wind; He who is realised when the senses are subdued; the Season; Beautiful to look at, Time; the transcendent Lord who yet receives all supplicants, the Severe, He who makes everything abide in Himself, the Capable, Who affords repose to the afflicted, and One who is considerate to the whole world; the Expansive, He who stands stationary, the Measure, the Seed that is not spent, the Purpose (of all endeavor) but Himself devoid of any purpose of His own, the Great Treasury, the Great Enjoyer, the highly wealthy; the Undepressed, the most Expansive, Existence, the Sacrificial Post at which all meritorious acts are offered, the Great Sacrifice, the Hub of the wheel of constellations, the Moon, the Adept, Stript of all encrustations, of noble aspirations; the Sacrifices of different forms and Himself the minor gods and the Chief God propitiated by sacrifices; the Refuge of the good; One who notes everything, the Liberated Soul, the Omniscient and the Supreme Wisdom; He who takes excellent vows, of beautiful face, the Subtle, the Fine-voiced, the Giver of happiness, the Friend, the Captivating, One who has conquered anger, of heroic arms and One who tears to pieces (the unrighteous); He who makes the unenlightened slumber in His mystic Delusion, Master of Himself, the Ubiquitous, of manifold forms and acts, the Year, the Affectionate, Surrounded by His children, the Source of all precious things, the Lord of riches; the Safeguarder of *dharma*, the Maker of *dharma*, Himself endowed with Dharma, Himself Good and Bad, the Perishable and the Imperishable, who becomes the unknowing embodied individual Soul; the Thousand-rayed, the Performer of functions, and the Author who has laid down the definitions; Centre of an orb of rays, the Spirit that presides over the mind, Lionlike in strength, the great Lord of beings, the First God, the Great God, the God of gods, the Bearer of gods, and the Teacher; the Superior, the Shepherd, the Protector, Realizable by knowledge, the Ancient, the Bearer of the bodies of the beings, the Enjoyer of (everything), the great Boar-incarnation, the profusely Liberal; the Drinker of Soma offering and of nectar, the Soma offering, Victor over many, Foremost among the eminent, Modesty, Victory, the Truthful, Scion of Dasarha race and the Lord of the Sāttvata people (or worshippers); the Individual Soul, the Observer of individuals' humility, Bestower of Release, the immeasurably Powerful, the Reservoir of different orders of beings, the Spirit without any limitation, He who lies on the great Ocean after engulfing the world with it, the Terminator of the world; the Unborn, Fit to be worshipped, Existing in His own innate nature, One who has vanquished his enemies, the Rejoicer, Bliss, the pleasing and Gratifying, Of true virtue, He who measured the universe in three strides; the Great Sage and Teacher (of Saṁkhya) Kapila, the Knower of the created, the King, He who covered the universe in three steps, the Lord of the gods, He who incarnated as the Fish with the huge snout, the Death of the god of Death; the Great Boar-incarnation, Known through the Upaniṣads, Possessed of an excellent army, Having golden armlets, Dwelling in the heart, the Deep, the Impenetrable, the Hidden, Bearing the discus and the mace; Brahmā the Creator, Himself His accessory, the Unconquered, Sage Vyāsa, the Strong, One who unfailingly drags beings away at the time of destruction, Varuṇa the Lord of Waters, Sage Vāsishṭha, Standing like a tree, Seen in the lotus of one's heart, Himself of a great mind; Possessed of Lordship, Dharma, Renown, Beauty, Dispassion, and Freedom or He who knows the origin and end, the movement and rest of beings, Knowledge and Nescience, He who deprives one also of these excellences; the Joyous, the Wearer of a garland of sylvan flowers, Armed with the plough, the God, the Resplendent Sun-god, the Patient, the Supreme Path to salvation; Possessing an excellent bow, Śiva armed with the axe, the Awful, the Giver of wealth, Heaven-stretching, the codifier of all systems of knowledge, the Self-born Lord of Speech; Lauded by three (special) Sāman hymns, Himself the Sāman chant and its Singer, the Beautific end, the Remedy and the Doctor, the Promulgator of the Path of Renunciation, Quietude and the Quiet, the Final Rest, Peace, the Highest Refuge; of Beautiful form, Bestower of peace, the Creator, He who revels in his creation, Who reposes in the lily of the heart, Benefactor of the world, Lord of the world, He who shrouds Himself in His Mystic Power, Having eyes that rain one's desired objects, Lover of *dharma*; He who does not retreat, Whose mind is turned inwards on the Self, Who gathers up all things at the dissolution, Who brings on welfare, the Beneficent, Bearing the Auspicious mark of *Śrīvatsa* on His chest, the abode of the Goddess of prosperity, Lord of Supreme Energy, Chief of the gods that are endowed with power; Giver, Master, Abode, Repository, Producer, Bearer, Author and Maintainer of Prosperity; the Supreme God and the Prop of the three worlds; of beautiful eyes and limbs, of joys, the Rejoicer, the

Lord of the luminaries, of controlled and disciplined Self, of unsullied fame, the Dispeller of doubts; the Excelling, Possessed of eyes all round, He who has no master, Frequently changing and yet stationary, Reposing in earth (Immanent in His creation), the Ornament, Affluence, without Sorrow and the Destroyer of sorrow; having rays of light, Worshipped by all, the Vessel within which everything is, the Pure Soul, the Purifier, the Unobstructed and Unopposed Hero, of superior energy, of unlimited valor; the Killer of the demon Kalanemi, the Heroic, the Scion and chief of the Sura tribe, of the form of the three worlds, Lord of the three worlds, Endowed with power, Slayer of the demon Keśin, the Lord who removes bondage; the Lord of love, the Guardian of love, the Loving, the Lovable, the Promulgator of the spiritual tradition, Of undefinable form, the All-pervading Lord, the Unlimited, the Acquirer of riches; Favourable to the Brāhmaṇas, the Promulgator of penance and knowledge, the Creator, the Supreme Soul, the Promoter of Brahman-knowledge, Knower of Brahman, of the form of the Brāhmaṇa, Possessor of the knowledge (Veda) and the Beloved of the Brāhmaṇas; of giant strides and acts, the Superior Light, the Great Serpent, the Great Sacrifice, Sacrificer and Oblation; He who is to be praised, Who loves praises, the Praises, Himself the Praiser, Who loves to fight, the Full, the Filler, the Holy, of virtuous fame; Free from all disease; Fleet as the mind, the Maker of holy places, the Wealth-bearing, the Bestower of the higher wealth of Deliverance, the Son of Vasudeva, the Precious thing, Possessed of precious heart, the Offering; the Meritorious Path, Honour, Existence, Right Being, the Refuge of the good, having heroic hosts, the Chief of the Yadavā clan, the Abode of the good, He who had beautiful associations on the Yamunā; the dwelling-place of beings, Lord Vasudeva, the Repository of the Breath of all living beings, One for whom there is no sufficiency in anything; Humbler of haughtiness,

Bestower of rightful pride, Himself elated in His own bliss, One whom it is difficult to hold within one's heart, the Invincible; Who is of all forms, of huge form, of resplendent form, Devoid of form and at the same time taking manifold forms, the Latent, of a hundred forms and a hundred faces; the One, the Many, the Sacrifice, the Highest import of the words "Who," "What," and "That which;" Father of the world, Besought by the world, Scion of the Madhu race, Affectionate to His devotees; of golden hue and limbs, of excellent limbs, of pleasing ornaments on the arm, the Slayer of warriors, the Difficult, Void of all attributes, One who has quenced desires, the Immobile and the Mobile; without pride or false assumptions, Bestower of honour, the Honoured, the Owner of the world, the Bearer of the three worlds, of sublime Intellect, Manifested in the sacrifice, He whose objects are fulfilled, the truly Intelligent, the Support of the earth; the Fountainhead of light, Possessing splendor, Eminent among those bearing arms, the Reins of control, Control, the (always) Preoccupied, of many high reaches (i.e., many exalted aspects), the Elder brother of Gada; of four forms, four arms, four manifestations; the Resort of all the four castes of mankind, the Accomplished, Being in the four states of waking, dreaming, deep sleep and the fourth beyond them, the Knower of the four Vedas, of Whom all that exists is but a fraction; Who returns to the world again and again and thus retires not, the Unconquerable, He who cannot be trangressed, Hard to be attained and known, realised and held in mind with difficulty, the Slayer of the evil-minded foes; of auspicious form, He who takes the essence of things in the world, Who extends Himself gloriously and Himself snaps that extension, doing sovereign and great duty, Who has regulated the acts appropriate to each, the Author of scriptures; of special birth, the Beautiful, of melting heart, the precious Hub which holds together everything, of auspicious thought, the Adored, the Giver of food, the Snouted-Fish-incarnation, He who vanquishes even the most learned; Golden-bodied, the Unperturbed, Lord of all lords of speech, the Deep Lake, the Deep Pit, the Great Being, the Great Treasure; He who gladdens the earth and tears it up as well, (pure and fragrant) like a jasmine, Cloud of coolness and plenty, the Sanctifier, the Breath, Who drinks nectar, Whose body is immortal, All-knowing and All-facing; Easy, of noble Vow, the Realized Soul, the Victor over foes, the Tormenter of foes, the Huge Banyan, the Udumbara tree (like unto whose fruit that contains a host of flies inside, Who holds within Himself the whole living world), the Sacred Pipal, the Slayer of the demons Chanura and Agha; the Thousand-rayed, the Seven-tongued Fire, the State of Sublimity which is fed by the seven fuels, namely, fortitude, forgiveness, mercy, purity, prosperity, soft speech and non-enmity towards beings; Borne on the sacred Vedic hymns in seven metres, Devoid of form, Impeccable, Unimaginable, the Inspirer of fear as well as its destroyer; the Great One who is the Infinitesimal and the Infinite, the Lean and the Stout, the Qualified and the Unqualified, the Unsupported and Self-supported; of a beautiful mouth (wherefrom the Vedas issued); Forefather of all families and the multiplier of all families; Bearer of burdens, Procalimed (in the Vedas), who is always engaged in Yoga and is the Lord of those that practice it, the Bestower of all desires, the four stages of life and He who toils therein and is emancipated thereby, the Tree with the rich foliage of all the worlds, Who is borne fleet on the Wind; the Bearer of the bow and the science of archery; the Punishment, the Punisher and the Subjugation; the Unvanquished, the All-enduring, the Controller, the Controlling rule and the Control; Possessed of the luminous quality, the Good, the True, Intent on the True and Righteous, the Object of all seeking, Deserving of all pleasing things, Deserving adoration, the Doer of the pleasant and the Promoter of endearment; Moving in the skies, the

Light, Shining beautifully, the Enjoyer of Oblations, the Omnipresent, the Sun that absorbs water, shines in varied hues, urges and produces; and the God who has the Sun as His eye; the Endless, the Enjoyer of oblations, the Enjoyer (of all things), Giver of happiness, Born of many (in his incarnations for the protection of righteousness), Elder to all, He who is never despondent, Ever forbearing, the Foundation of the world, the Wonderful; the Old and Existing from ancient times, the Tawny, the Sun, He into whom creation dissolves at the deluge; Bestower of welfare, Maker of welfare, Welfare, Enjoyer of welfare and Capable Promoter of welfare; Devoid of severity, Adorned with earrings, Bearing the discus, Overpowering, of forceful ordinances, Transcending verbal knowledge and source, (yet) permitting verbal account; the Cool, the Bringer of the Night of Soul; not Cruel, the Delicate, the Capable, the Considerate, the Most Forbearing, the Most Learned, the Fearless, He whose praises it is holy to listen to or sing; He who helps men to cross over transmigratory existence, the Destroyer of evil acts, of the form of Merit, the Destroyer of evil dreams, the Annihilator of warriors, the Protector, of the form of all the good souls, the Life of all beings, Established all round; of endless forms, of endless fortune, One who has conquered anger, the Dispeller of fear, the Perfect, the Profound, the Director, the Commander, the Various Quarters (i.e., of the form of Space); without Beginning, the Imparter of Beauty to the terrestrial and celestial worlds, the Excellent Hero with beautiful armlets, Birth, the Primary source of humanity, the Terrible, of terrible Prowess; the Station of support, Himself unsupported by any, Smiling like a flower, the Ever awake, the Upwardly progressive, the Conduct of the righteous path, Giver of Life, the Lauded, the Guarantee (of fruits of actions); the Authority, the Abode of Life, the Sustainer of Life, Life of Life, the Truth, the Knower of Truth, the sole Soul, He who is beyond birth, death and old age; the Tree that pervades the three worlds of earth, ether and heaven, He who reaches beyond them too, the Father and the Great-grandfather, the Sacrifice, the Lord of the sacrifice, the Sacrificing Priest, the Sacrificial accessories, and Borne by the Sacrifice; the Bearer of the Sacrifice, the Performer of the Sacrifice, the aim of all Sacrifice, the Enjoyer of Sacrifice, the means of Sacrifice, He who brings Sacrifice to an end, the esoteric Sacrifice of Knowledge; the Food and indeed the Consumer of all as food; Himself His source, Voluntarily manifested, Who penetrates (as indweller of all beings or as the Boar-incarnation to salvage the submerged earth), the Singer of Sāman symphonies (in the plentitude of freedom), the son of Devakī, the Creator, the King, the Destroyer of sins; He who holds the Conch, the Sword, the Discus, the Bow and the Mace, the Discus-armed, the Unperturbed, He who can use anything as a weapon for striking.

Thus these Thousand from among the divine Names of the Great Keśava, fit to be sung, have been fully told. He who listens to this or recites it daily shall encounter nothing untoward here or in the hereafter. *** In the blessed who are devoted to the Supreme Lord, there will be no anger, no jealousy, no avarice, no evil thought.***

Note

[1] First published in *The Indian Heritage* (Bangalore: Indian Institute of World Culture, 1956), pp. 421-435.

VI

Beads on Strings: Concluding Reflections on the Power of the Name

(by William J. Jackson)

The Sanskrit word *mantra* has entered the English language in full force, and the concept is showing renewed vitality these days. Repeated phrases like "Just say no" and "I am somebody" are commonly referred to as "mantras." Any secretly repeated utterance which brings success or promises to aid in the struggle for survival or give an edge in a tense and competitive world is commonly called a "mantra." To repeat a message of hope (the "I had a dream" speech of Martin Luther King, or the Gettysberg address[1] or a poem or song) in trying situations such as prison, violent persecution or longstanding oppression is interpreted by many moderns not as a neurotic act but as utilizing a necessary weapon or tool for the mind. ("Mind-tool" is the literal root-meaning of *mantra*.) Perhaps it is a postmodern pragmatism – respect for an efficient minimalist means to an end, an admission that survival has its own logic, just as the heart has "reasons of its own," which gives new currency to this term today, beyond its technical meanings in Hindu and Buddhist practices. The older associations of mantras as mystical formulaic prayers to be used in meditation and religious practice are still prominent in both the West and the East. Like the Sanskrit term *karma*, the term *mantra* is now generally known in the Western world, where it is used in the media to mean any repeated slogan or message. Thus, in racist protests it may be said that a crowd is shouting "mantras" of hate. The meanings of words like "mantra" and "karma" shift when they become buzzwords in everyday English, but nevertheless some continuity with the original meaning being newly applied to a different culture remains.

The Diverse Ubiquity of the Name

"Names are magic." Walt Whitman
An American Primer

Ritual may well be the most pervasive form of religious activity, if we define ritual broadly as a conscious, repetitive, circumscribed mode of directing attention in which people attempt to transcend their individual limits. The saying of holy names may well be the most ubiquitous form in which people attempt to link themselves with a higher power. Devoted faith in the practice of calling on a divine name in prayer or incantation is probably the oldest and most widespread form of religious life in human history. Invocation of holy names in ritual has been a primary mode of attempting to contact the holy; perhaps it is the minimal means necessary for the existence of ritual and prayer. In India, mantras which include holy names are at the heart of many millennia-old religious traditions. The prophetic Western religions and the mystical Eastern ones both offer spiritual practices and articulate theologies in which the sacred Name is inextricably linked to the central mysteries of faith, and there is evidence that such practices have ancient roots. The ways holy names are thought of and used tell us fundamental things about different cultures and historical periods, revealing essential differences.

The ubiquity of holy names in human cultures, though it has not been attended to comprehensively by scholars, is well known, and has been written about by historians of religion and theologians, so much so that Simone Weil's statement from a half century ago: "All religions pronounce the name of God in their particular language,"[2] sounds rather commonplace today. Martin Buber's assertion ". . . all God's names are hallowed, for in them He is not merely spoken about, but spoken to. . . "[3] strikes a less iconoclastic and exclusivistic attitude than is often associated with prophetic traditions, and it shows the universalizing tendency at work in this century of greater global awareness. Of course fundamentalist views could be cited to show the belief that a particular name is the only true one, but such provincialism is not new. The universal prevalence of holy names does not mean that the ultimate being named is conceived in the same way, or that the use of holy names is necessarily similar in various cultures, or that even in a single tradition the meaning of the name has remained constant throughout the centuries.

* * *

Non-Hindu examples of names – Yahweh and Tao – can serve as illustrations of how concepts of names for the holy vary. Traditions surrounding these two have striking and well known statements of caution or warning about placing the name of the ultimate in ordinary categories. Yahweh is a name for the holy as the personal divine supreme being, the creator who named himself as unnameable. Tao is the formless holy or ultimate so mysterious it made men despair of ever being able to name it. Let us look at the differences more closely for a moment. The respective salient points about the names of the extraordinary and eternal in these traditions are fairly well known, though not usually juxtaposed.

The name of the deity of the Hebrew prophets of Israel was too holy for man to speak, so the four consonants YHWH – (with vowels borrowed from the name Adonai this tetragrammaton becomes "Yahoweh" or "Yahweh") – were substituted to indicate the unutterable. They were a sign for the ultimately significant One who was beyond symbolic images and should not be profaned by being spoken. The dead sea scrolls show a four dot ellipsis to indicate the same. A commandment forbad graven images and another prohibited the use of the name of God to manipulate divine will—magico-religious practices associated with neighboring Canaanites and Egyptians. Yet there is much mention of the name of the Lord in the Torah. In Exodus it is said that God revealed himself to Abraham, Isaac and Jacob as "El Shaddai" (God Almighty), not disclosing his name Adonai or Yahweh (Exodus VI. 2-6). Yahweh is explained as a form of the verb *hayah*, "to be." (Exodus III. 13-15) Asked by Moses who he should tell the Israelites has sent him, God says in a theophanic pun on the name Yahweh, "I am that I am; tell them *I am* sent you." The revelation of the name was a self-embodying of the divine originating a divinely-willed path, a way to be. The name comes up often in the Torah. In Jerusalem there was to be built a house in which His name would dwell. (Deut. XII. 5,11, 21) "He [Abraham] called upon the Name of the Lord." (Genesis XII, 8 and XIII, 3) "Because of the savour of Thy good ointments, Thy Name is as ointment poured forth." (Song of Songs I. 3.) In more recent times, the Hasidic movement in Judaism followed the charismatic activities of the Baal Shem Tov – whose name means "Master of the Holy Name." His mysterious powers and wisdom are indicative of mystical Hasidism's restoration of enchantment to the idea of the power of prayer. But in all these cases the deity named is the transcendent being to whom humans are answerable for their action.[4]

Turning to ancient China, ineffably mysterious and subtle beyond form, the eterna Tao, written like this: 道 is stand to be nameless (*wu ming*). Words, being man-made labels, cannot hold such a subtle reality as Tao, the invisible processes of which manifest as existence. Hence, Tao is *pu-k'o ming*, impossible to name. There are constant reminders in early Taoist literature of the limits of human language in the attempt to capture the holy's essence. In ancient Chinese thinking the giving of a name (*ming*) meant the evaluating and assigning of the thing named to a specific place in a hierarchical cosmos. Tao transcends these schematics. "It existed before Heaven and Earth. . . Its name (*ming*) we do not know; Tao is the byname that we give it. . . "[5] The real Tao is beyond wordy identities; it has no name (*pu ming-yu*) and cannot be named, hence any claims to do so are false or forgetful of the truth. Yet ultimately Tao is the only identity to be identified in a world where "the only constant is change" and this everlasting identification is as origin or mother of what we see. The ultimate transcends human sensibilities. Yet by using the makeshift convenience of the name Tao to stand for the unnamable, Lao Tzu, Chuang Tzu and others fathomed depths and conveyed wisdom about the interconnections among the levels – organic life, natural environment, culture and cosmos – to generations of Chinese. While the names for the "ten thousand things" of phenomenal existence are useful in organizing the world around one, domesticating wilderness and securing prosperity and good fortune, the unnamable Tao is unthinkable and unsayable, though not unknowable by experience in the lives of the humble and receptive. The named Tao is a mysterious harmony in which humans take part.

From these illustrations we can see different implications and problems regarding names of the ultimate in prophetic and mystical traditions. All humans use names; culturally conditioned personalities differ in their experiences and understandings of how names and the named relate and how religious people will regard the relationship.

*　　　*　　　*

The inevitable association between the name of an entity and its presence in the mind, or between the name and the nature or power of the referent named, is as old as the roots of human language. In India the inextricability of name and form, *nāma-rūpa*, is a primary intuition expressed often in philosophy.

The mind gets a "handle"[6] on a referent by way of the name. But that name is conceived to be not merely a neutral sign or label for the referent, because experientially it can be held inside the mind subtly, through repetition it can conjure up the idea of the thing for oneself and for others. It can help map a hidden territory. The power, the essence, the subtle essential archetypal referent is available to the religious imagination via the name. *Vocare est invocare*, "To say the name is to invoke the named," the Latin saying goes. Thus the name of the deity is a mystical key to operate the named in the religious imagination. The word "religion" may derive from *relegere*, "to repeat, go over" an incantation, a ritual repetition of sacred sounds, prayers and magic formulae, and the relation between the name and numinous power of a deity is very close in ancient Roman religion,[7] and in others.

As the reference to a transcendent deity or ultimate reality, and a means to reach that or be oriented in relation to that, the holy name has had power in the worldviews of tribal people, and of ancient Egyptians and Romans, as well as of Gnostics, Christians, Muslims, Buddhists, Sikhs, and many others.[8]

Nāma: Trajectories of Sacred Utterance in India

> "What was it in the older text which permitted the later author to give that new interpretation, what was it in the altered temper of the time which required him to do so?" J. L. Mehta[9]

To consider the uses of the holy names in India, we must follow trajectories of development over many centuries, and look into this central symbol's meanings as they are transformed, inquiring into the holy name as a central mystery capable of repeated, seemingly inexhaustible, unfoldings.

Richard Lannoy is on the right track when he lists three elements of continuity in Indian thought: 1. Authority of word, mantra, invoked name as "universal metaphysical principle." 2. The endless flux of all things. 3. The monistic concept not distinguishing among matter, life, and mind.[10] I would add that of these three it is the first – the word – which is perceived as most within human control. J. Frits Staal in his *Agnicayana* work characterized Vedic thought as an over-valuation of the word.[11] Perhaps we live in a time of cynically undervaluing the word as powerless in itself, though we think of it as quite powerful in the hands of a clever "spin-doctor." If so, it will take some effort to interpret the uses of holy names in terms of adherents of holy name traditions as well as in our own terms, to find categories that will do justice to the situation and not impose inappropriate ones.

* * *

In the introduction to a recent book he edited, *Secrecy in Religions*, Kees Bolle writes perceptively ". . . historically, an initial mystery in a religious tradition demonstrates its nature and its strength by igniting debates of increasing rational precision and practices that assume the reified presence of the initial mystery without exhausting the initial strength."[12] The use of mantra and holy name in India is a good example of an "initial mystery" of this kind.

Many Hindus believe that devotion through recitation and praise of divine names has roots in the Vedas. The Rig Veda has such expressions as "With songs I call to you, the great, the expansive, as to a cow. . ." – the idea being that the worshipper calls the name of the deity, as a cow is called by name when one wishes to milk her. It is also said that one becomes wise by praising the name of Viṣṇu, and that Viṣṇu's name inspires respect because of its inherent energy. (*tveṣám hyasya sthavirasya nāma* (VII. 100. 3)[13] In the *Śatapatha Brāhmaṇa* (XI. 2. 3, 3) we find the idea that by means of Name and Form, the impersonal Brahman was able to descend again and again into the world it had created.

The Vedic idea that "the gods love the indirect approach" (*pārokṣa*), preferring to be called upon allusively with cryptic mystical references to their powers, which are their synonyms, is well known. It is also said that it is really "the One" that is multinamed: "They call him Indra, Mitra, Varuṇa and Agni . . . To what is One the poets give many a name." (Ṛig Veda I. 164. 46) Invoking names and mantras was a most important element in sacrifices during the Vedic phase. The *praṇava* and *gāyatrī* mantras have been important initiatory and spiritual practices from ancient times. The power of certain names, letters, and sounds is discussed in the speculations of *mīmāṃṣā*, Upaniṣadic thinkers, and the grammarians. [14] The theory of inherent powers and meanings in syllabic sacred sounds is part of the *mīmāṃṣā* school of philosophy. *Mīmāṃsā* de-emphasized the importance of the gods and considered the holy Vedic language, Sanskrit, to be "an emanation of Being (*sat*) in sound (*śabda*); hence the power of the sacred mantras and of the Vedic hymns to touch the quick of truth and so to work magic."[15] The *Śvetāśvatara Upaniṣad* (IV. 1) speaks of the One as manifested first in sound vibration, and as having many kinds of power, through which the multiple sound vibrations which mark the beginning of the cosmic process were generated.[16] The grammarians focused on the inherent sound of syllables as partaking in the cosmic power which generated them as units of meaning.[17] Worship through recounting numerous sacred names is found in the *Śatarudriya* ("100 Names of Rudra"), a work within the *Śatapatha Brāhmaṇa*, a part of Vedic ritual literature. The *Jābālopaniṣad* states that *japa* (repetition) of the *Śatarudriya* expiates sin and releases one from the rounds of birth and death.[18]

The historical origins of the *tāraka mantra* of Rāma's name are not known; in the ancient lore of Banāras this is the holy prayer taught by Śiva to those who die in the holy city, ensuring them of release.[19]

* * *

In early Buddhism the question of efficacious sounds and prayers was a bone of contention at the Third Council of Buddhist monks. There Mahādeva's manifesto dealing with the power of repeated words raised controversy. And in the third century AD the mantra became more and more important in all forms of Buddhism. *Dhāraṇī* – tantric Buddhist formulas were taken to China in the third century AD. In the seventh century AD *Mantrayāna* Buddhism as the path to liberation, was flourishing in India. The Jains also developed theories and practices involving mantras. While heterodox (Buddhist and Jaina) ideas of tantric mantra were colored by the centrality of renunciation, Hindu interpretations had roots in Vedic sacrifice.[20]

* * *

In the *Mahābhārata* epic of classical Hinduism, which took shape beginning around 500 BC, there is a scene in which the hero Bhīṣma is dying, during which he tells the hero Yudhisṭhira that chanting the divine names of Viṣṇu purifies and leads toward the highest spiritual realization. The *Viṣṇu sahasranāma*, "thousand names of Viṣṇu,"[21] are enumerated then. It is a well-known story in India how the author-to-be of the Vālmīki *Rāmāyaṇa* epic was a robber named Ratnākara, and that when the seven sages taught him to repeat the name of Rāma it transformed him into Vālmīki, whose eloquence in praising Rāma have made him known to many millions.

Mantras after the Upaniṣadic phase were central in all kinds of worship, as is evidenced in the *purāṇas*, *āgamas*, and *saṃhitās*. Mantras were used as invocations, in praise, in meditation, and salutations. Mantra in yoga theory and practice, such as articulated by Patañjali, was used as a device for attaining a one-pointed mind, a necessity for *samādhi*. It is said in Patañjali's *Yoga Sūtras* (II. 44) that repetition of sacred words bring one into contact with the God worshipped. Mantras were of psychological assistance for the aspirant on the path of yoga. In yoga the instrumentality of the mantra is seen in the traditional etymology of the word mantra, in which it is broken into *man* for mind and *tra* for tool. Thus, mantra is said to be an instrument for disciplining the mind. The yoga *upaniṣads*, written after 800 A.D. discuss the doctrine of Nāda Brahman, divine vibration. Three major yoga texts of the medieval period, *Haṭha-yoga-pradīpika*, *Śiva-saṃhitā*, and *Gheranda-saṃhitā*, elaborate on the meaning of sacred sound and how it can lead to yogic realization.[22]

In early non-Sanskritic literature reverence for the name is also mentioned. The Tamil classic *Śilappadikāram* ("Anklet Epic"), written by the Jain poet-prince Ilango, some time between the second and sixth century A.D., mentions the five syllable mantra, "Nāmaḥ Śivāya." The *Tevāram* poets depict the power of *Nāmaḥ Śivāya* as a combination of heart-felt *bhakti* and the sacred sound's inherent power.[23]

As a spiritual practice of the early Tamil Vaiṣṇava saints known as *āḻvārs*, such as Nammāḻvār (6th century), name-reciting and chanting formed part of *Vaiṣṇava bhakti*'s popular religious appeal; in principle, it was a path open to all, the promise of more direct access to the divine.

The *purāṇas*, which date from the Hindu Classical and Medieval periods, contain passages on chanting the name, and list thousands of names, synonyms for Viṣṇu or Śiva, which serve as mnemonic devices to call to mind demonstrations of divine power such as the conquering of demons, and to depict facets of the deity's personality. Each name conveys a glory or conjures in the imagination an episode in the deity's *līlās* or divine play. Listening to Lord Viṣṇu's name, and chanting it are the first two of the "nine marks of devotion" listed in the *Bhāgavata Purāṇa*, which was written in the 9th or 10th century (VII. 5. 22-23). This *purāṇa* also states that it is well known that in the present age, the *Kali Yuga*, wise men worship through sacrifices which consist largely of chanting the Lord's names and singing his praises (XI. 5. 32). The *purāṇas* further depict the extraordinary power of devotion to the name. In the *Rāmāyaṇa*, Hanuman, for example, is empowered to perform great feats through his faith in Rāma's name, rather than through Rāma's personal presence. And Ajāmila, when dying, achieves salvation because the name of his son is Nārāyaṇa, and by luck he thinks of that in his last moments.[24]

* * *

The *purāṇas* were revised first to defend against the influences of Buddhism and various forms of Tantra, then later to incorporate popular tantric features. Tantra became an irresistable influence in all kinds of sectarian religion in India. Mantras were popularized in the *tantras*, which assimilated previous ideas about mantra in light of Śiva-Śakti theology, with Śiva as *Aśabda Brahman*, *bindu*, (the silent divine, seed) and Śakti as *Śabda Brahman*, *nāda*, *mantra* (the divine vibration, creation's waves). *Tantra* is a vast, often bewildering subject. In *tantra* the concidence of opposites and identity of microcosm (person) and macrocosm (universe) are experienced in a leap beyond conventional categories. Tantric practices include worship of gods and goddesses, therapeutic yoga exercises, esoteric ritual symbolism and gestures, and spoken and written mantras used as protective devices and invocations. M. Biardeau identifies the essence of *tantra's* mode: "Tantra is the attempt to employ desire (kāma) and all the values associated with it at the service of liberation." Systematically employing some existing vitality for the highest goal, tantra takes the raw condition which could be a liability, and utilizes it as an instrument of refinement. R. Gandhi identifies this aspect of *tantra* as a universal trait of the human condition: "Man is a *tantrika*, a converter of apparent handicap into supreme advantage. . . he is a biped and transforms the apparent handicap and awkwardness of two-footedness into the supreme advantage of a stance without which there would be no human love and communication . . . no interface in human life, no looking upwards, heavenward, no fear of falling which symbolizes our own heightened awareness of possibilities and responsibilities." Tantra uses the imagination's natural potential for a sense of magic in names and sounds.[25]

* * *

In the *bhakti* movement *japa*, repeating a holy name in a mantra, murmuring it day in day out, with or without beads to count the number of times, has been a most popular religious practice in most sects. It is often used in cultivating religious longing for the presence of the divine, while visualizing the beloved. It has often been used with breathing exercises and meditation on cosmic processes such as creation and dissolution.

The *Agastya Saṃhitā*, a ritual text on devotion to Rāma composed in the 12th century elaborates on a metaphysics in which the syllables of the holy Name, *Rā* and *ma* are seen as two aspects of the ultimate reality, the origin of all cosmic manifestations. The *Agastya Saṃhitā* instructs on worship of the Name through *japa* and visualizations.[26]

In an early 12th century Śrī Vaiṣṇava commentary on the *Viṣṇu sahasranāma* ("Thousand Names of Viṣṇu"), a protege of Rāmānuja named Parasara Bhattar, argues that singing and chanting the name are at least as important as any other *bhakti* discipline: "By uttering the two syllables, *Ha* and *ri*, one gets ready for the journey to heaven," and in the *Kali Yuga*'s end those who remember Viṣṇu's name "are the blessed and their souls realize immortality."[27] Vaiṣṇava saint Jñāneśvara, who lived in Mahārāṣṭra in the 13th century advised devotees to hold on to the supreme way of spirituality by chanting the holy name, and Nāmadeva, another Vaiṣṇava saint from Mahārāṣṭra in the 14th century, spoke of the name as eternal and divine, and advised attaining oneness with the supreme through saying the name. Caitanya (d. 1533) was a Vaiṣṇava enthusiast of *bhakti* in Bengal who began a tradition of group dancing and singing of divine names and deeds. Popular *bhakti* philosophy continued to develop enthusiasm for the name, extolled the name of God even above God, or at least equated the two, thus emphasizing the importance of verbal remembrance of the deity, as an access open when the way to meditation and philosophy was barred. For example, Tulsidās (d. 1632) advised: "When meditation on the personal God is distasteful, and the impersonal too is far away from the mind, remember the life-giving name of Rāma." This devotional outlook ameliorated, it is said, "the inexorability of fate and men in distress turned to God [through the name] as a sure shield against misfortune."[28]

It is said in the *Rāmarahasyopaniṣad*, a later Sanskrit work, that if one faithfully recites the name of Rāma 96 crore (960 million) times one will attain *siddhi* – yogic power. V. Raghavan points to Tyāgarāja as an example of this. Tyāgarāja is said to have had a vision of Rāma after twenty-one years of reciting Rāma's name, and to have been inspired afterwards to compose music. Mahātma Gandhi also relied heavily on the name of Rāma. He believed that overcoming evil thoughts could heal the body of all ills, and that to do this the Rāma-*nāma* mantra is "an unfailing panacea for all ills."[29]

Thus, in a wide range of Hindu traditions and circumstances the holy name was believed to have an inherent extraordinary potency, bringing one in touch with the being or reality named. Mantras are known for their instrumentality in breaking down perceived structures of time, language and mental concepts.[30] Rhythmic repetition affects the human organism when performed mentally; all the more so when acoustic vibrations make an impact on the nervous system. Rhythm potentially can re-empattern a person's thoughts, feelings, perceptions. The intuition of sound vibrations as an elemental physical fact of the microcosmic universe is a significant insight. (Contemporary physicists have arrived at this view from a different route. Technology can turn matter, such as coal, to dust by means of sound vibrations.)

* * *

A theory and practice of the sacredness of sound and its effects on the human nervous system was developed further in mystical directions by Indian musician-yogis. For example, it is said that "In the center of the body is the *prāṇa* (life-force, breath); in the center of the *prāṇa* is the *dhvāni* (sound); in the center of the *dhvāni* is *nāda* (musical sound, harmonious primordial vibration); and in the center of the *nāda* is Sadāśiva–

the Supreme Lord."[31] Thus, in *nāda-yoga* the vibration of chanting the name ultimately participates in the nature of that which is named. (In keeping with this concept, chants and songs are called the deity's clothing in a Tyāgarāja lyric.) The idea of the magical power inherent in the recited name and in the mantric vibrational force of sound was developed and culminated in masterpieces of devotional music created by Nāmasiddhānta and *bhajana sampradāya* saints of the Kāverī delta.

* * *

Popular lore about the name also indicates its usefulness in attempts to encompass differing communities and harmonize relations among sects and achieve peaceful co-existence. For example, there is the idea that the name Rāma is composed of the *Rā* syllable from the Vaiṣṇava mantra "Om namo Nā*rā*yaṇa," and of the Śaiva mantra containing the words "Na*maḥ* Śivāya." Thus, it is said, one is really worshipping both Viṣṇu and Śiva in saying "Rāma." Śiva, Lord of yogis, is pictured repeating Rāma's name, and Rāma worships a Śiva-*liṅgam* at Rāmeśvaram. Lakṣmīdhara, in a fashion often associated with *smārta advaita*, near the end of his *Bhagavannāma kaumudi* graphically depicted the oneness of Śiva and Viṣṇu:

> The one who (as Viṣṇu) created the Holy Ganges, letting it flow from his lotus feet, became so enamored of its powers of deliverance that he (as Śiva) allowed the river to come to rest upon his head. That one is our guru, he is the divine sovereign of our people."[32]

The Kāverī delta Nāmasiddhānta movement inherits this urge toward inclusive unity, tending through devotion to faith in the divine names to point beyond narrow sectarianism. Although arguments and speculations have been made for

Yakṣa, Vaiṣṇava, Śaiva, or Śakta origins of the practice of repeating a holy name they are inconclusive due to lack of decisive historical evidence. The first religious use of saying holy names on Indian soil cannot be known. But the source and the certainty as to which name was used first is not after all as important as the goal toward which it was adopted as a way. Suffice it to say that in India ritual, yogic, musical and *bhakti* beliefs all have tended to dispose Indians of various persuasions to repeat sacred names and powerful sounds as means to spiritual realization.[33]

* * *

Nāma*siddhānta* is used by Raghavan, to mean "the way of salvation by means of the name." The term *siddha* is closely associated with *tantra* traditions. Some tantric texts go back to the 5th century, and the oral tradition must go back to more ancient times, with roots in pre-Aryan civilization. As the *Śatapatha Brāhmaṇa* interiorizes the ritual cosmic sacrifice, tantra takes this trend even further. The goal of tantra, as I have said, is to realize the identity of opposites – Śiva and Śakti, Nirvāna and saṃsāra, eternity and time, spirit and matter, macrocosm and microcosm. Some *siddha* traditions are especially concerned with transforming the body to attain immortality. Mantra is an integral part of these traditions.[34]

Lakṣmīdhara, who lived during the 15th century, is one of the links between the Nāmasiddhānta saints and the name-reciting traditions which preceded them. Called the "first theoretician who systematized the philosophy which is familiarly known as the *Nāma-Siddhānta*,"[35] Lakṣmīdhara, who was a *smārta* Brahman, also wrote an important treatise on *Śrīvidya*, a commentary on *Saundaryalaharī*, concerning tantric Goddess worship. Lakṣmīdhara is said to have been a great authority on *Purva Mīmāṃṣā*, the school of thought in which the sounds of mantras have inherent powers and the gods themselves do not exist independently from their invocations. In his treatise on the name, *Bhagavannāma Kaumudi*, Lakṣmīdhara refers to revelation, tradition, legend and history (*Śruti*, *Smṛiti*, *Itihāsa* and *Purāṇa*), asserting that they share similar views on the power of the name to bring deliverance. In Lakṣmīdhara we find a combination of backgrounds: *mīmāṃṣā*, *smārta* traditions, *tantra* and *bhakti yoga*. Lakṣmīdhara was an intermediary who gathered previous traditions of the name, and Bodhendra in the Kāverī delta studied Lakṣmīdhara's work and patterned his teachings after it. Basing his philosophy on Lakṣmīdhara's stance he opened up the practice to popularization, giving access to more and more people.

* * *

If we simplify the trajectory of sacred utterances in India to a broad outline we find five basic forms of expression: 1. In Vedic sacrifices, mantras are essential formulae, concerned with *karman*. *Om* is the prime example, (and *gāyatrī*, with which Hindus are initiated and which is recited daily and at important rites) and interpretations of this use were made by *Mīmāṃsākas*, Upaniṣadic thinkers and grammarians. 2. In yoga the mantra is a mind tool, an instrument for liberation. The archetypal "king of yogis" is Śiva, the Hindu deity beyond the conventions of man, but Buddhist and Jain mantras might also be included here. Not all mantras are names, and not all names are mantras, but reciting a holy name in a mantric formula is intended to give the mind a spiritual activity to focus it in its urge toward self-mastery. 3. In ritual worship mantras invoking names are used in praise and incantations. The *Āgamas*, *Purāṇas*, *Saṃhitās* show development of piety in reverence for Viṣṇu, among others. 4. In Tantra, there is a faith in the magical power of the mantra, which may include a name of a Goddess. Tantra incorporated earlier uses of the mantra, and certain attractive aspects of it pervaded Śaiva, Vaiṣṇava, and Buddhist communities. 5. In the *bhakti* renewal the name of the beloved, often Rāma or Krishna, became a link to the personal deity, a way to saving grace. Often the name was joined with appealing music and other arts to bring out emotional flavors, longing and love. Saints of Viṣṇu, Śiva, Goddess devotion, and of the Muslim-Hindu synthesis, such as Kabīr, Nānak and the Sikhs are examples of this use. It would seem that in these five overlapping but somewhat chronological categories the last three seem to involve increasing popularization of the concept. The sacred utterance goes from the specialists (Veda-knowing priests), to the common man, and people of cultural creativity and universalistic tendencies, such as *smārta* Brahmans, were increasingly implicated especially in these last three.

* * *

It is no accident, I believe, that the recognized leaders of the Kāverī delta Nāmasiddhānta movement were Telugu *smārta* Brahmans. *Smārtas* from ancient times were carriers of the *smṛiti*, "that which is remembered," the body of law codes handed down traditionally. These *smṛiti śāstras* present a "liberal non-sectarian trend of guidance . . . " not advocating the cause of any particular sect, hence their custodians have tended to be a force for integrative harmony when faced with sectarian diversity. In a sense the *smārtas* advocated their own understanding of religious life, but affirmation of the different views which make up the whole is not simply one more partial view. To encourage spirituality in various communities is not to form a sect. Philosophical expansiveness and creative assimilation produce different works than stances and answers based on exclusiveness, avoidance and elimination. Certain key *Smārtas* have been culturally creative synthesizers who assimilated non-Brahman devotional practices to their own rituals, ultimately developing some of the bhakti practices which spread throughout India in early medieval times; they seem to have been the pre-Gupta preservers of Purāṇic legends, who served in temples and used the old non-Sanskritic stories to glorify their own deities in Sanskrit.[36]

The "composite character" of Purāṇic Hinduism and of the Purāṇic texts is due to *smārta* innovation responding to societal disintegration and Buddhist and Jain competition. Conservatively, they promulgated Vedic authority and caste values, but innovatively they popularized Brahmanic ideas among lower twice-born castes, women and *śudras* (lower caste people), and they promoted Vedic ideas among Vaiṣṇava and Śaiva worshippers. They answered the heterodox challenge and gave religious access to the many by shaping the Purāṇic outlook during early medieval times, helping *bhakti* fervor spread.

Some members of the *smārta* community have long been known for tolerance and a harmonizing philosophy which "toned down the sectarian bitterness which Pañcaratra and Āgamic [Vaiṣṇava and Śaiva] conflict tended to produce."[37] The *smārtas* developed the practice of selecting and worshipping an *iṣṭadevatā*, the chosen or favorite form of the divine. In this practice the guru, after observing the temperament of the disciple, chooses a name and form of the divine, Vaiṣṇava, Śaiva or Śakta which is sympatico with the worshipper. This is a more intentional and disciplined use of the Name than that offered in the previously cited teaching of Bodhendra, yet it allows for a measure of freedom of choice– it is not simply hereditary.

As one more example of the *smārta* tendency to encourage devotion to one's favorite form or conception of

God without denying others, *smārtas* developed a special worship service expressing that outlook. Probably long before the Hindu medieval period, which began around 500 AD), after the creator god Brahmā lost importance, *smārtas* evolved a kind of worship known as *pañcāyatana-pūjā*. In this worship the major deities of the five orthodox Brahmanical sects were worshipped aniconically. Different colored stones, believed to be pervaded by the deities' essences are placed on a metal plate called pañcāyatana: black (Viṣṇu), white (Śiva), red (Ganeṣa), metalic ore (the Goddess), crystal (the Sun). They are configured with the deity of preference in the center, and the other four in a peripheral square. Later, Rāma and Krishna *pañcāyatana* worship was developed also. Thus, *smārtas* worshipped deities other than their own chosen form, and also were able to be loosely or closely affiliated with particular sects in a harmonious participatory manner. Hence it was in character with their past to espouse devotion to various names of God, whether they be Śaiva, Vaiṣṇava or Śakta,[38] in the late medieval and early modern period.

The leaders of Kāverī delta Nāmasiddhānta, in part because they lived in Tamil Nadu, often wrote not in their mother tongue, Telugu, but in Sanskrit, like the *smārta* writers of the Purāṇas, and unlike the many sectarian *bhakti* leaders who used their mother tongues for religious writing. In their spoken teachings they employed the regional languages. Being conservative innovators they also sought, as earlier *smārtas* had, to carry forward essential traditions, yet to adapt to meet the chaos of changing times, the turbulence in society.

* * *

The term *smārta* concerns the memory; as bearers of *smṛiti* (the recalled revelation) the *smārtas* have the role of being the rememberers of religious identity, to keep continuity with the past progressively. Memory in itself, always and everywhere, has to do with a "then" pictured "now," a previous situation, re-conceived at a subsequent time. Preservers of an essential thread or core of religious life, renewers of coherence, guardians of a viable orthodox tradition, *smārtas* have often served as intermediaries and transmitters handling and handing over the sacred ways of "then" in the crisis-ridden "now." It may be that the *smārta* Hindu metaphysics, with the concept of the inextricable nature of *nāma* and *rūpa*, emphasizes continuities, while prophetic faiths emphasize radical disjunctions. Study of the ways Name is conceived in religions offers an entry to a consideration of the presuppositions and character of Eastern and Western faiths.

* * *

Since humans are destined to repeat willy-nilly (because we naturally echo pop music, jingles from commercials, buzzwords and catch-phrases; but in a deeper sense because the organic lifemode itself is one of cycles, rhythms, oscillations – all life shares the code of DNA, following repeated patterns) why shouldn't postmodern people seek out and find the mantras which will help them and further the lifestream, use the seed-sounds worthy of refrain, whether Shalom or As Salamu Alaikam, Amen or Om, God bless or Namu Amida Butsu, Hail Mary or Jai Mahādevī, to make the best of one's time, marking it with awareness?

Further Reflections on Theories and Practices of the Name

The "meaning" of name repetition is that it goes round and round again until "meaning" in relative terms, rational and irrational, is left behind in immediate experience, as in ecstasy, trance, satori, transcendence. If beads represent time, name incarnates the Named to become the moments filling time, continuously transforming the passing into the eternal. Name is an entrance to experiencing consciousness in terms of mythical realms.

* * *

Why is veneration of the Name(s) so pervasive, so important? Seen from the level of logic, language and philosophy, the use of holy Names by religious people seems rooted in the mind and its labelling: "there are certain things of which the reality is not only known through, but is inseparably bound up with, *consists in*, the name by which it is called."[39] The range of interpretations along this line of thought runs from theism to sophisticated philosophy and ritual theory of *mīmāṃsā*. Humans everywhere pretend that these sounds they make are the names of the one they love, the ultimate bearer of all names, which is ultimately nameless (because nonhuman). The art of naming is very human. Name is the receptacle into which humans pour hopes, feelings, fears, joys, need for connectivity.

"It is through the name that the poet keeps hold of his vision, which is then able to unfold itself by virtue of this retention," according to Martin Heidegger. And ". . . poetry is. . . a state of knowing and feeling a name," acording to Gertrude Stein.[40]

* * *

Mantras, being multivalent instruments, are used and interpreted in a variety of ways. Harvey P. Alper in the introduction to *Understanding Mantras* writes "they are one of the structural pivots around which a mature and sophisticated society has organized its life. Traditional Indian society is predicated on its belief in the efficacy of the well-spoken human word and the well-made ritual gesture. May we explain mantras scientifically at the same time that we appreciate them personally" and "open up a new perspective. . . on the variety of Indian religious life and on humanity's capacity to give voice to that beyond which there is nothing more."[41] Thinkers with fixed ideas (if that is not a contradiction in terms), over-conditioned with presuppositions, subconsciously defending their own Christian or other Western orientations, are not up to this challenge. They are unable to see beyond the clever constructions they have worked so hard to build up. The "personal" side of Alper's suggestion is foreign to them, because they have been observing like voyeurs through a one-way mirror for so long. In that case, what to do to expand the possibilities of revisualization and understanding? One recourse is to see what glimpses our Western poets have opened on this. For example, Robert Bly and Octavio Paz.

* * *

From the level of organic life, cellular processes, seen in wonder by the poet, the same question about the why of the name's importance takes us to different views. American poet Robert Bly entitled one of his prose poems "The Origin of the Praise of God" which I quote in part here:

> "My friend, this body is made of bone and excited protozoa! And it is with my body that I love the fields. How do I know what I feel but what the body tells me? * * * . . . The sound that pours from the fingertips awakens clouds of cells far inside the body, and beings unknown to us start out on a pilgrimage to their Savior, to their holy place. Their holy place is a small black stone that they remember from Protozoic times, when it was rolled away from a door. . . And it was after that they found their

> friends, who helped them to digest the hard grains of this world. The cloud of cells awakens, intensifies, swarms. The cells dance inside beams of sunlight so thin we cannot see them. To them each ray is a vast palace, with thousands of rooms. From the dance of the cells praise sentences rise to the throat of the man praying and singing alone in his room . . ."[42]

The poet's implication is that praise comes from deep within, a process of disclosure within organic life which rhythmically moves each being through time and wonder around and around. The poet reveals connections among levels of existence, and praise through the name makes of those perceived connections bridges, ways to participate in other levels.

Continuing the exploration with the intuition of a creative specialist in symbolic envisioning – the poet – consider Octavio Paz's thoughts on the "sonorous jewels" which mantras are. Paz believes Tantrism's essence lies in the mantras. "They are the heart of the religions of India. The *mantra* is the other face of yoga and, like yoga, it is not intellectual but practical and non-discursive. It is a means of obtaining certain powers. The recitation of the *mantra*, whether silent or aloud, lays down a bridge between the reciter and the macrocosm, as do the breathing exercises of the yogi. But the *mantra* is above all a ritual instrument, to be used either in collective rites or personal worship... specialists have not paid enough attention [to the aspect of mantras as] indicative signs, sonorous signs of identification. Each divinity, each guru, each disciple, each worshipper, each concept, and each moment of the ritual has a *mantra* appropriate to it. The poet Kanha has expressed it better than this complicated explanation I have given: the syllables (*bījas*) clasp the naked ankle of the yogini like a bracelet. They are sonorous attributes."[43] For the vision seeker, mantras and ragas are beautiful adornments, charms around the features of the sacred one. The name is the accessible fold through which the mystery is entered.

Paz goes on: "Neither Christian prayers nor litanies nor abracadabras and other magic formulas are the equivalent of the *mantras*. Perhaps poetry is, or is rather one of its manifestations – which Alfonso Reyes once called 'jitanjafors,' the nonconceptual explosion of the syllables, the joy, anguish, the anger, the desire expressed in them. It is a language beyond language, as in the poems of Kurt Schwitters, the interjections of Artaud, the serpentine, feline syllables of Michaux, the ecstatic vowels of Huidobro. . . [but] the Indians do not invent these 'sonorous jewels' – the guru passes them on to the disciple. Nor are they poems; they are verbal amulets, linguistic talismans, sonorous scapulars. A symbolic and hermetic language – genital words, phonetic and semantic couplings, jingling *mantra*s. . . A language that blurs the distinction between the word and the act, that reduces the sign to a mere signifier, that multiplies and changes the meanings of these signs, that conceives of itself as a game that is identical to that of the universe, in which the right side and the left side, the feminine and the masculine, fulness and emptiness, are one and the same – a language that means everything and nothing."[44]

* * *

Harvey P. Alper's *Understanding Mantras* gathers some of the best work done on mantras recently, revealing a general scholarly agreement on the fact that mantra is the prime model for religious speech in India. But because tunnel-vision Western scholars consider mantra non-scientific (though it has a logic of its own), and because it is used to attain this-worldy ends, and because words of love are embarrassing to persons speaking with strictly cool intellects, mantra has not been represented in Western studies in a way proportionate to its importance. In Alper's book several scholars' works are highlighted. Jan Gonda has several definitions of mantra: 1. invocatory formulas, words of praise with magic power; 2. counsel, plan, secret, etc. ; 3. potent sound letters bringing good luck and bhakti instruments of religious transfiguration. Agehananda Bharati defines mantra as a "quasimorpheme... based on codified esoteric traditions and transmitted in initiation from preceptor to disciple" saying mantra is meaningful "within the mystical universe of discourse . . . verifiable by what it effects . . . complex feeling-tone in the practicing person." Frits Staal sees mantras as pre-linguistic – "the predecessor" (though mantras have not died so this seems to me a misnomer) of "language in the process of human evolution," and as aids to reach mystical states of awareness (which are also pre-linguistic). The study brings out the conclusion that language is something with which people accomplish actions in the Indian experience, it is not just words for saying things. It is significant that mathematics, calculative abstract thinking as the model for "real knowing" predominates among the intellectual elite of the West (despite such developments as modern physic's "string theory" in which subatomic particles are modes of vibration), while linguistics as a systemic metaphor has had more resonance among the Indian elite. Continuous faith in mantras, and interpretation of the universe as being language-like, created by divine sound is characteristic of India. *Nāmajapa* is a kind of mantra usage to call out in love and finally identify with the holy.[45]

* * *

I find it frustrating and amusing (yet typical) that in his autobiographical statement V. Raghavan mentions mantra in a very unusual context but does not remark on its unusualness. (See page 326.) Isn't it typical that this kind of anomalous situation is found in practice in India but is *often* not reflected in the traditional scholar's articles? Traditional people, even though somewhat modernized, tend not to tackle what does not fit the conventional mold. I am referring to Raghavan's uncle learning mantras from a Muslim. Just this, the very unconsciousness and separation of the ideal traditional which is approved, and the actual happenstance which seems to fall outside the framework, would be interesting to explore – and it is not unlike the question: what effects did Islam have on Hinduism in bhakti and practices relating to the name? Evidence of interaction is scarce, in my South Indian research.

* * *

I spent part of the summer of 1989 in South India, interviewing leading members of Nāmasiddhānta including Krishna Premi of Paranūr, Veṅkaṭaraman Bhāgavatar of Tiruvidaimarudūr, Śrī Natarājan and G. S. Balasubramanyan of Govindapuram and R. Krishnamurthy of Tiruviśanallūr, the author of a scholarly book on Nāmasiddhānta. Krishna Premi whom I met in Madras left an impression of simplicity and quiet sincerity, serenity and friendliness. I met Veṅkaṭaraman Bhāgavatar, a blind bhajan leader at the Bodhendra math, both in Madras and in his home village of Tiruvidaimarudūr. Both he and Krishna Premi seemed very knowledgeable in the history and practices of Nāmasiddhānta. A lifetime of practice and expounding of Nāmasiddhānta has made each of these men articulate speakers on the way of the name.

Little statistical information is available on the number of participants in Nāmasiddhānta today, I found as I spoke with the above-mentioned leaders. This is a problem in studying the religious ideas and practices of a rather decentralized movement of loosely organized nonsectarian or intersectarian congregations spread throughout the region. Nāmasiddhānta's view that not institution, but inner practice is essential, accounts for its lack of coverage among scholars who think especially in terms of domination and simple sectarian categories. The practice of devotion to the name is not much noted, yet it is all pervasive, cuts across sect affiliation, and is a central path in Hindu faith.

* * *

Italo Calvino: Prior to name is narrative. True? The telling of stories allows certain relationships among elements and not others. Śiva (or Rāma or the Goddess) acts a certain way: names *depict* people's feelings about that activity. Rudra or Śiva can harm or help, and hope for his helpfulness causes men to name him "Auspicious." Calvino says relationships take on beneficial or malignant powers, called magical powers– they should have been called *"narrative"* power. Potentialities contained in the word, in its ability to link itself with other words on the plane of discourse, or to stand for the extraordinary to transform imaginatively – that is the power of the story-name. *Nāmāvalis*, strings of names in litanies, each calling to mind a story or vision of Śiva's, Viṣṇu's, Goddess' acts. Narrative and name are inseparable; recalling "who" requires name.[46]

* * *

East/West binary differences are telling. Western prophetic-root faiths are confrontative, dualistic; Eastern faiths tend to be incorporative monisms. There is prohibition against using the Name in Judaism; encouragement to say the Name in more playful non-linear Hinduism. Perhaps both –

prophetic concerns and mystic concerns – show indestructible human impulses: Hasidim, Sufis, Eckhart are mystics in prophetic faiths; Ram Mohan Roy, Taoist messiahs and others are prophets in mystic faiths. Their various views of the name tell much about each way of being religious.

Judaism: *He* mustn't be named. Taoism: *It* is unnameable. Tao Te Ching:[47] Tao is undifferentiated perfect "being before heaven and earth" and is "the mother of the world – I don't know its name. I will call it Tao if it must be named, its name will be the immense" (*ta*). This is a pun or soundplay: Tao chimes with *ta*. (The immense part played by seemingly chance similarity of sounds in the logic, use and thought concerning names – sign of the playfulness and serious forgetfulness of consciousness.) The Nameless is the origin of heaven and earth. The Named is the Mother of the 10,000 beings.

For Chinese mystics the holy is not just there in the emperor's presence. The power of the name to capture imagination, initiate transformation, impel reorientation. Take for example the quite namable names of the yogic focal point between the eyes, to be meditated upon, in Chinese *Golden Flower*:[48]

"Square inch field of the square foot house" "Yellow castle," "Terrace of Life," "Purple hall of the city of jade," "Heavenly heart, golden flower, primal pass," "Border regions of the snow mountains," "Germinal vescicle," "Space of former heaven," "Realm of greatest joy," "Land without boundaries," "Dragon castle at the bottom of the sea," "Altar upon which life and consciousness are made." Such names announce the extraordinary to be found within, intrigue, beckon, impress with awe and reverence. Calling to mind what happens there, what that secret place of higher consciousness in the human body does and is, with metaphors that resonate in the mystic imagination – intuitive poetic naming initiates an initiation into a program, implied in the metaphorical names. The names begin a process: "Understand life thus," they say.

Mystics would seem to name potent experiences of the sacred as "the attractive," "the foothold in the mystery," "bridge linking this to that," "path to wonder," "mark of distinction," "seed of program," "hint of what is," "revealer of the concealed." The names are promises of a joyful mind, they give the imagination a reminder and foretaste, an appetite, a hope, a reason to resolve to attain; they offer a quest to pursue, a piece of the ultimate in the bewildering profane. They keep a non-present entity in mind, keep its reality alive, a way to strive and express hope for its presence. Hans Georg Gadamer: "To name something is always to call it into presence." Susan Sontag, in a story writes: "I write your name. Two syllables. Two vowels. Your name inflates you, is bigger than you. You repose in a corner, sleeping; your name awakes you. I write it. You could not be named otherwise. Your name is your juice, your taste, your savor. Called by any other name you vanish. I write it. Your name." (Susan Sontag in "The Letter Scene," a short story.)[49] Name behavior, whether in sacred or profane relationship, follows certain patterns, structures in human consciousness. Naming as a form of identifying is peculiar to humans – animals use scents and other means. Singing to demarcate territory is not limited to birds.

* * *

Considering nametags for the ineffable as *exempla* from various cultures, side by side synchronically – Allah, Tao, Brahman – we make abstract generalizations about them. For the intent aspirant, one name "fills the horizon" – each is the world of meaning totality, though all are able to be that. The sacred has an abundance of names, and this causes confusion in those unused to varied abundance, those unable to be generous, those defensive against *other* names. But for the postmodern world an essential name for the holy, a name which perhaps many humans must learn to say, is "The Many-Named." But even this name should not be taken too literally, but must be translated into many deeper subtler understandings. The trouble with literalism is it stops at a convenient point and refuses to see further.

* * *

Names are problems for translators. They cannot be dealt with very richly by literalists.

Literalists, like reductive positivists, take the "objective world" as linear reality and cut the loops of reflexivity, common humanity (including oneself) and multivalent resonance. They deny human enigmas of ambiguity, insisting on comforting simplicity, resisting deeper demands of diversity. They refuse and secretly fear the depths of human nature, realms of the unconscious clinging to neat answers instead of feeling the questions of depth, the ultrasensitive consciousness which humans live by, the mystery which must be plumbed by art as well as science, playful imagination as well as deadly serious rationality and the controller's certainty.

The cynic is the master of misnomers, applying a twisted conclusion, a condescending interpretive label to that which when seen within a deeper context is a justice or a marvel or a pattern. Nihilism puts existence in a category labelled "ridiculous" or "trashbin," sees meaningless chaos and not cosmos. Thus nihilism is far from the idealist with faith in the Name and its power, far from the poetic experience, far from the gratitude of wonder, trust and hope, which are associated with devotion to the name.

* * *

At one end of the spectrum technical mantric lore (Muttusvāmī Dīkṣitar and Tyāgarāja were expert); at the other end the poor bhakta in personal act of simply *saying the name*, link to the source of order in the midst of chaos.

Without practices of the name, and without the root paradigms of saints, perhaps the goal of *mokṣa* would seem to have been a "casualty" of the *bhakti* movement, which in many forms has stressed the enjoyment of love more than the transcendence of release. In the *Mahābhārata*, Bhīṣma waits 54 days then dies with the name of Krishna. Later, when the ideal is so devoted to bhakti, release seems betrayal of the highest experience – which is enjoying one's love of the personal God, tastable via the name.

* * *

Do Indians believe in words too much, as is asserted by J. Frits Staal, who wrote of Vedic man's "overvaluation of the word"? John Kenneth Gailbraith similarly characterized Coomaraswamy. The florid rhetorical forms of Hindu expression contrast starkly with understated Zen. Do Indians tend to mistake pious sentiments in flowery words for holy being, vulnerable (like many modern voters) to the charms of eloquent speakers? The bhakti saints criticize verbal hypocrisy, hold up examples of true *bhakti* piety versus hypocritical "magpiety." It is as difficult for the mystic to make public the private as it is for the political interpreters of religion to make private the public – they are different temperaments interested in different things: outward dominance, inward illumination. The power and the glory.

The power of voiced hope, the power of the uplifted human voice in ritual, to give courage is remarkable. Name, and song, are heightened language, heights to which language points and leads. The name attunes mind to awareness of eternal cosmic system resonance: *Nāda*, Kepler's cosmic "music of the spheres."

* * *

Gandhi knew the power of names. He replaced the names for untouchables with the name "Harijans" – "Children of God" – to create a moral dilemma in Indians, to appeal to their conscience. He succeeded in making at least some impact. (V. Raghavan named The Kāverī delta *Nāmasiddhānta* movement to underline the power of the name, holding up Tyāgarāja as ideal fulfilment, as inspiration.) Confucius had a program for "rectification of names." Countless examples illustrate the power, for good or ill, of names – the importance of correct, right-mindful names in the orientation of a life-way. An ego-centered people, like those described in the Old Testament, who would "make a name for themselves," is shattered, scattered in bewilderment of tongues; but wherever even two or three are gathered in The Holy's Name the Holy is present, and the spirit unifies, calms, heals, makes whole. And good should be done "in Jesus' name." Thich Nhat Hanh's poem "please call me by my true names" identifies with all beings, the starving Ugandan child, the arms merchant, the raped twelve year old, the pirate rapist, and asks "Please call me by my true names,/so I can wake up,/ and so the door of my heart can be left open, the door of compassion."

* * *

Envisioned enchanting names of the holy were what the mantra-seeing *ṛiṣis* knew. The formless has many names but none are absolute: a central Vedic rule of thumb often ignored by Western conclusions about the Vedas.

Name potentially overrides space, cancels distances. Song overrides time, makes the sung seem present. Name is a pilgrimage home, a love-call embrace, an immediate refuge. Song is a ritual art, a satisfying self-forgetting, an entrancing uniter of realms. Chanting is purposefully playing with sound and hearing, exploring it within discipline, within limits, to flow beyond, to transcend. So the singer's being becomes a "withness."

* * *

Modern physics: Everything is vibration – empty space with rapidly vibrating subatomic particles. India's ultimate paradigm of reality is language, not math. Acoustic models: reality as good vibrations; persons participating in vibrations to praise the Holy. Name veneration as religion at its most basic. A use of voice, a directing of mind, a flow of feelings–in short a worship verging on contemplation. A participatory symbol – presentational – open to involve followers in a lifeway. A mode of healing – reharmonizing discordant parts. A name is the shortest distance between two beings– man and wife, child and parent, man and God. As such it is a way. Nāmasiddhānta rationale: Call out and find Him within. The Lord is always on call.

Hindus feel the unknowable is sayable. Ineffable but singable, tasteable, rollable on the tongue, churnable in the heart, it is the refuge reached via name. Name is evidence of existence, beginning point of faith, reliable designation, insignia of dominion.

Diana Eck said of the Hindu view: "to say there are 330 million gods is to say how many places one is capable of standing to see the divine," each religious tradition has its own valid way of naming the divine; each name is limited yet "fills the horizon" for the believer; each religious language is a language of praise.[50] This is neo-*syādvāda* ("somehowism") – all exist, function, have a place – admits what is, with *ahiṃsā*, innocent tolerance.

Bhakti: "It is your love itself I know when your *Name* comes to mind." Immediacy. When a child is calling the mother there is no thought like "This is her *name* I call." The child is calling *her*, not calling her name. Need is invoking being, not fooling around with sign. The name is the shortest *formal* prayer. Informal: groan, sigh, cry, "help," weeping.

* * *

Nāma always goes with *rūpa*, but *nāma* is not *rūpa*. Name is not form, yet mantra is a *form*ula, a *form*ulation– reifiable sound power standing for invisible form. Interiorizable, able to shake up your vocal cords, nasal cavities, your brain and chest, breathing and heartbeat, as well as brain patterns: alpha waves. Repeated patterns to stabilize mind's attention. Able to transform consciousness of experience. Able to bring near the visualized form through the direction of consciousness.

Dolphins and whales *ensonify* fish to prey upon them. Interesting verb, ensonify. The Lord is bound by sincere prayer. "By the repetition of [Viṣṇu's] name, man is undoubtedly liberated from all sins, which fly like wolves that are frightened by a lion."[51]

Names describe, characterize, make possible vivid recollection of the nature of the Divine. Allah alone is abstract unity; the 99 most beautiful names conjure up detail, nuance, revelations of relations. Allah becomes – the monolythic stone has facets which live, which support, which may be kissed, and against which the fallen may be dashed or revived, as the Named wills.

* * *

The primary Western sense is sight according to Aristotle. Vision "unveils countless differences," says Jacques Derrida.[52] The Primary Eastern sense: hearing, which glosses over many troubling fluctuations of change with a mysterious unity, a blending harmony – all of language is in AUM, all one vibration. One needs both noonday discernment and deep sleep at night. Mark Helpern wrote that "The European ideal is to commit difficult acts amid richness and overflowing beauty."[53] This is an ideal perfect for the ecstasies and agonies of colonizers. The Eastern ideal – also taken to extremes by the vivid religious exemplars – is to transcend limits and pain of life through renunciation of the personal and by adhesion to ultimate truth. This has taken various forms – yoga's *tapas*, Jainism's fast unto death, bhakti's singleminded chaste dedication to the divine Beloved, to name a few. Eternal undercurrent as absolute harmony. Benign (divine) circular (natural) existence.

In Banāras invisible Śiva whispers the *tāraka mantra*: to smooth the way, make the link, unify the little namer and the vast Named. On the cremation ground the constant chanting "Rāma nāma satya hai."

* * *

In North India there are "banks" for storing the accumulated pages of the name written millions of times. While Tulsidās and others spread the practice of repeating the name, the more recent popular discipline is writing the name in notebooks, which are stacked and baled together in the banks. These savings institutions are associated with the Rāmānandī organization. It is considered especially auspicious to see 125 karor names (1,250,000,000). There are name banks in Banāras, Ayodhya, and many "branch offices" in other parts of North India.[54] Most moderns cannot conceal their amazement at the astronomical numbers (such as one billion 250 million) involved in the writing of the name in the movement of the Rāmānandī banks. It reminds me that whenever I explain that South Indian Rāma bhakti composer Tyāgarāja is remembered for repeating his Rāma mantra 125,000 times a day for twenty-one years and fifteen days (for a grand total of 960 million times in all) – my listeners usually laugh. Even religious Hindus sometimes seem amused at the spectacle of a little human with a short attention span struggling to add up a staggering number of recitations.

In Tamil Nadu there are even humorous stories of Tenāḷi Rāma reciting a Kālī mantra the required 30 million times in one night. The goddess with her thousand heads appears and offers the clownish brahman either wisdom or wealth, which are contained in separate vessels. The daring fool Tenāḷi Rāma Krishna greedily drinks both, then makes matters worse by bursting into laughter. "Why?" Kālī asks. He explains "I thought I had it bad when I have to blow my nose – what a mess it must be for you, with your thousand noses!" Kālī curses him to be a clown, leaving him much as he was before his 30 million ejaculations.

If Kabīr had seen the banks filled with notebooks of Rāma's name, would he have mocked them, and exploited the counter-image for hidden wealth – blackmarket money – as a vivid currency for the independent religious imagination? "Plunder the name," he advises the sneaking-prone human.

The changing metaphors regarding the name over the centuries are revealing, and the development of movements beginning in inspired religious experience, such as a lowcaste Ālvār's ecstasy, and ending with an elitist institution. I sense too the loss of some meaning and impetus here. Why is 125 *karor* an auspicious number, and 125,000 an important target amount which can qualify one to become a member of the Bhakti Name Bank Society? Is there mention in the Bank's literature of the goal or climax of this exercise? In the *Rāmarahasyopaniṣad*, for example, Rāma promises that whoever recites his name 96 *karors* of times is liberated from all sin, and attains infinite existence-consciousness-bliss. The climax of a vision and inspiration is often found in the lives of earlier South Indian name reciters. Perhaps ecstacy is an embarrassment to sober accountants. It might be helpful to learn more about the social backgrounds of the "depositors" on the name banks. The metaphor has changed, but has this banking become their primary or only form of devotion? Do depositors also sing? While it's true you have to petition a bureaucrat, is there still nostalgia enough so that depositors also sing to the beloved king and praise his name with music? In any case this practice regarding the name seems a far cry from earlier saints who sang enthusiastically about instant gratification – the name was called nectar, sweets, sugar candy, a fountain, and medicine. Banking on the name in the North now seems a more sober kind of saving for a rainy day.

This illustration shows a woman's face tatooed with the Sanskrit word "Rāma." She is a member of the North Indian Rāmnāmi community.[55]

We can read many things into this text. Is the Rāmnāmi woman smiling behind her open secret, or grieving in the public humiliation of self-effacement? Only a veil of bliss – *his* name over her face – curtains her from him (not him from her); I think you can see her smile subtly at play beyond the gloomy purdah of his sign. In any case there is nowhere to hide in this life; her truth is written all over her face. That *is* life for this Rāmnāmi. The woman's etched face thus becomes for us a text of religious love. Her ever-speaking face is an incantation which effortlessly says it all, and this *protects* the silent dedication-marked nameless namer of Lord Rāma. Only a Rāvana would dare ravish or insult her, with the divine-name woven veil over her face. The tatooed face displays self-displacement, devotional effacement of the individual, and the humble nomination of oneself for full refuge and release. Tatooed with one's hoped-for future, one's visible obsession and sole refuge of hope. Not a skin-deep bond, the name like meditation calms and directs the mind, cultivating the ground for depth inspiration. The name is the shortest formal prayer, the tatooed veil of name is the most insubstantial material separating her from (and joining her to) her beloved. How much closer can one get – Rāma is in her heart and on her tongue, and on her skin his name is the surface with nothing intervening. She has surrounded her self with him; for others he may not be present, for her there's no way he can vanish. She holds him. He holds her within his holy name.

"Purity is one of the most attractive ideas the human race knows. The other is perfection. Purity is absence; perfection is fullness."[56] Nāmasiddhānta ultimately means "perfected fulfilment of human being through the holy name." Purity, always important in the Hindu structuring of human life, requires purging, refinement, in the bhakti period, though the name. Thus the name is most auspicious, pure, powerful, complete, perfect, able to transform mind, bring grace, save, liberate.

Notes

[1] Just as *Bande Mataram* by Bankim Chandra Chatterji became a mantric national anthem unifying members of the Indian Independence movement, "We shall overcome" has functioned as a powerful mantra for the civil rights movement in America and elsewhere. The power of chanting to give strength in trying circumstances has often gone unnoticed in the modern world, but there are many examples showing chants and songs are still effective equivalents of "Open Sesame!" Because these chants involve people in a voicing of hope and a heartening solidarity as well as focusing minds on an ultimate ideal or goal, they are more than mere slogans, and are akin to *mantras* in the original meanings of the term. I would include among these "All we are saying is give peace a chance," and "Amazing Grace. " Thomas Merton in the opening passage of his *Asian Journal* mentions "Christian mantras."

[2] Simone Weil, tr. E. Craufurd, *Waiting for God* (New York: Harper, 1973. First pub. Putnam's Sons, 1951), p. 182.

[3] Martin Buber, *I and Thou*, tr. R.G. Smith (New York: Scribner's, 1958), p. 75.

[4] *Old Testament* ideas about names are revealing. In Gen. II. 19 Adam names, therefore has power to control, the animals. The story of Babel is suggestive: men want to "make a name" for themselves and build a tall tower, and are scattered in a bewilderment of tongues, but wherever a few are gathered in the holy's name, unifying spirit is present. ". . . the *double-bind* of YHWH affording (with the name of his choice, with his name, we could say, Babel) translation and no translation." Jacques Derrida, "Apocalyptic Tone," *Derrida and Biblical Studies* volume of *Semeia 23*, ed. Robert Detweiler (Chico: Scholars Press, 1982), p. 64. See also Thomas J. J. Altizer, *The Self-Embodiment of God* (Lanham: Univ. Press of America, 1987). *Encyclopaedia Brittanica*, "Baal Shem Tov," p. 762. The Baal Shem Tov was a wonder-worker who effected cures with the sacred name of God, sometimes with amulets incribed with the divine name.

[5] *Encyclopaedia Brittanica*, "Taoism." p. 1037.

[6] "Handle" is an apt term used by amateur radio operators meaning one's code name to identify oneself "on the air."

[7] H. Wagenvoort, *Roman Dynamism* (Oxford: Blackwell, 1947), p. 78. Remarking on the oldest usages of the term *numen* (holy) in conjunction with *nomen* (name) in the 2nd century BC, Wagenvoort asks: "was the combination *nomen et numen*... a standing expression for the idea 'godhead,' so that... the name made the *numen* a god?"

[8] Elaine Pagels, *The Gnostic Gospels* (New York: Vintage Books, 1981), pp. xvi, 29, 112, 123-4, 149, 154, 164, 166. D.T. Suzuki, *Mysticism, Christian and Buddhist: The Eastern and Western Way*, pp. 123 ff. There is a Mongolian story of hell in which frozen people suffer. The only thing they can move is their lips, and all their lips can say is "Bu-" the first syllable of Buddha's name. But that is enough to save them, according to John Laughlin in a personal communication. *The Way of a Pilgrim* (tr. R.M. French, New York: Harper and Bros. , 1955) describes a Christian tradition of repeating Jesus' name thousands of times each day. Karl Barth in various theological writings and Herbert Gabhart in *The Name Above Every Name* (Nashville: Broadman, 1986) are other Christians involved in recovering the holiness and power of the name in Christianity. In black American churches, such as Zion Temple, First Pentecostal Church, in Cincinatti, new members are led to the upper room to "tarry with the Holy Ghost," they kneel and repeat the name of Jesus over and over until they speak in an unknown tongue. In Islam, the recitation (*zhekar*) of the names of Allah is the one practice followed by all schools of Sufism. In the Qur'an (XI. 41) we find the words of Noah to those escaping the deluge: "Board [the Ark]; in God's Name be its course and mooring. My Lord is forgiving, merciful."

[9] J. L. Mehta, "My Years at the Center: Some Reflections," *Harvard Center for the Study of World Religions Bulletin*, Winter 1978, p. 3. Reprinted in J.L. Mehta, *Philosophy and Religion* (New Delhi: Indian Council for Philosophical Research, 1990).

[10] Richard Lannoy, *The Speaking Tree* (London: Oxford Univ. 1975) pp. 271-280.

[11] J. Frits Staal, *Agni: The Vedic Ritual of the Fire Altar,* 2 vols. (Berkeley: Asian Humanities Press, 1983).

[12] Kees Bolle, *Secrecy in Religions* (Leiden and New York: E.J. Brill, 1987), p. 12.

[13] Ṛg Veda VIII. 65. 3 tr. Doris Śrīnivāsan, *Concept of the Cow in the Ṛg*

Veda (Banares: Motilal Banarsidas, 1979). Ṛg Veda II. 2. 26. cited by V. Raghavan: *āsya jānanto nāma cidviktana / mahatte viṣṇo sumatim bhajāmahe.*

[14] Shashi Bhusan Das Gupta, "The Role of Mantra in Indian Religion," *Bulletin of the Ramakrishna Mission Institute of Culture*, Vol. VII, no. 3, March 1956, pp. 49, ff.

[15] Heinrich Zimmer, *Philosophies of India* (New York: Meridian Books), 1957, p. 607.

[16] Das Gupta, "The Role of Mantra. . . " pp. 49, ff.

[17] Jan Gonda, "The Indian Mantra," *Oriens* 16, 1963, and *Notes on the Names and the Name of God in Ancient India* (Amsterdam: North Holland Pub. Co., 1970). See also Das Gupta, "The Role of Mantra. . . " pp. 49, ff.

[18] *Śatarudriya* in the *Śatapatha Brāhmaṇa*, *Jābālopaniṣad* 3.

[19] Diana Eck, *Banāras: City of Light* (Princeton: Princeton Univ. Press, 1982), pp. 246, 331, 332-4.

[20] Edward Conze, *Buddhism, Its Essence and Development* (New York: Harper, 1959), pp. 180-187. See also Octavio Paz, *Conjunctions and Disjunctions*, tr. H.R. Lane (New York: Seaver Books, 1982), pp. 79-80, and A. Bharati, *The Tantric Tradition* (London, 1965).

[21] *Viṣṇusahasranāma with The Bhāṣya of Śrī Śaṅkarācārya*, tr. R. Ananthakrishna Sastry (Madras: Adyar Library, 1980). T. M. P Mahadevan, *Viṣṇu-Sahasra-Nāma: A Study* (Bombay: Bharatiya Vidya Bhavan, 1976.

[22] Patañjali, *Yogasūtras*. Lama Anagarika Brahmacari Govinda, *Buddhist Meditation*, and *The Way of the White Clouds* (London: Hutchinson, 1968). Jan Gonda, *Notes on the Name. . .*

[23] *Śilappadikāra* XI. 128-130. Ilango's brother worshipped Śiva, it is said, so the mantra was familiar to him.

[24] *Śrīmad Bhāgavata Purāṇa*, translated by C.L. Goswami (Gorakhpur: Gita Press, 1971).

[25] Das Gupta, "The Role of Mantra. . . ", pp. 49, ff.

[26] For information on the *Agastya Saṃhitā* see Hans Bakker's study *Ayodhya* (Groningen: Egbert Forsten, 1986).

[27] Parasara Bhattar, *Śrī Viṣṇu Sahasranāma with the Bhāshya of Śrī Parasara Bhattar*, tr. and ed. A. Srinivāsa Raghavan (Madras: Sri Visishtadvaita Pracharini Sabha, 1983), pp. 58, 63.

[28] *Cultural Heritage of India*, vols. I-IV (Calcutta: The Ramakrishna Mission, 1956 (2nd ed.)). See also vol. IV, p. 22. The Tulasi Das

quote cited in this paragraph is from Dohavali 8, cited in *Cultural Heritage of India,* vol. IV, p. 403.

[29] *Rāmarahasyopaniṣad*, *The Spiritual Heritage of Tyāgarāja*, C. Rāmanujachari and V. Raghavan (Madras: Ramakrishna Mission, 19.) M.K. Gandhi, *Rāmanāma*, ed. Bharatan Kumarappa (Ahmedabad: Navajivan, 1949), p. 52.

[30] Heinrich Zimmer, *Philosophies of India*, pp. 607-8. Mircea Eliade, *Yoga: Immortality and Freedom* tr. W. Trask (Princeton: Princeton Univ. , 1969, 1970), pp. 198, 212-216, etc.

[31] ("In the center of the body is *prāṇa*; in *prāṇa*'s center *dhvāni*; in *dhvāni's* center *nāda*; in *nāda*'s center the Supreme Lord." *Śloka* 6, *Svarārṇava* manuscript found among Tyāgarāja's books. Journal of the Music Academy of Madras, vol. XXIV, 1953, pp. 1-12. *Rāmarahasyopaniṣad*, cited by V. Raghavan, *Spiritual Heritage of Tyāgarāja*, ed. C. Ramanujachari and V. Raghavan (Madras: Ramakrishna Mission, 1966, 2nd ed.). See Śarṅgadeva's *Saṅgīta Ratnākara* I. iii.

[32] T.M.P. Mahadevan, *Seminar on Saints*, p. 140.

[33] Charlotte Vaudeville asserts "The belief in the divine nature of the Name and in its infinite potency as a means of salvation is common to the Sānt and medieval Vaiṣṇava tradition: it is evidently a Tantric conception inherited by both." *Kabīr* (London: Oxford Univ., 1974), p. 141. Perhaps the enthusiasm of popular Śakta tantric traditions of magical formulae may have germinated seeds already present. There are Śakta tantric interpretations of the Rāma tāraka mantra. S. Shankaranarayana in *The Ten Cosmic Powers* (Madras: Dipti Publications, 1972) says that Śakti is the goddess Tāra, the power behind the avatāra of Rāma, and hence the Rāmanāma is famed as the *tāraka mantra*, mystical prayer enabling one to cross beyond worldly cares. The *Adbhūta Rāmāyaṇa* shows Sītā generating the goddess Kālī, able to do deeds of which Rāma is incapable. Tyāgarāja's song on Sītā's power has been interpreted along these lines by T.V. Subbarao, but not all agree. Among Tyāgarāja's contemporaries, Muttusvāmī Dīkṣitar was very much in the tantric tradition, and Śyāma Śāstri wrote many songs to the goddess. A.J. Alston, in *The Devotional Poems of Mīrabaī* (Delhi: Motilal Banarsidass, 1980), mentions that the earliest reference to the practice are Śaivite (p. 15). V. Raghavan in *The Spiritual Heritage of Tyāgarāja* says the Vedic mention of the praise of the name of Viṣṇu is the first source. A.K. Coomaraswamy in *Yakshas*, describes bhakti practices, including the repetition of the name, as originating with Yakṣa

worship. Conze emphasizes the Buddhist contribution. *Buddhism: Its Essence and Development* (New York: Harper, 1959) pp. 181 ff.

The late medieval Hindu tradition of devotion to the divine name in the North was espoused by Rāmānanda, the 14th century saint originally from South India, by his disciple Kabīr of the 15th century, and by Guru Nānak (d. 1537) and the Sikhs; as well as by Caitanya of Bengal (d. 1533). In the South such saints as Nāmadeva (14th century) and Tukāram of Mahārāshtra (d. 1649), Deccan saints Purandaradāsa (d. 1564) of Karṇāṭaka, Bhadrācalam Rāmadās (17th century) and Annāmācārya (16th century) of Andhra Pradesh, and various Bhāgavatas of Tamil Nadu were also exponents of devotion to the name.

[34] Buddhist tantras rose in prominence in the 7th century and later, as the Vajrāyana branch developed, and in the 10th and 11th centuries the Sahajāyana school rose in importance. In Sahajāyana 84 mystic siddhas are revered. In the 10th and 11th centuries Brahmanical, Buddhist and Jain sects of tantric culture intermingled, and new forms of esoteric religion emerged. Repetition of magical sounds was a key feature of these forms.

The Nātha Siddhas are an example of a North Indian yogic tradition of ascetics seeking *mokṣa*, freedom from rebirth. The Nātha sect originated from teachings of the Buddhist Siddhacaryas. One of the famous Nātha siddhas was Gorakṣa of the 12th century. Though associated with Śaivism the Nātha Siddhas also have strong Vaiṣṇava associations in the Western parts of India, Buddhist affiliations in Nepal and Eastern India as well as Jaina and Islamic relationships in certain regions.

The Avadhūta sect which emerged in the 14th century has affinities with the Nātha sect. The Nāthas, in their striving to attain physical immortality, are allied to the Raseśvara siddhas through exercises, purification and the use of elixirs. There are other kinds of Siddhas as well. There are different groupings and schools of South Indian siddhas, such as the eighteen Tamil Māheśvara Siddhas "belonging to the glorious tradition of the Suddhamārga 'purity path' of Jñāna Siddhas," including ancient philosopher Tirumular and famed Śaivite Saints Manikkavācakkar, Appar, Jñānasambandhar, and Sundara. These Siddhas are supposed to have condemned religious forms and rituals including the worship of divine images. They are remembered for their miraculous deeds and devotional lyrics. Instead of trying to revitalize the body so that it could never be destroyed by death, like the Raseśvara and Nātha Siddhas, the Māheśvara Siddhas hoped ultimately to dematerialize the body, so that it could disappear "in a celestial form from the world of sense" finding its permanent place "in the transcendental glory of God. The ascension of Jesus... bears the signature of a true Siddha." *Cultural Heritage of India,* vol. IV, pp. 300-301, 281, 304. For more on Jesus' associations with magical powers see Morton Smith *Jesus the Magician* (San Francisco, 1978). In some schemes the Siddhas are semi-divine beings who have achieved the utmost purity and perfection, inhabiting the atmosphere between earth and heaven. In the *Vahni Purāṇa* it is said there are 88,000 Siddhas in the sky North of the sun and South of the seven *ṛiṣis*. Monier-Williams, *Sanskrit-English Dictionary*, p. 1215. Sometimes the Siddhas are interchangeable with *sādhyas*, a Vedic term for illumined seers. In the North, Kabīr, a mystic exponent of the Name, is associated with tantric Siddhas: his poetic imagery draws on their practices and philosophy which center on a quest for immortality. Charlotte Vaudeville, *Kabīr*, pp. 96 ff.

Sadāśiva Brahmendra's life, of all the Nāmasiddhānta saints, seems most Siddha-like. In it we find a confluence of *bhakti*, *jñāna* and *siddha* characteristics. He has been called "the silent sage," and is depicted in artistic representations in full-bodied silhouette because he roamed naked. He was considered a *jīvan-mukta*, "one liberated while yet alive." He was called an "*avadhūta*," but this is an ambiguous term, sometimes used to denote a member of a specific religious order, other times used generally to mean a liberated ascetic. Literally it means "removed, shaken off, discarded." The *avadhūta* is one who has "shaken off" worldly attachments. In the *Bhāgavata Purāṇa* (Book XI) a young Brahman is called an *avadhūta*. He wanders the world freely, perfectly calm, wise and unattached, and he teaches king Yadu how to attain *mukti*, freedom. The iconoclastic North Indian saint Kabīr has been called "a great singer, and avadhut, an advocate of advaitavad [Monism]. . . " and the same has been said of Sadāśiva Brahmendra.

[35] T.M.P. Mahadevan, ed. *Seminar on Saints* (Madras: Ganesh, 1960), p. 140.

[36] Cultural Heritage of India, IV p. 5. C. Dimmitt and J.A.B. van Buitenen, eds. and trans. *Classical Hindu Mythology* (Philadelphia: Temple Univ. Press, 1978), p. 8. Also *Cultural Heritage of India*. vol. II, pp. 248-250. In some categorizations there are three kinds of Smārtas:

Smārta Brahmans, Smārta Pañcaratras, and Smārta Paśupatas. It is said that from the 3rd to 6th centuries AD the Purāṇas were recast to eliminate Tantric elements and to emphasize Vedic principles; from the 7th century with the rise of Tantrism, the Purāṇas were again recast to add Tantric elements. *Cultural Heritage of India,* vol. II, p. 251.

[37] *Cultural Heritage of India*, vol. IV, p. 5. See also previous note.

[38] T. K. Venkateswaran, pp. 146-147.

[39] J. L. Mehtā, leter to William Jackson from Jabalpur, Aug. 1986.

[40] Walter Biemel, *Martin Heidegger: An Illustrated Study*, tr. J.L. Mehtā, New York: Harcourt Brace Jovanovich, 1976, p. 154. Gertrude Stein, *Lectures in America*, New York: Random House, 1935; reprinted, Boston: Beacon Press, 1957, p. 233.

[41] Harvey P. Alper, *Understanding Mantra*, Albany: State University of New York, 1990, p. 14.

[42] Robert Bly, *Selected Poems*, New York: Harper and Row, 1986.

[43] Octavio Paz, *Conjunctions and Disjunctions*, New York: Seaver Books, 1982, p. 80.

[44] Ibid.

[45] Harvey P. Alper, *Understanding Mantra*. See pages 1-14, 48-95 especially.

[46] Italo Calvin, "Readers, Writers and Literary Machines," New York Times Book Review, September 7, 1986, pp. 2, 30-31.

[47] Tao Te Ching, chapter 25.

[48] *The Secret of the Golden Flower: A Chinese Book of Life*, translated and explained by Richard Wilhelm, translated from the German by Cary F. Baynes, New York: Harcourt, Brace and World, 1962.

[49] *The New Yorker*, Aug. 18, 1986.

[50] Harvard Magazine Nov. -Dec. 1986. p. 76. Diana Eck suggests that "to say there are 330 million gods is to say how many places one is capable of standing to see the divine."

[51] *Viṣṇu Purāṇa*, I. 1. 30.

[52] Jacques Derrida, "The Principle of Reason: the University in the Eye of Its Pupils," *Diacritics*, Vol. XIX (1983), p. 3-20.

[53] Mark Helpern, *A Winter's Tale*, New York: Harcourt Brace Jovanovich, 1984, p. 8.

[54] Phillip Lutgendorf, "Banking on the Name" paper delivered at the American Academy of Religion Conference, Chicago, 1988.

[55] Ramadas Lamb, "Rāmnām and the Rāmnāmis: The Transformative Power of the Name," paper delivered at the American Academy of

Religions Conference, Chicago, 1988. See Lamb's Ph.D. thesis on the Rāmnāmis, written as partial fulfilment of requirements for a doctorate at the University of California at Santa Barbara.

[56] Annie Dillard, *To Live by Fiction*, New York: Harper and Row, 1982, p. 171.

Passages in Praise of the Name Selected from Indian Traditions:

Jñānasambandhar, Tamil Śaivite, 7th century. From the *Tevāram*:

While asleep or awake, with a melted mind, contemplate every day the 'Five syllables' (Nāma Śivāya–Obeisance to Śiva); it is they that kicked the Death that came to Markandeya who adored the Lord's feet with a mind free from deceitfulness. III.22.1.

It is these 'Five letters' that remove the obstacles which come to those who hold their breaths in the body, light the bright-flamed lamp of knowledge, open up the other path to truth and adoration. III.22.3.

That which takes to the path of salvation those who recite it with love, melted heart and flowing tears, our Lord's Name, Namaḥ Śivāya, the Truth forming the import of all the four Vedas. III.49.1.

O my good mind! The Lord's Names are medicines; they are sacred mantras; they are the way to salvation in the other world; they are all the other good things too, through them all acute miseries are destroyed; contemplate only the Names of the Lord. III.92.1.

tr. V. Raghavan, *The Great Integrators: The Saint-Singers of India*, New Delhi: Publications Div. , Govt. of India, 1979 (Fourth ed.), p. 88.

Sundaramurti, Tamil Śaivite, 9th century:

[O Lord!] Without any other attachment, I cherished within my mind only Thy holy feet; I have been born with Thy grace and I have attained the state whereby I will have no rebirth. O benevolent Lord at Kodumudi [A Śiva shrine in Tamil country], worshipped and lauded by the learned! Even if I forget you, let my tongue go on muttering your mantra *Nāmaḥ Śivāya.*

W. T. DeBary, ed. *Sources of Indian Tradition*, Vol. I, New York: Columbia University Press, 1958, p. 350.

Verse attributed to *Śaṅkarācārya*, 9th century:

Prayer, sweet as the sweet melon
Makes even a dog-eater perfect;
Even a beggar walks without fear
With crores [tens of millions] of gold pieces.
O Aparna! this is the fruit of Thy *mantra*
entering their ears.
Who can say, O Mother!
The fruit which is born of the recitation
of Thy *mantra*?

Translated by Sir John Woodroffe, *Hymns to the Goddess*, Madras: Ganesh & Co., 1964 (third reprint), p. 188.

Bhāgavata Purāṇa, 10th century:

By merely chanting the names and glories of Śrī Kṛṣṇa one is freed from all attachments and reaches the Supreme. What is attained in the Satyayuga by one contemplating Lord Viṣṇu, in Treta by one who propitiates Him through sacrifices, and in Dwapara through worship of the Lord, is attained in the Kālī age merely by chanting the name and singing the praises of Śrī Hari.

Śrīmad Bhāgavata Mahāpurāṇa, Vol. II, tr. C. L. Goswāmī. Gorakhpur: Gītā Press, 1971, p. 1666.

"The articulation of a name of Viṣṇu – that is the only

thorough atonement for the sins of all classes of sinners, be one a thief, a drinker, one guilty of treachery to a friend, a Brahman-slayer, one sharing the bed of a preceptors wife, a slayer of a woman, a king, one's own parent or a cow, and whatever other sinners there may be; for thereby the Lord Viṣṇu's own mind is directed towards the utterer, who is thenceforward remembered by Him as his protege."

Bhāgavata Purāṇa, VI. 2. 9-10.

Tripurastotram, from the *Tāntrasara*

O Bhavanī! even an ignorant man
Who, meditating on Thy form,
recites Thy *mantra* a lakh of (100,000) times
Acquires all poetic power,
And those things in the three worlds
which are most difficult of attainment.
O Bhavanī! be gracious to me.

Translated by Sir John Woodroffe, *Hymns to the Goddess*, Madras: Ganesh & Co., 1964 (third reprint), p. 92.

Tirumaṅgaimannar, Tamil Vaiṣṇava, From *Periatirumoli* (I. 1. 90):

The name *Nārāyaṇa* will bless one with high birth and affluence; it will obliterate all the sufferings of the devotees; it will endow one with the heavenly state and the service of the Lord; it will bring success and all good things; it will perform for one more beneficial acts than one's own mother; that word I have found, the name Nārāyaṇa.

W.T. DeBary, ed. *Sources of Indian Tradition*, Vol. I, New York: Columbia University Press, 1958, pp. 351-352.

Jñāneśvara, Vaiṣṇava from Mahārāṣṭra, 13th century:

Oh Mind! Hold on with all your strength to the one

supreme principle (of spiritual exercise) – chanting the holy Name. Surely that will win the compassion of Lord Hari, the dispeller of all human misery. That holy Name is easy to chant. Always chant it with your heart filled with love for God. There is not a single principle to follow, beyond that of chanting the holy Name. If you inadvertantly take to any other path your life will go to waste in no time at all.

Jñānadeva says that for his part he now remains silent. But deep inside his heart the Lord manifesting himself carries on a spontaneous chanting of the holy Name, giving him inner peace and bliss of soul.

Marāthi *abhanga*, tr. by Dr. Brahmananda Mavinkurve in personal correspondence from Prasanthi Nilayam, Andhra Pradesh, 1989.

Nāmadeva, Vaiṣṇava-Santa from Mahārāṣṭra, latter 14th century:

Literal Translation of Nāmdev's *Philosophy of the Divine Name*:

I. The Name permeates densely the sky and the lowest regions and the entire universe. Who can tell to what depths in the nether regions and to what height in the heavens It extends? The ignorant undergo the eighty-four lakhs of species of births, not knowing the essence of things. Nāmdev says the Name is immortal. Forms are innumerable, but the Name is all that.

II. The Name itself is form; and form itself is Name. There is no distinction between Name and form. God became manifest and assumed Name and form. Hence the Name the Vedas have established. Beware, there is no *mantra* beyond the Name. Those who say otherwise are ignorant. Nāmdev says the Name is Keśava Himself. This is known only to the loving devotees of the Lord.

III. The all-pervading nature of the Name can only be

understood when one recognizes his 'I.' When one's own name is not recognized, it is impossible to get the all-pervading Name. When one knows oneself, then one finds the Name everywhere. To see the Name as different from the named creates illusion. Nāmdev says, 'Ask the Saints.'

IV. None can realize the Name by practice of knowledge, meditation or austerity. Surrender yourself first at the feet of the Guru and learn to know that 'I' myself is that Name. After finding the source of that 'I,' merge your individuality in that one-ness, which pervades beyond *dvaita* and *dvaitatita*, that Name has come into the three worlds. The Name is Para Brahman itself, where there is no action arising out of duality.

Talks with Śrī Ramana Maharshi, Tirivannamalai: Śrī Rāmanāśramam, 1978 (sixth ed.), pp. 416-417.

Lakṣmīdhara, *smārta* Brahman, 15th century:

Recital of the Divine Name leads to the extinction of sin; the continued repetition of the Name strengthens the good *vāsanas* [experiential impressions which produce patterns of behavior] connected with the connotations of the Name and eliminates the bad *vāsanas* which strengthen the tendency to sin; this generates the impulse to serve the devotees of the Lord; their infectious zeal in describing His manifold glory induces Naiṣṭiki Bhakti, unshakable elevation; then follow in succession the abolition of sorrow, the exaltation of the soul, the realization of the Highest which is Truth and therefrom *mukti*.

From *Bhagavan Nāma 'Kaumudi* in N. Raghunathan's article "Bodhendra and Sadguruswamy" in *Seminar on Saints*, Madras: Ganesh, 1960, pp. 133-140.

Narasiṃha Mehtā, 15th century Gujarāti Vaiṣṇava. Gujarāti bhajan:

Whoever repeats "Rāma-*nāma*" has all the sacred rivers in his body.

Caitanya Mahāprabhu, Bengali Vaiṣṇava, 1485-1533:

Teachings of Lord Caitanya:

1. Glory to the Śrī Krishna *saṅkīrtana* which cleanses the heart of all the dust accumulated for years and extinguishes the fire of conditional life, of repeated birth and death. This *saṅkīrtana* movement is the prime benediction for humanity at large because it spreads the rays of the benediction moon. It is the life of all transcendental knowledge. It increases the ocean of transcendental bliss, and it enables us fully to taste the nectar for which we are always anxious.

2. O my Lord, Your holy name alone can render all benedictions to living beings, and thus You have hundreds and millions of names like Krishna and Govinda. In these transcendental names You have invested all Your transcendental energies. There are not even hard and fast rules for chanting these names. O my Lord, out of kindness You enable us easily to approach You by Your holy names, but I am so unfortunate that I have no attraction for them.

3. One should chant the holy name of the Lord in a humble state of mind, thinking oneself lower than the straw in the street; one should be more tolerant than a tree, devoid of all sense of false prestige and should be ready to offer all respect to others. In such a state of mind one can chant the holy name of the Lord constantly.

4. O almighty Lord, I have no desire to accumulate wealth, nor do I desire beautiful women, nor do I want any number of followers. I only want Your ceaseless devotional service birth after birth.

5. O son of Mahārāja Nanda Krishna, I am Your eternal servitor, yet somehow or other I have fallen into the ocean of birth and death. Please pick me up from this ocean of death anbd place me as one of the atoms at Your lotus feet.

6. O my Lord, when will my eyes be decorated with tears

of love flowing constantly when I chant Your holy name? When will my voice choke up, and when will the hairs of my body stand on end at the recitation of Your name?

7. O Govinda! Feeling Your separation, I am considering a moment to be like twelve years or more. Tears are flowing from my eyes like torrents of rain, and I am feeling all vacant in the world in Your absence.

8. I know no one but Krishna as my Lord, and He shall remain so even if He handles me roughly by His embrace or makes me brokenhearted by not being present before me. He is completely free to do anything and everything, for He is always my worshipful Lord unconditionally.

International Society for Krishna Consciousness translation.

Purandaradāsa, Vaiṣṇava of Karnāṭaka, 1480-1564, Kannada bhajan:

Need he who sings the name of Hari stand in fear of hell itself?
Can there ever be a deer who has no fear of the lion?
Can there be darkness which is not afraid of the sun?
Is there a hill impervious to the thunderbolt of Indra?
Is there someone fearless when all is inundated by the great flood? Need he who sings the name of Hari stand in fear of hell?
Jalajanabha, Govinda, Janārdana, Kalusha Harana, Karirāja Rakshaka—
All are names which fulfil one despite what one may lack.
There is no snake alive which does not fear Falcon Garuda;
There is no leaf of grass which a blazing fire cannot consume

Need he who sings the name of Hari stand in fear of hell itself?
It is enough if, with devotion to You, Purandara Vitthala,
One utters Your name and calls your other names—Narahari, Nārāyaṇa, Keshava. . . Need he who sings the name of Hari stand in fear of hell?

Harināma kirtane anudinava, adapted from translation by Sitaramiah, *Purandaradāsa*, New Delhi: Publications Div., Govt. of India, p. 35.

Say "Hari Nārāyaṇa, Hari Nārāyaṇa," Mind, say "Hari Nārāyaṇa!"
Narada planted in this world the seed of the Name, Nārāyaṇa;
And with the fervent boy Dhruva it became a sprout;
And with that best devotee Prahlāda it became a shoot;
With king Dharaniśa Rukmaṇgada the Name became a bud;
With Bhīṣma, grandfather of the Kauravas, it blossomed into flower. Say "Hari Nārāyaṇa. . ."
With Draupadī, Arjuṇa's wife, the Name became a growing fruit;
With Gajendra it became a half-ripened fruit;
With Śuka the twice-born sage it became a fully mature fruit.
Ajāmila, who said Your Name on his deathbed, ate the fruit and savored its juice. Say "Hari Nārāyaṇa. . ."
When there is a name which gives everything one needs
Why bother with fire sacrifices, codes of conduct, mantra, tapas?
Remember Lord Purandara Vitthala with complete concentration,

O mind, and say "Hari Nārāyaṇa. . . "

Tr. by T. S. Parthasarathy and William Jackson, Kannada text in *Bhajana Ratnākara*, p. 346.

From the *Rāmakarṇāmṛita*, a later Sanskrit text:

Obeisance unto the Raghurāma-Mantra– the Mantra made potent and worshipped by the great *munis* (sages) and yogis like Brahmā etc. , the Mantra that can destroy poverty, sorrow and the diseases of birth and death, the Mantra which is the only safe canoe to ferry one across the ocean of metempsychosis, and which removes the greatest of fears.

Oh mind! Drink the medicine in the form of Śrī Rāma's name which will remove all infatuations, which will give one the mental attitudes and beatitudes of great munis; which will uproot all the demons, which will annihilate the cycle of births and deaths, which gives endless bliss to its devotees and which is an effective life-giving medicine in all the three worlds and which fetches one all the virtues!

Rāma Mantra is the most effective weapon in destroying the enemy; which is worshipped by the Upanishadic expressions; which will help one to rise above Saṃsāra; which will enable one to get rid of attachments at the opportune time; which confers every kind of wealth, and which can revive one from the bite of the snake sorrow. O tongue! Repeat always this Śrī Rāma Mantra which will make life fruitful.

For all embodied beings who are devoid of the discerning faculty, living for the most part by evil deeds like killing, the name of Rāma is the most powerful source of liberation. It shine in the heart of yogis as Truth and Bliss. All the Vedas worship it. It is the seat of all fortunes. By contemplating Rāmanāma unceasingly one gets liberated.

From the *Rāmakārṇāmṛita*, quoted in *Śrīmad Rāmāyaṇam and All Round Success*, Madras: The Little Flower, 1963, pp. 26, 34, 72, 80.

Kabīr, Vaiṣṇava Bhakta, Muslim pir, Sikh Bhagat, Kabīrpanthi avatār, 15th c.

The Greatness of Prayer (Sumirana):

If you can plunder, plunder,
let the Name of Rām be your booty!
[Otherwise] later you'll repent,
when you breathe your last! (3)

Call and cry for Kesau [the Lord],
do not endlessly sleep:
If day and night you cry piteously,
He will hear you in the end. (4)
Kabīr, it is no easy task
to invoke Hari's Name:
As when playing above a stake, [like an acrobat]
he who falls is lost! (5)

Repeating 'Thou, Thou', I became Thou,
in me, no 'I' remained:
Offering myself unto Thy Name,
wherever I look, Thou art! (6)

[True] Bhakti is adoration of Hari's Name,
all else is boundless torment!
[To worship] in soul, words, and deeds,
such is the essence of Prayer, [says] Kabīr. (7)

If the devotee has a thought,
let it be [but] of Hari's Name:
Any thought which is not for Rām
is but the noose of Kal [dragging one to hell]! (8)

They who know not love and tenderness,
whose tongue repeats not [the Name of] Rām,
Those men were born in the world in vain
and so went to perdition! (9)

Millions of actions are instantly erased
by invoking the Name, just a little,
But merits heaped up for endless ages,
without the Name, will lead you nowhere! (11)

Long is the road, far off is the house,
rugged is the path, beset with dangers:
O Saints, tell me, how can man obtain
the inaccessible Vision of Hari? (12)

The Name of Rām is the essence of Reality,
the *tilak* of the three worlds:
The servant Kabīr applied it to his forehead
and he shone in matchless beauty. (13)

Kabīr, invoke Rām confidently
as long at the lamp-wick [is burning]:
When oil has run out, the lamp will go out,
then you will sleep day and night. (16)

If you can plunder, then plunder
that treasure of Rām's Name:
When Kal seizes you by the throat,
the tenth door will be blocked! (22)

Kabīr, I keep repeating it
and every one can hear:
By invoking Rām, man is saved,
without it, all is grief! (25)

Says Kabīr, I have told them
and so have Brahmā and Maheś—
Rām's Name is the essence of Reality:
such is my teaching for all! (26)

Tr. Charlotte Vaudeville, *Kabīr*, Oxford University Press, 1974.

If saying Rāma gave liberation,
saying candy made your mouth sweet,
saying fire burned your feet,
saying water quenched your thirst,
saying food banished hunger,
the whole world would be free. S. 40

If you don't see, if you don't touch,
what's the use of the name?
If saying money made one rich,
nobody would be poor. S. 40
Tr. Linda Hesse, *Bijak of Kabīr*, pp. 31-32.

Guru Nānak, Punjabi Founder of the Sikh Faith, 1469-1539.

(Suniai sidh pir sur nath)
By hearkening to the Name,
The disciple becomes a Master,
A guide, saint, a seraph;
By hearkening to the Name
The earth, the bull that bears it
And the heavens are unveiled.
By hearkening to the Name
Man's vision may explore
Planets, continents, nether regions.
Death vexes not in the least

By hearkening to the Name,
Those that hearken to the Name;
They are beyond Death's reach.
Saith Nānak, the saints are always happy;
By hearkening to the Name
Sorrow and sin are destroyed.

tr. V. Raghavan, *The Great Integrators: The Saint-Singers of India*, New Delhi: Publications Div., Govt. of India, 1979 (Fourth ed.), p. 126.

Rāmadās of Bhadrācalam, Telugu Rāmabhakta of the 17th c. (*Dennatiko*)

1. When shall I drink the nectary juice
   of Rāma's purifying name?
   When after worshipping shall I hold
   his holy feet in my heart?
3. When will I have a steady mind
   always discarding wavering qualities?
   When will I recite the saving name
   of the Lord with its five truths?

Āyyāvāl, South Indian Telugu *smārta* Brahman, 17th century:

Are you not the supremely compassionate one! O Lord, you are on the look-out for some pretext to save people: when words such as *ahara* ("bring"), *prahara* ("take away"), and *samhara* (destroy), containing the syllables *ha* and *ra* are spoken by them, you think that they are uttering your Name (Hara) and save them.

From the hymn *Śivabhakti Kalpalatika* tr. by Vandana Mataji, *Nāma Japa*, Bombay: Bharatiya Vidya Bhavan, 1984.

Bodhendra, South Indian Telugu Brahmin, 17th century:

This is the concluding view that is shown. In whatever way, under any circumstances by the performance of the chanting and singing of the Name, all sins get destroyed and release does happen, whether the Name is recited by woman or man. It may be by any man [of any caste or position], or by one insane, by one having faith or without faith. It may even be by one for the sake of the removal of the distress created by thieves, [wild animals like] a tiger, or any disease. It may be for obtaining non-eternal results in the form of *dharma*, *artha* or *kāma* or for the sake of other gifts.

Tr. by V. Raghavan, from the *Nāmāmṛitarasayana*, quoted by Raghavan in the introduction to *Ākhyāṣaṣṭi*.

Sant Tukāram, Vaiṣṇava from Mahārāṣṭra, 17th century

The Name of the Lord is the seed and also the fruit which springs therefrom. It is the highest religion, the good deed and worship. It is the essence of all religious practice. It banishes all trouble, for where the Lord's devotee sings His name and performs the Nāma Saṅkīrtan all virtues combine and dwell there. When the Lord enters the heart and ascends the throne all that is good makes its appearance there, and as a result of His entrance pain of transmigration ends for the devotee. So do not fear to follow the tenets of the faith in which you are born, all that is necessary is to repeat the name of Lord Vithal constantly.

Bhavan's Journal, Vol. VII, no. 13, Jan. 22, 1961.

Mīrābaī, Vaiṣṇava from North India, 16th century:

The King prepared a cup of poison
Which they gave to the princess to drink.
She drank it up
Like the foot-wash of the Lord,

Singing the glories of Govind.
I have drunk from the cup
Of the Holy Name,
And nothing else pleases me. . . (40)

I have practiced remembrance of Thy Name
In my heart, day and night.
Again and again I call upon Thee
In grievous affliction. . . (63)

O my Beloved, I have felt the attraction
Of the holy Name. I have heard
That those who take the Name are saved,
The whole rock-hard world melts to water.
I have earned no merit
And have amassed much demerit through sin.
The courtesan who taught her parrot
To repeat the holy Name
Was transported to the heaven of Vishṇu.
The elephant only half-pronounced Your Name,
Yet all his troubles came to an end.
Descending from Garuda, You came running on foot,
And all his re-birth in animal wombs
Came to an end.
You exempted Ajāmila from his sins
And his fear of death melted away.
He sang the holy Name
Simply by calling for his son,
This the whole world knows.
You recognize faith when you see it,
And grant boons to those who seek refuge
With a pure heart.

Mīrā is Your servant,
Accept her as Your own!

Tr. A. J. Alston, *The Devotional Poems of Mīrabaī,* Delhi & Varanasi: Motilal Banarsidass, 1980.

Tulasidās, North Indian poet-saint writing in Hindi, 1532-1623.

Let anyone accept any *sādhana* (spiritual exercise),
he is free to follow its pursuit.
But to me Thy Name is the granter of all boons.
The various paths outlined in the Vedas
for the emancipation from
Karma, upāsana and jñāna (wisdom) are all good,
But I seek only one shelter and that is Thy Name,
I seek nothing else besides.
Has not Thy Name, O Lord,
made the very stones swim in the ocean
and also helped the monkeys to cross the waters?

In the Kālī Age, knowledge, dispassion, yoga,
and samādhi are of no avail.
Constantly repeat the name of Rāma,
with unwavering faith;
Greater than austerity, pilgrimage, oblation,
charity, disciplines and fasts
Is the repetition of the name of God, O Tulasidāsa.

Barava Rāmāyaṇa, *Cultural History of India,* IV, p. 403.

What instruction does the great Lord Śiva give the dying
Upon the banks of the Ganges in Kāśi,
the land of Dharma?
Hara tells them of the glory of Rām's Name,
and he himself recites it,

From age to age this universe has known it
  and the Vedas too describe it.

Tulasidāsa's *Vinaya Patrika*, tr. F. R. Allchin, *The Petition to Rāma*, London: George Allen Unwin, 1966, p. 206.

Tyāgarāja, Telugu-speaking *smārta* Brahman in Tamil Nadu, 1767-1847:

What joy could there be beyond this ecstasy, O Rāma
When there is unanimity in the meeting of devotees
Could there be any bliss greater than this, O Rāma?
In devotion they dance, they sing tunefully
Praying that the Lord appear before them
It is enough to merge one's mind in Him
What happiness could ever surpass this bliss, O Rāma?
When one says 'I am He' forgetting the body
With its bundle of senses, singing the Lord's glories
What joy could there ever be beyond this ecstasy,
  O Rāma
When I murmur over and over Your Name
These worlds seem to shine divinely!
O Prince Whose career is praised by Tyāgarāja
What happiness could ever surpass this bliss, O Rāma?

Tr. William Jackson, *Tyāgarāja: Musician Saint of South India–The Exploration of a Religious Life and Legacy,* Ph.D. Thesis, Harvard University, 1984.

Rāmakrishna Paramahaṃsa, Bengali Shakta, 19th century:

Japa means silently repeating God's name in solitude. When you chant His name with single-minded devotion you can see God's form and realize Him. Suppose there is a piece of timber sunk in the water of the Ganges and fastened with a chain to the bank. You proceed link by link, holding to the chain, and you dive into the water and follow the chain. Finally you are able to reach the timber. In the same way, by repeating God's name you become absorbed in Him and finally realize Him. – Rāmakrishna Paramahaṃsa.

From *The Gospel of Śrī Rāmakrishna: Originally recorded in Bengali by M., a disciple of the Master*, tr. Swami Nikhilananda. New York: Rāmakrishna-Vivekananda Center, 1973, pp. 878-9.

Those who invoke the Name of God become saints. Krishna Kishore was a saintly man of Ariadaha. One day he went on a pilgrimage to Vrindavan. During his journey he became thirsty and, seeing a man near a well, asked him to draw a little water. The man excused himself, saying he was of a very low caste, being a cobbler, and so, unworthy to offer water to a Brahman. Krishna Kishore then said to him: 'Purify yourself by pronouncing the name of God! Say: Śiva! Śiva!' The man obeyed and then offered the water to drink and that orthodox Brahman drank it! How great was his faith!. . . Caitanya and Nityānanda used to transmit the Name of Hari (the initiation into ritual invocation, *japa yoga*) to everyone including pariahs and embraced them all. A Brahman without this love is no longer a Brahman; a pariah with this love is no longer a pariah. Through bhakti an untouchable becomes pure and is raised up. – Rāmakrishna Paramahaṃsa. *L'Enseignement de Rāmakrishna*, pub. by J. Herbert.

Ramana Mahārshi, Tamil Śaivite, 20th century:

Devotee: What is the result of 'Rāma Japa' (repetition of Lord Rāma's name)?

Mahārshi: 'Rā' is Reality, 'Ma' is the mind; their union is the fruit of 'Rāma Japa.' Utterance of words is not enough. The elimination of thoughts is wisdom. It is the Absolute Existence.

Talks with Śrī Ramana Mahārshi, Tiruvannamalai: Śrī Ramanasramam, 1978 (sixth ed.), p. 189.

Śrī Aurobindo, Bengali synthesizer of yogas, 20th century:

The Word repeats itself in rhythmic strains;
Thought, vision, feeling, sense, the body's self
Are seized unutterably and he endures
An ecstasy and an immortal change. . .

Śrī Aurobindo *Savitri*, Pondicherry: Śrī Aurobindo Ashram, 1954, p. 426.

Ramchandra Gandhi, twentieth century philosopher, North India:

["At the end of one's life, to utter with one's last breath] 'Hey Rāma!' is a consummatory extreme thanksgiving invocation of Rāma who is God, a rare and holy final accomplishment. Only the rarest bhakta of Rāma invokes Rāma undespairingly and unpetitionarily as death suddenly and unexpectedly takes him. All of Gandhi's life was an immersion in Rāma Nāma, vehicle and śakti of the whole man and his civilization, metaphysical Indian civilization which the satyagrahi was pitting against anti-metaphysical, unspiritual, grasping bullying unbelieving modern times, also against cowardly decaying Indian society and hard hearted privileged Indian individuals and classes unmoved by the plight of starving servile millions." *I Am Thou*, Poona: Indian Philosophical Quarterly Pub., 1984.

Passages on the Name from Other Traditions

The suinymous mysticism of *Alfred Tennyson*, English poet:

". . . a kind of waking trance. . . I have frequently had, quite up from boyhood, when I have been alone. This has come upon me through repeating my own name two or three times to my self silently, till all at once, as it were, out of the intensity of consciousness of individuality, individuality itself seemed to dissolve and fade away into boundless being, and this not a confused state, but the clearest of the clearest, and the sweetest of the sweet, the weirdest of the weirdest, utterly beyond words where death was an almost laughable impossibility, the loss of personality (if so it were) seeming no extinction, but the only true life. I am ashamed of my feeble description. Have I not said the state is utterly beyond words? . . . By God Almighty! There is no delusion in the matter! It is no nebulous ecstasy, but a state of transcendent wonder, associated with absolute clearness of mind.

Memoirs of Alfred Tennyson.

Shi-ite Muslim use of name-repetition:

"The Shi-ite Muslims venerate Ali, Muhammad's son-in-law. The devotion of a Persian dervish to Ali's name in the 19th century for thirty years was described by a traveller: The dervish had vowed thirty years previously never to use his throat and tongue except to always utter Ali. "He thus wished to signify to the world that he was the most devoted partisan of that Ali who had been dead a thousand years. In his own home, speaking with his wife, childen and friends, no other word but 'Ali!' ever passed his lips. If he wanted food or drink and anything else, he expressed his wants still by repeating 'Ali!' Begging or buying at the bazaar, it was always 'Ali!' Treated ill or generously, he would still harp on his monotonous 'Ali!' Latterly his zeal assumed such tremendous proportions that, like a mad man, he would race the whole day, up and down the streets of the town, throwing his stick high up into the air, and shriek out, all the while, at the top of his voice 'Ali!' This dervish was venerated by everybody as a saint, and received everywhere with the greatest distinction."

Arminus Vambery, His Life and Adventures, Written by Himself, London, 1889, p. 69.

Shinran, Japanese, 1173-1262, devoted to Buddha Amitabha:

"Shameless though I be and having no truth in my soul,
Yet the virtue of the Holy Name,
the gift of Him who is enlightened,
Is spread throughout the world through my words,
Although I am as I am. . .
Through the Merciful One's Name
one's human failings are no bar to saving grace."

Howard Thurman, a black Christian preacher travelling in India in the mid-twentieth century:

After preaching a sermon in the Anglican cathedral in Madras, Howard Thurman was chastised by a young Indian with tears in his face: "You did my Master wrong tonight – it was a terrible thing. . . You preached your entire sermon and not one time did you call my Savior by name – by name – not one time."

Though the Indian agreed with Thurman that the words he had spoken were true to Jesus' teachings, and that he sensed Jesus' spirit in the congregation's midst, the rebuke was not taken back: "You did not call Him by name. And it is important that His name be lifted up, that He might draw all men unto Him."

Paraphrased from Howard Thurman's *With Head and Heart*, New York: Harcourt Brace Jovanovich, 1979, p. 117.

R.D. Ranade, 20th century Mahārāṣṭran mystic and scholar of Hindu mysticism:

"Finally, in regard to the value of the Name, the mystics of India are no less insistent upon its efficacy than their compeer mystics of the West. Indeed, if there is any bond of unity more than any other between Hinduism and Christianity in their teaching about the realisation of God, it is their identical insistence on the efficacy of meditation by means of the Name. It is not only in Christianity, however, that the name assumes such gigantic power. Even in the Egyptian and Hebrew religions, we find the same insistence upon the efficacy of the Name. 'The very first Egyptian God Ra effected his own creation by the utterance of his own portentous name, and then created all the things of the universe. 'Similar again is the attitude of the Hebrews towards the name Yahweh; while Christianity insists that God's name is above everything else 'Hallowed by Thy Name,' 'the Name above every name.' It is, however, not merely on the name of God that Christianity insists, but even on the name of Jesus. Even the utterance of the name of Jesus would be as good as the utterance of the name of God. In his *Virtues of the Holy Name of Jesus*, Richard Rolle tells us: 'O Jesus, verily Thou Whom we call Saviour dost save man, and therefore Jesus is Thy Name. Ah! Ah! that wonderful Name! Ah! That delectable Name! This is the Name that is above all names, without which no man hopes for salvation. Verily, the Name of Jesus is in my mind a joyous song, and heavenly music in mine ear, and in my mouth a honeyed sweetness. Wherefore no wonder, I love that Name which gives comfort to me in all my anguish.' And the *Cloud of Unknowing* says that one might utter any name of God one pleases. Indeed, the shorter it is, the better: 'And if thee list have this intent (of union with God) lapped and folden in one word, for thou shouldest have better hold thereupon, take thee but a little word of one syllable: for so it is better than two, for ever the shorter it is the better it accordeth with the work of the Spirit. And such a word it this word God, or this word Love. Choose thee whether thou wilt, or another: as thee list, which that thou likest best of one syllable. And fasten this word to thy heart, so that it never go thense for thing that befalleth. This word shall by thy shield and thy spear whether thou ridest on peace or war. With this word thou shalt beat on this cloud and this darkness above thee. With this word thou shalt smite down all manner of thought under the cloud of forgetting'." R. D. Ranade, *Mysticism in India: The Poet-Saints of Mahārashtra.*

Gary Snyder, American Zen Buddhist and Shamanist poet and environmentalist:

"Most sacred songs are composed of magical words which no one knows the literal meaning of, or perhaps only a small priestly class, but the people at large do not know the literal meaning of them. Having the Roman Catholic services in Latin adds to the magic for most people. Many different traditional religions utilize archaic languages in their services for the magical power of this unintelligibility. . . In the case of, say, Hinduism and Buddhism. . . we have Mantras, and we have Dharanis. Mantras are little short magical songs which are part translatable, but in part perhaps not; famous example: *Om Mani Padme Hum: Om*, magical seed syllable, *Mani*, translatable word meaning jewel, *Padme*, translatable word meaning 'in the Lotus,' *Hum*, non-translatable word indicating victory. *Om* and *Hum* are what you call seed syllables. They are not part of any language construction. They are used only in special context. In magical Sanskrit, there are a number of what are called 'seed syllables,' which are theoretically the building blocks of all languages in Sanskrit theory, and are used sometimes all by themselves, sometimes in mixture with nonwords to create the Mantras, which are magical power, meditation phrase songs, with many different uses."

Gary Snyder, *The Real Work: Interviews and Talks 1964-1979*, pp. 182-3.

VII
APPENDICES ON V. RAGHAVAN

V. Raghavan's Autobiographical Reflections (Written in 1968)

Family Background and Connections with Musicians[1]

Mention may be made of my maternal grandfather Śrī A. Nārāyaṇaswāmī Iyer, the first Tamil Vakīl (advocate) at Tiruvārūr. He came of a stock of Vaidikas steeped in Sanskrit from the village of Nannargudi; his cousin (Ammanji) Raju Ganapathin was a contemporary and friend of Mm. Raju Śāstrigal and was well versed in Mantra-Śāstra, and had *siddhi* (accomplishment) in *Bala-mantra*. Nārāyaṇaswāmī was a *yajusha* Ganapathin and he was put in charge of the Veda Paṭhaśala at Vedāranyam; and although young, he was able to manage also the economic affairs of the Trusts and Endowments of the Yazhpanam merchants made in the Vedāranyam very well. The English Collector who saw his capacity called him and asked him to pass some tests in the Civil and Criminal Procedure Codes which he said should be of very little strain to one who mastered so much of the Vedas. Young Nārāyaṇaswāmī accordingly passed and became the first Vakīl at Tiruvārūr and was known for continuing his orthodox activities along with his work as a Vakīl. Whenever Mm. Raju Śāstrigal came to Tiruvārūr for Tyāgarāja *darśanam* (to see a holy person or image and be blessed)[2] he stayed with this maternal grandfather of ours.

Near Tiruvārūr is a village called Kootampadi where

some of Appayya Dīkshita's descendants had settled. The Kootampadi people had a house in Tiruvārūr a few houses to the west of our maternal grandfather's; but Mm. Raju Śāstrigal preferred to stay with our grandfather. The contacts had continued and at one stage, as my mother's sister had told me, there had been serious talk of my mother being given in marriage to Yajñaswāmī Śāstrigal.

Nārāyaṇaswāmī Iyer's second son N. Mahādeva Iyer, my mother's younger brother, who passed away in 1967, was a very well-known lawyer in the whole of Tanjore District for a number of years, and retired as Government Pleader at Tiruvārūr; he was devoted to a number of religious activities, himself being a Subrahmaṇya Upāsaka. He was very good in Sanskrit, particularly on the literary and aesthetic side, and was a pioneer in organizing musical activities in Tiruvārūr. He was a great personal friend of Pushpavanam who was very much under his influence and stayed with him in his house often.

Mahādeva Iyer looked after the medical treatment of Pushpavanam during his last days at Tanjore. Mahādeva Iyer discovered also Chidambaram Śrīraṅgāchāriār, father of Embar Vijayaraghavachariar and had arranged in our own house at Tiruvārūr several series of Harikathās (musical discourses) on the *Rāmāyaṇa* epic, the *Bhāgavatha Purāṇa*, the lives of the Nāyanmārs (South Indian Śaivite saints), etc. Along with him Jagannātha Kavi stayed in our house at Tiruvārūr more continuously. Jagannātha Kavi was a young Telugu poet who composed admirably both in Telugu and Sanskrit songs and verses for Śrīraṅgāchāriār for his Harikathās. There was also a gifted Tamil composer of Mayuram, Tyāgarāja Deśikar (an *oduvar*). The compositions in Tamil, Telugu and Sanskrit of these two composers may still be heard in many of the performances of Embar Vijayaraghavachariar. I can recall the days and the occasions when these composers wrote some of these pieces and the lively atmosphere of their being given the contexts of their producing the compositions and reading them out and their being rendered in music and enjoyed. Along with Harikathā Kalakshepams, there were also in those days Vedaparāyana *ghoṣthis* going on in our house during the annual festival at the Tyāgarāja temple. A memorable and complete series of *Bhāgavata Purāṇa* expositions by a renowned pandit Raṅgasamudram Veṅkaṭarama Śāstrigal which filled the gaps when there were no Harikathās. Then there were music series connected with Rādhā Kalyāṇa Utsavam which was an annual feature in which all top musicians of those days with a number of accompanists staged the older·type of long drawn kutcheries. There was hardly a stalwart of the music world of those days who had not come and sung there and stayed at our house.

During this time there was also staying in our house for a number of years Papanāsam Śivan as a young bachelor, singing his songs and doing *bhajanas*. It was towards the end of his stay with us at Tiruvārūr that he was married. It was in continuation of this association, that I began to take interest in him afterwards in Madras, in the forties. It was I who brought him into the motion pictures, first for the Sītā Kalyāna produced at Kolhapur for which I wrote scenario and dialogue and from which his new life as a cinema composer started.

Mahārājapuram as a youngster had his debut at the *Gṛihapraveśam* of my uncle's house, which became a well-known rendezvous and port of call for musicians. His legal help was freely available for musicians and dancers. It was a litigation that brought Bharatam Nallūr Nārāyaṇaswāmī Iyer to our uncle and the association continued over years. When these were all coming from outside, there were the native local masters of Nāgaswāra, notably Tiruvārūr Swāmīnāthan and his brother Kittuchami, the former being the father-in-law of the late Flute Swaminathan Pillai of Tirupambaram. As I have narrated in the Preface to my Patel Lectures, along with the above, must be mentioned, the Bhajanas carried on in the month of Māргasirsha for which traditional Bhajana experts used to come from neighbouring villages and I fell in line with them and became engrossed in *Giri-pradakṣinam* (circumambulating the holy mountain) and *bhajana* recitals.

On my father's side my grandfather Śrīnivāsa Iyer was a powerful figure well-known for his capacity in dealing with men and things. A tall, strong man, he owned 15 *vaḷis* at Pavitramanikkam on the border of Tiruvārūr and was a Karnam of that village. My father's elder brother Rāmaswāmī Iyer was a Magistrate with Civil and Criminal duties known for his strictness and integrity, and he had left a lasting impression in our family. I myself was given the *śarman* after his *śarman*, at the time of my *upanāyanam* (initiation). . . My mother and my mother's sister were interested in devotional literature and there was the practice in the family of getting by heart a large number of *stotras* (verses), *Ārya Dvisati* (*Lālita Stave Ratna*) of Durvāsas and the *stotras* of Śrīdhara Veṅkaṭeśa Āyyāvāl being two of their favorites; I still cherish the copy of the collected *stotras* of Āyyāvāl in *grantha* script (an old form of written Tamil) used by my aunt. They along with the other *stotras*, I got by heart when I was quite a young boy. During my boyhood I got by heart quite a large number of *stotras* long and short.

Sanskrit Background

Both my parents passed away while I was seven. My father's sister who was devoted to traditional learning and in the old world way, was a capable manager of domestic affairs, took charge of our family; she put me and my young sister and my maternal uncle's son under a Sanskrit Pandit, Sengalipuram Appaswāmī Śātrigal, pupil of Mahāmahopadhyāya Kodavasal

Narsimhāchāriar. With this *pandit* (scholar) I learned Sanskrit in the traditional style in addition to the Sanskrit as second language in the School where we had a very competent *pandit* in Nārāyaṇa Vejapeyar also. I must mention also an interesting person who created a lot of enthusiasm in my young mind, an old lady named Sundari Patti of Chai, who had mastered Sanskrit and could converse in Sanskrit with pandits. She was a friend of my mother's sister and often checked up our progress in Sanskrit and I learnt some Sanskrit compositions from her, notably a very good Rāmāyaṇa *odam* (boat song) in Sanskrit which is still un-published and was probably composed by one of her ancestors. There was also another lady distantly related to us, Kutti Āmmāl alias Lakshyanandam who had taken to Vedānta philosophy and read Sanskrit *advaita* (monism) works with wellknown pandits. I have mentioned these two ladies in my account of Woman Sanskritists which I wrote in Tamil long ago in *Kalaimaṅgal.*

In the school Sanskrit was only my second language and my optional subjects were Chemistry and Botany. When I came for a admission in Presidency College, Madras, I wanted to pursue Botany in which I had done special work even while in the fifth and sixth Form even at that time I had compiled a glossary of plants, trees, creepers etc. in Sanskrit literature with their in Tamil name and Sanskrit name and Botanical and common English names.

Owing to the communal politics of the Justice Party at that time which had affected seriously College-admissions, I could not get a seat in Botany and I had to take a new group in which I was the sole student, – Ancient History (Greek and Roman), Logic and Sanskrit in all the three of which I got Distinction in the Intermediate Examinations. Of course my Sanskrit grounding was already very good and I remember that the very first set of Sanskrit verses which I composed are dated during the years of my Intermediate course in Presidency College.

In addition to the practice of writing out *stotras* and getting them by heart, there also the practice of keeping Diaries and notebooks in which all good and quotable verses interesting from one point of view or other, heard or read, were written out and also by heart if possible.

My maternal uncle Mahadeva Iyer had his own private Subhāshita notebooks. This he had imbibed from Tiruviśanallūr Raghava Śāstrigal who, as stated elsewhere, was related to us; he was Indian Industrialist Rājarāma Śāstri's elder brother and father of R. Ramachandran (of Gemini). Raghava Śāstrigal (one of Dhanam's sons-in-law) was perhaps as much a savant of Sanskrit as of music and was the brother's son of Tiruviśanallūr Rāmachandra Śāstrigal. I had picked up the habit of keeping my own *Subhāshita* notebook and getting by heart best verses from my early days; this steadily grew with the development of my own studies. When I happened to live in Triplicane during my Sanskrit Honours course especially, not a day passed without my spending at least three hours with Raghava Śāstrigal, reciting Sanskrit verses of special beauty and taking down from him verses which I did not know. In fact I possess two or three books written in the hand of Raghava Śāstrigal containing select verses from all over Sanskrit literature, which he left with me before he died. It was Raghava Śāstrigal who had taught Kumārasambhava to Sirkali Sundrachariar, a family friend, my uncle and aunt having lived sometime in Egmore along with Sundrachariar's sister who had married in Dewan Bahadur T. Rangachariar's family.

The contacts with Sundrachariar which began in Triplicane and in the Sanskrit Academy were a renewal of old ties. Outside of my academic studies one of the most effective influences which widened my study and appreciation of

Sanskrit classics, was that of Sundrachariar. It is through his inspiration that I took to the reading and mastering of the *Bhāgavata Purāṇa* and *Mahābhārata* epic systematically, getting by heart several portions of the *Bhāgavata* especially. It is on coming to know of this that my Prof. Kuppuswāmī Śāstrigal asked me to speak in those days on the Gītā Day; and I spoke on the *Bhāgavata* and Gītā at V.P. Hall when Śrī K. Chandrasekharan was the Secretary, and again on the Greater Gītā at the Ranade Hall. The late Padmanabha Śāstrigal who was my teacher in Vyākaraṇa in the Presidency College called me and fondly expressed his joy at my mastery of the *Bhāgavata* when I was so young. Falling in the line of the earlier formative forces in the field of *bhakti* and *bhajana*, the *Śrīmad Bhāgavata Purāṇa* has been the mainstay and force in all my later writings reaching up to *The Spiritual Heritage of Tyāgarāja*.

In addition to the musical background derived from early life at Tiruvārūr, academic interest in music and dance and in the Sanskrit texts thereon started with a fresh zest when I had to deal, during my Ph.D. work, with *Matsya Śāstra* with Abhinavagupta's commentary and several allied works. During this time I was in close associations with the late Śrī K.V. Ramachandran with whom we had all lived at Luz Corner for some years. K.V. Ramachandran and I had jointly pursued work on behalf of music, dance and dance-drama and we two were the first to go to some of the Tanjore Villages and to bring to light the traditional Nātakas of the Bhāgavatas at Merattūr, Soolamangalam etc.

Although engrossed in academic research and scientific study, edition of texts and scrutiny of manuscripts and the pursuit of logic and philosophy, there had been a persistent urge almost from the very beginning towards original literary activity which started expressing itself through Sanskrit verses, prose, plays, skits, essays, *stotras*, etc. in Tamil and English. However, considering the domestic circumstances, a career was not possible without a permanent employment in this country, although one of my twins in this line of activity, Manjeri S. Iswaran, classmate from Intermediate, thought otherwise. The latter discovered rather late in his life that I was right and one required a permanent position both financially and otherwise to be able to pursue writing activity. If I had been otherwise placed in private life, I wonder whether I would have become at all a research scholar or a University man, and whether I would not have gone away to the field of free lance writings or of journalism. I had actively cultivated the associations of the leading writers in all the languages of India and had been fairly intimate with several of them occupying front ranks in their own languages.

In the young days of consuming energy and overflowing enthusiasm, when one was bursting with ideas, I had written out for several friends film scenerios of *stotras* from epics, *purāṇas* and Sanskrit classics, of course without any business knowledge or inclination to make money out of them.

Other Acquaintances and Formative Influences

A. Narayanaswami Iyer, my maternal grandfather, had a younger brother named A. Śrīnivāsa Iyer who married the sister of Tiruviśanallūr Rajaram Śāstrigal (Indian Industrialist) and died prematurely. He was a brilliant person and had been selected for Provincial Civil Service along with N. Gopalaswami Iyengar, R. Śrīnivāsa Iyer (later Accountant General), and others of that time. He was also a man of striking qualities which endeared him to all. It happened that in George Town, Madras my elder maternal uncle who had been also selected for such Service was living with my mother's sister who had become widowed when quite young. At that time, they were living together with B. Rajam Iyer, author of *Kamalāmbāl Charitram* and *Rambles in Vedānta.* Rajam Iyer took a fancy for A. Śrīnivāsa Iyer and it has been handed down in our family that Rajam Iyer had Śrīnivāsa Iyer in mind when he drew some of the pictures in *Kamalāmbāl Charitram*, his unfinished story in English entitled "True Greatness of Vasudeva Śāstrigal" included in the *Rambles.* There is also an episode in the *Kamalāmbāl Charitram* of a bogus *sadhu* deceiving a person. This, we have been told, was an account of an actual incident which happened at Tiruvottriyur for my elder maternal uncle V. Subramania Iyer with all of whom Rajam Iyer was living.

One of the formative influences during the two years of my Intermediate Study (when I was living with my eldest brother next to Mylapore Club) was my frequent visits to the Rāmakrishna Maṭh where some of the Swamijis took to me, and I spent hours with them whenever I went there. Even while in the S.S.L.C. I had read Vivekananda's Lectures and the interest grew, as time passed, in the Vivekananda Ramakrishna lectures and movement. Later association developed further through the *Vedānta Keśarī* journal and Rāmakrishna Mission International Centres all of which were visited by me in Europe, U.S. and South East Asia. There is hardly a leading Swamiji in the Rāmakrishna Missions from California to Singapore with whom I have not come into contact.

Mention may also be made of the early development of interest in Tagore. In S.S.L.C. I stood first in English among those who passed from the Government High School, Tiruvārūr. Among the books I received as present was Tagore's *Gora.* During my two years of Intermediate study, I had read a great deal of Tagore literature and I even now preserve my notebook of those days in which I had in my own way imitated *Gītāñjali*, *Gardener* etc. All these lead up to the threshold of the Sanskrit Honours which I took in the teeth of domestic opposition, my brothers pressing me to take up History or Economics. After obtaining distinction in Sanskrit and with all the earlier interest in Sanskrit, I had come to know by reports about Prof. Kuppuswāmī Śāstrigal. N. Gopala Iyer of Mannargudi who was an advocate in Tanjore, who as younger brother had married my maternal uncle's daughter, had been a hotel-mate of Kuppuswāmī Śāstrigal and he introduced me to Professor. Professor used to take snuff in those days and Gopala Iyer and he were snuff-chums and they were together messing in the same hotel in the Kucheri Road at just the place where the Matthala Narayanan Street takes off.

Studiousness and academic distinction in my generation in the family were first seen in the case of my eldest brother V. Balasundaram who came out with a brilliant record in School and college, particularly in mathematics. He was a pet of Mr. Littlehall who wanted him to go up for further studies in mathematics. He unfortunately chose the career of an Advocate in the Metropolis for which he was temperamentally not suited, despite his talents. Balasundaram had also a keen literary flair and was given to wide reading in English literature and was particularly good in Shakespeare.

Another interesting personality in my family may be mentioned, – my father's sister's husband Vaidyanātha Śāstrigal of Erukkur on the Kolli dam. A Sāmavedin like us, and a Mirasdar, he took a fancy for starting a business, and having thereby lost his Estate, he fell upon his Vedic learning and training. He learned also *mantras* to cure severe reptile bites and skin eruptions from a Muslim and his house became a most crowded center for people who came for his cures.

It was during the several public activities in Madras in the field of Sanskrit and Indian Culture that I became intimately associated with late S. Satyamurthi the political leader of whose oratory, like many other youngsters of the time, I had been a regular listener and admirer. This also proved a sort of renewal of older family ties and his father-in-law (father of his second wife) was a class-mate and kinsman of my father. When Satyamurthi was living in Triplicane my contacts with him were very frequent.

Notes

[1]Xerox copy of typed manuscript obtained from V. Raghavan's daughter, Nandini Rāmani, Madras.

[2]See his *Tyāgarāja Śatakam*, edited by V. Raghavan.

Dr. V. Raghavan, A Personal Reminiscence

(by Milton Singer)

Professor William Jackson has kindly invited me to add a personal recollection of my association with Dr. Raghavan in the 1950s and 1960s. Since I am neither a Sanskritist nor a historian of religion as he is, I shall not try to comment directly on his interesting study. Instead, I shall describe the circumstances under which I came to know Dr. Raghavan and some of the important contributions he generously made to a joint co-operative project to enlist Indian scholars in a research program launched in 1951 by Robert Redfield at the University of Chicago and supported by the Ford Foundation.

The general objective of the program, as we formulated it at the time, was "to co-ordinate and to improve methods for the comparative study of the major contemporary civilizations of Asia and of their interactions with the West." With the help of Professor Gustave von Grunebaum, then at the University of Chicago, and Professors Arthur Wright at Stanford and John Fairbank at Harvard, the project had already enlisted the co-operation of scholarly specialists on Islamic and Chinese Civilizations respectively to join the program. The decision to add specialists on Indian civilization was made in 1953. My wife and I travelled to India in 1954-55, 1960-61, and in 1964, and the Redfields went in 1955 for this purpose. Before going to India, I prepared myself by attending classes and lectures at the University of Pennsylvania during the Autumn of 1953 in Professor W. Norman Brown's program of South Asia Regional Studies and during the Winter of 1964 at Berkeley in Professor David Mandelbaum's seminars and lectures.

The decision in 1953 to concentrate on India was in part influenced by the presence in the United States of some six anthropologists who had recently done field studies in Indian villages. Although Redfield was at that time interested in extending anthropological studies beyond the small "primitive isolate" and to include complex cultures and living civilizations, he thought that the extended method should begin "from the bottom up," with village studies. His Swedish lectures on *The Little Community* (1955) sketched the rich conceptual resources that had become available for the practice of an extended anthropological method. It was, however, a bit of a revelation to hear the anthropologists who had done some Indian village studies declare in the Chicago *Village India* seminar of 1954 that a village study was not the only way to enter Indian civilization (see Marriott, 1955, especially the Foreword and Editor's Preface). At about the same time, the cultural role of cities in the formation, maintenance, and transformation of particular civilizations was explored somewhat speculatively in a joint paper which Redfield and I presented to a symposium on Urbanism organized by Bert Hoselitz, the economic historian (Redfield and Singer, 1954). Our paper posed, but did not argue, the question of how the great and little traditions of a civilization and its great and little communities, as Redfield labelled them, within a middle range time-perspective of several thousand years, could be related to the structures and processes which anthropologists studied in contemporary short-run field studies. With the benefit of hindsight we can now say that my encounter with Professor M.N. Sirnivas's monograph *Religion and Society among the Coorgs of South India* (1952) in Philadelphia and Berkeley and with Dr. V. Raghavan in Pune in 1954 provided the essential concepts and information needed to answer the questions raised in Chicago in 1954 by the *Village India* seminar and the paper on "The Cultural Role of Cities."

My first meeting with Dr. Raghavan took place in Pune at the Deccan College. The occasion was a seminar on interdisciplinary Indian Studies which Dr. S.M. Katre, the linguist, had helped to organize and report (Katre, 1955). This seminar had been conceived in Chicago by a group consisting of Robert Redfield, Norman Brown, Robert Crane, Chadbourne Gilpatric, Daniel Ingalls, David Mandelbaum, Philips Talbot, and Dr. S.M. Katre. I participated in this conference, held on April 30 and May 1, 1954. The conference was intended to complement the seminar on Indian villages that had extended over the 1954 Spring Quarter with successive reports by anthropologists who had recently completed village studies–Oscar Lewis, Bernard Cohn, Gitel Steed, David Mandelbaum, Kathleen Gough, McKim Marriott and Alan Beals. These reports were assembled and edited by Marriott in the volume *Village India* and published by the University of Chicago Press in 1955.

The Indian village seminar concluded that village studies were not the only method for launching a study of Indian civilization, and the conference on Indian thought discussed other possible approaches including literary, linguistic, philosophical, and historical studies. Robert Redfield's program for intercultural and interdisciplinary studies, which had started in 1951, was also discussed at this meeting. One practical proposal that emerged from these discussions was to enlist the co-operation of a group of outstanding Indian scholars to make suggestions for some possible interdisciplinary studies. Since Professor Norman Brown, Professor Katre and I were all planning to be in India during 1954-55 we agreed to help organize and chair a seminar on Interdisciplinary Indian Studies to be held, at Dr. Katre's invitation, in the Deccan College. Fourteen Indian and six American scholars were invited to this seminar.

In a preliminary report of the seminar issued by the Deccan College the purpose and agenda were described as follows:

Seminar On Interdisciplinary Indian Studies

A seminar on Interdisciplinary Studies was held at Poona on November 18, 19 and 20, 1954 under the auspices of the Deccan College Post-Graduate and Research Institute. The seminar was convened by W. Norman Brown, Professor of Sanskrit and Chairman of South Asia Regional Studies at the University of Pennsylvania, and Milton Singer, Professor of the Social Sciences at the University of Chicago.

The purpose of the Seminar was to bring together some Indians and some Americans seriously concerned with the future of Indian studies in the United States and in India for an exchange of views and for the exploration of possibilities of specific forms of co-operation.

The agenda for the Seminar was set as follows:

Thursday:	Welcome by S.M. Katre,
2-30 to 5 p.m.	Introductory Comments by D.R. Gadgil.
	Purpose and Background of the Seminar, statement by Milton Singer.
	Trends in Indian Studies in the United States, statement by W. Norman Brown.

Friday: 1-30 to 5 p.m.	Variety and integration in the Pattern of Indian Culture, discussion to be opened by V. Raghavan.
	Variety and Integration in the Pattern of Indian Languages, discussion to be opened by S.K. Chatterjee.
	What Do Village Studies Tell Us About Indian Culture and Society? Discussion to be opened by V.M. Dandekara.
Saturday: 10 to 12-30 p.m.	The Planned State in Ancient and Modern India, discussion to be opened by A.S. Altekar and D.G. Karve.
Saturday: 2-30 to 5 p. m.	The Study of Urban Castes and Classes and their Political Economic Roles, discussion to be opened by D.R. Gadgil.
	Present Status and Needs in Social Science Studies in India, discussion to be opened by D.N. Majumdar.
Sunday:	Sightseeing: (Visit to Karla, Bhaja, Bedsa, and School of Yoga at Lonavala).

Summaries of papers were presented and discussed by the participants as indicated in the published report of the Seminar edited by Professor S. M. Katre and published by the Deccan College in 1955. My own presentation described the Redfield program, a nine-page description of which was also circulated. The discussions supported interdisciplinary approaches, although at least two participants were skeptical of anthropological approaches. Dr. Raghavan's paper on "Variety and Integration in the Pattern of Indian Culture" was astonishingly close to Redfield's approach. Taken together with his warm personal invitation to Madras City, we were persuaded to make a preliminary visit, the result of which was a decision to spend about three months there in 1954-55, learning what was happening to Hinduism in a metropolitan center. Return trips in 1960-61 and in 1964 were chiefly devoted to follow-up studies in Madras.

It would be difficult to exaggerate Dr. Raghavan's influence on my research and writing on Madras, especially during the first trip in 1954-55. As my principal guide on the first visit, he introduced me to a circle of important cultural and spiritual leaders, and also recommended a series of cultural events for me to observe as they happened; many of these were announced in an English language daily. His ever-ready willingness to answer my questions and to discuss the meanings of these events, at his office or in his home, as well as to read and comment on what I wrote about them, no doubt influenced my interpretations as they did those of many other visitors who were beneficiaries of Dr. Raghavan's guidance.

My interpretations of Redfield's program, particularly as modified by M.N. Śrīnivas' 1952 conceptions of "Sanskritic Hinduism" and of "Sanskritization," led me to formulate the research question as "What Happens to Sanskritic Hinduism (as a great tradition) in a Metropolitan Center (such as Madras)?" Dr. Raghavan's qualifications to throw light on this question, as a Sanskritist and cultural leader, are quite evident. The explanation of his influence then needs to be considered as a matter of convergence and conjuncture between Dr. Raghavan as an outstanding Sanskritist, and Smārta Brahman, and the Redfield-Śrīnivas framework which I brought to India.

This convergence has been cited and discussed in my book *When a Great Tradition Modernizes* ([1972] 1980).

Dr. Raghavan was not my main guide during the second trip in 1960-61 when I did an intensive study of the Radha-Krishna bhajans in Madras City, or during the third trip when I studied industrial leaders and their Hindu ethic. Although Dr. Raghavan continued as a friend and consultant on these later trips, he also encouraged me to study the anti-Brahman and non-Brahman sects.

The encounters with Krishnite Smārta Brahmans in the Bhajans, and also with Brahman and non-Brahman Vaishnavas, Shaiva Siddhantas, as well as with the secular anti-Brahmans (D.K. and D.M. K.) contextualized for me the institutions and functionaries to which Dr. Raghavan introduced me–the Shiva temple and its temple priests in Mylapore, the Music Academy and such star performers as Balasaraswati and Subhalakshmi; the Kuppuswāmī Shastri Sanskrit Academy; Vaishnava temple in Triplicane, Śrī Vaishnava acharayas and schools at Perumbudur; the pilgrimage center at Tirupati, among others.

Perhaps the most important person to whom Dr. Raghavan introduced me was the Shankaracharya in his ashram at Kanchipuram. In addition to being revered by Dr. Raghavan and his family, the Shankaracharya was considered by many at that time to be the most influential spiritual leader in South India and was routinely referred to as "His Holiness." In my two interviews with him, he impressed me strongly with his dedicated intelligence, wide knowledge, and good sense. Dr. Raghavan's elder son, age 14 at the time, accompanied me on the first interview (for descriptions of the interviews see *When a Great Tradition Modernizes*, pp. 86-89, 341-42, and passim). Three of Dr. Raghavan's students, Sundaram, Janaki, and T.K. Venkateswaran, were also helpful guides in Madras. For

"T.K.'s" special role see my *Krishna* volume (Singer, ed. [1966] 1968).

One of the first ceremonial events to which Dr. Raghavan invited us was in a village near Madras. Many of Dr. Raghavan's friends also came to watch it because they said it was an authentic traditional folk performance which they called "making the god dance." By moonlight, the images of Shiva and Parvati astride two giant logs carried by about six men on their shoulders forward and back accompanied by the music of long pipes, truly appared to be doing a transcendental dance.

Other memorable performances to which Dr. Raghavan accompanied me were a temple floating festival and a Śiva night at the Mylapore temple. As several men pulled a wooden platform on which images of Shiva and Parvati were seated around a temple tank, Dr. Raghavan commented that all the "attentions" shown to an earthly ruler are shown to the divine images. "It is a cool moonlight night: the people have come out after a warm day; it would be pleasant for anyone to take a ride on the temple float. . . " (Singer [1972] 1980: 117).

On the great night of Śiva (Mahāśivaratri) at the end of February when Śiva is honored at the Mylapore temple, Dr. Raghavan and his entire family came with offerings of fruits and flowers and made the rounds of all the shrines. The temple was very crowded on this occasion, although Dr. Raghavan explained that the crowds did not constitute a "congregation" in the Western sense. They were simply a group of worshippers come to celebrate the festival (Singer, ibid, 116-117).

Before leaving Madras in the Spring of 1955, I was intrigued by the similarities in structure, functions, and contents of the calendrical temple festival and the domestic life cycle rituals such as a first and sixtieth birthday. The further analogies of such rituals with the more informal ceremonies of bhajans, puranic and epic recitations and dramatizations, and the performances of music, dance, and drama suggested the generic concept of "a cultural performance" as multimedia enactments of puranic and epic episodes which were identified as encapsulated specimens of indigenous cultural traditions and distinctive group identities. The recurrence of similar processes of changes in various cultural performances provided important markers for the study of the effects of urbanization on cultural change and continuity (Singer 1955, 1959, [1972] 1980).

A general conclusion I drew from these encounters with traditional institutions, functionaries, and cultural performances was that Dr. Raghavan's Madras and environs were more of an "orthogenetic" and sacred center than the modern "heterogenetic" metropolitan center I had imagined. Dr. Raghavan agreed with this conclusion and cited some of his own historical studies in support. A recent historical study by an urban historian at first contrasted Madras and Madurai as a colonial port city and a ceremonial center respectively, but later the author was impressed by the number of temples in contemporary Madras (Lewandowski 1977, 1980). A contrast between ancient coastal Puhar, near Madras, and the inland capital of Madurai has been interpreted by my colleague A.K. Rāmanujan in terms of Redfield's heterogenetic-orthogenetic contrast. (For further discussion of this question see my papers "Purusha and Modular as Architectural Symbols" and "The Symbolism of the Center, the Middle, and the Periphery.")

One explanation of Dr. Raghavan's significant influence on my observations and interpretations during our first visit to Madras in 1954-55 is to be found in a general convergence between his conception of Hinduism as a dynamic product of the historic interactions of Sanskritic cultural traditions and of popular practices and beliefs, on the one hand, and the Redfield-Śrīnivas conceptualization of an all-India Sanskritic Hinduism on the other hand. I first noticed such a convergence when Dr. Raghavan presented his paper on "Variety and Integration in the Pattern of Indian Culture" at the Poona seminar in 1954. Robert Redfield also recognized the relevance of the paper for his conceptions of the structure and organization of tradition and cited it in his book *Peasant Society and Culture* (1956). In the Fall of 1955, when Professor Redfield participated in a Madras conference, he heard Dr. Raghavan and Dr. M.N. Śrīnivas discuss their respective interpretations of the "Sanskritization" process, the former accenting the linguistic-cultural aspects of the process, while the latter emphasized its role as a mechanism of upward social mobility in the caste hierarchy (A. Aiyappan and L.K. Bala Ratnam, eds., 1956). We submitted both the Raghavan paper on "Variety and Integration in the Pattern of Indian Culture" and the Śrīnivas paper on "Sanskritization and Westernization" to the *Far Eastern Quarterly* which published them in 1956.

While the general convergence of our approaches and Dr. Raghavan's generous willingness to place his profound knowledge of Indian culture and of the local scene at my disposal did much to smooth my way on this first field study, there were still many surprises and unexpected encounters. The details are described in my book *When a Great Tradition Modernizes* ([1972] 1980). Several amusing examples will be mentioned because they changed my conception of the relations of an anthropologist to "native" informants. One such informant impatiently responded to my elementary questions by saying "you sound like a child asking these questions." Another informant, a Śrī Vaishnava ritual specialist, kept referring to "P.C." while describing his and his father's duties. Finally, I asked who or what is "P.C."? He said, in a tone of mock surprise, "you are an anthropologist and don't know Tylor's *Primitive Culture*!" He then launched into a very knowledgeable discussion of Tylor's distinction between animism and animatism. These and many other examples soon convinced me that many of the "informants" I interviewed were "learned informants." Later at an AAA meeting I tried to persuade my colleagues to recognize such a category even among so called "primitive" cultures such as Malinowski's Trobrianders and Turner's Ndembu. Indeed, when observing a ritual specialist and astrologer from Kerala conduct elaborate one-year and sixty-year ceremonies in a Madras household, while the male family members and friends sat on the floor commenting on the regional differences in the ceremonies, partly for my benefit and partly out of genuine curiosity about the proceedings, made me feel that I was attending a high level seminar with live demonstrations. [Kerala ritual specialists have a high reputation for preserving traditional rituals. cf. Moore 1989, Staal 1983, Wood.] This and other experiences such as my interviews with the Śaṅkaracharya at Kanchi not only convinced me that I was conversing with "learned informants," but also that I was being educated by thoughtful and articulate teachers. Once, when I was returning with Dr. Raghavan from a local festival, we encountered a small group in a street bhajan. The leader of the group, who knew Dr. Raghavan, asked him if I were a Hindu. Dr. Raghavan said that I was not, but that I was doing a "scientific study" of Hinduism. Today I am no longer sure I would accept this description. In any case, several years later, Dr. Raghavan sent a completely unsolicited letter to the President of my university describing my Madras study and expressing satisfaction with the way it had been carried out.

Before the first trip to India, when I was listening to Professor David Mandelbaum's lectures on the "Peoples of

India" in Berkeley during the Winter quarter of 1954, an experienced social anthropologist advised me not to spend time reading "all those Indian epics and myths," but to go and settle in a village, learn the local language and do an intensive field study. It was already too late to take his advice at that time since I had spent the Fall quarter of 1953 at the University of Pennsylvania listening to Professor W. Norman Brown's lectures on the texts of ancient Indian civilization and Professor Stella Kramrisch's slide-lectures on ancient Indian art and sculptures, attending classes in Hindi, on the ethnographic sources for South Asian anthropology, and participating in a faculty seminar on Oriental mythology. Yet in one respect I did follow that senior anthropologist's advice: when in India and Madras, I spent very little time reading myths and epics, or books and articles on other topics for that matter. I was much too busy meeting people, observing all sorts of cultural events (including epic and puranic dramatizations), interviewing, travelling and attending meetings, to have time for much reading. This was a paradoxical situation, for India has a very old learned and literate tradition and Dr. Raghavan was an outstanding representative of that tradition who specialized on the performing arts and in collecting and cataloguing thousands of Sanskrit, Pali, and Tamil manuscripts, and was himself the author of over 30 books and 300 articles. As an M.A. and Ph.D. in Sanskrit language and literature and comparative philosophy, and trained under Professor S. Kuppuswāmī Śāstri, he had the academic qualifications and the scholarly productivity to become the Professor and Head of the Department of Sanskrit at Madras University. But he carried all that academic scholarship lightly and did not overwhelm with it people who consulted him. In all the years that I knew him, I can recall only about six of his papers and four or five books which he called to my attention and presented to me. The articles included the papers on "Methods of Popular Religious Instruction in South India," "Variety and Integration in the Pattern of Indian Culture," "Some Leading Ideas on Hindu Thought," "Some Madras Musicians in 1800." The books included *The Great Integrators: The Saint-Singers of India*, *Anarkali: A New Sanskrit Play in Ten Acts*, *The Heritage of Tyāgarāja*, *Bhoja's Sringara Prakasa*, and the UNESCO *Heritage of Sanskrit Literature*.

One reason for Dr. Raghavan's restraint was probably his desire to call my attention to works that would be of immediate relevance to my research interests, as most of the articles and books were. In fact, his classification and description of the three paths in Hinduism–*Karma Marga*, *Bhakti Marga*, and *Jñāna Marga*–provided an overall framework for understanding what was happening to Hinduism in Madras, and for suggesting an analogy with the historic interpretations of *works*, *faith*, and *knowledge* in the West.

Although years later Dr. Raghavan sent me a thick printed volume of his complete bibliography, I do not think that he expected me to comment on the length and scope of that volume. From my association with him, I believe that what really mattered to him as a creative participant in a great living Sanskritic tradition was to keep that tradition alive in the face of hostile movements to suppress or obliterate it. As Dr. Raghavan wrote in his Patel lectures:

> Emotional integration which helps to sustain territorial integration is an achievement on a different plane and is a matter of culture, personal, social and national. The recreation of an image of ourselves as members of a country in a physical sense, and a culture in a spiritual sense, is the prerequisite for the development of a sense and feeling of belonging to one nation. The learned pursuit of Indology has

done the basic service to the nation of recovering the national image and the image of a national tradition to which Indians belong. (*The Great Integrators*, 1966: 15).

References

Appadurai, A. and C.A. Breckenridge. 1976. The South Indian Temple: authority, honor and redistribution. *Contributions to Indian Sociology*. 10, 187-211.

—. 1981 *Worship and Conflict Under Colonial Rule: A South Indian Case*. New York: Cambridge University Press.

Aiyappan, A. and L.K. Bala Ratnam, eds. *Society in India*. Madras: S.S.A., 1956.

Brown, W. N. 1966. *Man in the Universe: Some Continuities in Indian Thought*. Berkeley: University of California Press.

Fairbank, John K., ed. 1957. *Chinese Thought and Institutions*. Chicago: University of Chicago Press.

Katre, S.M. ed. *Seminar on Interdisciplinary Indian Studies*. Poona: Deccan Post-Graduate College, 1955.

Kramrisch, S. 1946. *The Hindu Temple*. Calcutta: University of Calcutta Press.

Kroeber, Alfred L. 1963. *An Anthropologist Looks at History: Selected Essays*. Ed. by Theodora Kroeber. Foreword by Milton Singer. Berkeley: University of California Press, 1963.

Lewandowski, S. 1977. Changing Form and Function in the Ceremonial and the Colonial Port City in India: An Historical Analysis of Madras and Madurai. *Modern Asian Studies* 2: 183-217.

—. 1980. The Hindu Temple in South India. In A. King, ed., *Building and Society*. London: Routledge and Kegan Paul.

Mandelbaum, D.G. 1956. The Study of Complex Civilizations. *Current Anthropology*. Chicago: University of Chicago Press.

—. 1970. *Society in India*. 2 vols. Berkeley: University of California Press.

Marriott, McKim. 1955. *Village India*. American Anthropological Association Memoir and University of Chicago Press.

—. 1959. Changing Channels of Cultural Transmission in Indian Civilization. *Intermediate Societies, Social Mobility and Communication*, V. Ray, ed. Seattle: American Ethnological Society.

Moore, M.A. 1989. The Kerala House in a Hindu Cosmos. *Contributions to Indian Sociology*, 28 91): 169-202.

Raghavan, V. 1955. Some Leading Ideas of Hindu Thought. *The Vedānta Kesari* 16, No. 10, 344-49.

—. 1956. Variety and Integration in the Pattern of Indian Culture. *The Far Eastern Quarterly* 15 (4).

—. 1958. Popular and Classical Music. *Journal of the Music Academy*, 28: 100-106.

—. 1959 [1958]. Methods of Popular Religious Instruction in South India. In M. Singer, ed. *Traditional India: Structure and Change*. Philadelphia: American Folklore Society.

—. *Bhoja's Sringara Prakasa*. Madras: Punarvasu, 1963.

—. 1966. *The Great Integrators: The Saint Singers of India* [Patel Memorial Lectures], Publications Division, Government of India Press.

—. 1968. *Bibliography of the Books, Papers and Other Contributions of Dr. V. Raghavan*. Ahmedabad: The New Order Book Co.

—. 1972. *Anarkali: A New Sanskrit Play in Ten Acts*. Madras: The Samskrita Ranga.

Rāmanujan, A.K. 1970. Towards an Anthology of City Images. In R.G. Fox, ed. *Urban India: Society, Space and Image*. Durham: Duke University.

Redfield, Robert. 1953a. Relations of Anthropology to the Social Sciences and the Humanities. *Anthropology Today*. Arthur L. Kroeber, ed. Chicago: University of Chicago Press.

—. 1953b. *The Primitive World and Its Transformations*. Ithaca, N.Y.: Cornell University Press.

—. 1955a. *The Little Community: Viewpoints for the Study of a Human Whole*. Chicago: University of Chicago Press.

—. 1955b. The Social Organization of Tradition. *The Fair Eastern Quarterly* 15 (1): 13-21.

—. 1956a. *Peasant Society and Culture: An Anthropological Approach to Civilization*. Chicago: University of Chicago Press.

—. 1956b. Primitive and Peasant: Simple and Compound Society. Published in part in *Society in India*. A. Aiyappan and L.K. Bala Ratnam, eds. Madras.

—. 1962. *Human Nature and the Study of Society*. Margaret P. Redfield, ed. (Papers, vol. 1). Chicago: University of Chicago Press.

Redfield, Robert and Milton Singer. "The Cultural Role of Cities." *Economic Development and Cultural Change*, 1954: 53-73.

Singer, Milton. 1955 The Cultural Pattern of Indian Civilization. *The Far Eastern Quarterly* 15 (1).

Singer, Milton ed. 1958-59. *Traditional India: Structure and Change*. American Philosophical Society.

—. 1964a. The Social Organization of Indian Civilization. Diogenes. Reprinted in *When a Great Tradition Modernizes: An Anthropological Approach to Modern Civilization*. N.Y.: Praeger, 1972.

—, ed. [1966]. *Krishna: Myths, Rites and Attitudes*. Chicago: University of Chicago Press, 1968. Foreword by D.H.H. Ingalls.

—. [1972]. *When a Great Tradition Modernizes: An Anthropological Approach to Indian Civilization*. Chicago: University of Chicago Press, 1980.

—, ed. 1973. *Entrepreneurship and Modernization of Occupational Cultures in South Asia*. Durham, N.C.: Duke University Press.

—. 1976. "Robert Redfield's Development of a Social Anthropology of Civilizations." In *American Anthropology: The Early Years*. Ed. by John Murra. St. Paul: West Publishing Co.

—. 1988. David Mandelbaum and the Rise of South Asian Studies: A Reminiscence. In P. Hockings, ed. *Dimensions of Social Life: Essays in Honor of David Mandelbaum*. Berlin: Mouton de Gruyter.

—. 1988. Symbolism of the Center, the Periphery, and the Middle. L. Greenfeld and M. Martin, eds. *Center: Ideas and Institutions*. Chicago: University of Chicago Press.

Singer, Milton B., and Bernard S. Cohn, eds. 1968. *Structure and Change in Indian Society*. Chicago: Aldine Publishing Co.

Śrīnivas, M.N. 1952. *Religion and Society among the Coorgs of South India*. London and N.Y.: Oxford University Press.

—. 1956. Sanskritization and Westernization. *Far Eastern Quarterly* 15 (4).

—. 1962. *Caste in Modern India and Other Essays*. Bombay: Asia Publishing House.

—. 1966. *Social Change in Modern India*. Berkeley: University of California Press.

Staal, F. 1983. *Agni: the Vedic Ritual of the Fire Altar*. 2 vols. Berkeley: Asian Humanities Press.

Turner, V. 1967. *The Forest of Symbols*. Ithaca: Cornell University Press.

—. 1974. *Dramas, Fields, and Metaphors*. Ithaca: Cornell University Press.

—. 1979. *Process, Performance, and Pilgrimage*. New Delhi: Concept Publishing Co.

Tylor, E.B. [1871]. *Primitive Culture: Researches into the development of mythology, philosophy, religion, language, art, and custom*. 2 vols. London: 1873.

von Grunebaum, G.E. 1955. Islam: Essays in the Nature and Growth of a Cultural Tradition. *American Anthropological Association Memoir*. London: Routledge and Kegan Paul, 1955, 1961.

von Grunebaum, G.E. 1962. *Modern Islam: The Search for Cultural Identity*. Berkeley and Los Angeles: University of California Press.

Wright, Arthur F., ed. 1953. Studies in Chinese Thought. *American Anthropological Association Memoir*. Chicago: University of Chicago Press.

—. 1960. The Study of Chinese Civilization. *Journal of the History of Ideas* 21 (2).

—, ed. 1964. *Confucianism and Chinese Civilization*. N.Y.: Atheneum.

VIII

Bibliography

Primary Sources: Nāmasiddhānta Texts

Nārāyaṇa Tirtha, *Kṛṣṇalīlātaraṅginī*. Madras: Vavilla, 1967. (Sanskrit text in Telugu script.) For a more recent edition in Devanāgarī script, with English translation, see *Śrī Krishna līlā taraṅginī*, translated by B. Natarājan, Madras: Mudgala Trust, 1988, volume 1. 1990, volume 2.

Sadāśiva Brahmendra, *Śivamanasikapūjā Kīrtanani Ātmavidyāvilāsa*, Madras: Śrī Kamakoṭi Kośaṣṭhānena Prakāsitam, 1951. Translated into English and Tamil by V. Narayanan.

Sadgurusvāmī, *Bhajana Ratnākara*. ed. K. Pancapagesa Iyer, Madras: author, 1972.

_____________, *Bhakti-samdeha-dhvanta-bhaskara*, ed. A.B.S. Rāmasvāmī, rev. ed. New Delhi: Delhi Bhajana Samaj, 1958.

Śrīdhara Veṅkaṭeśa Āyyāvāl, *Śāhendravilāsa*, (ed. V. Raghavan), Tiruchi: Tanjore Saraswati Mahal Library, 1952.

__________________, *Gaṅgaśatakam*.

__________________, *Ākhyāṣaṣṭih śatakam*, (ed. V. Raghavan), Kumbakoṇam and Madras: Kāmakoṭi Kośaṣṭhanam, 1944. No. 15 contains introduction, No. 25 contains text.

Śrī Bodhendra Sarasvati, *Bhagavan-nāmāmṛita rasodayam; Nāma rasayanam; Nāma suryodayam; Nāma taraṅgam; Harihara bhedadikaram; Harihara advaita bhūṣanam; Mūrthabrahma vivekam; Bhagavan nāmāmṛita*. Manuscripts at Saraswati Mahal Library, Tanjore.

__________________. *Harihara advaita bhuṣanam*, ed. T. Chandrasekharam, Madras: Government Press, 1954.

Upaniṣad Brahman, *Upeya-nāma-viveka* (ed. V. Raghavan), Madras: Adyar Library, 1967.

The Vaiṣṇavopaniṣads (including Rāma-tapinīyupaniṣad, Rāmarahasyopaniṣad, Kalisamtaranopaniṣad, Gopālatapīntyupaniṣad. Adyar: Theosophical Society, 19 .

Viṣṇusahasranāma with the bhasya of Saṁkarācārya, tr. into English by R. Ananthakrishna Sastry, Madras: Adyar Library, 1980.

Lakṣmīdhara, *Bhagavannāma Kaumudi*, Kasi: Prakāśasthānam Acyutagranthamālā Kāryālayaḥ, 1907.

Rāma-Tapanīya-Upaniṣad (also the *Rāma Upaniṣad* with the commentary of Nārāyaṇa, ed. by Vindhyeśvari Prasāda Śarman; also the *Hanumaduktarāma Upaniṣad*), Banaras: Benares Printing Press, 1879.

Selected Secondary Bibliographic Sources

Harvey P. Alper, ed. *Understanding Mantras*, Albany: State University of New York, 1989. (See especially p. 359 "The Significance of Names" and p. 327 and following, "A Working Bibliography for the Study of Mantras.")

____________, "Regression Towards the Real," *Parabola* 8, no. 3: pp. 72-81.

F.R. Allchin, "The Place of Tulsī Dās in North Indian Devotional Faith," in *Journal of the Royal Asiatic Society*, 1966, pts. 3 and 4, pp. 128-9 especially.

Thomas J. J. Altizer, *The Self-Embodiment of God*, Lanham: University Press of America, 1987.

Sinnappah Arasaratnam, *Merchants, Companies and Commerce on the Coromandel Coast, 1650-1740*, Delhi: Oxford Univ. Press, 1986.

Guy L. Beck, *Sonic Theology: Hinduism and Sacred Sound*, Columbia: University of South Carolina Press, 1993.

Joachim Ernst Berendt, *Nada Brahma: The World is Sound*, Rochester: Destiny Books, 1987.

Agehananda Bharati, *The Tantric Tradition*, London: Rider and Co., 1965.

Usha R. Bhise, "The Importance of *Naman* in the Ṛgveda," All-India Oriental Conference Summary of Papers, 25:2-3.

Madeleine Biardeau, *Sphota siddhi (La Demonstration du Sphota) par Mandana Misra, introduction, et commentaire par Madeleine Biardeau, texte etabli par N.R. Bhatt avec la collaboration de T. Ramanujam*, Pondichery: Publications de l'institut francais d'indologie, 1958.

John Blofeld, *Mantras, Sacred Words of Power*, London: Allen and Unwin, 1977.

A.K. Coomaraswamy, "Spiritual Authority and Temporal Power," in *American Oriental Society Journal*, New Haven: AOS, 1942.

Harold Coward, *Sphota Theory of Language*, Delhi: Motilal Banarsidass, 1980.

______________ and Krishna Sivaraman, eds., *Revelation in Indian Thought*, Emeryville, Calif.: Dharma Publishing, 1977.

Francis X. D'Sa *Sabdapramanyam in Sabara and Kumarila: Towards a Study of the Mimamsa Experience of Language*, Wien: De Nobili Research Library, 1980.

Alain Danielou, *Hindu Polytheism*, New York: Bollingen, 1964, especially pp. 334-349: "The Thought-Forms or Mantras."

Raghav Chaitanya Das, *The Divine Name*, Bombay, Author, 1954.

Shashi Bhusan Das Gupta, "The Role of Mantra in Indian Religion," *Bulletin of the Rāmakrishna Mission Institute of Culture*, Vol. VII, no. 3, March 1956, pp. 49-57.

_____________, "Some Later Yogic Schools," *Cultural Heritage of India*, vol. 4, Calcutta: The Rāmakrishna Mission, 1956, pp. 291-299.

R. De Smet, "Nāma Japa in Christianity," *Mountain Path*, Tiruvannamalai, Ramanashram, April 1981, pp. 91-93.

Louis Dumont, *Religion/Politics and History in India: Collected Papers in Indian Sociology*, Paris: Mouton, 1970 (first pub. 1962).

Eknath Easwaran, *The Mantram Handbook*, London: Routledge and Kegan J. Paul, 1978.

Franklin Edgerton, *Mīmāṅsā Nyāya Prakāsa or Āpadevī: A Treatise on the Mīmāṅsā System by Apadeva, Translated into English, With an Introduction, Transliterated Sanskrit Text, and Glossarial Index*, New Haven: Yale Univ. Press, 1929.

Maryla Falk, *Nāma-rūpa and Dharma-rūpa*, Calcutta: Univ. of Calcutta, 1943.

Richard Fox, ed. *Realms and Regions in Indian History* (includes "The Segmentary State in South Indian History" by Burton Stein) forthcoming. Durham, NC.

M.K. Gandhi, *Rāmanāma*, ed. Bharatan Kumarappa, Ahmedabad: Navajīvan, 1949.

L. Gardet, "Un Probleme de mystique comparee: la mention dun Nom divin. . . " in *Revue Thomiste*,(?) 1952, pp. 642-679; 1953, pp. 197-216.

Nadiedja Gorodetzky, *The Prayer of Jesus*, Oxford: Blackfriars, 1942.

Jan Gonda, "The Indian Mantra" in *Oriens* 16, 1963. pp. 244-297. (Also included in Jan Honda's *Selected Studies*, Leiden: E.J. Brill, 1975.)

__________ *Medieval Religious Literature*, Wiesbaden: Otto Harrassowitz, 1977, especially pp. 267-270.

__________ *Notes on the Names and the Name of God in Ancient India*, Amsterdam: North Holland Pub., 1970. Verhandelingen. . . series number 4, deel 75.

Jan Gonda, *Vision of the Vedic Poets*, The Hague: Mouton and Co., 1963. Republished in New Delhi: Munshiram Manoharlal, 1984.

Kathlen Gough, *Rural Society in Southeast India*, Cambridge: Cambridge Univ. Press, 1981.

Lama Govinda, *Foundations of Tibetan Mysticism, According to the Esoteric Teachings of the Great Mantra*, London: Rider and Co., 1959, 1967.

John Stratton Hawley and Mark Juergensmeyer, *Songs of the Saints of India*, New York: Oxford Univ., 1988.

J.C. Heesterman, *The Inner Conflict of Tradition: Essays in Indian Ritual, Kingship, and Society*, Chicago: Univ. Chicago Press, 1985.

Heinrich Heiler, *Erscheinungsformen und Wesen der Religion*, Stuttgart: W. Kohlhammer Verlag, 1961, pp. 276, 341 ff.

Norvin J. Hein, "Caitanya's Ecstasies and the Theology of the Name" in *Hinduism: New Essays in the History of Religion*, ed. Bardwell L. Smith, Leiden: E.J. Brille, 1976, pp. 19-32.

W. Heitmuller, *Im Namen Jesu*, Gottingen: Vandenhoeck and Ruprecht, 1903.

Arthur Maurice Hocart, *Kings and Councillors*, Chicago, 1970 (first pub. 1936).

______________________, *Kingship*, Oxford, Oxford Univ. Press, 1927.

K.R. Śrīnivāsa Iyengar, ed. *Guru Nānak: A Homage*, New Delhi: Sahitya Akademi, 1973.

T. Izutsu, *Language and Magic*, Tokyo: Keio Institute of Philological Studies, 1956.

Mohanlal Bhagawandas Jhavery, *Comparative and Critical Study of Mantraśāstra, with Special Treatment of Jain Mantravada. . .* Ahmedabad: Sarabhai Manilal Nawab, 1944.

E. Kadloubousky and G.E.H. Palmer, *Writings from the Philokalia on Prayer of the Heart*, London: Faber and Faber, 1951.

R. Krishnamurthy, *Saints of the Cauvery Delta*, New Delhi: Concept Publishing Co., 1979.

T.S. Kuppuswamy Śāstri, "Rāmabhadra-Dīkshita and the Southern Poets" (including Āyyāvāl) in The Indian Antiquary, July 1904, p. 187.

Richard Lannoy, *The Speaking Tree*, London: Oxford Univ. Press, 1975.

David Ludden, *A Peasant History of South India*, Princeton: Princeton Univ. Press, 1985.

T.M.P. Mahadevan, ed., *A Seminar on Saints*, Madras: Ganesh and Co., 1960.

Louis Massignon, *Essai sur les origines de lexique technique de la mystique musulmane*, Paris: P. Geunther, 1922.

J.L. Mehtā, *Religion and Philosophy*, New Delhi: Indian Council for Philosophical Research, 1990.

A.L. Mudaliar, ed., *Bibliography of the Books, Papers and other Contributions of Dr. V. Raghavan*, Ahmedabad: New Order Book Co., 1968.

B. Natarajan, *Śrī Krishna Leela Taraṅginī by Nārāyaṇa Tirtha*, Vol. I, Translation and Notes in English. Madras: Mudgala Trust, 1988.

Andre Padoux, "Contributions a l'etude du mantrasastra: I, La selection des mantra (mantroddhara)," *Bulletin de l'Ecole francaise d'extreme-orient* (Hanoi) 67: pp. 59-102.

___________, "Some Suggestions on Research into Mantra," *Indologica Taurinensia (Turin) 6: pp. 235-39.*

T. S. Parthasarathy, *Music Composers of India,* Madras: C. P. Rāmaswāmī Aiyar Foundation, 1982.

V. S. Pathak, *Smārta Religious Tradition,* Meerut: Kusumañjali Prakashan, 1987.

Hanuman Prasad Poddar, *The Divine Name and its Practice,* Gorakhpur: Gorakhpur Press, s. d. (Same as Jan. 1938 Issue of *Kalyāna Kalpataru* Journal?)

Swami Pratyagatmananda, *Japasutram, The Science of Creative Sound,* Madras: Ganesh and Co., 1971.

Krishna Premi, *Gospel of Mahātma Sree Sree Krishna Premi* tr. Śrī Natesa Prabhu, Paranur: Premika Grandha Prakaṣa Sabha, 1983.

V. Raghavan, "Bhāgavata Purāṇa," *Vedānta Kesari,* Oct. 1965.

___________ed., *Composers* (Cultural Leaders of India Series), New Delhi: Publications Division, Ministry of Information and Broadcasting, Govt. of India, 1979.

___________ed., *Devotional Poets and Mystics,* Vols. I and II. New Delhi: Publications Division, Ministry of Information and Broadcasting, Govt. of India, 1978, 1981.

___________ *The Great Integrators,* New Delhi: Publications Division, Ministry of Information and Broadcasting, Govt. of India, 1966, 1969, 1976, 1979.

___________ *The Indian Heritage,* Bangalore: Indian Institute of World Culture, 1956.

___________ "Nārāyaṇa Tirtha," Madras: Śrī Nārāyaṇa Tirtha Festival Celebration Committee, Tirupunturutti, (s. d.).

___________"Sadāśiva Brahmendra" in *Service* II,ii, April 1952, pp. 84-85, 88.

___________, and C. Ramanujachari, *The Spiritual Heritage of Tyāgarāja,* Madras: Rāmakrishna Math, 1966, page 107 ff.

____________, "Śrī Sadāśiva Brahmendra's Atma-Vidyāvilāsa," in *Vedānta Keśari* XXXVII, viii, Dec. 1950, pp. 301-304.

____________, "The Tattvasaṁgraha Rāmāyaṇa of Rāmabrahmānanda," in *Annals of Oriental Research*, Vol. X, pt. 1, Madras: University of Madras.

V. Raghavan, "Upanishad Brahmān, His Life and Works," *Journal of the Music Academy* of Madras, Vol. XXVII.

____________, "Vak Devata," *Dilip*, May-June, 1975.

Rāmakrishnayya, *Telugu Literature Outside Telugu Country.* Telugu Series, no. 9. Madras: Univ. Madras. [s.d.]

R.D. Ranade, *Mysticism in India: The Poet-Saints of Mahārashtra*, Albany: State Univ. of New York, 1983 (reprint).

J.F. Richards, ed., *Kingship and Authority in South Asia*, Madison: South Asia Studies, Univ. Wisc. Madison, Publication Series, #3, 1978. (Articles by Heesterman, Burton Stein, Ronald Inden.

Nilakanta Śāstri, *A History of South India*, Madras: Oxford University Press, 1976, 1981.

Robert P. Scharlemann, ed., *Naming God*, New York: Paragon House, 1985.

Frithjof Schuon, *Language of the Self*, tr. M. Pallis and M. Matheson, Madras: Ganesh and Co., 1959.

____________, The Transcendent Unity of Religions, New York: Harper and Row, 1975.

S. Seetha, *Tanjore as a Seat of Music*, Madras: Univ. of Madras, 1981.

B.A. Selatore, *Social and Political Life in the Vijāyanagar Empire*, Madras: B.G. Paul, 1934, (especially vol. II).

Bhadrashila Sharma, *Mantrasiddhi ka upaya*, Prayag: Kalyan Mandir, 1969.

T.R. Sharma, *Studies in the Sectarian Upaniṣads*, Varanasi and Delhi: Indological Book House, 1972, pp. 27, 111, 120.

James Silverberg, *Social Mobility in the Caste System in India: An Interdisciplinary Symposium.*

Milton Singer, ed. *Krishna: Myths, Rites, and Attitudes*, Chicago: Univ, of Chicago, 1966, (Especially pp. 90-172).

C.K. Śrīnivāsan, *Marāṭha Rule in the Carnatic*, Annamalai: Annamalai University, 1944.

J. Frits Staal, ed., *Agni: The Vedic Ritual of the Fire Altar*, 2 volumes, Berkeley: Asian Humanities Press, 1983.

_______________"Ritual, Mantras and the Origin of Language," *Amrtadhara, Professor R.N. Dandekar Felicitation Volume*, Poona, 1984, pp. 403-25.

Burton Stein, *Peasant State and Society in Medieval South India*, Oxford: Oxford Univ. Press, 1980.

K.R. Subramanyam, *The Marāṭha Rājas of Tanjore*, Madras, 1928 (Delhi: AES reprint 1988).

D.T. Suzuki, *Mysticism: Christian and Buddhist, the Eastern and Western Way*, New York: Collier, 1962, pp. 123-157.

Stanley J. Tambiah, "The Magical Power of Words," *Man* 3, o. 2:pp 175-208. (Also included in Stanley J. Tambiah's *Culture, Thought and Social Action: An Anthropological Perspective*, Cambridge: Harvard Univ. Press, 1985).

Kailash Vajpeyi, *The Science of Mantras, A Manual for Happiness and Prosperity*, New Delhi: Arnold Heineman, 1979.

Swami Vivekananda, "On Mantra and Mantra-Chaitanya," in *Complete Works*, Calcutta: Mayavati Memorial Edition, 1962, vol. 7, pp. 407 and following.

Vandana-Mataji, *Nāma Japa: Prayer of the Name in the Hindu and Christian Traditions*, Bombay: Bharatiya Vidya Bhavan, 1984.

Charlotte Vaudeville, "The Cult of the Divine Name in the Haripath of Dñyāndev" in *Wiener Zeitschrift fur die*

Kunde Sud-Und Ostasiens, 12-13, 1968-69. Leiden: Brille, p. 395 ff.

Archmandrite Kallisto Ware, *The Power of the Name, the Jesus Prayer in Orthodox Spirituality*, Oxford: Fairacres Publishers, 1977.

Alex Wayman, "The Significance of Mantras, from the Veda Down to Buddhist Tantric Practice," in *Buddhist Insight, Essays by Alex Wayman*, ed. G. Elder, Delhi: Motilal Banarsidass, 1984.

Albrecht Friedrich Weber, "Vac und Logos," *Indische Studien*, Vol. 9, Berlin 1965, pp. 473-80.

Sir John Woodroffe, *The Garland of Letters*, Madras: Ganesh and Co. , 1969, pp. 305-313, "Mantra Sādhana."

Index

Abdul Rahim Khankhana 59
Abdur Rahim Khani Khan 166
Abhinavagupta 210
Advaitin sannyāsins 148
Advaita 202
Advaitasiddhānta xi
Agastya Saṃhitā 259
Aldous Huxley 95
Alfred Tennyson 312
Allah 103, 281
Allama Prabhu 55
Allā mahādevī 55
Ananda K. Coomaraswamy 90
Ananta 113
Anāhata nāda 179, 180
Annamācarya 229
Apabhraṃśa 49
Appar 51
Appayya Dīkṣita 210
Aristotle 281
Aruṇagirināthar 53
Asceticism 2
Aśoka 37
Aurangzeb 8
Avadhūta 23, 131, 290
Avatārs 47
Avyakta 179
Ayodhyā 25
Ayyāvāl 80
Ācāryas 47
Ākhyāṣaṣṭi 70, 80, 123, 124, 126, 213
Ālvārs 51
Āṇḍāl 51
Ātman 136, 138
Ātmavidyāvilāsa 25, 132, 134
Āyyāvāl 9, 19, 70, 110, 121, 213, 306
Āyyāvāl Festival 128

Baal Shem Tov 250
Bangalore 37
Bankim Chandra Chatterji 286
Basava 55
Beauty ix
Bees viii
Bhadrācalam 190
Bhadrāchala Rāmādas 61
Bhagavad Gītā Bhāsya 115
Bhagavad Gītā 67, 160, 206
Bhagavan Nāmāmṛita 346
Bhagavan Nāmāmṛitārṇava 70
Bhagavan nāma 70, 113
Bhagavan-nāma bhuṣana 111
Bhagavannāma Kaumudi 17, 116, 263, 347
Bhagavatsṃdarbha 213
Bhajana Ratnākara 346
Bhajana sampradāya 27, 29, 33, 119, 142, 148
Bhajana 21, 30, 109
Bhajanasampradāya 225

Bhaktamālā 57
Bhakti 281
Bhakti 62, 264
Bhartṛihari 210
Bhaṭṭa Tota 155
Bhavabhuti 157
Bhāgavata dharma 112
Bhāgavata 161, 162, 163, 165
Bhāgavata 35, 151, 152, 190, 220
Bhāgavatars 31
Bhāgavata Purāṇa 50, 60, 64, 69, 79, 144, 159, 211, 214, 257, 295, 323
Bhoga 53
Bhūpatirājapuram 28, 143
Bhūṣana 70
Boar 143
Bodhendra xii, 9, 15, 110, 113, 114, 116, 307, 346
Bodhisāttva 135
Bopadeva 56, 160
Brahman 139
Brahmā sūtras 210
Brahmendra 9
British 10
Bṛihadaraṇyaka Upaniṣad 156
Buddha's name 287
Buddhism 255
Buddhist 169

Caitanya 35, 60, 61, 213, 259, 299
Cakravaka 171
Campū 9
Caṇḍāla 122
Caṇḍīdās 60
Caryā-gītas 49
Cātaka 171
Chanda Sahib 24
Chandogya Upanisad 155
Charaka 231
Charlotte Vaudeville 289
Chinese mystics 275
Clement of Alexandria 93
Colonialism 97
Confucius 279
Coromandel 7

Daharākāśa 138
Dakṣiṇamūrti mantra 23
Dara Shikoh 180
Daśarathi Śarakam 189, 195
Deva's 113
Devatā Nāma Māhātmya 71
Devāra 51
Devī-mahātmya 60
Dharmavijaya Campū 126
Dharmavijaya 9
Dhvāni x
Diana Eck 280
Divya-nāma-samkīrtanas 226
Divyabandham 51
Dutch 7, 10

Egypt 180
Ekāntada 55
Ekojī 8
European rivalry 7
Experience ix
Expiation 17

F. Schwartz 11
Farquhar 13
Four ācāryas 29
Frank Clooney 6
Frithjof Schuon 91, 98

Gai Eaton 97
Gandhi 231, 260, 279
Gaṅgā 20, 122, 123, 128
Garga 98
Gary Snyder 316
Gertrude Stein 268
Gītagovinda 59, 144
Gnosis 92
Gnosis 95
Golconda 186
Golden Flower 275
Gopanna 189
Gopāla Bhaṭṭaka 213
Gorakhnātha 49
Granth Saheb 58
Guṇatrayaviveka 204
Guru 98, 99
Guru 47
Guru Nānak 169, 305

Haidar Ali 11
Hans Georg Gadamer 276
Hari-hara bhedadhikkāra 116
Hari-hara-advaita-bhūṣaṇam 116
Haribhaktisudhārṇava 151
Haridāsas 55
Harvey P. Alper 268, 271
Hinduism 92
Hiraṇyagarbha 206
Hiuen 16
Howard Thurman 314
Hypocrisy 278

Ingalls xvii, 3
Integrations 62
Integrators 3
Islam 273
Iṣṭa-devata 111, 221
Italo Calvino 274
Itihāsa 48

J. Frits Staal 253, 272
J.L. Mehta 4, 252
Jacques Derrida 281, 286
Jagannātha 17
Jaimini's 6, 208
Jain 169
Jainism 49
Jan Gonda 272
Japa 94, 102, 103, 258
Japamāla vii
Japji 172
Japyeśa 219
Jayadeva 29, 59
Jīvanmukta 132, 135
Jñānasambandhar 294
Jñāneśvara 50, 56, 259, 296
John Kenneth Gailbraith 278

Kabīr 59, 188, 283, 303
Kali Yuga xiv
Kali 65, 68, 72
Kalidāsa 73, 157
Kalisantaranopaniṣad 66
Kanakadāsa 56
Kanha 270
Kapila 163, 164
Karṇāṭaka 54
Kashmir 58
Kashmir Śaivism 210
Kaumudi 113
Kavis 155
Kāñcīpuram 18, 110, 200
Kāverī xii, 218

Kāverī delta xiv, 126
Kees Bolle 253
Kena Upaniṣad 173
Kīrtana 226
Krishna 20, 186
Krishna Premi 273
Krishna-līlā-taraṅgiṇī 27, 142, 143, 146, 150, 346
Kṛiti 226
Kṣetrayya 186
Kumārasambhava 157
Kumbakoṇam 22
Kun 181

Lakṣmīdhara 17, 114, 261, 262, 263, 298, 347
Lallādevī 58
Liṅgayariar 120
Liṅgāyats 55
Logos 180

M. Biardeau 258
Madhavācārya 56
Mahābhārata 161, 234, 255, 278
Mahāliṅga Svāmī 128
Mahārāṣṭra 56
Maitri Upaniṣad xiv
Majma-ul-Bahrain 180
Mantra vii, 231, 247, 270, 281
Mantropadeśa 189
Manu 164
Manucci 126
Maṇḍana 209, 210
Maṇḍukya Upaniṣad 204
Marātha xvi, 126
Marāṭha kings 7
Mark Helpern 282
Martin Buber 249
Martin Heidegger 268
Marudānallūr 112
Matsya Purāṇa 16
Mānava-dharma-śātra 102
Māṇikkavāchakar 50, 51
Mārā 78
Māyā 175
Measure viii
Merattur 152
Metaphysics 96
Milton Singer 328
Missionaries 126
Mīmāṃsā 208
Mīrābāi 57, 307
Monism 62
Mother 281
Mughals 7
Muhammad 105
Music 106, 224
Muslim 18

Nada Brahma: The World is Sound 348
Nadukkaveri 149
Nagaratnāmmāl 37
Nakedness 23
Name 5, 64, 101, 176, 196
Name 62
Name banks 282
Name of Rāma 205
Name-consciousness 214
Nammālvār 51, 256
Narasī Mehtā 35, 57, 298
Naukā Carits 70
Nāda x, 50, 223, 224, 260
Nāda-upāsana 137

Nālātiram 51
Nāma kīrtana 81
Nāma 203
Nāma-sankīrtana 109
Nāmadeva 259, 297
Nāmasiddhānta vii, 12, 201, 262
Nāmasiddhānta 36
Nāmaṣṭaka 213
Nāmāmṛita Rasāyana xii, 70, 115, 205
Nāmāmṛita Rasodaya 70
Nāmāmṛita Sūryodaya 70
Nāmdeva 57
Nānak 58, 62
Nārada 60, 66, 70
Nārāyaṇa Tīrtha 9, 26, 142, 148, 149, 206, 346
Nātha Siddhas 290
Nāthamuni 51
Nāyak xv, 7, 126
Nāyanārs 51
Neo-syādvāda 280
Nilakantha Dīkṣita 157
Nirguṇa Brahman 170
Nivedita 48
Niyogis 12
Non-sectarian 31

Octavion Paz 270
Old Testament 279
Om 103
Oṃkār 182, 208
Origins 262

Padma Purāṇa 82, 160, 205
Pañcāyatana-pūjā 266
Para Brahman 211
Paramaśivendra Sarasvatī 132
Paramārtha Prakāśa 49
Paraṇava 156
Parasara Bhattar 259
Parijataharaṇa nāṭka 152
Participatory 280
Patanjali 94
Patañjali's Yoga Sūtras 256
Patronage 21
Paṭṭinattār 53
Pārijāta haraṇa 144
Perennialism 91
Poetry viii
Postmodern 267
Poṭana 225
Prabodhasudhākāra 174
Prahlāda 164
Praṇava 103
Prasād 20
Prayāg 29
Prāyaścittam 17
Pudukoṭṭai 23, 132
Purandaradāsa 55, 300
Purāṇas xiii, 48, 257
Purāṇic Hinduism 265
Purity 285
Purva Mīmāṃṣā 262
Pūjā 223

R. Gandhi 258
R.D. Ranade 314
Raghuvaṃsa 157
Ramana Mahārshi 311
Ramchandra Gandhi 312
Rantideva 164
Rasa 2
Raskhan 59, 166

Rādhākrishna Bhajana Maṭh 112
Rāma 192, 195, 221
Rāma Rahasya 72
Rāma uttara tāpani 73
Rāma-Tapanīya-Upaniṣad 72, 347
Rāma-nāma 206, 231
Rāmabrahmānanda Sarasvati 72
Rāmacaritamānasa 167
Rāmadās 306
Rāmakarṇāmṛita 302
Rāmakrishna 99
Rāmakrishna Paramahaṃsa 95, 310
Rāmamāhātmya 71
Rāmarahasya Upaniṣad 205, 207, 212, 260, 283
Rāmataraṅgacandrikā 206
Rāmatāpinī 205, 212
Rāmāliṅgasvāmī 54
Rāmānanda 35, 50, 59
Rāmānuja 50
Rāmāprasad 60
Rāmāyaṇa 71, 159
Rāmāyya 55
Rāmdās 57
Rāmdhum 232
Rāmnāmi 285
Release 5
René Guénon 90
Rescue 193
Richard Lannoy 253
Riddle 175
Rigveda 155
Ritual 248, 263
Robbers 21
Robert Bly 269
Roman 252
Rules 204
Rūpa 213
Ṛg Vedic hymns 64
Ṛiṣis 47, 155, 279

Sadāśiva 9
Sadāśiva Brahmendra 22, 131, 346
Sadgurusvāmi xii, 11, 27, 29, 111, 346
Saguṇa Brahman 170
Sahāja 49
Saint 4
Samādhi 4, 19, 133
Samārtha 57
Sambandhar 51
Samsāra 2
Sannyāsin 27, 148
Sanskrit xiii
Santaranopaniṣad 72
Sanyāsa 228
Saṅgatis 227
Sarabhojī II 30
Schuon 91
Self 101
Semmangudi 26
Shi-ite Muslims 313
Siddha xi, 262
Siddhas 53, 290
Siddhānta xi
Siddhānta Kalpavalli 133
Siddhi 133
Silhouette 26
Simone Weil 248
Sir George Grierson 59, 166
Sister 48
Sivājī 8
Smārta 13
Smārta xiii, 33, 35, 221, 264, 265

Somasundara 120
Sonic Theology: Hinduism and Sacred Sounds 347
Sound 173
Sphoṭa 209
Srinivasa Iyer 26
St. Marcarius of Egypt 93
Stomach ache 29
Subhāṣitas 49
Sufism 103
Suicide 17
Sultan-ul-Adhkar 181
Sundaramūrti 51, 294
Sundarar 51
Susan Sontag 276
Sūtra Bhasya 135
Swaz-i-Mutlak 181
Śabda Brahman 156, 211
Śabda 177, 180, 181, 209, 214
Śahajī 131
Śaivasiddhānta xi
Śaṅkara 3, 48, 50, 67, 103, 114, 135, 156, 208, 209, 214
Śaṅkaradeva 60
Śarabhojī 23
Śatapatha Brāmaṇa 254
Śatarudrīya 64, 255
Śāhaji 8, 9, 111, 120, 125
Śāhendravilāsa 9, 121, 124, 125, 346
Śilappadikāram 256
Śiva 21, 263, 274
Śiva-mantra 206
Śivamanasikapūjā Kīrtanani 346
Śivapañcākṣari 206
Śivarāma 132
Śivavāktar 53
Śrāddha rites 20
Śrāddha 122
Śri Aurobindo 48
Śrīdhara Veṅkaṭeśa Āyyāvāl 119, 120, 121, 346
Śrīvidya 262
Śūnya 62
Śvetāśvatara Upaniṣad 254

Taittirīya Upaniṣad 158
Tamil Māheśvara Siddhas 290
Tani Shāh 187, 194
Tantra 257, 262, 263
Tao 249, 251
Tatooed face 285
Tattva-sāṁgraha-rāmāyaṇa 72
Tāntra 49
Tāntrasara 296
Tāñjāvūr xv
Tāraka mantra 2, 13, 73
Tāraka nāma 220
Tāyumānavar 54
Tenāḷi Rāma 283
Tevāram 256
Thich Nhat Hanh's 279
Tiruchirāpalli 24
Tirumaṇgaimannar 296
Tirumazhiśai 53
Tirumūlar 53
Tiruppughazh 54
Tiruppunturutti 151
Tiruvaiyāru 218
Tiruvāchakam 51
Tiruvārūr 218
Tiruvidaimarudūr 128, 273
Tiruviśanallūr 9, 19, 111, 121, 131
Tiryvāimozhi 51
Tondaiman 23

Tradition 98
Transcendent 2
Triuviśanallūr 128
True devotee 222
Tsiang 16
Tukārām 57, 307
Tulasi 59
Tulasidās 166, 259, 309
Tyāgarāja 11, 61, 73, 75, 76, 77, 82, 83, 84, 85, 146, 196, 217, 310

Ultramundaneity 26
Unity 95
Unstruck music 179
Uñchavṛitti 31
Upaniṣad Brahman 367
Upaniṣad Brahmayogin 200
Upaniṣad Brahmendra 146
Upāya 203
Upeya 203
Upeya nāma-viveka 74, 200, 207, 213, 347
Uttararāmacarita 157

V. Raghavan xv, 14, 272
Vallabhācharya 59
Varada Rāmadās 188
Varaha 28
Varahūr 143, 149
Varnāśrama dharma xiii

Vāk's 156
Vālmīki 78, 168, 256
Vedic sacrifices 263
Veṅkaṭaraman Bhāgavatar 273
Vibrations 280
Vice 28
Vidyāpati 59
Vijayanagara xv, 34
Vision viii, 4
Viṣṇu Purāṇa 67, 79, 156, 159
Viṣṇu Sahasranāma 64, 67, 232, 234, 255, 347
Viśva 81
Vīraśaiva 55
Voice 27
Vyāsa 161
Vyāsarāya 56

Word 179

YHWH 286
Yahweh 249, 250
Yajñavalkya 148
Yakṣagana 189
Yoga 49
Yoga 157, 183, 256, 263
Yogi 137
Yogīdu 49

Zhekar 287

PLACES ASSOCIATED WITH NĀMASIDDHĀNTA

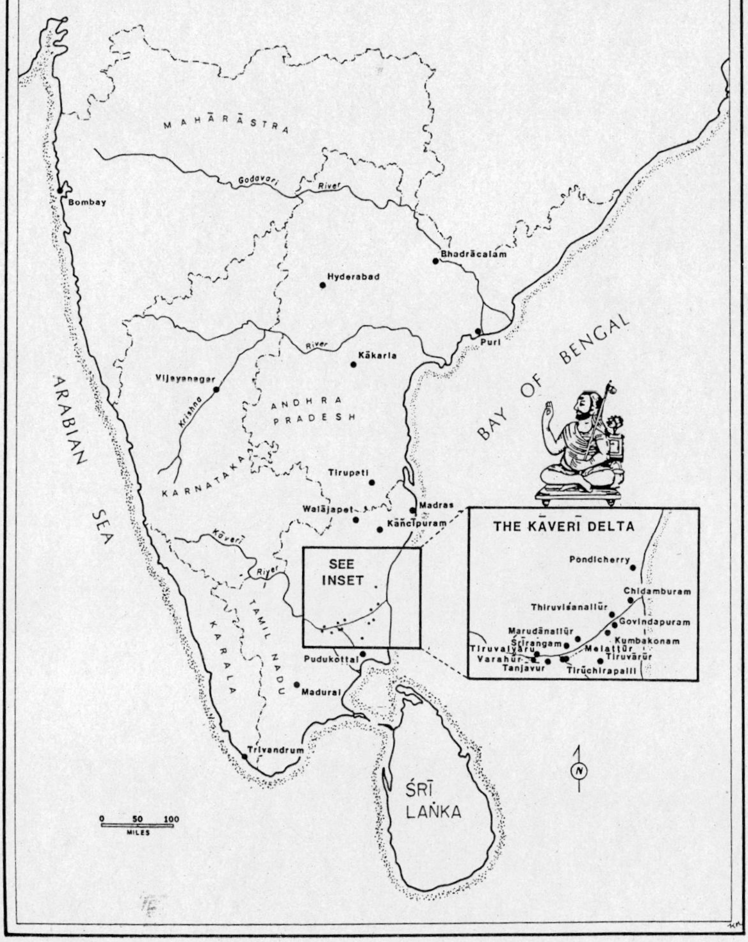

* R. Krishnamurthy of Coimbatore author of *Saints of Cauveri Delta*, is the photographer responsible for the photos of Bodhendra, Sadaśiva Brahmendra, Sadguru Svāmī, and locations associated with Āyyavāl.
* The Photo of Dr. V. Raghavan is courtesy of his daughter, Nandini Ramani, and photos taken in Tiruvidaimarudur are courtesy of Veṅkaṭaraman Bhāgavatar.
* The cover photo is of a female member of the Rāmanāmī Samāj, an untouchable devotional movement in Central India. The primary practice of its members is the chanting of the name "Rām" the most powerful name of God to them. They also wear it on their clothing, as well as tattoo themselves, often extensively, with the name in Sanskrit characters.
  The photo was taken by Ramdas Lamb, a professor of Religion at the University of Hawaii.

Dr. V. Raghavan

The Āyyāvāl Maṭh in Tiruviśanallūr

Sadāśiva Brahmendra

Nārāyaṇa Tīrtha

Śrī Bhagavannāma Bodhendra

The well in the Āyyāvāl maṭh, from which the Goddess Gaṅgā is believed to have manifested herself in response to the prayers of Āyyāvāl.

The lane leading from the Āyyāvāl math to the Kāverī river, along which Āyyāvāl is said to have encountered a starving caṇḍāla, whom he fed.

Veṅkaṭaraman Bhāgavatar of Tiruvidaimarudūr

Bhajana celebrations held in Veṅkaṭaraman Bhāgavatar's home

Bhajana celebrations held in Veṅkaṭaraman Bhāgavatar's home